Race, Oppression
and the Zombie

CONTRIBUTIONS TO ZOMBIE STUDIES

White Zombie: Anatomy of a Horror Film. Gary D. Rhodes. 2001

The Zombie Movie Encyclopedia. Peter Dendle. 2001

*American Zombie Gothic: The Rise and Fall (and Rise)
of the Walking Dead in Popular Culture*. Kyle William Bishop. 2010

*Back from the Dead: Remakes of the Romero
Zombie Films as Markers of Their Times*. Kevin J. Wetmore, Jr. 2011

*Generation Zombie: Essays on the Living Dead
in Modern Culture*. Edited by Stephanie Boluk and Wylie Lenz. 2011

*Race, Oppression and the Zombie: Essays on Cross-Cultural Appropriations
of the Caribbean Tradition*. Edited by Christopher M. Moreman
and Cory James Rushton. 2011

Zombies Are Us: Essays on the Humanity of the Walking Dead.
Edited by Christopher M. Moreman and Cory James Rushton. 2011

The Zombie Movie Encyclopedia, Volume 2: 2000–2010. Peter Dendle. 2012

Great Zombies in History. Edited by Joe Sergi. 2013 (graphic novel)

Unraveling Resident Evil: *Essays on the Complex Universe
of the Games and Films*. Edited by Nadine Farghaly. 2014

"We're All Infected": Essays on AMC's The Walking Dead
and the Fate of the Human. Edited by Dawn Keetley. 2014

Zombies and Sexuality: Essays on Desire and the Walking Dead.
Edited by Shaka McGlotten and Steve Jones. 2014

Race, Oppression and the Zombie

Essays on Cross-Cultural Appropriations
of the Caribbean Tradition

EDITED BY
CHRISTOPHER M. MOREMAN *AND*
CORY JAMES RUSHTON

CONTRIBUTIONS TO ZOMBIE STUDIES

McFarland & Company, Inc., Publishers
Jefferson, North Carolina

LIBRARY OF CONGRESS CATALOGUING-IN-PUBLICATION DATA

Race, oppression and the zombie : essays on
cross-cultural appropriations of the Caribbean tradition /
edited by Christopher M. Moreman and Cory James Rushton.
p.   cm.— (Contributions to Zombie Studies)
Includes bibliographical references and index.

ISBN 978-0-7864-5911-7
(softcover : acid free paper) ∞

1. Zombies — Social aspects.   2. Zombies — History.
3. Folklore — Caribbean Area.   4. Caribbean Area — History.
5. Caribbean Area — Social conditions.   6. Caribbean Area — Race relations.
I. Moreman, Christopher M., 1974– II. Rushton, Cory.
GR581.R34 2011   398.209729 — dc23   2011021467

BRITISH LIBRARY CATALOGUING DATA ARE AVAILABLE

On the cover: Poster art for the 1943 film
I Walked with a Zombie (RKO Radio Pictures/Photofest)

Printed in the United States of America

McFarland & Company, Inc., Publishers
Box 611, Jefferson, North Carolina 28640
www.mcfarlandpub.com

Acknowledgments

We would like to thank all of the contributors to this volume, for their patience as we moved through the process, and for their efforts and timeliness as we moved it forward. We'd also like to thank all of the people who submitted proposals to our initial call for papers (we received over 120 proposals), though we could choose only a fraction of them. We would also like to send a blanket thank you out to all of our colleagues who encouraged us in our interest in zombies, at our respective institutions as well as at conferences and other events. Thanks also to Theresa Duran for her index. We must also give thanks to the good people at Piper's Pub in Antigonish for pouring the libations from which the seeds of this whole idea originally grew.

Table of Contents

Introduction: Race, Colonialism, and the Evolution of the "Zombie"
CORY JAMES RUSHTON and CHRISTOPHER M. MOREMAN   1

I — Haitian Origins: Race and the Zombie

1. New South, New Immigrants, New Women, New Zombies:
   The Historical Development of the Zombie in American
   Popular Culture
   ANN KORDAS   15

2. Hurston in Haiti: Neocolonialism and Zombification
   RITA KERESZTESI   31

3. Putting the Undead to Work: Wade Davis, Haitian Vodou, and
   the Social Uses of the Zombie
   DAVID INGLIS   42

4. Guess Who's Going to Be Dinner: Sidney Poitier, Black
   Militancy, and the Ambivalence of Race in Romero's
   Night of the Living Dead
   BARBARA S. BRUCE   60

II — The Capital of the Dead

5. Time for Zombies: Sacrifice and the Structural Phenomenology
   of Capitalist Futures
   RONJON PAUL DATTA and LAURA MACDONALD   77

6. Zombified Capital in the Postcolonial Capital: Circulation
   (of Blood) in Sony Labou Tansi's *Parentheses of Blood*
   ELIZABETH A. STINSON   93

III — Culturally Transplanted Zombies

7. Zombie Orientals Ate My Brain! Orientalism in Contemporary
   Zombie Stories
   ERIC HAMAKO   107

8. Post–9/11 Anxieties: Unpredictability and Complacency in
   the Age of New Terrorism in *Dawn of the Dead* (2004)
   BECKI A. GRAHAM   124

9. The Rise and Fall — and Rise — of the Nazi Zombie in Film
   CYNTHIA J. MILLER   139

10. Eating Ireland: Zombies, Snakes and Missionaries in *Boy
    Eats Girl*
    CORY JAMES RUSHTON   149

11. It's So Hard to Get Good Help These Days: Zombies as a
    Culturally Stabilizing Force in *Fido* (2006)
    MICHELE BRAUN   162

IV — *The Future of Zombie Understandings*

12. Zombie Categories, Religion and the New False Rationalism
    EDWARD DUTTON   177

13. Nothing but Meat? Philosophical Zombies and Their
    Cinematic Counterparts
    DAVE BEISECKER   191

Bibliography   207
Filmography   219
About the Contributors   223
Index   225

Introduction

Race, Colonialism, and the Evolution of the "Zombie"

CORY JAMES RUSHTON and
CHRISTOPHER MOREMAN

Jamie Russell (2005) might have been correct when he stated that zombies had been ignored by critics of horror (p. 7), but that does not mean that zombies have been universally ignored by the academy, as a recent article by Sarah Juliet Lauro and Karen Embry makes clear: "The ubiquity of the metaphor suggests the zombie's current cultural currency" (Lauro and Embry, 2008, p. 86). Zombies are now receiving a great deal of attention because they are both symbolically prolific and textually ubiquitous:

> Because the zombie travels so widely, and across so many fields, it has become a very familiar character, one that participates in narratives of the body, of life and death, of good and evil; one that gestures to alterity, racism, species-ism, the inescapable, the immutable. Thus it takes us to "the other side"—alienation, death, and what is worse than death: the state of being undead [Webb and Byrnand, 2008, p. 83].

Still, at least prior to our current moment, the academic zombie, when it has come to the attention of scholars, has lurched down some very narrow (but nonetheless suggestive and fruitful) paths. The academic world knows five things about the zombie trope, and these things have come to be taken as truisms. One, that the zombie began as something associated with Haiti, and further with a religion the West once called Voodoo and now, in an age of greater cultural tolerance, calls Vodou. Two, that as a result of this, the zombie is best understood in the postcolonial mode, and says as much about "Western" fears as it does about any Haitian reality. Three, that George Romero redirected zombies in a fundamental way in 1968, when he reimagined them in *Night of the Living Dead* as cannibalistic ghouls who replicate themselves through infection, and that Romero's casting a black actor as his hero was ground-breaking in some way that critics still fail to agree upon (in part because Romero himself has sent mixed messages concerning whether that casting was a political statement or not). Four, that Romero's 1978 follow-up film, *Dawn of the Dead*, again re-cast the zombie, now as a symbol for mindless consumerism, thereby establishing zombie narratives as a potential location for critiques of late capitalism. Finally, the modern academic probably knows that Deleuze and Guattari proclaimed the zombie to be the "only modern myth" in *Anti-Oedipus*, lending the motif a certain cultural cachet.

1

The present volume is largely concerned with the Caribbean or Haitian zombie, a creature that comes from the African roots of Caribbean religion; a forthcoming companion volume, *Zombies Are Us: Essays on the Humanity of the Walking Dead*, will explore the many cultural uses of the zombie in the years following the release of George Romero's first two films. Whatever the truth which lies behind the legend of the Caribbean zombie, it is worth remembering that this legend has been reimagined in the West at least twice: once in the early twentieth century, where films like *White Zombie* summoned the zombie in the service of various Caucasian fears and racisms, and a second time when the resulting North American construction was further modified by George Romero in the classic *Night of the Living Dead* and its first sequel, *Dawn of the Dead*. The "real" Haitian zombie is not only revenant but phantom, the subject of competing ethnographic and historical claims, seemingly eclipsed by a scarier, more ghoulish Hollywood descendent. This introduction will argue that the Haitian zombie has not disappeared as fully as it might seem — the Caribbean roots of "the only modern myth" remain the first and perhaps best way to explain and explore all modern manifestations of zombieness.

The Caribbean Origins

Though the official state religion of Haiti is Catholicism, the vast majority of Haitians practice the religious syncretism that is Vodou, a tradition that is often misunderstood at best, and vilified at worst. The term "Voodoo" is now differentiated from Vodou, as it has come to encompass every ignorance of the true religion. Voodoo, as distinct from Vodou, should be used to signify the racist image of a devil-worshipping, black-magic wielding, and uncivilized tradition imagined by Western popular culture. Vodouisants (practitioners of Vodou) in New Orleans often refer to their spirituality as Voodoo, differentiating the "darker" elements as Hoodoo. The choice of terminology here includes an element of sensationalism, as "Voodoo" has become a huge tourist attraction in the Big Easy, but the distinction between a legitimate religious tradition and some form of dark art is maintained. The spiritual tradition more properly called Vodou is a loosely affiliated, syncretistic religion originating primarily in Haiti (though aspects of it can be found throughout the West Indies, and similarities exist with traditions such as Santeria and Candomblé), that combines elements of a variety of African spiritualities, most prominently from the West African kingdom of Dahomey (modern-day Benin), with Roman Catholicism and "New World" native spirituality. The religion began when slaves of wide-ranging African backgrounds were brought together in what became the hub of the slave-trade — Haiti. Huge numbers of Africans from varied tribal affiliations and cultures were forced to find common ground as they were gathered to the island of Hispaniola. This common ground included collective spirituality as these diverse peoples were systematically "converted" to the Catholic Church. Vodou resulted from an amalgam of beliefs and traditions of a people who were at once forced to accept, and yet collectively rejected, a colonial religion of oppression while they struggled to retain some sense of African identity and culture. Voodoo, which we might take as a term of derision, ought to be taken not to refer to the Haitian religion but rather only applies to negative and racist constructions. Far from being the object of Hollywood horror, this perversion of Haitian religion, long proffered by fearful American slave-holders and Christian clergy alike, still appears today: evangelist Pat Robertson explained, in response to the massive earthquake that hit Haiti in January, 2010, that the island nation's independence, and subsequent misery and poverty, were set in motion when the Haitian people "swore a pact to the Devil" during their successful revolution of 1791–1804. The distinction between Voodoo and Vodou will be maintained throughout the chapters in this volume, with Vodou being the preferred spelling of the religious tradition, and Voodoo reserved for sensationalistic, horrific, or racist depictions of it.

Zombies, for their part, represent in the African tradition not simply the walking corpses of the Western imagination but are synonymous with a wide range of monsters. Bratty children are sometimes themselves called zombies, or frightened into behaving by the threat of zombies under the bed. Spirits of the dead, people transformed into animals, and tiny fairy folk can all be designated zombies (see Ackermann and Gauthier, 1991; Niehaus, 2005). Aside from being scary monsters, what all of these ideas share in common is an idea of subjugated agency. Karen McCarthy Brown defines the zombie as "either the disembodied soul of a dead person whose powers are captured and used for magical purposes, or a soulless body that has been raised from the grave to do drone labor in the fields" (Brown, 2005, p. 9638). The former suggestion of the zombie as disembodied spirit is more often referred to as the *zombi astral* and has not translated into the Western imagination. The latter concept of the revenant corpse remains what most of us would now recognize as a zombie proper. Aside from the varied suggestions as to what zombies may signify, there is also some degree of uncertainty as to where the term originates. It has been suggested that the term derives from West African words for "fetish" (*zumbi*) or "spirit/god" (*nzambi*); certainly, both of these might more easily be associated with the *zombi astral*, which can be bought and kept as charms for luck and health. Another relation is to the Louisiana Creole *jumbie* (thought to itself derive from the Spanish, *sombra*, being a ghostly shade or perhaps the French, *les ombres*, shadows) which can signify either an evil curse or a ghost. It may just as easily be a French patois derivation, a favorite of one of the authors (Moreman), of the words *sans vie*, a possibility particularly fitting considering the relationship between the zombie and the slave in Haiti (cf. Kordas, this volume). Whatever its etymology, it seems clear that the zombie as walking corpse is particularly attached to Haiti, while the *zombie astral* as captured soul (often held in a jar for future and nefarious use) is more popular in Africa. The Haitian derivative is suggestive of the unique conditions of slavery and Catholic doctrine. Catholicism was known and had been successfully amalgamated into some African spiritualities, but in Haiti it was rejected as the religion of the "white man's God."

The zombie in Haitian folklore is believed to be the product of evil magics employed by a dark priest known as a *bokor*, or sorcerer, to be distinguished from the benign priest and priestess, the *houngan* and *mambo*. According to Wade Davis' controversial ethnography, the production of a zombie serves a social corrective function as only deviants are made into zombies (Davis, 1985; Davis, 1988a). Whether or not this is the case, Haitians hold the possibility of one's being transformed into a zombie — a mindless slave risen from the dead by evil magic — as very real, even enacting laws prohibiting zombification.

As with Vodou/Voodoo, the wildly disparate forms taken by the zombie in the western imaginary can be problematic. Lauro and Embry suggest a triple nomenclature:

> Given the fact that there are multiple valences in play, it seems best to designate the distinction typographically: there is the Haitian *zombi*, a body raised from the dead to labor in the fields, but with a deep association of having played a role in the Haitian revolution (thus, simultaneously resonant with the categories of slave and slave rebellion); and there is also the *zombie*, the American importation of the monster, which in its cinematic incarnation has morphed into a convenient boogeyman representing various social concerns. The *zombie* can also be a metaphoric state claimed

for oneself or imposed on someone else. This zombie has been made to stand for capitalist drone (*Dawn of the Dead*) and Communist sympathizer (*Invasion of the Body Snatchers*), and, increasingly, viral contamination (*28 Days Later*). In its passage from zombi to zombie, this figuration that was at first just a somnambulistic slave raised from the dead became evil, contagious, and plural. Our manifesto proclaims the future possibility of the *zombii*, a consciousless being that is a swarm organism, and the only imaginable specter that could really be posthuman [Lauro and Embry, pp. 87–8].

No lesser a light than Slavoj Žižek disagrees, drawing on Lacan and arguing that the undead of *Night* "are not portrayed as embodiments of pure evil, of a simple drive to kill or revenge, but as sufferers, pursuing their victims with an awkward persistence, colored by a kind of sadness ... *because they were not properly buried*," like Antigone's family and Hamlet's father (Žižek, 1992, pp. 22–3). This sadness would seem to be rooted firmly in the Haitian zombi, rather than the initial walking corpses of Romero's film, which appear first in a graveyard (the very definition, one would think, of being properly buried).

Lauro and Embry's third version, the zombii, is a riposte to Haraway's idea of the cyborg, the posthuman who has evolved through a mingling of self and machine, and does not necessarily directly concern us here: except that the academic zombie, as a nearly-empty signifier carrying a few key-but-infinitely-interpretable features (strength through swarming, lack of individuality or identity), does seem to embody a kind of consciouslessness. The zombie comes to represent whatever we fear most from Others, not just in individual texts, but in the criticism itself. To borrow Lauro and Embry's terminology, by recasting the zombi as zombie, Romero created something which could legitimately be both Other and our own spectral, feared future at the same time.

The threat is that of assimilation to an inexorable collective, and is the same fear we see at work in *Star Trek*'s Borg: the absolute loss of identity in the service of an unknown and unknowable, in fact unachievable because non-existent, goal. The Haitian zombie could be called the living dead in a metaphorical sense, especially after Davis: the Marxist *homo laborans* in the service of a master, with an emphasis on being either dead and acting alive, or alive and acting in an unconscious way that is like death in its lack of individual consciousness. Romero's "living dead" were another matter entirely: "...the zombie, by its very definition, is anticatharsis, antiresolution: it proposes no third term reconciling the subject/object split, the lacuna between life and death. The zombie is opposition held irrevocably in tension" (Lauro and Embry, p. 94). For Lauro and Embry only the post-human zombii suggests the "possibility of a negation of the subject/object divide ... a paradox that disrupts the entire system" (Lauro and Embry, p. 94). Only by metaphorically escaping its Caribbean roots could the zombie become a signifier which points beyond the system itself: George Romero effected that escape, albeit partially by accident.

Zombie Swerve: "...to all the undead around the world..."

With this immortal line, a newly-zombified DJ in Santa Monica sends a record out to the growing zombie hordes in 1988's *Zombi 3* (dir. Lucio Fulci). The zombie apocalypse, in this film, is the result of American military experiments with a chemical compound called "Death One," experiments which take place not in the United States, but suggestively in its former colony, the Philippines. Lucio Fulci's unofficial sequel/prequel to Romero's *Dawn of the Dead*, known most often as *Zombi 2*, locates the birth of the zombie in the Caribbean, from which it spreads to New York and the rest of the world; by 1988, the unofficial sequel to that unofficial sequel took its cue once again from broader trends, including the chemical-origin stories found in John A. Russo's also-unofficial sequel series starting with *Return of the Living Dead* (1985), where zombie outbreaks occur as a result of exposure to 245-Trioxin (itself based on "Trixie," the chemical compound which causes insanity in Romero's 1973 *The Crazies*, remade in 2010). The chemical or viral cause has since become the most common in-text explanation for zombie outbreaks (although less common than aporia, the lack of explanation, or sometimes an ambiguous cacophony of competing explanations).

In many respects it looks as though the Haitian zombie is a thing of the past, permanently eclipsed by the success of Romero's cannibals. Romero's own use of the "Voodoo" explanation was brief: a single line in which *Dawn*'s Peter recalls that his grandfather, a Trinidadian priest, used to say that when hell was full, the dead would walk the earth. But for Romero, this is merely one of a host of explanations provided within his films, a plethora which makes it impossible to pinpoint a particular cause (and which, in turn, was deftly satirized in *Shaun of the Dead* (2004), when the protagonist flips through a host of television channels all offering different explanations). Still, the viral/chemical explanation is everywhere: *28 Days Later* and its sequels on film and in graphic novels, the *Resident Evil* franchise, Max Brooks' novel *World War Z*, etc.). The Vodou zombie is, by contrast, relatively hard to find: there is the film adaptation of Davis's *The Serpent and the Rainbow*, and hints in such low-budget films as *Enter Zombie King* or Godsmack's 1998 heroin anthem, "Voodoo." In Andy Duncan's short story "Zora and the Zombie," Zora Neale Hurston, a central figure in American reception of the Haitian zombie, is depicted experiencing odd events and meeting Felicia Felix-Mentor, the "zombie" photographed for her 1937 book *Tell My Horse* (see Rita Keresztesi, this volume). Duncan notes that Hurston is almost unknown in horror circles today: "I marvel that many readers, judging from their comments, never heard of Hurston. Had I realized beforehand that this story would be many readers' introduction to her I wouldn't have dared write it." Romero's reinvention seems to hold the field.

If the Haitian zombie is not completely gone from western pop culture, its presence is often muted at best, indeed often roped to the later Romeran or viral form of the zombie. There have been some attempts to combine the two species of zombie into a single narrative, with limited success. The 2005 Irish comedy *Boy Eats Girl* is one of a handful of texts which attempt to combine the two traditions: the zombie crisis is caused by a voodoo ritual, but the zombies are cannibalistic because a key page of the manuscript was missing when the ritual was performed (for more, see Rushton, this volume). Similarly, *Zombiez* (also 2005), often described as a hip-hop zombie film and with an all African American cast, uses Romeran cannibal zombies but prefaces itself with a screenshot explaining that the living dead could be created through pharmaceuticals, specifically the "pufferfish" — the overt reference to a 1982 study by an unnamed pharmacologist is certainly intended to imply Wade Davis (*The Serpent and the Rainbow* came out in 1985, but Davis' article in the *Journal of Ethnopharmacology* appeared in 1983). This admittedly oblique return to the Haitian zombie reflects the film's desire to be an African American zombie film, however unsuccessfully.

Max Brooks' popular parody *The Zombie Survival Guide* (2003) invokes the Haitian zombie as one of many metatextual jokes. After much discussion concerning zombie traits, Brooks' narrator turns to the "voodoo zombie" in order to distinguish the two species:

> It is true that the word "zombie" originally comes from the Kimbundu word "nzúmbe," a term describing a dead person's soul, and yes, zombies and zombification are integral parts of the Afro-Caribbean religion known as voodoo. However, the origin of their name is the only similarity between the voodoo zombie and the viral zombie [Brooks, 2003, p. 20].

Brooks does not privilege one or the other in diegetic terms: the *Survival Guide* posits that both kinds of zombie are real and might be encountered. The narrator, however, is manifestly less concerned with the voodoo than the viral. When his discussion turns to the possibility of controlling the viral zombie, the narrator's mildly sardonic voice comes to the fore: "Several times headstrong humans have insisted they could simply command their living dead attackers to stop. As cold, rotting hands grabbed their limbs and dirty, worn teeth bit into their flesh, these people discovered, too late, what they were dealing with" (p. 22). It is a theme Brooks comes back to in his novel, *World War Z* (2006), when a communications expert who ran Radio Free Earth during the conflict discusses various misconceptions the global communications network was designed to address; in doing so, she rehearses a list of zombie qualities derived from various Romeran texts:

> There were so many misconceptions: zombies were somehow intelligent; they could feel and adapt, use tools and even some human weapons; they carried memories of their former existence; or they could be communicated with and trained like some kind of pet. It was heartbreaking, having to debunk one misguided myth after another. The civilian survival guide helped, but it was still severely limited [Brooks, 2006, pp. 196–97].

Besides the sly reference to his own earlier *Zombie Survival Guide*, Brooks has taken deliberate aim at several previous zombie narratives, including some by Romero himself: intelligent zombies (*Land*); zombies who remember (the original *Dawn* and *Day*); zombies as pets or companions (*Day of the Dead, Shaun of the Dead,* and *Fido*). Brooks even has an in-text explanation for some of these "misconceptions": the "quisling"—humans driven mad by the disaster, and have come to believe that they are themselves zombies (Brooks, 2003, pp. 157–59). All proof of in-fighting among zombies, and by extension all that Brooks declares non-zombie behavior, can be attributed to these quislings.

More often, however, the Haitian zombie is eclipsed altogether. Perhaps no greater example can be found than that of Simon Garth, a 1973 Marvel Comics attempt to cash in on the sudden popularity of zombies following *Night*. In the short-lived *Tales of the Zombie*, Steve Gerber and others tell the story of Garth, a businessman who is sacrificed one night to the spirits of the *loa* only to arise as an undead creature controlled by whoever holds the key to an amulet around his neck. The priestess who is initially supposed to kill him reveals herself to be his "trusted Creole secretary" Layla; the ritual is inadvertently completed only when another of Garth's employees stabs him with the ritual knife while he is fleeing the voodoo practitioners. *Tales of the Zombie* is an anthology series, full of voodoo stories in the old EC Comics horror mode, and long prose attempts to "explain" Voodoo/Vodou to comic book fans or to review zombie-themed films like *Night*, the 1974 blaxploitation zombie movie *Sugar Hill* (later edited for television as *The Zombies of Sugar Hill* and not to be confused with the 1994 Wesley Snipes gangster film), and the James Bond vehicle *Live and Let Die*. Despite the heavily traditional zombie stories in this series, when Marvel published a re-imagining of Simon Garth's story for its adult MAX imprint in 2006, Garth became a bank teller with Layla as his co-worker; the zombie threat in this new version is not Voodoo, nor is it individual. Instead, the plot is highly derivative of the *Resident Evil* series: the army has been experimenting with a virus, and Garth is only involved because he and Layla have been taken hostage by thieves who then drive into the contaminated zone. The final symbolic rejection of the text's Haitian-tinged origin comes when the re-imagined Layla is quickly dispatched by a random zombie: even in a heavily ameliorated form, most modern zombie narratives have no place for a priestess of the *loa*.

Consumption: Not Just for Tuberculosis Anymore

Despite the proliferation of potential meanings, the zombie is associated with capitalism above all else: "Capitalism, we suggest, works as an analogue of zombiedom because it too is predicated on insatiable appetite, and the drive to consume," write Webb and Byrnand; later in the same article, they argue that Romero's films "are particularly good examples of zombie films that lay down the terms by which the zombie trope 'reads' capitalism" (p. 90–1). The argument is the wrong way around: Romero's films do indeed "lay down the terms" precisely by not being "good examples"—they are the progenitors of the trope itself, particularly *Dawn*, which takes much of its lasting power from its at-the-time unique setting in a shopping mall. If *Night* reimagined the raised dead as cannibalistic, infectious ghoul rather than victimized laborer, *Dawn* further reimagines that ghoul's cannibalism as symbolic of endless (indeed pointless) consumption. In a fundamental sense, the Haitian zombi—a symbol of the *bokor* or master's appetite, for wealth, sugar, white women, what-have-you—is not gone, but has rather been invested with that very appetite in its own right; in the absence of consciousness, that appetite is both undefined (in the sense that the zombie wants only to ingest the humanity it once shared) and all-encompassing (to eat or turn all human life is to destroy all value, as civilization collapses with the disappearance of its human inventors and inhabitants). In fact, the viral zombie is not only the consumer or the market, but is capital itself: "Capitalism has the same heartless all-consuming character, particularly in its pure form in which the 'invisible hand' of the market is supposed to bring about a dynamic equilibrium between supply and demand.... The problem is that capital doesn't care, and doesn't weigh human costs. It is simply zombie—hungry, and hence focused on feeding and expanding regardless of the consequences" (Webb and Byrnand, p. 93; but explored more thoroughly in Chris Harman, 2009; and Datta and MacDonald, this volume). As Stinson argues, in this volume, the zombie-as-capital trope has been adopted in Africa, the ultimate (linguistic) homeland of the zombie; Jean and John Comaroff (1999) have also noted this trend in South Africa. Steve Shaviro argues that this adoption of the Romeran zombie, which "originally came into American culture from distorted accounts of Haitian vodoun," are now coming back full circle: "...the periphery indulges in a sort of reverse exoticism, as it appropriates the mythology of the imperial center," no longer "workers and producers, but figures of nonproductive expenditure" (Shaviro, 2002, p. 289). Third World discourse now consumes the American zombie in turn, putting it to work in opposition to the domination of First World economic models. The Caribbean zombi, it could be argued, has not been replaced at all, only reinscribed, and thereby made more powerful.

Even otherwise exclusively diegetic matters could be explained through the lingering influence of the zombi in its American descendent. The fast/slow debate—which concerns the definition of the "realistic" speeds at which an undead corpse could reasonably be expected to move—makes little sense without the Haitian zombi, the catatonic victim of poisons or spells whose mobility is limited by a lack of consciousness or agency. Arguments mounted in the defense of the Romeran zombie's slow movement range from the likelihood of broken bones which cannot subsequently heal (which seems unreasonable when we are talking about living corpses in the first place) to their narrative nature as a group monster: "Zombies have no individual identity, but rather get their power from membership in a group: It's easy to kill one, but 1,000 indomitable flesh eaters may just overwhelm you" (Levin, 2004). The Vodou zombie is still here, in the central lack of agency and individual will which it bequeaths to Romero's otherwise-distinct creatures. The Romeran zombie's ability to infect the living and create more unthinking members for the group is a more perverted inheritance: instead of a bokor laboriously raising undead servants, the creatures raise themselves. In effect, zombies are now self-colonizing, following patterns set up long before the living victim was ever born. The master-figure is eliminated, particularly in texts which do not seek to locate the origins of the zombie outbreak anywhere in particular, leaving the zombie open to a greater range of symbolic possibilities: shopper-as-zombie, stripper-as-zombie, Walmart-employee-as-zombie.

A true "'zombie manifesto' is one that cannot call for positive change, it calls only for the destruction of the reigning model" (Lauro and Embry, p. 91), a "monstrous future," a phrase they borrow from Franco Moretti (2005, p. 95, n. 26): "...the monster expresses the anxiety that the future will be monstrous" (Moretti, p. 84). The zombie calls for revolution without goals. But Moretti is worth quoting at greater length here, as his observation comes from a discussion of Dracula and Frankenstein's monster, creatures very different from the zombie/zombi in their resolute individuality, even if they flirt with the same ideological preoccupation with capitalism, a society split between the capitalist and the worker, bourgeois and proletariat:

> The literature of terror is born precisely *out of the terror of a split society*, and out of the desire to heal it. It is for just this reason that Dracula and Frankenstein, with rare exceptions, do not appear together. The threat would be too great: and this literature, having produced terror, must also erase it and restore peace. It must restore the broken equilibrium, giving the illusion of being able to stop history: because the monster expresses the anxiety that the future will be monstrous. His antagonist — the enemy of the monster — will always be, by contrast, a representative of the present, a distillation of complacent nineteenth-century mediocrity: nationalistic, stupid, superstitious, philistine, impotent, self-satisfied. But this does not show through. Fascinated by the horror of the monster, the public accepts the vices of its destroyer without a murmur.... The monster, then, serves to displace the antagonisms and horrors evidenced *within* society *outside* society itself [Moretti, pp. 83–4].

The zombi and its master, whether the Béla Lugosi of *White Zombie* or the *bokor* of Davis's study, can with some effort be fit to this model: Lugosi's Legendre and his ally, the plantation owner Charles Beaumont, will both fall to their deaths, freeing at least their white female victim Madeleine, and thus erasing terror and restoring peace. (Simon Garth, in his earlier version, plays out something of this tension: he has two named employees, the loyal Layla and his traitorous gardener Gyps, both of whom play different roles in reducing the capitalist himself to commodity). The viral zombie does not fit this pattern in quite the same way: in the classic Romeran film and its successors, the zombie outbreak is often not contained — the stopping of history is not illusory at all, the destruction of the reigning model is complete. In Romero's films and other texts like *The Walking Dead*, Moretti's model is reversed. The reigning model is recalled over and over again only to be destroyed almost as many times as it is invoked: in Kaufman's Fiddler's Green (*Land of the Dead*, 2005), the unnamed village in the woods in Carrie Ryan's novel *The Forest of Hands and Teeth* (2009), or the quasi-utopian prison setting of Image Comics series *The Walking Dead*'s third and fourth volumes. Further, while the protagonists of the viral zombie narrative are as flawed as those in Moretti's texts, those flaws condemn these various protagonists in a way that is meant to be noticed: Kim Paffenroth's Christian reading of Romero's films is correct that the human characters have a better chance of survival when they avoid self-centered and stupid behaviors (Paffenroth, 2006). Webb and Byrnand observe: "In story after story, there seems to be no limit to the survivors' rage, or their incapacity to empathize with one another" (p. 86). Even when survivors do show empathy or tolerance, their actions have less effect in the world than the more routine dark actions. In *Land of the Dead*, the heroes flee their city, eschewing the opportunity to attack and possibly destroy the zombie horde; in doing so, they circumvent the class struggle at the heart of Romero's films. Crucially, they do not solve that problem, the central political or social dilemmas of class conflict and human alienation bequeathed to the viral zombie by its Haitian zombi forebear.

Not all zombie aficionados are enamored of the signifying undead. Mark Kidwell's comic book series *'68* was originally envisioned as a series which would come between story arcs for a series focused on a reimagined Barbara (from *Night*) but set in Vietnam (a one-shot was released in 2007, a mini-series began in 2010, both from Image Comics). Kidwell describes the genesis of the series: "Basically, I started thinking about the year in which the original Romero film was shot (1968) and started wondering what was going on in the rest of the world at the time"—thus *Night* meets the 'Nam comic, not surprising given that much of the critical response to *Night* considered the Vietnam War an important context for the film (Hervey, 2008, pp. 95–8). Originally planned as a tie-in, Kidwell remarks that "Upon later reflection the property was judged strong enough to stand on it's [sic] own and is no longer part of the NOTLD series. It stands on it's own as an original property." Asked about the zombie genre's tendency towards socio-political relevance, Kidwell makes a case for kind of apolitical generic purity:

> I gotta tell ya, I'm not a fan of mixing political commentary with horror. I know, I know ... a lotta folks will grind on and on about the "consumerism" subtext of Romero's *Dawn* and the underlying "Dangers of Nuclear Testing" themes of films like *The Hills Have Eyes*. I'm here to assure you that more people (like me) came out of *Dawn of the Dead* after their initial viewing saying, "Man, did you see that fuckin' guy's head explode?" or "I lost it when that dude bit a chunk outta that lady's arm!" As far as my intent goes, the only statement being made with *68* is about sticking by the people you care about, until the end (or after) in the face of something horrible [Bough, *Revenant* online, 2006].

Earlier, Kidwell had belied his own avowed distaste for themes on exactly the latter issue, the "brotherhood felt among the troops and the willingness of fellow soldiers to walk through fire to save their brothers in arms." In that, Kidwell is expanding on one of Romero's key tropes — the coming-together of a group of survivors in the face of horrific calamity — and simultaneously rewriting Romero's third film, *Day of the Dead*, with its portrait of disaffected and cruel soldiers who share a vague sense of fellowship with each other in opposition to the scientists and civilians with whom they are saddled. To take 1968 and reinvent it as a glorification of military idealism is itself "mixing political commentary with horror."

But for Kidwell, as for others, it is mostly about the gore. The recent Dynamite series *Raise the Dead* (2007) has been specifically marketed as a counter-text to *The Walking Dead*, widely seen as an intelligent but slow series about the psychological damage caused by a society-wide catastrophe. As the reviewer for *Ain't It Cool News* puts it: "*The Walking Dead* is still a quality read about the emotional toll a zombie apocalypse has on the human spirit, but this is a zombie book that doesn't forget to put the bite into its story." Shades of Anton Chekhov: if there's a zombie in the room in Act 1, it had better eat someone's entrails in Act 3. The issue is a deeper one than it may first appear, having led to a continuing division in the zombie genre: social relevance versus the splatter films early critics saw even in *Night* and its successors. *Night*'s co-writer, John Russo, has argued that the social relevance of Romero's own films has been overstated:

> A lot of the critics have jumped off the deep end in likening the ghouls to the silent majority and finding all sorts of implications that none of us ever intended. I think George wants to encourage

that kind of thinking on the part of some critics. But I'd rather tell them they're full of shit [Russo in Hervey, p. 24].

Even as the cinematic zombie comedies (*Shaun of the Dead*, *Fido*) invest their stories with heady doses of social and political commentary, B-movies and graphic novels reiterate the buckets of blood approach, tragedy divested of all meaning: the best example is Peter Jackson's aptly titled 1992 film *Braindead* (released in North America as *Dead Alive*).

The Question of Ben

To be fair to Russo, his skepticism may be partially rooted in precisely the factor that caused critics to take *Night* seriously in the first place: the gore was, for the time, excessive, but the casting of a black actor as the film's protagonist — and then having a posse (which has seemed obviously modeled on a lynch mob to many viewers and critics) execute that protagonist at the end of the film — virtually by itself created an intense critical interest. The casting of Duane Jones as Ben has been dismissed by Romero himself as "an accident. The whole movie was an accident" (Romero in Hervey, p. 24). As Hervey puts it, the crew's on-site discussions of the film's themes, the collapse of the traditional family and the possibility of revolution, never overwhelms the finished product: "...*Night*'s implications hit audiences more powerfully for not being laboured over: they're genuine subtexts" (Hervey, p. 26). Even Ben's death is the result of several "accidents": Jones has said he suggested Ben's death as the only ending that wouldn't "read wrong racially"; the final cut of the film omits a line in which the Sheriff regrets the mistaken shot which brings Ben down (Hervey, pp. 113–5).

Jones' observation was confirmed when producer Russell Streiner (who also appears in the film) observed that the audience at the film's opening night, largely African American, responded by stating that the film could only end with "Whitey" destroying the character, eliminating the specter of an able black leader (Hervey, p. 115). Max Brooks, in the section of his *Survival Guide* dedicated to "historically recorded attacks," tells the fictional story of a 1762 zombie outbreak occurring in Castries, St. Lucia. Both reinscription of the Caribbean zombie as viral and allusion to *Night*'s ending, Brooks' short narrative twice states that Africans are particularly capable of combating zombies. The first is during the initial outbreak:

> An outbreak of indeterminate source began in the poor white area of the small, overcrowded city.... Several free black and mulatto residents realized the source of the "illness" and attempted to warn the authorities. They were ignored. The outbreak was diagnosed as a form of rabies [Brooks, 2003, p. 201].

Once civil authority has completely broken down and the island's white population takes refuge in two fortresses, the slave and free black populations join forces and in "a slow, deliberate wave, they cleared St. Lucia in seven days" (202). Once British and French reinforcements arrive, the slaves are re-enslaved and the island's free blacks are executed, and the incident is officially remembered as a slave uprising. Just as Ben "must" be killed by a fearful white power at the end of his narrative, so does the black population of St. Lucia.

The Only Modern Myth

It is tempting to think that Deleuze and Guattari's observation, that the zombie is the only modern myth, is routinely cited not because it is a particularly interesting or even accurate observation, but because Deleuze and Guattari are in that rare category of academic superstar. The full quote is this: "The only modern myth is the myth of zombies — mortified schizos, good for work, brought back to reason" (Deleuze and Guattari, 1983, p. 335). For Lauro and Embry, the viral zombie posits the end of revolution itself, in a flattening of all expectation, all personal or class ambition. "When we become zombiis, when we lose our subjectivity and the ability to rationalize, there will be no difference between the two. Therefore, when we truly become posthuman, we won't even *know* it" (Lauro and Embry, p. 108). In Romero's *Dawn of the Dead*, Peter guesses that the dead are flocking to the mall because "this place was important to them" in life; the analogue character in the 2004 remake, Kenneth, says the same thing, but only in a deleted scene. We won't know it when it happens, indeed.

The cultural currency of the zombie, rooted in a fluidity which allows the trope to be used in a variety of academic disciplines and cultural contexts, the very openness of the metaphor — paradoxically now moves hand-in-hand with the waning of the genre itself. Although many critics, including some in this volume, note the increasing popularity of the zombie towards the end of the twentieth century, there are signs that the nearly-unstoppable zombie hordes have finally met their match: over-saturation.

Contributors to the Present Volume

Ann Kordas traces the origins of the zombie in the American imagination, providing an overview of the evolution of the monster from its Haitian origins as it slowly spread to North America. Rita Keresztesi focuses on *Tell My Horse: Voodoo and Life in Haiti and Jamaica*, published in 1938, the product of an ethnographic study conducted by novelist and folklorist, Zora Neale Hurston. Hurston has been lauded as a great African-America writer, but her work on Vodou remains controversial — likely the result of lasting biases against the subject matter as much as criticisms of the book's form or scholarship. At least as, if not more, controversial than Hurston in the field of zombies is Wade Davis. Sociologist David Inglis unpacks the lasting prejudices attached to Vodou and the zombie, and their study, through a detailed discussion of the controversy surrounding Davis's ethnobotanical work, much of which has been accepted by the popular imagination despite heavy criticism from within certain segments of the academy. Barbara S. Bruce continues the discussion of the racial elements of the zombie in discussing the role of Duane Jones, the black star of George Romero's low budget horror *Night of the Living Dead*, in contrast to the mainstream celebration of "the first black superstar" (Bruce, this volume), Sydney Poitier. Though both Poitier and Hurston are celebrated as African Americans, the zombie as racialized symbol remains an object of derision. Ronjon Paul Datta and Laura MacDonald change course in moving from racial aspects of the zombie to interpreting the creature from a Marxist perspective. The notion that the zombie might represent a criticism of capitalism has been prevalent since Romero's *Dawn of the Dead*, but the Haitian background to the zombie also forces us to consider economic issues in relation to the zombie. Elizabeth A. Stinson brings the racial, economic, and neocolonial discussion of "zombified capital" into focus with a close reading of Congolese dramatist Sony Labou Tansi's play *Parentheses of Blood*. Eric Hamako further shows how the zombie symbolizes the racial and socioeconomic "Other," imbued with Orientalist qualities such as an insatiable yet asexual hunger for the flesh, unintelligibility, implacability, and a horde-like social-structure that threatens to pollute heteronormative white family structures and racial purity. Becki A. Graham brings the logical conclusions of the preceding chapters into the modern day as she relates depictions of the modern zombie to the threat, real or imagined, of terrorism. Here, the racist fears of American slave-holders experienced with the successive/ful revolution(s) in Haiti are recognized in modern fears of the Other assaulting America. As far as monsters imbued with meaning go, Cynthia J. Miller exposes the heights to which the zombie has been vilified as she notes the correspondence between them and that greatest villain of the Western imagination — Nazis. Miller examines the relationship between these two monsters as she explores the sub–sub-genre, whose comedy value often outweighs the severity of its subject matter, of zombie–Nazi films that have appeared since World War II. Exploring yet another cultural milieu for zombie meanings, Cory James Rushton examines the Irish film *Boy Eats Girl*, which sees zombies embodying cultural paralysis and presents an argument for a religio-nationalist resurrection for Ireland and its identity. If zombies are so often seen as a "destabilizing force that shatters [everyday life]" (Braun, this volume), Michele Braun offers the recent film *Fido* as a corrective in its portrayal of a post-zombie-apocalyptic world in which the zombie cannot necessarily be controlled, but might at least be understood and incorporated into the world. Edward Dutton and Dave Beisecker both wonder at the myriad possibilities of interpretation opened up by the "post-modern" zombie. Beisecker offers a philosophical analysis of what it means to be a zombie, engaging with the ongoing debates of consciousness studies and the ramifications that zombies, philosophical and otherwise, might have for materialism. Dutton then engages in a rebuke of Ulrich Beck's notion of "zombie categories" — categories that are maintained and yet have become empty of meaning in a post-modern word — arguing instead for a rationalist perspective on metaphors.

PART I

Haitian Origins:
Race and the Zombie

1

New South, New Immigrants, New Women, New Zombies
The Historical Development of the Zombie in American Popular Culture

Ann Kordas

In 1791, a slave rebellion erupted in the French colony of Saint-Domingue (now the country of Haiti) on the Caribbean island of Hispaniola. The rebellion quickly grew into a revolution, and from 1791 to 1804 enslaved people of African descent attacked the French planters who owned them and the soldiers and civil servants who maintained French rule on the island. Fleeing the violence and bloodshed, many planters left the island, taking their slaves with them. Many of these unwilling immigrants settled in and around the city of New Orleans, which, until 1803, was under French rule. The slaves from Saint-Domingue brought to this soon-to-be-American city a complex set of religious beliefs. These Haitian beliefs and the rituals associated with them, known as Vodou, were derived from spiritual beliefs and practices indigenous to western and central Africa, the regions from which the Haitian slaves had come. Once in the United States, some (but by no means all) of these beliefs combined with the beliefs of American-born slaves, Native American practices, and European folk traditions to create the uniquely American religion called Voodoo, which quickly became popular among people of both African and European descent living in the region. One belief that the Haitian slaves do not seem to have brought with them was a belief in the creature now most associated in the American imagination with the folklore of Haiti—the zombie. Indeed, the zombie did not become widely known in the United States until the 1930s. However, almost as soon as the Haitian zombie entered the American imagination, American popular culture, especially Hollywood films, transformed the Haitian zombie into a creature that revealed more about the hopes and fears lurking in the American psyche than in the Haitian one.

This transformation is the subject of this chapter, which will focus on the historical development of the zombie in American popular culture. The development in the United States of the folkloric character called the zombie has been long and complex. The zombie has at different times possessed many different traits and represented many different things. Zombies have been regarded both as creatures of horror and creatures of despair, objects to be alternately feared and pitied. The very nature of the creature, a voiceless being lacking a will and intellect of its own, made the zombie a blank slate upon which the concerns, hopes, and fears of white Americans could be written. Little more than an extension of the will of its master, the zombie of the American imagination and of American popular culture easily became whatever the American public wanted it to be. It is my contention that both the zombie and the zombie master came to represent those elements of society which America's white middle class found disturbing or troublesome and over which it wished it could exert control. Cultural representations of the zombie in the United States have thus been intimately linked with cultural ideas regarding African Americans and other people of color, southern and eastern European immigrants, and "modern" women — elements considered potentially dangerous to white, middle-class society in the early twentieth-century. Because perceptions of "dangerous" peoples varied, so did perceptions and depictions of the zombie change to reflect these fears.

The Original American Zombi

Although Haitians believed in the existence of several different types of zombies, twentieth-century Americans recognized only one. According to Haitian belief, zombies could take many different forms. A zombie could be a soul stolen from a living person by a magician to be used to bring luck or to heal illness. A zombie could also be a dead person who had willingly, at the time of death, given his or her body to the Vodou gods to use as a receptacle. Finally, a zombie could be a reanimated, mindless, soulless corpse taken from its grave to serve the master who had awakened it. It was this form of the zombie that captured the American imagination in the early twentieth-century.

Although the majority of Americans did not become aware of the "existence" of the reanimated corpse called the zombie until the early twentieth century, some nineteenth-century Americans were aware of a creature called a "zombi" (spelled without the final "e") that slightly resembled the "captive soul" version of the Haitian zombie. Nineteenth-century Americans, however, were unaware of the connection between this usually innocuous creature and Haitian Vodou beliefs. The first American zombi was not a mindless body controlled by an evil master but an entity of considerably more power and autonomy. The word "zombi" first appeared in an English-language publication in the United States in a short piece of fiction entitled "The Unknown Painter," a reprint of a story from *Chambers' Edinburgh Journal*, which appeared in an 1838 edition of an Ohio newspaper called *The Alton Telegraph*. In the story, which is set in seventeenth-century Spain, "zombi" is applied to a spirit whom a young African slave claims appears in the studio of his master, the Spanish painter Murillo, at night and works, very skillfully, on paintings being created by Murillo's apprentices. The Spanish painters unanimously reject the boy's explanation for the changes made to their canvasses during the night and imply that faith in the existence of "the Zombi of the negroes" is found solely among Africans. This story evidently struck a chord with American readers. Stories of helpful African creatures no doubt helped to assuage the guilt felt by whites in a slave society, and the tale was reprinted several times in local newspapers throughout the nineteenth century ("A Story of Murillo's Pupil," 1879). By the mid-nineteenth century, the word "zombi" had thus come to be associated in the minds of some Americans with a creature of African "origin" that willingly performed services for whites.

The association of the word "zombi" with powerful spirits of African origin also appeared in other fictional works published in newspapers in the late nineteenth-century and the first decades of the twentieth. In "Last of the Caribs: A Romance of Martinique," published in *The Decatur* [Illinois] *Daily Review* in 1879, a Carib Indian informs a group of French children of "the sorceries of Zombi (a negro fetich)" (*sic*) which protect the man from harm. In another story, "The Marathon Mystery," a white man's Creole mistress speaks of "zombi" as a spirit that lives "in the air, in the earth, everywhere" (Stevenson, 1906, p. 14). Reference to "zombi" as an African spirit appeared in non-fiction works as well. For example, a 1902 newspaper article referred to the "Zombi" (spelled, in this case, with an upper-case "z") as a god worshipped by voodoo practitioners (Rhodes, 2001, p. 75). How widespread familiarity with the zombi spirit was in the United States in the nineteenth and early twentieth centuries is unclear. However, the word *zombi* was apparently in common enough use "in nurseries and among the servants" in "the Southern States" to merit its inclusion in a dictionary of uniquely American terms as a word meaning "spirit" or "ghost" (Schele DeVere, [1872] 2009, p. 138).

Another "Zombi" (this time spelled with a capital "z" and used as a proper noun) was also familiar to some Americans in the nineteenth century. "Zombi" was the name attributed to the leader of various pre–nineteenth-century, non–American slave revolts. The date and location of these revolts differed (and it is unclear if a rebellious slave named Zombi ever actually existed or was simply a folk hero created by unfree African laborers), but the character of Zombi remained the same.

Although a slave named Jean Zombi is credited in some French accounts with a leadership role in the Haitian slave revolt which ended with the declaration of Haiti as an independent republic in January 1804, references to Jean Zombi did not appear in any English-language publications during the nineteenth or early twentieth centuries (Rhodes, p. 75). While non French-speaking Americans may not have known of this Zombi, others were familiar with the exploits (whether real or fictional is unclear) of another rebellious slave who was called simply Zombi. This report, a reprint of "Extracts from the Modern Traveler," which described a seventeenth-century slave rebellion in Pernambuco, Brazil, appeared in the Wisconsin newspaper *American Freeman* in May 1845. In this account, printed in a publication that appealed to a readership of free African Americans and whites with abolitionist sentiments, Zombi appears as a heroic figure who leads a group of fellow slaves out of captivity. In the story, the rebel slaves not only escaped from the Portuguese, but they also created their own "black Kingdom in the New World." Zombi's followers, readers are told, built a city "possessed [of] a certain degree of magnificence" and made Zombi their "elective monarch." The author of the tale equates Zombi's followers with "the founders of Rome"; in the manner of the first Romans, who acquired wives by kidnapping the Sabine women, the rebel slaves carried off women from Portuguese estates. Lest otherwise sympathetic white readers be repelled by the thought of possible miscegenation, the story specifies that the men "[swept] the neighboring plantations for every *woman of color*" (emphasis mine). These heroic slaves died as bravely as they lived; when the Portuguese finally recaptured their capital, Zombi and his men "[threw] themselves down the rocky side of the fort." In case the truly noble nature of Zombi and his fellow rebels had escaped notice, the author concludes by informing readers that "had their success been equal to their bravery, their right to make slaves of the whites would have been ... as good as that which the Portuguese had to enslave them."

Thus, long before the publication in 1929 of William Seabrook's *The Magic Island*, an account of the author's travels in Haiti, which is credited with introducing the wandering corpse reanimated through Haitian Vodou rituals known as a zombie (spelled with an "e") to the American public, awareness of the supposed existence of a powerful entity or being (whether supernatural or human in nature) called a "zombi" did exist. However, with the appearance of *The Magic Island*, all references to "zombis," whether in the guise of helpful spirits, Vodou gods, or heroic slave leaders, disappeared from American publications and presumably from the American psyche as well. Following publication of *The Magic Island*, the only "zombies" in American popular culture were the walking dead of Haitian folklore.

New South, New Zombie

Why did the concept of the zombie as a reanimated, mindless corpse so quickly replace the earlier understanding of the zombie as a creature entirely spiritual in nature in American popular culture? Although it cannot be said that all (or even most) Americans in the nineteenth and early twentieth centuries were aware of the spirit of apparently African origin called the zombi or of rebellious bondsmen surnamed Zombi, various references to these types of "zombis" had appeared in American fiction and non-fiction for nearly one hundred years. Why, then, should both the "zombie spirit" and the "real" Zombi be so rapidly supplanted by a very different vision of the zombie as weak instead of powerful, docile instead of rebellious, and pitiful instead of awe-inspiring?

The sudden popularity of the Haitian zombie may perhaps be explained by the nature of the creature itself. The Haitian zombie did resemble the American zombi spirit in some crucial ways. It was a supernatural entity clearly associated with the belief system of people of African descent. It performed services for both Africans and non Africans. Like the rebellion-leading human Zombis, the zombie was, in essence, a slave. However, the Haitian zombie possessed traits that these earlier "zombis" did not. It may have been these unique traits that appealed to Americans (at least white, middle-class Americans) and made the zombie a more desirable creature than the zombi. At the very least, the characteristics of the Haitian zombie made it, in many ways, a less frightening being than the zombis of nineteenth-century America.

Perhaps what pleased white Americans most about the Haitian zombie was that it was not really a very frightening creature. Although the zombie could be made to harm the living, it did not (it could not) do so of its own volition. Indeed, it was the living being who created the zombie and directed its actions who constituted the true danger. Although in William Seabrook's book and other early "non-fiction" accounts of the Haitian zombie, zombie makers were of African ancestry, in fictional accounts, zombie makers were often white.

This depiction of blacks as helpless creatures was undoubtedly appealing to many white Americans. Americans of European ancestry in both the north and south had long feared African Americans, despite the fact that, in most regions of the United States, whites substantially outnumbered blacks, and, in every region, whites held superior economic, social, and political power. Prior to the abolition of slavery in the United States with the ratification of the Thirteenth Amendment in 1865, white southerners had lived in fear of slave revolts. Even many northern whites who otherwise disliked the institution of slavery feared that if African American slaves were set free they would rise up and slaughter white Americans in revenge for their suffering. Both before and after the Civil War, many Americans both north and south feared that African American servants (whether enslaved or free) would poison them (Litwack, 1979, pp. 62–63, 66; Genovese, 1972, pp. 615–17; Jordan, 1968, pp. 110,

115). So strong was this belief (which had little basis in fact) that even white abolitionists occasionally succumbed to it; the nineteenth-century African American artist Edmonia Lewis was dismissed from Oberlin College, a hotbed of abolitionist sentiment and a bastion of liberal thought, after two young white women living in the same boarding house falsely claimed that Lewis had tried to poison them (Bearden and Henderson, 1993, pp. 57–60). Although such fears were not completely without justification, nineteenth-century slave revolts were relatively few in number and easily quashed. With the exception of the August 1831 rebellion led by Nat Turner in Southampton County, Virginia in which 55 whites died, most revolts resulted in few white fatalities (Genovese, pp. 587, 592, 594). Nevertheless, white fears of African American violence persisted in the post–Civil War period.

In the post–Civil War New South, white anxieties concerning African Americans were linked not just to fears of potential black violence but to white resentment of the new control over their own labor now exercised by African Americans. No longer able to demand free labor from African Americans, white planters needed to attract willing workers and pay them (albeit poorly) for their labor. This situation was complicated by the fact that following the Civil War, many African American men sought employment outside the cotton fields, or, if they did perform agricultural labor themselves, tried to keep their wives and children from fieldwork. Furthermore, following the Civil War, many African Americans, now able to travel freely, moved westward, and, by the beginning of the twentieth-century, many African Americans had also begun to move to northern cities in search of work in communities where the lynching of black men was not a common occurrence or a source of public entertainment as it was in the South.[1]

Fear of physical harm at the hands of African Americans and fear of economic hardship as the result of the inability to command African American laborers led many white southerners in the late nineteenth and early twentieth centuries to yearn for a black labor force of contented, willing, docile workers. These yearnings were satisfied in numerous ways. Fictional tales of the antebellum south recounted halcyon days of yore when happy, eager slaves willingly worked to please kind, benevolent masters and beautiful southern belles. Stories by white authors told of slaves who willingly denied themselves opportunities to be free in order to save their beloved masters from Yankee soldiers (Hale, 1998, pp. 51–58, 60, 70–71). The image of the gentle, willing, white-loving laborer appeared in novels and short stories, in advertisements for a variety of products and services, on product labels, and on "collectibles" (e.g., smiling Mammy potholders and bottle openers) kept in white homes to replace and remind housewives of the vanished happy servants of yore. Certain categories of African American servants — especially the Mammy — were transformed into icons celebrated in poetry, prose, film, and art for their love and devotion (Hale, pp. 98–101, 111, 151–53, 155–60, 163–64).

The Haitian zombies who appeared in works like William Seabrook's *The Magic Island*, in short stories, and in motion pictures like *White Zombie*, the 1932 Victor Halperin film which was the first movie to feature zombies, were akin to the fictional Mammies and devoted antebellum field hands who served to assuage southern guilt and reassure white Americans that African Americans had been (and could be again) willing workers who posed no threat to white power or physical safety. Seabrook's and Halperin's zombies were essentially harmless creatures who, while they resembled contemporary African American laborers in appearance, possessed "desirable" qualities that white employers wished for (but found lacking) in the New South's African American workforce.

In many ways zombies were the perfect laborers. Although zombies were capable of performing physical labor, they lacked all traces of intellect, volition, or self-awareness. They could not think or speak, and they felt no pain. Completely lacking in emotion, they felt no anger or resentment and had no desires of their own. The person who unearthed a corpse and made it into a zombie had complete control over the reanimated body and could order it to perform any task that he or she wished. Zombies had no desire or ability to resist. They had no memories of their former lives. Although they needed sustenance and shelter, zombies required only minimal attention. Insensible to cold, they could be dressed in rags. Lacking a sense of taste, zombies could be fed the blandest, most inexpensive foods. Indeed, zombie folklore insisted that under no circumstances could zombies be fed meat or any food containing salt; if zombies consumed these forbidden substances, they would cease to be zombies and would revert to being immobile corpses (Seabrook, 1929, pp. 93, 95–99, 101). Zombies were not only "content" to be treated poorly, they seemed to demand it.

In many ways, the Haitian zombie displayed many of the stereotypical characteristics of antebellum African American slaves while lacking the "troublesome" qualities of free African American laborers. Accounts of zombies authored by Americans or appearing in American newspapers emphasized the zombie's lack of intellect just as racist descriptions of African Americans commonly described them as limited in intelligence or possessing the minds of children. Despite this supposed lack of intellect, however, zombies, informants routinely stated, could be taught to perform "simple tasks." In most accounts and early zombie films, zombies are typically shown performing the type of work that had commonly been assigned to African American slaves. They work in the fields, harvest crops, and work in sugar mills. One of William Seabrook's informants specified that zombies served as "drudge[s] around the habitation or the farm, [performing] dull heavy tasks" (Seabrook, p. 93). Zombies, like slaves, were not autonomous and had no control over their working conditions. As the character Murder Legendre in *White Zombie* explains to his guest, the French planter Beaumont, the workers in his sugar mill, all of whom are Haitian zombies, are the perfect employees: "They work faithfully, and they are not worried about long hours." In the event that they did not work hard enough or fast enough, zombies could be "beat[en] ... like a dumb beast"; free laborers could not be abused with impunity (Seabrook, p. 93). Zombies could presumably be beaten so easily because they did not possess the same ability to feel pain as did living beings. In this respect, zombies further resembled African American slaves in the eyes of many white Americans. In the nineteenth century, many whites had believed that African Americans were less sensitive to pain than were people of European ancestry, and white physicians often performed surgical procedures on black patients without the use of anesthesia (Pernick, 1985, pp. 155, 156). Furthermore, zombies, like slaves but unlike other employees, were a form of chattel whose labor could be rented or otherwise conveyed to others. Several sources specified that the creator of the zombie, usually described as an evil sorcerer, "can assign his authority over the zombie to someone else" ("Interesting Facts," 1943, p. 3).

Zombies did not, however, resemble *free* African American laborers. Zombies did not complain about their pay or working conditions and did not abandon their employers in search of better conditions. Zombie workers, unlike free laborers, could be created on demand to satisfy the needs of the employer. In *White Zombie*, Murder Legendre tells Beaumont that it would be easy to create a zombie workforce for his plantation. Zombies received and required no compensation for their labor other than minimal shelter and meager rations. Finally, if one wished to dispense with one's workers, this could more easily be done with zombies than with living workers. Workers who had been dismissed or mistreated might harbor resentment against a former employer and try to harm him or his business in some way. Troublesome zombies could be destroyed as easily as they were created; at the end of *White Zombie*, the zombie army of archfiend Murder Legendre is quickly dispensed with by a rather dimwitted American who "tricks" them into walking off a cliff. (He stands on the edge of a cliff and simply steps aside when the zombies march towards him.)

Claims that white Americans regarded zombies as ideal workers are not entirely speculative in nature. In *The Magic Island*, William Seabrook describes supposed encounters between zombies and the living. Although Seabrook claimed to have seen zombies only once, he recounts tales told to him by Haitian informants in which they described their contact with zombies.[2] One of the most detailed accounts in the book related the story of a married couple from the province of Columbier. In 1918, Seabrook's chief informant, a Haitian farmer named Polynice, told him, a man named Ti Joseph and his wife Croyance brought a group of male and female zombie laborers from a rural area bordering the Dominican Republic. (The Josephs apparently purchased the zombies from someone else. The details of the story indicate that they did not know enough about zombies to have been able to create them on their own.) The zombie workers, the informant claimed, were destined to work on sugar plantations owned by Hasco (the Haitian-American Sugar Company), a company that both refined sugar and produced rum. Whether or not the labor of these men and women had in fact been purchased by Hasco is unclear; what is clear, however, is that both Seabrook and his informant apparently believed that "zombies" would have been sought after by this company, which paid "low wages, twenty or thirty cents a day," and would have made ideal employees (Seabrook, p. 95).

The zombie was thus an ideal worker who could solve many of the labor problems of late nineteenth- and early twentieth-century America. Such creatures were certainly not to be feared. Indeed, depictions of zombie workers could serve to assuage employers' fears. Why then were zombie films considered horror films? The object of terror in the zombie film was not the black zombie. The truly terrifying creature was the zombie master, the creator and controller of zombies. The zombie master evoked fear not by making zombies of people of African descent but by using his ability to control these creatures to harm whites. Even more terrifying was the zombie master's ability to make zombies of white men and (especially) white women. Harm done to blacks did not frighten white Americans; the zombie master's power to harm whites and reduce them to a servile condition similar to that of blacks was the true source of horror.

What made the zombie master an even more frightening figure was his or her ethnicity; in zombie films the zombie master was often a person of non Anglo-Saxon ancestry. In the 1935 film *Ouanga*, for example, the zombie maker is a young woman of mixed European and African ancestry (Dendle, 2001, pp. 130–31). Similarly, in a later film, 1943's *I Walked with a Zombie*, a white woman, the wife of a wealthy plantation owner, is transformed into a zombie by the black leader of the local vodou/voodoo cult. The zombie priest not only possesses the ability to call her to him when he wishes, but he also apparently has the ability to manipulate whites who have not been transformed into zombies into doing his bidding. In another film of the 1930s, Victor Halperin's *Revolt of the Zombies* (1936), recruits from French Indochina are turned into bullet-proof zombies by a Cambodian zombie master and sent to attack Austrian soldiers in their trenches during World War I. For Americans living in the first half of the twentieth century, the thought that non Anglo-Saxons could command such power was disturbing for a variety of reasons.

New Immigrants, New Zombie Makers

If the zombie reminded white Americans of African American laborers, the zombie master called to mind a variety of troubling associations. In early accounts of Haitian zombies, the zombie master was usually black. He or she was often claimed to be a Vodou priest or priestess who controlled, through a combination of fear and religious devotion, the behavior of the black community. African American religious leaders had been feared by white Americans long before the appearance of the Haitian zombie master in American works of fiction and non-fiction. Enslaved African American spiritual leaders had often served as a locus of power and authority that stood in opposition to white slave owners and the legal and political institutions that they controlled. The knowledge that African American religious leaders could stir up anger and rebellion caused some slave owners to grant the right to preach only to those who could be counted upon to emphasize the need for good Christians to submit to their masters and quietly endure the privations of the temporal world (Raboteau, 1978, pp. 212–14, 218, 220, 238; Genovese, p. 259, pp. 587–88). Fear of the power of black religious leaders was not necessarily unwarranted; Nat Turner, the leader of the most deadly slave revolt in American history, gained credibility in the slave community as a result of his reputed gift for prophecy. Indeed, Turner's revolt was sparked by a solar eclipse which Turner interpreted as a sign from God indicating that the time had come for slaves to free themselves (Genovese, pp. 271–72, pp. 592–93; French, 2004, p. 42). Turner's rebellion aroused such fear of African American religious leaders among whites that, following his defeat, many southern states passed laws forbidding African Americans to preach and allowing them to attend religious services only in the presence of whites (Genovese, p. 257; Johnson, 1966, pp. 161, 163). In twentieth-century zombie literature, fear of African American religious leaders was superimposed on Haitian zombie makers.

Not all zombie masters in American literature and film were of African descent, however. They were all, however, non Anglo-Saxon. In the film *White Zombie*, for example, the zombie master is clearly eastern European (even if his last name is French). In *Ouanga*, the heroine, a white woman, is nearly transformed into a zombie by a woman of mixed African and European ancestry (Dendle, 2001, pp. 130–31). In *Revolt of the Zombies*, the original zombie master is Cambodian; he is murdered soon after the beginning of the film by General Mazovia, an Allied officer of uncertain ethnicity (Serbian? Russian?) who hopes to learn for himself the secret of creating zombies. Clearly, by the 1930s, the zombie master had come to represent other fears as well.

Although the presence in American society of large numbers of free African Americans was a significant source of anxiety for white Americans in the late nineteenth and twentieth centuries, they were not the only source of anxiety. While white southerners employed Jim Crow laws to control the south's black population, white, native-born Americans in the industrialized north sought to control another group of potentially dangerous people — immigrants from southern and eastern Europe. Before the Civil War, immigrants to the United States had come largely from the British Isles and northern Europe. With the exception of the Irish, most were Protestant and assimilated without great difficulty into American society. Most of the United States' small Jewish population were middle-class practitioners of Reform Judaism and blended fairly easily into the Protestant communities in which they lived. Following the Civil War, however, the nature of American immigration changed. Beginning in the 1870s and reaching a peak in the 1910s, the majority of European immigrants came from Italy, Greece, and the empires of Russia and Austria-Hungary. Most were

Roman Catholics, Orthodox Jews, or members of various Orthodox Christian churches; very few were Protestant. Many were uneducated, and the majority were quite poor. As America's cities swelled with the new immigrant population, many white, middle-class Americans feared that this would bring an end to native-born, Protestant hegemony (Higham, 1963, pp. 38–40).

Fear of the new immigrants was closely linked to the assumption that the religious beliefs of these newcomers and the political traditions of their native lands would make them unsuited to life in a democratic society. People who supposedly had depended upon the Pope or the Russian Czar to make all decisions for them would, many nativists argued, be unable to think for themselves or make good political choices. In the words of Ohio Congressman Michael Foran, who introduced legislation in 1884 that would prohibit the immigration of contract laborers, "This class of immigrants care nothing about our institutions, and in many cases never even heard of them.... They, as a rule, do not become citizens, and are certainly not a desirable acquisition to the body politic" (Zolberg, 2006, p. 194). Such people, Foran argued, "are not freemen, and very many of them have no conception of freedom" (Zolberg, p. 195). Many American Protestants feared that Roman Catholics in particular would continue to follow the commands of the Pope and not those of American political leaders (Higham, p. 180).

Other fears centered on the high birthrate of the new immigrants and the low birthrate of white, native-born, middle-class Americans who, by the 1910s, typically produced an average of two children per marriage (D'Emilio and Friedman, 1988, p. 174). Many American politicians and social reformers railed at the unwillingness of white, native-born women to bear large numbers of children and accused middle-class men of allowing their bodies to become weak and sickly (Putney, 2001, pp. 4–5, 31, 32, 34). Oliver Wendell Holmes, for one, was horrified by the large numbers of "soft-muscled, paste-complexioned-youth as ... never before sprung from loins of Anglo-Saxon lineage" (Putney, p. 31). From the White House, President Theodore Roosevelt inveighed against impending "race suicide" (Putney, p. 34). As the Anglo-Saxon, Protestant middle class died out as a result of their failure to reproduce, nativists argued, southern and eastern European Catholics and Jews would become the dominant elements in society. What remained of the native-born middle class would become second-class citizens in their own land and would be forced to sit idly by as armies of Roman Catholics, recruited from the ranks of the Knights of Columbus, delivered America into the hands of the Pope (Blee, 1991, p. 87).

In the West, the fears of white, native-born Americans were slightly different. Workmen in California feared the arrival of Jews and Italians less than they did the immigration of thousands of Asians to the cities and farmlands of the West Coast. In an attempt to keep the Asian immigrant population (especially the Chinese population) from growing too quickly, the federal government, at the behest of Western politicians and labor leaders, passed laws limiting the number of Asians allowed to enter the United States. Fears of domination by Asians are reflected in a scene in *Revolt of the Zombies*. In this film, after the Cambodian priest Tsiang has sent his Asian zombie army to attack the Austrian trenches (with disastrous consequences for the Austrians), officers from both sides of the conflict assemble and agree that the ability to create zombies cannot be left in the hands of a Cambodian. A German general appeals to the Allied officers by reminding those present of their shared "European-ness." "I am not here to plead the cause of the Central Powers," General von Schelling insists, "but that of modern civilization. In the name of humanity, you must not go further with your experiments. It may mean the destruction of the white race."

Fears of the new immigrants were thus clearly reflected in zombie films which portrayed non Anglo-Saxon zombie masters seizing power from their social superiors and interfering with the reproductive capacity of white Americans. This fear forms the basis of the narrative in 1932's *White Zombie*. The star of the film, Hungarian immigrant Bela Lugosi, plays the zombie master Murder Legendre, an archetypal villain of indeterminate origin, though it is obvious that he is "foreign." Legendre is swarthy with luminous, dark eyes. Unlike the other male characters, who are clean shaven, he sports a goatee. He speaks English with a heavy Eastern European accent. Although no mention is made of Legendre's religion, the inside of his home resembles the interior of a Gothic cathedral complete with pointed arches, stained glass windows, and cruciform-shaped stone carvings, implying that he is Roman Catholic. He is clearly not of Anglo-Saxon origin, and, despite his surname, does not appear to be French either. He thus represents a mysterious alien presence to the American main characters Neil and Madeleine, to the French planter Beaumont, and to the black Haitians. Fear that lack of deference and unbridled reproduction on the part of newly arrived European immigrants would undermine America's social fabric is reflected in Legendre's actions. Legendre, although seemingly of humble origin, has acquired great wealth and power through his ability to reproduce. Legendre, however, does not reproduce by fathering children; Legendre's reproductive superiority lies in his ability to create, at will, armies of zombie laborers and bodyguards. The zombies who toil in his fields and his sugar mill are the source of his wealth and whatever claim to social status he might have.

Despite his great wealth and grand home, Legendre, the film makes evident, has not been accepted by Haiti's social and political elite. Legendre, however, does not accept the fact that Haiti's elite will not recognize him as an equal, and his resentment of this treatment forms an important part of the film's plot. The film's narrative revolves around the wedding of Madeleine to Neil, a young American working in Port-au-Prince. During the voyage from the United States to Haiti, Madeleine meets and becomes friendly with a fellow passenger, a wealthy planter named Beaumont. Beaumont clearly occupies the highest social position of anyone in the story. Despite the fact that he speaks English without an accent, he is clearly a wealthy European, presumably of French heritage. Beaumont owns a large estate and a beautiful home decorated in a "European" fashion. The house is large with high ceilings. Paintings and tapestries adorn the walls. The rooms are filled with heavy, ornate furniture that seems to be of medieval provenance. Chandeliers hang from the ceilings, and vases filled with cut flowers adorn every room. Beaumont's house servants, which include a butler and two maids, are white and wear uniforms. The first time Beaumont appears on screen he is shown in his office wearing formal riding attire. Later, he is shown wearing a tuxedo.

While on board the ship, Beaumont asks Madeleine to allow him to host her impeding wedding at his estate, and she accepts his generous offer. Beaumont, however, has ulterior motives. He has fallen in love with Madeleine and wants her for his own. Upon his arrival in Haiti, Beaumont approaches Legendre and asks him to cast a spell that will put Madeleine under his [Beaumont's] control. Legendre has, in effect, been commissioned by Beaumont, his social superior, to perform a service for him. Legendre, however, also covets Madeleine and uses his powers not only to place Madeleine under Beaumont's control but to place Beaumont under his.

Although Beaumont's mad desire for Madeleine drives him to seek Legendre's help, it is clear that he is repulsed by the zombie master. When Beaumont first approaches Legendre to request his assistance, Legendre reaches out his hand to Beaumont. Beaumont, however, refuses to shake hands. Although outwardly Legendre appears to accept the slight with equanimity, even subsequently addressing Beaumont deferentially as "monsieur," a close-up of Legendre's withdrawn hand, which he has contorted into a shape somewhere between a fist and a claw, reveals his true feelings. Although Beaumont initially is able to assert his superiority over Legendre, by the end of the film, the situation has been reversed. Suffering from the effects of a magical potion that Legendre has placed in his wine, a potion which will soon turn him into a zombie, Beaumont, speechless and barely able to move, reaches out his hand to grasp Legendre's in a gesture of supplication. Legendre, however, is unmoved by Beaumont's appeal for mercy and instead takes the opportunity to gloat at his fall: "You refused to take hands once. I remember. Well, well. We understand each other better now." Unopposed by the helpless Beaumont, Legendre now takes control of Madeleine for himself. Legendre has, in effect, reversed the social order. He has attacked his superior to steal "his" woman.

Legendre's destruction of Beaumont is not the first occasion on which Legendre has used his "reproductive" abilities to gain control over his superiors by turning them into zombies. When Legendre arrives at Beaumont's house to help him remove Madeleine's body from her tomb, he introduces Beaumont to the group of zombies he has brought with him to carry the coffin. Attending upon Legendre are, among others, a vicar, a former (French) Haitian Minister of the Interior, a (French) captain of the Haitian gendarmerie, and the former (French) "high executioner." Legendre has made all of these men, his superiors, men who once held positions of authority in Haitian society, into zombies as punishment for having wronged him in the past. Instead of submitting to the powers that be, Legendre takes revenge against his superiors by making them his servants.

If part of the purpose of zombie fiction and zombie films, however, was to reassure white, middle-class audiences that dangerous elements in American society would not prevail, Legendre's attacks on his social betters cannot be allowed to succeed. The aristocratic Beaumont must triumph over Legendre, and he does. At the film's climax, which takes place in Legendre's home/fortress, Neil arrives to rescue Madeleine accompanied by a seemingly German missionary. Their bravery and heroism (characteristics which Neil has not previously displayed) are proclaimed to the audience by the fact that both men are attired in white clothing and ride white horses. Neil, however, cannot save Madeleine without assistance. Neil is a weak man, the type of fragile, sickly, "paste-complexioned" white collar worker that middle-class social reformers decried. Following Madeleine's death, Neil, rather than learn the truth, retreats to the local tavern to drown his sorrows. Spurred to action by the missionary, an acceptable northern European companion, Neil falls ill on their journey to find Madeleine, and the elderly missionary must go on without him. At one point in the rescue attempt, Neil is rendered unconscious, and Legendre nearly succeeds in making Madeleine kill him. Neil does ultimately (perhaps accidentally) succeed in destroying Legendre's zombie bodyguard, but Neil is no match for Legendre himself. However, just as Legendre is about to finally destroy Neil and gain full control over Madeleine, Beaumont, who is also dressed in white despite the fact that his actions have previously been quite villainous, appears. With his last ounce of strength and last iota of free will, he pushes Legendre from a cliff into the sea and follows behind him, atoning for his own sins and saving Madeleine and Neil. The message is clear: Beaumont must triumph over his presumptuous inferior and save Anglo-Saxon women for Anglo-Saxon men.

Legendre's attacks on Beaumont and Neil and his attempted theft of Madeleine reflect fears of middle-class, native-born Americans that the new immigrants would rise in society partly through their attempts to co-opt and control Anglo-Saxon women. In *White Zombie*, however, Madeleine could not have been so easily transformed by Legendre if she herself had not been somewhat complicit in Beaumont's "theft" of her. Had Madeleine possessed the reticence and timidity of earlier generations of American women, she would never have been in danger. Many of the dangers posed by the new immigrants were closely connected to another troublesome element in twentieth-century American society — the New Woman.

New Woman, New Zombie

The stereotypical New Woman, who appeared in the United States in the late nineteenth- and early twentieth-centuries, was a young woman who delighted in engaging in pursuits previously thought acceptable only by men. The New Woman was usually well educated, often having attended or graduated from college. She was interested in political issues and social problems. She might work outside the home, at least until she married. When she married, she married a man whom she expected to be more than a provider; the New Woman sought a husband who would treat her as an equal partner in marriage and be both a true companion and a compatible sexual partner. The New Woman dressed more provocatively than did women of earlier generations; by the 1920s this meant sleeveless dresses, relatively short skirts, and sheer stockings. The New Women cut their hair and used cosmetics. They drank and smoked cigarettes, and they sought entertainment in public places such as movie theatres, dance halls, and night clubs where they were often accompanied by young men. The New Woman was also more likely to read and talk about sex than women of earlier generations, and a substantial number engaged in intercourse (usually with their fiancés) before they were married (Cott, 1987, pp. 147–51, 156; Latham, 2000, pp. 18–20, 26, 30–31–59; Ullman, 1997, pp. 18–22, 23).

While some Americans welcomed the appearance of the New Woman, many feared that these young women were a dangerous, uncontrolled element in American society. Others believed that their entrance into public places of entertainment and their unsupervised socializing with men exposed them to harm. Fears that young women would be preyed upon by villainous men were reflected in a widespread fear of "white slavery" that pervaded American society in the early twentieth-century. White slavers were thought to lure young women with promises of entertainment or protestations of love, imprison them, and consign them to a life of sexual slavery in either American or foreign brothels. Fears of both unchecked female sexuality and white slavery quickly found their way into American popular culture; novels such as Reginald Kauffman's *The House of Bondage* (1910), plays, and films such as *Traffic in Souls* (1913) featured "modern" women and white slavers in their plot lines. Significantly, many of the white slavers of American popular culture were immigrants of non-northern European ancestry. Indeed, the Eastern European trafficker in young women became a standard element in films and popular fiction (D'Emilio and Friedman, pp. 208–09; Grittner, 1990, pp. 3, 61–63, 69, 109–10, 114, 115; Ullman, p. 5).

Like other films of this early period, zombie films incorporated themes of sexual transgression and white slavery into their plots. While the Haitian zombie was generally a black male, the zombies of Hollywood film were often white and female, and the zombie master assumed the character of a white slaver. Originally, the character of the zombie had had no sexual dimension to it whatsoever. Indeed, what could be less sexual than a walking corpse? This very quickly changed, however, and, during the 1930s and 1940s, the zombie came to be associated with moral transgression, especially sexual transgression.

Stories about the creation of zombies changed to reflect this new dimension of the zombie. William Seabrook's original informants described the creation of zombies in vague terms. A corpse was "taken from the grave and endowed by sorcery with a mechanical semblance of life" (Seabrook, p. 93). No information was given regarding what types of people were most likely to become zombies after death. Indeed, Seabrook's informants seemed to indicate that any and all people were vulnerable. By the 1930s and 1940s, however, more details had been added to the zombie creation account; stories about zombies, such as the 1943 article "Interesting Facts About Zombies — The Walking Dead," now added the important element that "zombies [were] sinners. Anyone who sins in the West Indies becomes prime zombie material, if someone was hurt by the sin" (p. 3). LeRoy Antoine, an advisor on the film *I Walked with a Zombie*, who had "studied the voodooism of his native Haiti," also believed (or at least told motion picture directors and journalists that he believed) that moral transgression during one's lifetime rendered one vulnerable to becoming a zombie after death. Significantly, the example that he provided was one of sexual transgression: "As an illustration, a Haitian has a good looking wife, and another Haitian comes along and steals her. That is a sin, and the wife stealer immediately becomes good zombie material" (Foster, 1942). Although the sinner and prospective zombie in the example provided by Antoine was a man, the offense for which the man was punished — adultery — was a sin requiring the complicity of a woman. In the film, *I Walked with a Zombie*, the eponymous zombie is Jessica Holland, the wife of British planter Paul Holland. Jessica is transformed into a zombie at her mother-in-law's behest after she makes plans to run away with her husband's half-brother, Wesley Rand. Other connections between sinful behavior and the zombie made more explicit reference to the sexual transgressions of women. In the article "Interesting Facts About Zombies," the writer assured readers that, because people became zombies only as a result of sinful behavior, "If you keep your skirts clean, you have nothing to worry about" (p. 3). Rather than using other colloquial expressions meaning to act appropriately, the unknown author chose an expression which, through its explicit reference to a skirt, connoted the sexual transgression of women.

Women, of course, could sin sexually in a variety of ways, some of which were more forgivable than others. At one end of the spectrum were "white slaves," sexually innocent women who were either lured into a life of prostitution by a man (usually as a result of their ignorance and naiveté) or kidnapped and physically confined in a brothel. These fears of unwitting women forced into a life of sin, a "fate worse than death" as such a life was described in the language of the nineteenth century, by nefarious men (and occasionally women) of non–Anglo-Saxon ancestry is clearly reflected in the films of the 1930s and 1940s that feature "white zombies." The connection between white slavery and the creation of zombies is alluded to several times in *White Zombie*. In the film, Madeleine unwittingly becomes prey to Beaumont when he "seduces" her by offering her the use of his mansion for her wedding and promising to have her fiancé Neil transferred to New York to work for him as his agent. The shipboard "seduction" of the innocent young woman journeying to an unknown land was a standard trope of late nineteenth- and early twentieth-century white slavery literature and film. Upon arriving in Haiti, Madeleine and Neil travel to Beaumont's home, where he is arranging a wedding ceremony for them. Likewise, in stereotypical white slavery narratives, the young woman was often tricked or forced into a life of prostitution through the guise of a sham marriage. Ernest A. Bell's "true" account of the white slavery trade, *Fighting the Traffic in Young Girls*, for example, informed readers that, according to "Mrs. Ophelia L. Amigh, superintendent of the Illinois State Training School for Girls

... runaway marriage is a favorite trick of the White Slaver." According to Amigh, such marriages were often the culmination of romances that began aboard summer excursion boats (Bell, 1911, p. 251). This was a favorite element in works of white slave fiction. Appropriately enough, Madeleine is transformed into a zombie at her wedding supper at the home of her shipboard "seducer" Beaumont.

Beaumont accomplishes this feat by placing a bit of a magical potion that he has received from his acquaintance, zombie-maker Murder Legendre, in a flower that he then gives to Madeleine to sniff. (Once again, Madeleine willingly, if unwittingly, assists in her own destruction: After Beaumont unsuccessfully begs her to abandon Neil and marry him as he is walking her to the altar, Madeleine, instead of becoming incensed at Beaumont's egregiously bad behavior, smilingly accepts the poisoned flower as a final gift from him. A woman of the nineteenth century would have refused to accept such a gift from a man who had acted so inappropriately). Significantly, another way to deliver the potion to the victim that Legendre has suggested to Beaumont would be to place a small amount in a glass of wine. Later in the film, Legendre uses this very method to administer the potion that turns Beaumont into a zombie.

The use of a magical powder or potion to turn both Madeleine and Beaumont into zombies is an interesting element in the film's narrative. Although zombie films and literature did not usually provide many details regarding how zombies were created, the use of potions or powders is never hinted at. However, according to white slavery tales, placing sleeping drops in a glass of alcohol, tea, or lemonade was a standard method of abducting young women.[3] This resemblance between white slavery literature and the film's narrative does not seem to have escaped the notice of at least some members of the audience. So closely does the potion-wielding Legendre resemble a white slaver that a 1932 review of the film described the character as "a sinister fiend who traffics in the exhumation of ... bodies" ("Theatre and Stage News," 1932, p. 4). "Trafficking" in "bodies" was at the time a phrase closely associated with the activities of white slavers.

The connection between Beaumont's and Legendre's villainous intentions and white slavery was further emphasized by the text, design, and placement of newspaper advertisements for *White Zombie*. Many of the ads for the film emphasized Madeleine's sexuality and physical beauty. Advertisements frequently featured drawings of women who appear to be either naked or wearing see-through clothing. The text of the advertisements often emphasized the sexual dimension of the narrative and blamed Madeleine's fate on her own desires. One advertisement succinctly summarized the plot as follows: "A beautiful girl turns from her lover on her bridal night ... turned into a ZOMBIE and made slave to a fiend's passion!" The accompanying picture shows a small, apparently naked woman caught in rays emanating from Bela Lugosi's eyes (*White Zombie* advertisement, 1932). The combination of white slavery, women's sexuality, and a plantation setting as essential elements in the zombie narrative was further emphasized by the ad's placement next to one for the film *Cabin in the Cotton*, which featured the come-on "Flaming Passions Behind Modern Slavery" and indicated that the passions in question were those of "A planter's daughter seeking a thrill..." (*Cabin in the Cotton* advertisement, 1932).

Although Madeleine had acted innocently when she "betrayed" Neil, other zombie films depicted women who had willingly transgressed sexual conventions. In *I Walked with a Zombie*, Jessica Holland is clearly depicted as the initiator of the adulterous relationship between herself and her brother-in-law. Wesley Rand, her illicit lover, is depicted as a weak alcoholic who cannot control his own urges, and Jessica's mother-in-law requests that a zombie priest transform Jessica into a zombie after she becomes disgusted by Jessica's displays of pleasure at her ability to manipulate men. In *Revolt of the Zombies*, Armand Louque uses his ability to create zombies to force Claire Duval, his former fiancée who jilted him in order to marry his friend, into marriage. Women who had knowingly and deliberately violated the sexual rules of society were often presented as villainous and, as villains, were sometimes cast in the role of zombie-maker and not as the more pitiable zombie. In the film *Ouanga*, for example, Clelie, a woman of mixed African and white descent, attempts to transform a white woman into a zombie. Clelie's actions are motivated by her desire for the white woman's fiancé. Clelie is a true villain, for she has broken a number of taboos. A woman, she has attempted to manipulate the behavior of a man. A person of mixed race, she has dared to attack a white woman in order to marry a white man. Clelie's crime may extend even beyond this. The white couple whose marriage Clelie wishes to prevent are named Adam and Eve (Dendle, 2001, pp. 130–31). Clelie is thus seemingly attempting to destroy the future of the human race by interfering with the ur-parents of all humankind. Clelie is thus guilty of both violence toward whites and an attempt to annihilate humanity through her inversion of the social and sexual order.

Although sexual transgression, whether unwitting, as in the case of Madeleine, or deliberate, as in the case of Clelie and Jessica Holland, was always presented as dangerous and undesirable in zombie films, such films did not reject women's sexuality completely or condemn the new morality of the New Woman out of hand. Indeed, lack of sexual desire on the part of women is depicted as unnatural, and the New Woman, the woman who is a romantic companion, intellectual equal, and sexual partner combined, is portrayed as men's true desire. In films of the 1930s and 1940s, the husband or fiancé of the female zombie is never the one who places her in this situation; instead, another person (usually another man) gains control over the wife/fiancée and manipulates her for his own purposes. Modern men, the films make clear, do not want zombies for wives. Although a female zombie (completely uncontrolled by her husband/master, always silent, possessing no desires of her own) would have made an ideal wife for many men during an earlier period in history, the female zombie is depicted as an imperfect wife for the modern age.

This sentiment is made clear in a scene in *White Zombie*. Beaumont, having followed Legendre's instructions, has been successful in transforming Madeleine, the object of his desires, into a zombie. In the scene, Beaumont, now supposedly in possession of all he needs to make him happy, gazes upon Madeleine. Attired in a dress with long sleeves, and a full, bell-shaped, floor-length skirt, a fitting costume for a middle-class woman of the nineteenth century but not the twentieth, she plays a tune on a piano, a fitting occupation for a nineteenth-century wife. Madeleine does not speak; her face is blank, emotionless. Beaumont approaches her and speaks to her. He implores her to respond, to show some trace of feeling. Madeleine is unresponsive. Beaumont pleads with Legendre to return her to her earlier state. Despite Legendre's mocking reminder that if Madeleine does regain her senses she will certainly become aware of what Beaumont has done and hate him for it, the distraught Beaumont insists that he does not want Madeleine as a zombie. He is willing to risk Madeleine's displeasure and begs Legendre to restore her true nature. Beaumont clearly does not want a "traditional" wife. He fell in love with Madeleine not just because of her beauty but because of her modern traits. The passionless zombie is old-fashioned and ultimately unappealing; the New Woman is what men really desire. Only the truly perverted Legendre wants a zombie for a wife.

Zombie films and zombie fiction of the twentieth century played a complex role in

American culture. Zombie films and zombie literature conveyed to viewers and readers the dangerous nature of new elements within American society — new immigrants, modern women, unrestrained sexual behavior, and a middle class more interested in having sex for pleasure than for reproduction. These works of literature and film used the characters of the zombie and the zombie master to reiterate warnings and reinforce sentiments conveyed to the public by other means in other venues. Besides serving to warn white, middle-class Americans yet again of the dangers lurking in the modern world, zombie films and literature also sought to reassure white, middle-class Americans by presenting images of docile laborers, heroic northern European men, and beautiful women restored to their husbands after having learned of the dangers attached to modern behavior. The very "emptiness" of the zombie, which made the creature the perfect vessel to convey various fears, doubts, and concerns, and the ease with which this "monster" could be defeated made it the ideal cultural repository for the anxieties and interests of the twentieth century and a fixture in American popular culture.

NOTES

1. For information on "spectacle lynchings" in the early twentieth century, see Hale (1998, 199–239).

2. Seabrook did not believe that zombies were reanimated corpses or attribute their existence to supernatural forces. Instead, Seabrook seems to have believed that zombies were living people who, because of mental illness, brain injury, or mental retardation, acted like mindless automatons. Their disability made them prey to unscrupulous people seeking inexpensive labor (Seabrook, 100–02).

3. The use of a powder or potion to destroy one's victims also fits within many of the other "destroy the Anglo-Saxons" narratives that were well known to middle-class Americans. Murder Legendre attacks his victims in precisely the way that many whites feared African Americans (like Edmonia Lewis) would attack them — through mixing poisonous powders or potions in their food. Similarly, nativist literature circulated by the Ku Klux Klan in the 1920s warned Protestants that their Catholic neighbors would one day rise up against them and "secretly use the poisonous cup" and other murderous implements to destroy all non–Catholics (Blee, 1991, p. 87).

2

Hurston in Haiti
Neocolonialism and Zombification

RITA KERESZTESI

In her historical cultural ethnography *Tell My Horse: Voodoo and Life in Haiti and Jamaica* (1938), Zora Neale Hurston includes a startling photograph of a Haitian woman, "the broken remnant, relic, or refuse of Felicia Felix-Mentor in a hospital yard" (Hurston, [1938] 1990, p. 179). According to the script under the photograph, she is a zombie (p. 180). Hurston is both fascinated and repulsed: "And the sight was dreadful. That blank face with the dead eyes. The eyelids were white around the eyes as if they had been burned with acid. It was pronounced enough to come out in the picture" (p. 195). The photograph shows the zombie in a hospital gown that reveals only a glimpse of her humanity in the small detail of her embroidered dress worn under a shapeless frock. While in Haiti on a research trip to collect materials for her book on Voodoo[1] practices in the Caribbean, Hurston heard from Dr. Rulx Leon, Director-General of the Service d'Hygiene, that "a Zombie had been found on the road and was now at the hospital at Gonaives" (p. 195). She immediately traveled to the site to observe the Zombie. Hurston, who herself was initiated as a Voodoo priestess both in New Orleans and later in Haiti, is surprised by her own reactions to the living-dead with whom she comes face to face: "There was nothing that you could say to her or get from her except by looking at her, and the sight of this wreckage was too much to endure for long" (p. 195). During her visit to the hospital, Hurston was allowed to take some pictures of the Zombie: "I took her first in the position that she assumed herself whenever left alone. That is, cringing against the wall with the cloth hiding her face and head. Then in other positions. Finally the doctor forcibly uncovered her and held her so that I could take her face" (p. 195). This is the image she includes in the book.

Tell My Horse is a rich mix of genres that record the author's experiences, impressions, and reflections on her ethnographic research trips to Jamaica and Haiti. What holds the different pieces together is her interest in understanding the Neo-African religion of "Voodoo" already driven underground by the time she made her visits to the Caribbean between 1936 and 1938 (with a brief break when she returned to the United States for a couple of months due to poor health).[2] According to Ishmael Reed's "Foreword" to a recent edition of the book (1990), Hurston tackles such diverse topics as "the botany, sociology, anthropology, geology, and politics of these nations" (xii). Reed commends Hurston's innovative writing techniques, which would lead her text to be read as "the postmodernist book of the nineties" (xv). But more importantly, he commends her for writing seriously on the controversial topic of Voodoo spiritual practices that Reed defines as:

> ... less a religion than the common language of slaves from different African tribes, thrown together in the Americas for commercial reasons. This common language was feared because it not only united the Africans but also made it easier for them to forge alliances with those Native Americans whose customs were similar. Voodoo has been the inspiration for the major slave revolts in this hemisphere [xiii].

Here Reed interprets Voodoo, or Hoodoo, as less of a religious practice and rather as a unifying political expression and tool for revolt. "Hoodoo" is often used to refer to African American traditional folk magic, also known as conjure, which incorporates practices from African and Native American traditions. In this sense, Voodoo is a syncretic transcultural entity that is resistant to discourse of domination and power, such as Christianity and plantation slavery. What is controversial about Hurston's reading of Voodoo is that she exposes its negative use to cover up and code, literally and bodily, indentured servitude in Haiti.

In this article I follow Reed's lead in discussing Hurston's fascination with zombies, specifically the case of Felicia Felix-Mentor, in politically motivated and socially and historically situated terms. In her account of the practice of Voodoo, what Reed initially defines as "the Neo-African religion practiced in Haiti," Hurston pays particular attention to the "main loas (gods), their need, their desire, and their powers" and to the "strange phenomenon" of "possession" "during which a mortal is taken over by a god" (xiii). The title of the book, "tell my horse," refers to the Creole phrase, "Parlay cheval ou," which, according to her biographer, Valerie Boyd, Hurston had heard daily while in Haiti (Boyd, 2003, p. 320). Possession in the practice of Voodoo is a state when a person, usually a woman and/or from the lower classes, is not in control of his or her actions and is not responsible for the words uttered; he or she is "mounted" by the god Guede who speaks and acts through the person mounted (like a horse). According to Boyd:

> A spirit, "with social consciousness, plus a touch of burlesque and slapstick," as Hurston described him, Guede always began his caustic commentary with these words: "Tell my horse." Often, too, Haitian peasants used this phrase as a disclaimer — feigning possession by Guede in order to express resentment of the upper class, to make devastating revelations about their enemies, or to otherwise say things they lacked the courage to say in their ordinary unmounted state [p. 320].

In this sense, being possessed or mounted by the god are masked forms of social critique and resistance in a tradition similar to the "carnivalesque" Mikhail Bakhtin describes in *Rabelais and His World* (1984) or, rather, to a Caribbean version of carnival observed on several of the islands in the West Indies.[3] While Bakhtin focuses on the subversive class and gender ramifications of European Renaissance carnival, the Caribbean Carnival was, and still is, an expression of and reaction to colonial occupation and plantation slavery in racial terms. Similarly, in Haiti, Vodou has functioned not only as a religious practice and but also as political speech that can unite groups of people of African descent against French colonials or, later, occupying American troops, as well as against the class privileges of and exploitation by the Creole upper class. Hurston's use of the English transliteration of the Haitian Creole term for her title signals her own intent to speak bluntly about issues of colonial oppression as well as of class and gender antagonisms in the neocolonial Caribbean context. For example, in her chapter on "Women in the Caribbean," she openly critiques sexist discriminatory practices both in Jamaica and Haiti. In line with the forced adoption of Euro-colonial values, in the Caribbean, women of African descent were considered of less value within the social strata: they were also less educated and often did the menial physical labor of loading banana boats, coaling ships, or working in the rock quarries. Upper-class and mulatto women are somewhat better off. As Hurston comments on gender- and class-discrimination:

> This sex superiority is further complicated by class and color ratings. Of course, all women are inferior to all men by God and law down there. But if a woman is wealthy, of good family and mulatto, she can overcome some of her drawbacks. But if she is of no particular family, poor and black, she is in a bad way in that man's world. She had better pray to the Lord to turn her into a donkey and be done with the thing. It is assumed that God made poor black females for beasts of burden, and nobody is going to interfere with providence [Hurston, (1938) 1990, p. 58].

Her message was repeated in *Their Eyes Were Watching God* (1937), the novel she wrote during this same period, between her Caribbean travels.

The literary critic Robert E. Hemenway ([1977] 1988) finds *Tell My Horse*— along with Boyd (2003) later — to be lacking in organization, depth, and analysis. Hemenway complains that the talented novelist and trained folklorist Hurston is "not a political analyst and traveloguist" (pp. 248–49). He calls her views naïve since she "praises the nineteen-year occupation of that country [Haiti] by American marines, attributing solvency and political stability to the American influence." He blames her for giving too much credence to oral traditions while making "no attempt to compare these legends with historical facts" (p. 249). Both Hemenway and Boyd declare the book to be a novelistic failure — because it does not adhere to generic rules or disciplinary boundaries, even though it was a commercial success in England where the book was published under the title, *Voodoo Gods: An Inquiry into Native Myths and Magic in Jamaica and Haiti* (see Boyd, p. 322). Hurston's book has gotten little critical attention in literary circles since its publication, except, maybe, from Ishmael Reed who celebrates the postmodern quality of Hurston's writing. Reed also appreciates Hurston's critical voice that takes on the male chauvinism of Afro-Caribbean societies and her keen eye that can see the protest elements in Voodoo. In my reading, Hurston's political critique and thinly masked social analysis make *Tell My Horse* particularly interesting. She is one of the first African American writers to notice and draw attention to the rigid class, gender, and color stratifications within black communities in the United States and the Caribbean.[4] Hurston sees not only superstition and magic in the figure of the zombie, she also notices the less obvious practices of social and bio-chemical engineering at work in turning women and able-bodied men into cheap sources of labor — a sociopolitical variation on what W. J. T. Mitchell calls "biocybernetic reproduction" in art and culture (Mitchell, 2003, p. 1).

Mitchell rewrites Walter Benjamin's modernist manifesto on the consequences of the new technologies of the work of art in the context of our current age of "biocybernetic reproduction." He places those issues — biological, technological, ethical, and political — in the larger context of the relation between "bios" and "cyber." The new mode of "biocybernetic reproduction" is a "a rewriting of the traditional dialectics between nature and culture, human beings and the tools, artifacts, machines, and media" (p. 5). The relation of the Cyber to Bios, i.e., that of the Word (or Code) to the Image it explains, is also the mechanism at work in turning humans into zombies. Zombies may be viewed as the Voodoo versions of what we today call cyborgs. Mitchell's term also functions as a tool for periodization, because the age of "biocybernetic reproduction (high-speed computing, video, digital imaging, virtual reality, the internet, and the industrialization of genetic engineering) dominates the age that we have called 'postmodern'" (p. 8). Mitchell describes biocybernetics as an "attempt to control bodies with codes, images with language"; then he suggests that the "one task of art in the age of biocybernetic reproduction [is] to reveal the codes and expose the illusion of the ultimate mastery of life" (p. 21). Similarly, Hurston is interested in breaking the code behind the production of zombies, to unmask the supernatural and expose the interested intention behind the "natural." Hurston opens "Chapter 13, Zombies" of *Tell My Horse* with the probing question: "What is the whole truth and nothing else but the truth about Zombies?" (Hurston, 179). In the rest of the chapter she seeks the truth, or rather, the code behind the image of the zombie, Felicia Felix-Mentor, as if confessed under oath in a courtroom.

Since the very definition of the zombie is that "it" lacks language, will, or consciousness, Hurston finds herself in the position of having to prove to the world (mainly to her American unbelieving readers)— through the medium of photography — that zombies do exist. The camera therefore serves as witness to an experience that otherwise eludes linguistic representation or rational logic. The zombie belongs to the realms of the Lacanian Real that is foreclosed to the Symbolic or Imaginary orders. It eludes language and interpretation. Her task is to capture the Real at the level of the Imaginary through photography. The image captures the surface of the elusive Real and gives an access to imagining a reconnection of the Real to the Symbolic order. Thus Hurston's photograph serves as evidence of and witness to the supernatural phenomenon of zombification for a skeptical American audience that wants evidence and responds favorably only to the legal, scientific, or rational language of the Symbolic order. Hurston starts her chapter on zombies with a comparison between American and Haitian perceptions of and approaches to death and dying: "Here in the shadow of the Empire State Building, death and the graveyard are final. It is such a positive end that we use it as measure of nothingness and eternity. We have the quick and the dead. But in Haiti there is the quick, the dead, and then there are Zombies" (p. 179). Since Western rationality can only believe in facts, and since "[w]hat is involved in the 'give man' and making Zombies is a question that cannot be answered anywhere with legal proof" (p. 189), Hurston resorts to the one medium that comes the closest to factuality, the documentary technology of photography. Because the zombie cannot give an account of his or her story, the image must speak for itself, what Mitchell calls the "word-image dialectic" (Mitchell, p. 6). In capturing the un-capturable, Hurston gives witness and evidence to a phenomenon that escapes both reason and language. She breaks the rules of secrecy and magic and translates the practice of Voodoo into the neocolonial practice of turning people into objects, humans into slaves and machines.

When discussing the American occupation of Haiti, indeed Hurston writes about the events in celebratory terms. But I believe that her voice is ironic and her message is dialogic, as usual. Since she is writing for a predominantly white American audience, she performs both a complicit praise for American imperialistic aggression as well as a scathing critique of the American occupation of Haiti in particular, and of neocolonialism in general. Therefore, to read her analysis of early twentieth-century Haitian society and politics as a purely monologic text is a mistake. Hurston's earlier ethnographic text, *Mules and Men* ([1935] 1990), offers a key to unlocking her rich prose that masquerades as an insider's depiction of African American folklore for white audiences but with a wink to her true audience of Black folks in her introduction to that text:

> Folklore is not as easy to collect at it sounds. The best source is where there are the least outside influences and these people, being usually under-privileged, are the shyest. They are most reluctant at times to reveal that which the soul lives by. And the Negro, in spite of his open-faced laughter,

his seeming acquiescence, is particularly evasive. You see we are a polite people and we do not say to our questioner, "Get out of here!" We smile and tell him or her something that satisfies the white person because, knowing so little about us, he doesn't know what he is missing. The Indian resists curiosity by a stony silence. The Negro offers a feather-bed resistance. That is, we let the probe enter, but it never comes out. It gets smothered under a lot of laughter and pleasantries.

     The theory behind our tactics: "The white man is always trying to know into somebody else's business. All right, I'll set something outside the door of my mind for him to play with and handle. He can read my writing but he sho' can't read my mind. I'll put this play toy in his hand, and he will seize it and go away. Then I'll say my say and sing my song" [2–3].

Hurston demonstrates her trickster character who can play to two audiences simultaneously, satisfying them both but with different results. White readers can read her writing but its true meaning stays inaccessible to them. Her "feather-bed resistance" leaves them comforted but not informed.

In *Tell My Horse*, Hurston legitimates a creative space for her surprise critique within the context of Haitian social racial relations: she prepares a sympathetic audience by not condemning the American occupation immediately but, at an opportune moment, she pulls off her most effective piece of evidence for critique from her magician's hat, the shocking photograph of the zombie. The readers cannot help but feel empathy for the plight of Haiti's living dead and, ultimately, for the cause of Haitian independence, both political and economic. The neo-colonial U.S. occupation in 1915 was driven by imperialist competition. The government "saw military occupation as a way to establish political and economic dominance [in] Haiti and secure a base of power in the region" (Scott, 2004). While it is true that the American general public was not well informed of the violence and economic exploitation that accompanied the United States Marine Corps' nineteen-year long occupation of Haiti, by the time of Hurston's visit to Haiti, these facts were well known. For example, between "1918 and 1932 *The Nation* magazine carried more than fifty articles and editorials on conditions in Haiti. Evidence of torture and massacres uncovered by *The Nation*'s 1920 inquiry into the American occupation of Haiti led to a congressional investigation and helped bring the island independence in 1934" (Heuvel, 1990).

     According to a 1920 article in *The Nation*, the occupation also resulted in the resuscitation of the old Haitian law of "corvee," the practice of forced road labor, transplanted to the colonies from feudal Europe. The American occupiers proudly pointed to the newly built military roads which,

     ... were in large part built by Haitian slaves ... under American taskmasters. An old Haitian law of corvee, or enforced road labor, rarely if ever invoked, authorizing three days' work in each year on roads about the citizen's domicile, was made the excuse for kidnapping thousands of Haitians from their homes — when they had homes — forcing them to live for months in camps, insufficiently fed, guarded by United States marines, rifle in hand. When Haitians attempted to escape this dastardly compulsion, they were shot [Seligman, quoted in Heuvel].

Because the regions that most heavily relied on corvee slavery responded to such renewal to slave labor with resistance and extreme violence, the then brigade commander of Haiti was forced to formally abolish the practice by 1919. It is not hard to see the parallels between the foreign occupiers' use of the practice of corvee slave labor and the neo-colonial practice of zombification Hurston discusses. Moreover, Nancy Cunard's 1934 anthology, *Negro*, which was an ambitious effort to showcase the cause of the "New Negro," much more so in scope than Alain Locke's earlier anthology from 1925, contained a short piece on "Hayti" by Grace Hutchins. Hutchins labels the U.S.'s role as "Wall Street's occupation of Hayti" and describes it as "one of the bloodiest chapters in the history of American imperialism" (Cunard, 2002, p. 288). She also describes the practice of *corvée* as slavery being revived by the marines. Similarly, in W. E. B. DuBois's assessment, the American occupation of Haiti was a "violation of the independence of a sister state," causing the death of 3,000 Haitians, all for "the pushing of the monopoly claims of an American corporation which [held] a fraudulent charter" (Christol, 1991, p. 61).

Hurston uses several techniques to give validity to her topic of bringing reality and political meaning to the phenomena of zombies and zombification in Haiti: she relies on the use of photography, on information gained from folklore, and on the evidence of six case studies. One of the case studies is the story of Felicia Felix-Mentor. Hurston relies on the old saying that seeing is believing, thus her most convincing tools prove to be the photographs she takes:

> ... I had the good fortune to learn of several celebrated cases in the past and then in addition, I had the rare opportunity to see and touch an authentic case. I listened to the broken noises in its throat, and then, I did what no one else had ever done, I photographed it. If I had not experienced all of this in the strong sunlight of a hospital yard, I might have come away from Haiti interested but doubtful. But I saw this case of Felicia Felix-Mentor, which was vouched for by the highest authority. So I know that there are Zombies in Haiti. People have been called back from the dead [p. 182].

While seeing is not always believing, taking a photograph may be equal to a legal oath of telling "the whole truth and nothing else but the truth" — of zombies. Therefore, after having created an interested audience for her cause to draw attention to the renewed use of indentured servitude that borders on new practices of slavery, practically, in the U.S.'s backyard, Hurston uses the masters' tools — reason and the fascination with photographic images as evidence — to dismantle illusions about United States foreign policy decisions and of self-righteous notions of justice, freedom, and democracy. Once Hurston has established her credibility (with her camera and the authority of a famous male doctor who calls her attention to the case and invites her to meet the unfortunate woman), she can offer her shocking explanation and scathing social critique of a hidden system of indentured servitude and slavery aided by medicinal drugs and masked by the mystery and fear surrounding Haitian Vodou practices.

Hurston supplies several interpretations to the image of this "cyborg" and to the systemic process of zombification in Haiti. Moreover, she offers a political analysis of the social system that necessitates the existence, or to use Mitchell's term "biocybernetic reproduction," of human beings as laboring machines or indentured servants. Having authenticated the validity of her encounter with a real zombie, she sets out to find a rational and plausible explanation to a seemingly irrational and downright dangerous phenomenon: "Now, why have these dead folk not been allowed to remain in their graves? There are several answers to this question, according to the case" (Hurston, [1938] 1990, p. 182). In order to get to the "truth" of the matter, she leads her American readers through a series of possible though still "fantastic" — as Tzvetan Todorov (1973) and Rosemary Jackson (1988) use the category of "the fantastic" for the literary genres of subversion — explanations. Thus, by the time she gets to her most horrifying explanation — a drug-induced state of slavery — it seems a likely answer to her initial question:

> **A** was awakened because somebody required his body as a beast of burden. In his natural state he could never have been hired to work with his hands, so he was made into a Zombie because they wanted his services as a laborer. **B** was summoned to labor also but he is reduced to the level

of a beast as an act of revenge. C was the culmination of "ba' Moun" ceremony and pledge. That is, he was given as a sacrifice to pay off a debt to a spirit for benefits received [Hurston, (1938) 1990, p. 182].

The medium through which such a violation of personal integrity takes place is the "bokor" who sucks the soul out of the victim. Bokors are said to be Voodoo initiates who perform acts to harm. The differences between the good and the harmful in Voodoo are often too close to call. As Hurston explains: "But it is not always easy to tell just who is a houngan and who is a bocor. Often the two offices occupy the same man at different times" ([1938] 1990, p. 189).

More recent ethnographic studies have established a connection between the role bokors played in pre-colonial African societies and their colonial transplants mostly in Haiti, but also in the larger context of the African Diaspora (cf. Metraux, 1972). "Voodoo" priests generally function as the overseers or "masters of the land" by maintaining social order. In the context of Haiti, bokors were linked to the bands of escaped slaves or Maroon societies that organized revolts against the French in the late eighteenth century. These secret societies are believed to have used the botanico-chemical process of zombification as a form of capital punishment, but never as a random act. It is also important to point out that while zombification can be linked to poisoning, the powders and potions derived from the Datura plant (also known as the "Zombie cucumber" in West Africa as well as in Haiti) and tetrodotoxin derived from a dried fish do not work without the societal logic of crime committed and its due punishment recognized as legitimate by rural Voodoo societies (see Davis, 1983; 1985; 1988a).[5] The vast majority of Haitian peasants do practice Voodoo. Voodoo societies function as systems of education, law, and medicine and as the enforcers of the code of ethics that regulate social behavior (similar to practices along the West coast of Africa). Rural Voodoo (or Bizango) societies practically control everyday life and function as practitioners of power alongside and often in opposition to the official Haitian government (Del Guercio, 1986). While Voodoo societies had been in the past the facilitators for order and positive social change, such as organizers or supporters of slave revolts, it is important to point out that the creation of a masked system of slavery is eerily reminiscent of externally imposed slavery by an occupying force, such as the French or later the United States. Therefore, I would like to suggest that we should distinguish between the two modes of slavery: slavery in the African context that functions more like indentured servitude and is only temporary, and slavery in the Americas, which is permanent and is better described by what Aimé Césaire calls "thingification" (1972, p. 21).

Since the fear of being turned into a zombie is mostly held by "the common people" ([1938] 1990, p. 181), Hurston suggests that Haitian society — seemingly divided into two classes — actually has a third class, that of zombies, which functions as a hidden slave system under neo-colonial circumstances.[6] Once someone is turned into a zombie, there is no return to humanity or to one's previous class status, unless the bokor who initiated the zombification dies: the "resurrected body [is] being dragged from the vault ... and set to toiling ceaselessly in the banana fields, working like a beast, unclothed like a beast, and like a brute crouching in some foul den in the few hours allowed for rest and food. From an educated, intelligent being to an unthinking, unknowing beast" ([1938] 1990, p. 181). Such "abject" beings, as Julia Kristeva (1982) uses the term, then not only pay for other people's debts, they also provide easy profits to those who are initiated to the secrets or can afford the services of a bokor. The bokors function as the slave traders as well as slave drivers in this market of human souls. To prevent rebellions, this technologically improved version of slavery (it even functions more efficiently than the "replicant" system within the speculative fictional world of *Blade Runner*, where the humanoid robots can and do rebel) has all the benefits of the system without its messiness (of rebellions and of the inefficiency of forcing individuals to act against their will). Zombified slaves are chemically induced "docile bodies" who labor away efficiently and with hardly any risk of sabotage. As Hurston's contemporary, the previously mentioned Grace Hutchins "of the Labor Research Association" comments citing G.G. Balch's *Occupied Haiti*, in Nancy Cunard's *Negro*:

> ... Forced work on the highways, called the *corvée*, had been abandoned in this Negro republic but was revived by the marines. "Unwilling workers were impressed.... They were sometimes manacled like slaves, compelled to work for weeks with little or no pay and inadequate food, and shot down if they attempted to escape" [Cunard, p. 288].

According to the ritual of zombification, as Hurston observes it, a zombie once taken from his or her home and carried past by the house after death in a ritualistic forgetting ceremony is immune to memories from the past:

> If the victim were not taken past his former house, later on he would recognize it and return. But once he is taken past, it is gone from his consciousness forever. It is as if it never existed for him. He is then taken to the hounfort and given a drop of liquid, the formula for which is most secret. After that the victim is a Zombie. He will work ferociously and tirelessly without con-sciousness of his surroundings and conditions and without memory of his former state. He can never speak again, unless he is given salt. "We have examples of a man who gave salt to a demon by mistake and he come man again and can write the name of the man who gave him to the loa [god]," Jean Nichols told me and added that of course the family of the victim went straight to a Bocor and "gave" the man who had "given" their son [(1938) 1990, pp. 183–84].

After describing the "living-dead" with the help of information gleaned from Haitian oral traditions, Hurston tells six more stories that testify to the facts "regarding Zombies with names and dates [who] come from all parts of Haiti" ([1938] 1990, p. 192). Case number five is the story of Felicia Felix-Mentor. Before telling the story, Hurston again presses for her most plausible explanation for the existence of Zombies. While at the Hospital at Gonaives, she discussed "the theories of how Zombies came to be" with the doctors, after which:

> It was concluded that it is not a case of awakening the dead, but a matter of the semblance of death induced by some drug known to a few. Some secret probably brought from Africa and handed down from generation to generation. These men know the effect of the drug and the anti-dote. It is evident that it destroys that part of the brain which governs speech and will power. The victims can move and act but cannot formulate thought. The two doctors expressed their desire to gain this secret, but they realize the impossibility of doing so. These secret societies are secret. They will die before they will tell. They cited instances. I said I was willing to try. Dr. Legros said that perhaps I would find myself involved in something so terrible, something from which I could not extricate myself alive, and that I would curse the day that I had entered upon my search [196].

To support the theory of the intentionally induced zombie state for someone else's profit, Hurston finally tells Felicia Felix-Mentor's story. She was thought to be dead for twenty-nine years when in October 1936 she turned up at her father's farm saying, "I used to live here" (196). But again, the code eludes the image, and besides being identified by her brother and husband, who had long since remarried, the zombie's existence is relegated to secrecy and mystery: "How did this woman, supposedly dead for twenty-nine years, come to be wandering naked on the road? Nobody will tell who knows. The secret is with some bocor dead or alive" (197). Hurston ends her chapter with the story of a Port-au-Prince woman who wanted to marry off her five daughters by hiring two little zombie-girls who are forced to pray on behalf of the unmarried daughters. Since four of the five daughters had been already divorced, Hurston flippantly concludes: "For it is said that nothing gotten through 'give man' is permanent. Ah Bo Bo!" (198).

Robert Hemenway does not dwell much on this period of Hurston's life and accepts her mission in Haiti and Jamaica as a matter of fact: "While many believed that zombies represented only a superstitious fear held by the ignorant, Zora was not so sure. Whether the condition resulted from a bokor's sucking out the soul of the victim prior to death, administering a secret poison, or calling on some Petro god, she was willing to accept the existence of zombies as fact" (Hemenway, [1977] 1988, p. 250). Even though Hurston was warned not to study the rituals of the Petro gods (but rather those of the Rada gods), Hurston made some effort to learn the ways of the Petro loas who were associated with evil acts, such as human sacrifices and the worshipping of the devil (see Hemenway, pp. 246–47). Hemenway, though, takes note that: "Months after the initial warnings, in late June, 1937, she began to see what people had been hinting at. While deep in her studies in a remote part of the bush, she was taken violently ill" with symptoms of "gastric disturbance" (p. 247). In Hemenway's description, Hurston was convinced that "her illness and her Voodoo studies were related" (p. 248). After the illness, she backed away from her intense studies and returned to the United States where she finished *Tell My Horse*.

Hurston's later biographer, M. Genevieve West, dedicates more attention to Hurston's interest in "Voodoo." In her reading: "Hurston's discussion of secret societies, zombies, and 'give man' in *Tell My Horse* suggests that her research might have represented a threat to the secrecy necessary for making zombies and for the operation of secret societies such as the Sect Rouge. If she were indeed poisoned, fear of disclosure seems a likely motive" (West, 2005, p. 130). West concludes that since Hurston backed away from her desire to learn further about Voodoo, secret societies, and zombies, her illness was connected, at least in her mind, to her curiosity and investigative ethnographic work. The previous six months Hurston spent in Jamaica were dedicated to the study of another secret society, the Maroons of Accompong, a community that is located in the hills of St. Elizabeth Parish and which was founded by the descendants of Africans who escaped slavery. There, too, Hurston made contact with a medicine man with extraordinary powers (West, p. 129). What connects the disjointed narratives of the book is Hurston's desire to reveal "hidden truths": "In titling the collection *Tell My Horse*, Hurston hoped to convince readers that she was merely the channel by which the truth about Voodoo traveled, but American readers were not quite sure what to make of her treatment of Haitian life and culture" (West, p. 131). West then goes on to focus on the book's structure, its publication history with Lippincott, and its unfavorable reception in the U.S.

Hurston gets as close as she can to a plausible explanation that connects the spiritual practice of zombification with a system of indentured servitude right after the conclusion of the nineteen-year long United States occupation of Haiti. The photograph she takes of the zombie is her attempt to make magic intelligible. She tries to explain what Kristeva calls the state of "abjection[, which] notifies us of the limits of the human universe" (Kristeva, p. 11). The sphere of abjection, the state where the "I" and subjectivity give way to a state in-between subject and object, i.e., where the self is sustained only through loathing and/or possession by the other (Kristeva, p. 10). The "abject I" lacks agency in relation to the other who keeps her/him/it in emotional and/or physical bondage. As Kristeva explains:

> We are no longer within the sphere of the unconscious but at the limit of primal repression that, nevertheless, has discovered an intrinsically corporeal and already signifying brand, symptom, and sign: repugnance, disgust, abjection.... The *symptom*: a language that gives up, a structure within the body, a non-assimilable alien, a monster, a tumor, a cancer that the listening devices of the unconscious do not hear, for its strayed subject is huddled outside the paths of desire [p. 11].

Since the abject body evades language (and the positive ego-building energy of desire) — it cannot speak because it is denied subjectivity, moreover, as in the case of zombies, is also denied access to memories and thinking in general. Therefore, if abjection is the death of the remembering and willful subject, then writing and supplying a story to the living-dead is a form of resurrection (i.e., the catharsis from a polluted and also silent state through the Logos, see Kristeva, pp. 16–31). Hurston, even at the price of her own health, attempts to break the code of silence and abjection, the code that turns human beings, often women and the poor, into zombies. By telling their stories, giving credit to the disenfranchised mode of knowing via oral traditions, folklore and hearsay, and by supplying the photographic image to the un-knowable or unseeable, she "resurrects" them as subjects, as human beings. By taking the zombie's picture Hurston makes her visible and unique, worthy of a story. By telling the stories of abject bodies, she reasserts the zombie into human history and explains its position in Haitian society — as an illicit way of settling a score, economic or moral.

Brinda Mehta suggests that in Haiti, the feminine divine force of Ayida-wédo is complimentary to the masculine presence of Damballah, the male serpent Vodou god that originated from African (Dahomean) cosmology (Mehta, 2002, p. 654). Mehta situates the feminine divine power in the context of a forgotten colonial past on Haitian grounds. She advocates, by following others such as Simon Gikandi and Myriam Chancy, among others, to read Haitian history within the double legacies of colonization and slavery:

> In other words, ancestral memory is resurrected through the ritualistic act of naming evidenced in story telling, dance and music rituals that locate Mother Africa as the primary origin. Women's connection to this origin is particularly crucial to their subjectivity given the fact that they have been forced to identify with male-doctored points of reference that have resulted in their subsequent cultural and historical isolation and alienation. Chancy posits the theory of "culture-lacune" as the necessary script for reading Haitian women's absence that had traditionally led to their marginalization. However, she assert that rather than accepting the passive dictates of historical erasure, Haitian women have defined a women-centered culture that has emerged from the very silencing to which it has been subjected [Mehta, p. 661].

Mehta connects women's alienation within Haitian society to a long history of "alienating forces of geographical dispersal and social fragmentation that were a result of colonization" (p. 663). In the contexts of the slave trade, the physical and spiritual diaspora of Africans, and the long history of colonization, zombies take on a special significance.

Mehta suggests, as does Hurston, that "zombification" is often "the sign of a cruel family punishment for having violated its codes of conduct" (Mehta, p. 667). She then quotes Maximilien Laroche, who states that death in Haiti assumes "a menacing form in the characters of the zombie ... the legendary, mythic symbol of alienation ... the image of a fearful destiny ... which is at once collective and individual" (in Mehta, p. 667). Therefore, in Mehta's interpretation, zombies come to symbolize "the disastrous impact of colonization and slavery on Haitians, zombification led to a particular condition of soulless-ness that stripped individuals of their creative, spiritual and human potential by reducing them to a robotic state of (non)-existence" (Mehta, p. 667) — the state Kristeva calls abjection. Furthermore, Mehta adds the dimension of gender to that of the colonial context in which even women of the upper classes can be the victims of zombification: "Women suffered a further level of eroticization and objectification when their state of complete passivity incited male fantasies of domination. The zombification of beautiful, upper class white or light-skinned mulatta women, in particular, has constituted a recurrent theme that has haunted the Haitian cultural and literary male imaginary" (p. 667). The practice of zombification often crosses racial, color, and class lines, making the victims available and accessible to those who are in lesser social standing, thus creating an upside-down power structure, not unlike during times of carnival in the rest of the Caribbean. But, while carnival is a temporary reversal of power, zombification is arbitrary in terms of its length and there is no guarantee that one can return to her or his original status.

Hurston's encounter with the zombie leads her to uncover a larger issue than the spiritual practices of "Voodoo." She unearths a case of chemical and social engineering that she understands as a revival of the slave system and the remnant of colonization, re-enacted by the American marines during her time. Soon after, she leaves Haiti abruptly, complaining of physical ailments, and abandons the process of her initiation into Haitian Voodoo practices. While her fascination with Voodoo stays with her till the end of her life — she wrote a column entitled, "Hoodoo and Black Magic" for the *Fort Pierce Chronicle* from 1957 to 1959 — she never returns to her interest with such intensity as before.

NOTES

1. Though "Vodou" is the more appropriate term for the Haitian religion, "Voodoo" is often used to denote the Louisiana variant of this tradition, into which Hurston was originally initiated. Since Hurston uses "Voodoo" almost exclusively in her book, I will use this spelling throughout this chapter.

2. In March of 1936 Hurston was awarded a Guggenheim Fellowship to study West Indian Obeah practices. The next month she set out for Jamaica where she spent half a year, after which, in September of the same year, she traveled to Haiti. After a brief return to the United States, she went back to Haiti and stayed till the next September on a renewed Guggenheim Fellowship. Once back the United States, in February 1938, she wrote *Tell My Horse* and published the book later that year. She recorded her Caribbean travels in Maitland, Florida.

3. For a discussion of the history and political meaning of the Caribbean Carnival, see Aching (2002), Cowley (1996), Harris (1999), and Liverpool (2001), among others.

4. The only two contemporary literary texts that I can recall that deal with sexism and colorism are a short story, "The Wife of His Youth" by Charles W. Chesnutt, published in the *Atlantic Magazine* in 1898, and the other, a lost classic novel by Hurston's fellow Harlem Renaissance writer, Wallace Thurman, *The Blacker the Berry*, published in 1929.

5. Note that Davis's findings have been hotly contested. See David Inglis' contribution to this volume. Eds.

6. Neocolonialism or neocoloniality can be generally and briefly defined as the Ideological State Apparatus of advanced imperialism that replaces the more overt repressive systems of colonial administrations. Nations, corporations, and international organizations such as The World Bank, the International Monetary Fund, or the World Trade Organization, and in particular the United States, aim to control other nations through indirect means. In lieu of direct military-political control, neocolonialist powers employ economic, financial and trade policies to dominate less powerful countries. Besides such economic controls, other sectors, such as language, culture, education, and healthcare are also under the powers of globalization and Westernization as well as Americanization.

3

Putting the Undead to Work
Wade Davis, Haitian Vodou, and the Social Uses of the Zombie

DAVID INGLIS

"Although they have no tongues, zombies [can] speak of a particular time and place" [Comaroff and Comaroff, 1999, p. 289].

Most representations of zombies occur in the realm of popular fictions. But what happens when the undead escape from the confines of popular culture and enter into realms where their presence is regarded as unwanted intrusion and uncanny intervention? What transgressions occur when the zombie leaves the world of horror films and dime-novels, and starts to stalk the halls of academia?

This chapter depicts and analyzes just such a situation, depicting some of the fraught relations that can pertain between academia on the one hand and zombies on the other (Olsen, 1986). It does so by examining the case of the Canadian ethnobotanist Wade Davis, whose autobiographical book *The Serpent and the Rainbow* (Davis, 1985), and its more "academic" sequel, *Passage of Darkness* (Davis, 1988a), contended that zombification, far from being a mythical process, was a really existing social and pharmacological phenomenon, fundamentally rooted in the social structure of contemporary Haiti. According to Haitian peasant folklore:

> by magical or other unknown means a person may die and be transformed into a creature of living death called a zombie. This living-dead entity is said to have no will of his own, but can be made to perform slave labor. Opinion is divided as to the process by which this transformation can be made to occur. Some Haitians appear to prefer the magical explanation, while others believe that a poison is used by malevolent practitioners to cause the change [Anderson, 1988, p. 121].

It is important to note that the Haitian conception of the zombie is not at all like the flesh-eating and often fast-moving ghoul of horror films since the 1960s. The latter is very much a contemporary creation, in large part popularized by the American film-maker George A. Romero's highly influential zombie films, beginning with *The Night of the Living Dead* in 1968, and now a mainstay of cinema and video-gaming world-wide. The fear that is embodied in the Haitian figure of the zombie is not the Euro-American one of the dead returning to visit a cannibalistic holocaust on the living, but rather involves dread of the body snatcher — the zombie master — who takes the living body and destroys the soul within it, creating a living dead being who endlessly obeys his will (Sheller, 2003, p. 168). Thus the Haitian fear is not *of* zombies, which is the Euro-American disposition. Rather, the anthropological record is replete with cases of Haitians taking in and caring for people they believe to be zombified relatives (Littlewood and Douyon, 1997). The fear is instead of *becoming* a zombie, deprived of all free will and enslaved to a powerful, predatory master. Clearly this fear harks back in certain ways to the brutal conditions of plantation life during the colonial period (Dayan, 1998). While the Haitian conception has clearly acted as a source of inspiration for the mass-mediated Euro-American notion, nonetheless the latter has evolved quite markedly over time away from the former. Early Euro-American horror fiction did indeed draw on the Haitian idea of the passive living-dead under the sway of a cruel zombie master — the films *White Zombie* (1932) and *I Walked with a Zombie* (1945) are cases in point. Such fictions clearly could make the symbolic connection between the inhuman conditions of the Caribbean sugar plantation during the centuries of slavery — the Haitian zombie's birthplace as it were — and the dehumanizing and deadening effects of large-scale factory labor, creating resonances for film audiences of the 1930s and 1940s (McIntosh, 2008). But after Romero's highly influential reworking, the cannibalistic, aggressive and increasingly mobile figure of the zombie has come to resemble less and less the tragic, passive figure of the Haitian imaginary (Mohammad, 2006, pp. 93, 101)

Davis's audacious claim was that the Haitian beliefs actually represent really (although rarely) occurring practices, and that the Haitian view that a poison is deployed to "make" zombies is actually true. Davis's argument has three elements: a *social structural and functionalist* argument (zombification is a form of social control); a *materialist-pharmacological* argument (zombification is made possible by the creation and use of certain poisonous powders made by sorcerers); and a *cultural-psychological* argument which knits the other two elements together (the powders only have a strong effect on victims because the latter strongly believe in the existence of zombies, very much fear being made into one, and when the powders are administered, think they really are being turned into a zombie).

Thus according to Davis on the basis of his fieldwork in Haiti, zombies (*zombi*, in the transliteration of Haitian Creole parlance that Davis uses) "really exist," as they are the drug-addled subjects of powerful secret societies, which are centered around Vodou ("Voodoo" in the Western derogatory sense) beliefs, that are endemic within Haitian society, and which grew out of the secret associations that slaves brought over with them to Haiti from west Africa and which flourished amongst the bands of maroons — rebellious runaway slaves — who waged war on the French authorities during the last days of colonialism. At the behest of these societies, sorcerers use certain pharmacological weapons, powders based around the lethal drug tetrodotoxin (TTX), to psychologically enslave their chosen victims, allegedly putting them to work in conditions of never-ending subjugation. The victims are those individuals who have transgressed certain community norms — such as getting rich at the expense of one's family and neighbors — which the secret societies monitor and police in the interests of social stability in rural Haiti. While Davis admits that cases of zombification are rare — as he puts it, there is no assembly-line of zombies in Haiti — nonetheless the phenomenon is real, as it is rooted in the Haitian social structure, is at the epicenter of the Vodou belief-system, and can be empirically documented. Davis's two books on the subject were intended as comprehensive documentations of the reality of zombification, and were presented by the author as pioneering ethnographic and pharmacological treatises that would prove once and for all that zombies "really exist" (even if only sporadically).

The publication of the two books, especially the first, whipped up various storms — a feeding frenzy by journalists very keen to exploit a highly newsworthy item; the piquing of interest in otherwise scholarly materials by Hollywood producers, leading to the transformation of *The Serpent and the Rainbow* into a film directed by horror film auteur Wes Craven; and a series of increasingly rancorous academic polemics in which Davis was accused, among other charges, of vulgar self-promotion, of outrageous sensationalism, of methodological naivety, of falsifying data, and of setting back the anthropological study of Haiti by fifty years. These controversies created a cultural complex involving vexed issues to do with death, mortality, colonialism, race, and the limits of scientificity. They raised pointed issues about who is authorized to speak about whom, how one can write about certain problematic topics without toppling into sensationalism and the worst kind of stereotyping, and, above all, about what happens when a symbol — in this case, the zombie — moves from domains where it has hitherto been sequestered (here, the worlds of superstition and popular entertainments) into others where it seems to have no place, in this case the hallowed groves of academe.

I contend here that underlying all the various polemics against Davis voiced by his critics is the fear that by treating the zombie *ontologically* (as a "real" entity) rather than merely *representationally* (that is, as only a symbol to be found in certain kinds of folklore and popular fiction), fundamental rules about the nature of "proper" scientific scholarly conduct were broken, these in turn underpinned by deeply held assumptions about what is intellectually respectable to "believe in" and to turn one's attention towards. Beyond the scholarly merits or demerits of Davis's claims, as these have been identified by the critics, and beyond their veracity or otherwise, what was at stake in the zombie debates involved the consequences of importing into "respectable" realms the *disreputable* figure of the zombie, associated with the cheapest and most vulgar kinds of fictions, especially given that the latter was being presented as a really "living" (but at the same time, "deadened") entity. Taking such a possibility seriously seems inappropriate and foolish, perhaps even mad. Davis's thesis provoked a whirlwind of condemnation in large part because he, presumably unintentionally, unleashed an uncanny figure into places it normally is not allowed to go. In this paper, I will trace out the various ways in which Davis's fieldwork and writing on zombies broke all sorts of rules, and how in doing so, he has left a troubling legacy as to how one might think about the social significance of zombies.

Haiti and the Undead

> "...one speaks only of death and zombies in Haiti."
> — René Depestre (in Dayan, 1993, p. 148)].

As the leading Haitian author René Depestre notes, the zombie is one of the motifs apparently irrevocably associated with Haiti, both by Haitians themselves and by foreigners. The beliefs held by the Haitian peasantry as to the existence of zombies "have always engaged the curiosity of outsiders and the interest of anthropologists" since the late nineteenth-century onwards (Yasumoto and Kao, 1986, p. 747). The outside world's fascination with zombie lore is both generated by, and very much contributes to, more general perceptions of Haiti, "a place so often imagined as excess, and dismissed as savage," as one of the foremost modern commentators on Haitian affairs has phrased it (Dayan, 1993, p. 136). As a *Vanity Fair* journalist put it in 1989, at the height of fears in the U.S. that Haiti was the original source of the AIDS pandemic then spreading across North America, "Haiti is to this hemisphere what black holes are to outer space" (cited in Farmer, 1992, p. 4).

On this recurring stereotypical view, which has informed foreign (especially North American) opinion about Haiti for more than a century, the country is "a pre-industrial society inhabited by ignorant, diseased peasants oblivious to the outside world" (Farmer, 2006, p. 50). But as one of the leading critics of this kind of view, the American doctor Paul Farmer (ibid.), notes, Haiti as a geo-political and cultural entity is actually a "creation of expansionist European empires"—in this case, the French imperial state—and thus "a quintessentially Western [and modern] entity," rather than the insular pre-modern enclave untouched by modernity, progress and civilization imagined by foreign observers. As Sheller (2003, p. 165) argues for the islands of the Caribbean more generally, these have been constructed by Western racializing discourses as either havens or hells that were "beyond the modern, even as modernity created [them]."

In Haiti's case, European and North American negative depictions of the country as a feverish inferno of Voodoo-induced depravity were very much stimulated by racist fears over what was in the nineteenth-century a glaring socio-political anomaly, the world's first "black republic." This was a modern polity founded through the revolutionary activities of former slaves, who had managed through impressive military strategizing to overthrow the rule of the French imperial masters in 1804. A thoroughly modern state created and run by blacks was a focus of both fascination and repugnance in post–Enlightenment Europe and North America. At one level, the revolutionary birth-pangs of the Haitian Republic constituted "the crucible, the trial by fire for the ideals of the French Enlightenment," as here were the ideals of liberty (in the strongest sense — freedom from slavery), equality and fraternity being put into practice not by the revolutionary bourgeoisie of Paris but by the apparently wretched former slaves of the French plantation colony of San Domingue (Buck-Morss, 2009, p. 42). That those hitherto kept in the most wretched conditions by European masters could overthrow the latter and found a Republic based on the most contemporary enlightened ideals, was very much a source of fascination and wonder in early nineteenth-century Europe, catching the attention, for example, of the young Hegel, whose master-slave dialectic can be read as an explicit theorization of Haitian socio-political conditions (ibid.). But as the early idealistic days degenerated into brutal internecine rivalry among the revolutionary leaders, Western observers began to look at Haiti not with admiration but with increasing disgust. This has arguably been the recurring pattern ever since, the apparent fall from grace of the early Haitian Republic and its relinquishing of the promise of modernity leading to "images of revulsion and hostility in the Western imagination ... images of the unspeakable and mysterious" that have been renewed and recycled ever since (Arthur and Dash, 1999, p. 315).

Within this primarily negative nexus of foreign images of, and thoughts about, Haiti that have pertained ever since, (mis)representations of Vodou, the belief-system of the Haitian peasantry, have been central. Vodou was from the late eighteenth-century the majority religion of the slaves, and then ex-slaves, of the countryside, a system of thought that could borrow certain images from the Republic's official religion, Roman Catholicism, but which has stood firm against repeated attempts by the Church and metropolitan political elites to eradicate it or diminish its influence (Philippe and Romain, 1979). Despite being a vibrant system of thought that has changed its contours over time as Haitian society itself has changed (Dayan, 1998), it remains the case today that Vodou is "one of the most caricatured religions in the world" (Dutton, 1993, p. 136). It remains swathed in mystery, an unsavory enigma that is the staple resource of horror fiction writers the world over. As Mintz and Trouillot (1995, p. 10) put it, "Vodou[n] has fascinated anthropologists and sensation-seekers alike. Few, other than believers, know exactly what it is," even if foreigners think they know what it is. The caricatured Voodoo beloved of foreign observers "conjures up visions of mysterious deaths, secret rites ... dark saturnalia," even if the reality is, of course, much more mundane (Metraux, 1972, p. 15, cited in Farmer, 1992, p. 3).

The relentlessly negative portrayals of Vodou as "Voodoo" spring in large part from sensationalistic, mostly fictional travel literature of the later nineteenth- and early twentieth-centuries. Perhaps the first to popularize the subsequent rigid clichés about Vodou as involving notorious rites and cannibalism was the work of the former British consul Spenser St. John, whose 1884 memoir *Hayti, or the Black Republic* caused a sensation in Victorian England with its lurid tales of murder, despotism and the rampant wickednesses of Voodoo superstition. However, the high-water mark of such depictions came during the period of the U.S. occupation of Haiti (1915–34), when a slew of sensation-mongering books appeared, often written by former members of the American forces stationed in the country, and appearing under such dime-store titles as *Black Baghdad* and *Cannibal Cousins*. Richard Loederer's *Voodoo Fire in Haiti*, which first appeared in German in 1932, also added more fuel to the fire, with its vivid images of power-crazed Voodoo priests presiding over wild orgies and the cooking of stews with human flesh as the main ingredient. The *New York Times* reporter William Seabrook also made a vital contribution to the purple prose of the period with his 1929 travelogue *The Magic Island*, depicting a Voodoo ceremony in this manner, reminiscent of the worst Bacchanalian excesses imaginable: "...in the red light of torches, which made the moon turn pale, leaping, screaming, writhing black bodies, blood-maddened, sex-maddened, god-maddened, drunken, whirled and danced their dark saturnalia" (Seabrook, 1929, p. 13). Seabrook also first popularized the figure of the zombie, paving the way for its use in American films — the first of these, *White Zombie*, starring Bela Lugosi as a nefarious Voodoo priest with the power to create the living dead, appeared only three years later, in 1932. These sorts of books — and later, films — were not only designed to titillate the palates of European and North American audiences keen to hear of wild revels and anthropophagous feasts. They also served to justify morally and politically the U.S. occupation, by representing the population as wholly unable to conduct themselves in anything approaching a civilized manner. Zombies figured very much within this cultural nexus, for as Newitz (2006) argues, when racial difference cannot be talked about explicitly because of broader social norms silencing its explicit enunciation, it can be covertly depicted through representations of differences between dead and alive bodies, and by extension "dead" and "alive" cultures: in this case, the forward-looking, progressive, modernity-embracing and -creating social order of whites, as opposed to that of blacks, which is supposedly stuck within a mire of savage, backward-looking custom and superstition. In this sense, the zombie can operate as a potent coding of racial and cultural divides, standing as an uncanny emblem of a wider barbarity. Yet ironically, the cultural roots of the zombie in Haiti itself are very much connected to ex-slaves' fears of a return to an enslaved condition. Whereas whites construed the zombie as all that was vile about Haiti, black Haitians understood the zombie within a nexus of folk memory about the brutality of the white slave-masters and their power to destroy a slave both physically and spiritually (Dayan, 1998).

Although the particular political juncture of the American occupation has now passed, the images thrown up by it still haunt Western imaginaries in the contemporary period. As Arthur and Dash (1999, p. 319) put the point, "the time-honored clichés of the supernatural" forged a century ago have perpetuated "the image of Haiti as the land of the zombie." And such images seem to be eternally recurring. As mentioned above, in the 1980s there was a widespread belief in the U.S. that AIDS had originated in Haiti, and that its generation was somehow connected to Voodoo rituals, although in actual fact the disease arrived in Haiti from North America, carried most likely by sex tourists (Farmer, 1992). Journalistic coverage of this issue in the early 1980s drew with ease upon the range of images elaborated more than sixty years before. Thus the apparently abnormally high rate of AIDS infections among Haitians could be reported as "a clue from the grave, as though a zombie, leaving a trail of unwinding gauze bandages and rotting flesh, had come ... to pronounce a curse" on the depraved creatures called Haitians and the whites depraved enough to have sexual congress with them (cited in Farmer, 1992, p. 2).

It was not just tabloid journalism that reached towards this stock of imagery. In 1986, the apparently respectable confines of the *Journal of the American Medical Association* ran an article entitled, "Night of the Living Dead," which contained these assertions: "Do necromantic zombiists [sic] transmit [AIDS] during voodooistic rituals? ... Even now, many Haitians are voodoo *serviteurs* and partake in its rituals ... [they] may be unsuspectingly infected with AIDS by ingestion, inhalation or dermal contact with contaminated ritual substances, as well as by sexual activity" (Greenfield, 1986, p. 2200, cited in Farmer, 1992, p. 3). In the same vein, it was alleged at the time in quite "respectable" outlets that many Voodoo priests were homosexual, that they used their powers to cajole would-be sexual partners into submission, and that they spread AIDS because of their widespread use of infected blood samples in their ceremonies (Moore and LeBaron, 1986).

It was in these sorts of ways that an association was built up in the 1980s that to be a Haitian was automatically to be an AIDS carrier. In this way, the earlier images of Voodoo and zombies were put to new purposes, at the same time as being rejuvenated by their association with matters of highly contemporary, and potentially global, concern. Such images again resurfaced in the later 1980s and 1990s, during the times of Haiti's political crises — starting with the overthrow of the regime of the younger Duvalier in 1986 — and further American interventionism (Fatton Jr., 2002). Once again, ideas as to Haitians being congenitally unable to govern themselves effectively came to the fore, and once again, this situation could in part be ascribed to the supposed stranglehold of Voodoo over the Haitian imagination (Brown, 1989).

A PhD on Zombies

It was against and into this highly charged political and cultural background that Wade Davis went to Haiti to find zombies and those who make them. One can imagine the great splash one could make at graduate seminars and academic conferences by announcing that one's fieldwork had proven that zombies "really exist." This is apparently precisely what happened at the XIth International Congress of Anthropological and Ethnological Sciences in Vancouver in 1983, when Davis made exactly that kind of pronouncement in a paper he presented in a slot he filled at the last minute in place of an absent delegate. Rumor spread like wildfire that a graduate student, newly returned from Haiti, was making such sensational claims (Farrer, 1988). Davis had indeed recently returned from the field, having spent the period from April to November 1982 in Port-au-Prince and rural Haiti. The first written fruits of the fieldwork appeared later in 1983, in a paper with the provocative title "The

Ethnobiology of the Haitian Zombi" (Davis, 1983), which appeared in the *Journal of Ethnopharmacology*. This was an obvious outlet for a scholar in ethnobotany (the study of how particular non–Western societies use particular drugs for medical and religious purposes), and one which was bound to reach the right kind of audience for a young and ambitious entrant into the field.

Davis had impeccable academic credentials: undertaking a PhD within the respected Botanical Museum at Harvard, under the supervision of the doyen of ethnobotany worldwide, Professor Richard Evans Schultes. The outlandishness of the claims being made was mitigated by the fact that funding for the project had come from such august sources as the American National Science Foundation, the Wenner-Gren Foundation for Anthropological Research, and, from Davis's homeland, the Canadian Social Science and Humanities Research Council. But while one might expect students and scholars to be funded to carry out research on folkloric *beliefs* about Haitian zombies, it remained the case that providing money for work that alleged they were in fact *real*, was definitely out of the ordinary. Indeed, from the very beginning of the project, the assumption animating it was that not only was zombification a real process, but that it held the promise of opening up a potentially astounding pharmacological secret. The idea of sending a student to Haiti had come from Nathan S. Kline, a psychopharmacologist then in charge of the Rockland State Research Institute of New York. Kline had worked in Haiti for thirty years at the time of his contacting the Harvard Botanical Museum, establishing the only psychiatric facility in the country at that time. Along with Haitian colleagues, he was convinced that zombies were indeed real, and not only part of the rich folkloric culture of the Haitian peasantry.

This belief was mounted upon two apparently well-documented cases of actual zombification. Although stories of the existence of zombies are reported to be endemic among the Haitian peasantry, and although Article 246 of the Haitian Penal Code treats zombification as a form of murder and punishable as such, what has long bedeviled the attempts of those seeking to prove that zombies are real is lack of evidence as to actual cases of those who have apparently "come back from the dead." Kline had two such cases that seemed highly plausible: 58-year-old Clairvius Narcisse, who had appeared near his home village 18 years after being buried in 1962, and 33-year-old Francine Illeus (known locally as *Ti Femme*), who had been declared dead in 1976 and had reappeared post-mortem after 3 years. In the former case, the death had been registered at an American-run clinic, making in Kline's view the likelihood of false diagnosis of death much more unlikely than if Narcisse's death had been registered by local officials or his family. Surely the American physician who had certified that Narcisse was dead must have had good grounds for thinking he was dealing with a corpse? But as Narcisse had apparently risen from the grave, it seemed plausible to claim that he had merely had *death-like symptoms* which would have compelled even a highly trained doctor to certify death. Narcisse's case seemed to suggest that he had only looked as if he was dead when he was certified as such. So the puzzle was posed as to how this could be.

Part of the folkloric tradition had it that the sorcerer, the *bokor*, could create a poisonous powder that was deployed as part of the magic ritual of zombification. Following the lead of an early quasi-anthropological study by Zora Neale Hurston (Hurston, [1938] 1990), it could be hypothesized that Narcisse's symptoms may have been induced by such a powder. The capacity to render a person sufficiently comatose to seem dead to a trained eye, but which nonetheless would allow them to be resuscitated later, by means as yet unknown, promised to be of vast pharmacological interest, including possibly being used to subdue

NASA astronauts on future long-term space flights. So it was with the bizarre conjunction of the hyper-modernity of space exploration with the apparently quintessentially pre-modern folkloric figure of the zombie — each pole mediated by the possible pharmacological sophistication of Vodou *bokors* and their "zombie powders," a potion both deeply "traditional" and yet potentially astoundingly future-oriented — that Kline approached Richard Evans Schultes in search of a young, keen, adventurous ethnobotanist who could collect some samples of "zombie powder." This was a feat that had never been achieved before, either by foreign investigators or by interested parties among Haiti's urban elite. For this task, Schultes put forward Davis, who had already proven his fieldwork credentials in strenuous investigations in the Amazon jungle for his undergraduate dissertation. As Davis subsequently presented it, Kline had put the project to him in these terms: he was not just to go to Haiti, but to go "to the frontier of death" itself (1985, p. 25). As it turned out, Davis was perfect for the task, at least in terms of the capacity for garnering vast publicity — but then also notoriety — for what became known as the "zombie project."

Davis was duly dispatched to Haiti in early 1982, his activities during the next several months being written up in *The Serpent and the Rainbow*. After a second brief trip to Haiti in 1984, he had not only collected eight samples of so-called zombie powder, but also interview material with various individuals supposedly connected to zombification, including Clairvius Narcisse himself, and some participant observational material on the events taking place within the secret societies. The connection Davis made between the zombie powder and zombification on the one side, and the secret societies on the other, had come about as a result of reading the-then novel material of the Haitian anthropologist Michel Laguerre (1989), which had argued that the secret societies, known by at least some Haitians as "Bizango" societies, existed to defend local community interests against what members saw as the depredations of outsiders, especially as regards the buying of land. Davis extrapolated from this account in two ways.

First, Davis laid emphasis on the justice-meting powers of the secret societies among members of the community itself, with sins against communal norms being punished by an elaborate system of judgments and reprimands. Second, zombification is understood by Davis as the ultimate capital punishment, the most severe retribution that can be handed out by a secret society to an errant individual. The zombification is carried out by the *bokor*, acting for the secret society, as a carefully calibrated act of communal vengeance on the most reprehensible miscreants. It is emphatically not, Davis warns, either a random or criminal act, but rather the severest sanction of the secret society acting as the guarantor of local social stability. In that sense, zombification is a highly moral act, for even if it is greatly feared by the peasantry it in effect protects them from evil-doers. The great fear of zombification is what keeps Haitian peasant society functioning: what seems a terrifying threat to the individual is actually a mechanism that guarantees the well-being of the whole social order, and necessarily so, as without the terror induced at the thought of becoming a zombie, the justice of the secret societies would be impotent. The pharmacological agent of this (on Davis's view) essentially Durkheimian mechanism of community retribution against the deviant is the zombie powder, which renders the victim unable to show to those around them when s/he is "dying" that s/he is in fact not dead when s/he has been pronounced to be so.

On Narcisse's testimony, he had been quite conscious and able to perceive events around him, all the way through his supposed "death," including the horrifying ordeal of being buried alive, but he had been in no way able to signify this either to the doctors who certified him deceased or, later, the mourners at his funeral. He had been reduced by the zombie powder to being a wholly passive witness at, and to, his own death, rendered wholly in the power of the *bokor* who had administered it. When he was dug out of the grave, less than 24 hours after he had been certified dead, he remembered in the interview with Davis being beaten violently by a number of shadowy figures and then led off to labor in the fields in a remote part of the island where no-one would recognize him. Apart from the trauma of the burial alive, Davis conjectured, on the basis of endemic folkloric beliefs about there being another powder which "revived" the buried person once they had been taken from the grave, that Narcisse may well have been dosed with another drug at the point of exhumation, one which had the power to help erase his memory and put him into the stupefied condition necessary to keep him in the pacified state of the zombie for an indefinite time:

> The victim, affected by the drug, [and] traumatized by the set and setting of the graveyard and immediately beaten by the zombi maker's assistants, is bound and led before a cross to be baptized with a new zombi name. After the baptism, he or she is made to eat a paste containing a strong dose of a potent psychoactive drug which brings on an induced state of psychosis. During the course of that intoxication, the zombi is carried off to be sold as a slave laborer, often on the sugar plantations [Davis, 1983, p. 101].

Thus there must exist two kinds of zombie powders, a "before" one which renders the victim totally helpless to the point of seeming lifeless to all witnesses, and an "after" one, which keeps the recently-exhumed unfortunate in a condition of suspended mental animation. The eight different powders which Davis eventually collected from various *bokors* were of the first type. He claimed that their main psychoactive ingredient was tetrodotoxin (TTX), which was derived from particular species of puffer fish to be found off Haitian waters. Powders of the second type were not collected, although Davis was convinced their main ingredient was *Datum stramonium*, a plant which was known in local patois as *concombre zombi*, "the Zombi's cucumber," an apparent gesture in the direction of its pharmacological purpose within Vodou circles.

Davis's orientation to the zombie phenomenon was that of the ethnobotanist, a specialist who has to span two specialist worlds, that of the ethnologist and that of the natural scientist. We saw above that there were three parts to his argument — the social (zombification is a punishment inflicted on malefactors by the secret societies), the pharmacological (the toxic nature of the zombie powders), and the cultural/psychological. As regards the latter, which connects the other two elements, Davis constantly emphasizes that "any psychoactive drug has within it a completely ambivalent potential. Pharmacologically it introduces a certain condition, but that condition is mere raw material to be worked by particular cultural or physiological forces and expectations" (1985, p. 151). Thus the zombie powders could only "work" effectively on a person who believed strongly in the possibility of zombification.

Other foreign observers had long noted the widespread use of tales about zombies to teach children about social mores, those mores themselves structured by the Vodou belief system (Huxley, 1966). If that was the case, then a person brought up within such a context would be very predisposed to believe that what was happening to them was indeed really turning them into a zombie. Davis argues that it is the belief that one could be made a zombie that ensures that the zombie powders have the effects that they do on those undergoing zombification. A person brought up within the Vodou world-view — which Davis views as an all-encompassing cosmology from which the Vodouisant cannot escape (e.g., 1985, p. 82) — believes that the *bokor* really has the power to turn them into a zombie through sorcery. The *bokor* has at his disposal a range of magical acts, all of which are aimed at capturing the *ti bon ange*—the "little good soul"—of an individual, a key notion in Vodou cosmology according to Davis. When a *bokor* captures the *ti bon ange* he can either create a *zombi cadavre*—a physical zombie, of the kind that is made to look dead, buried, then uncovered—or a *zombi astral*—a zombie of the spirit, a non-corporeal zombie, a spirit kept in a small vessel like a pot, indicating that the *bokor* has complete control over his or her soul. Zombies of the spirit are far more common than zombies of the flesh. Indeed, Davis and other observers have pointed out that when a foreign investigator tries to procure a zombie, it will inevitably be a *zombi astral* that is offered by informants. On one memorable occasion, Davis (1985, p. 186) was told by some contacts that they had come to sell him some *zombis astrals* as they thought he would have difficulty getting a *zombi cadavre* through United States immigration and customs!

The first written fruit of Davis's researches was the 1983 paper mentioned above, which reported interim findings. This was almost immediately picked up by the august British medical journal *The Lancet* (1984), which reported Davis's findings without demur, but did mention—in an uncharacteristic aside—that Ian Fleming might have appreciated this research as James Bond was poisoned by tetrodotoxin in the novel *Dr. No.* The paper became the basis for the semi-popular book—part research report, part first-person-narrated travelogue, part adventure story—*The Serpent and the Rainbow*, the text of which in turn was reproduced in large part for its more explicitly "academic" sequel, *Passage of Darkness: The Ethnobiology of the Haitian Zombie*, published by the University of North Carolina Press (Davis, 1988a).

If one reads all three texts, one is struck by the fact that Davis is masterful at integrating earlier material into later publications, with the final publication in the series very much reading as a comprehensive synthesis of the various elements and genres upon which the ethnobotanist, practitioner of a discipline that is itself a hybrid between anthropology and pharmacology, has to draw. Apart from the latter two elements, *Passage of Darkness* also contains material from psychology, medicine, sociology, politics and history—in the latter case, not just of Haiti, but of Western modernity too, especially as regards the history of vexed attempts to define precisely what "death" is and how to diagnose it. Not even the severest critic of Davis could plausibly claim that he does not write well. In fact, far more than the travelogue-cum-adventure text of *The Serpent and the Rainbow*, the "academic" tome of 1988 reads marvelously well, the sections on Haiti's brutal history of slavery, colonialism, and the first successful slave rebellion in history, being particularly superbly rendered because of their concise but vivid conjuring-up of the bloody events leading to the creation of the first independent "Black Republic" in 1804. Even the potentially very dry material to do with the pharmacological properties of particular species of puffer fish—allegedly the source of tetrodotoxin in the zombie powders—is presented in a way that is clear and interesting to the non-scientist. But it would be his obvious literary talents that would get Davis into some of the biggest controversies surrounding the zombie project.

From Field to Film

Responses to Davis's claims have ranged from the ecstatically excited to the angrily denunciative. On its publication in 1985, *The Serpent and the Rainbow* became a subject of some notoriety and—that rare thing—a work by an academic which became a best-seller in the U.S. and other territories.

The popularity and notoriety were very much augmented when shortly after publication, the rights to the book were bought by the film producers David Ladd and Doug Claybourne (Robb, 1998). Wes Craven, riding high with the recent success of his film *A Nightmare on Elm Street* (1984), was brought on board the project, which, with a budget of 11 million U.S. dollars, was far more generously resourced than most genre films of the time. The relatively large budget was won in spite of what Craven has presented as a bias against films about zombies: "I kept running up against this problem people had with the subject matter. As soon as you say 'voodoo' or 'zombie' people think it's some old B-film" (Robb, 1998, p. 128). Ironically, the B-films Craven here refers to are the very ones from the 1930s and 1940s that were inspired in large part by Seabrook's sensational travelogue about Haiti mentioned earlier. So there was an attempt by the director to distance himself from such fare, and to produce a piece that was more ethnographically "realistic." Craven noted that Davis had managed to show that Voodoo is "a racially-despised sub-culture ... which is totally misrepresented, because we've made it into this dark, nasty thing, but it's really like Catholicism" (ibid., p. 132), attempting to demonstrate that Voodoo/Vodou is actually "really all right" as it is just like the very religion, Catholicism, that throughout the history of Haiti has been trying to stamp Vodou out for nearly two hundred years (Rey, 2004). The historical irony here — that the film purported to present Vodou in a positive light, while actually depicting it in the usual highly caricatured and sensationalistic manner — seemed rather lost on the director.

The large budget indicates that the film-makers originally intended something somewhat different from a standard horror film. Interviews with Craven from the time and after indicate that he saw the adaptation of the book as allowing him to escape the more narrow confines of his chosen genre. He regarded it as an opportunity to make a more "adult" film than he had made hitherto, especially as the screenplay depicted the villains of the piece — those who control the zombification process — not as the secret societies but rather the Tonton Macoute, the Duvalier regime's notorious secret police. This was a very significant change in emphasis from the book, where the Tonton Macoute very much play a background role. Davis notes that part of the initial success of the Duvalier regime was to embrace Vodou as a de facto unofficial state religion, rather than reject it as previous regimes in Port-au-Prince had, in order to gain more effective control over the countryside. Duvalier Senior also courted *bokors* and recruited them into the secret police apparatus itself, presenting himself, in his look and overall demeanor, as the greatest of all Vodou priests. But one gets very little sense from Davis's account of how the Tonton Macoute may have affected the very nature of the secret societies themselves, usurping their alleged role as expressions of community justice as Davis had claimed, a point made by various academic critics as we will see. By placing the secret police at center-stage, albeit in a curious and sensationalized way, Craven and the screenwriter, Richard Maxwell, were arguably correcting one of the ethnographic failings of Davis's account, namely its relative shunning of political realities and the social changes effected by them.

Despite this — no doubt unintentional — development, Craven, the producers and subsequent fans of the film have all taken Davis's account as unalloyed ethnological fact, a quite different perspective than that taken by Davis's academic audience. As Craven put it, "there is indeed a tribal judgement where a person who affronts the tribe is made into a zombie" (Robb, 1998, p. 126). Craven has subsequently said that he immersed "himself in voodoo lore to maintain the film's authenticity" (Muir, 1998, p. 132). Defenders of the film have argued that while the screenplay had to get away from "the often dry and scientific prose of Davis' true-life account" (ibid., p. 126), nonetheless the essential "truth" of the book was maintained, in spirit if not to the letter. That truth is maintained despite the addition of the following elements in the film that were not in the book: the hero (now called Dr. Dennis Alan — he has a doctorate, an accomplishment that Davis at this point did not have) is buried alive and is himself zombified; a whole series of dream sequences are added, including the constant reappearance of a desiccated zombie bride, and a large snake appearing out of one character's mouth; and the addition of a monstrous villain — a recurring motif in Craven's filmography — who is the head of the Tonton Macoute, and who has the power to enslave all and sundry, especially political malcontents, through his zombification sorcery, which is presented as truly "magic" rather than pharmacological and cultural, as in the book.

For advocates of the film — generally hardcore fans of Wes Craven — the adaptation is "an astonishingly complex film" that, despite the fantastic plot additions, really lifts the ethnological lid off of what really happens in Haiti (ibid., p. 143). This is also the view of some subsequent viewers of the film, as a glance at the user reviews of the film's IMDB.com webpage amply testifies, a location where it seems that at least some viewers know about the source material, take it as factual, and seemingly wholeheartedly accept the existence of efficacious zombie poisons.[1]

For academic critics, however, the prose of the source material is neither "dry" nor "scientific," but rather reads as easily as fiction as it does as science, and "falls into the fuzzy realm of literary anthropology previously reserved for writers like Carlos Castaneda" (Dutton, 1993, p. 148). Even more so, the film has taken a battering from the academics who have watched it — or at least claim to have done so. These critics have argued that the film is a fairly tawdry attempt to cash in on Davis's scholarly credentials — the very credentials that such critics dispute, as we will see. The really existing Haitian dread of *becoming* a zombie is too difficult and too interior a subject to film, so that that sentiment, which Davis emphasizes over and over again, while still present to some degree in the film (especially in the attempt to evoke horror in the audience with a sequence in which the hero is buried alive), is mostly ditched in favor of the standard post–Romero trope of *fear of* zombies (Koven, 2008). In so doing, Craven and his colleagues created "grist for the mill of yet another sensation-mongering American ... film about bloody, sexually licentious" voodoo, the very set of clichés that Craven had initially tried to avoid, not least because he felt that by basing the film on Davis's book, he had source material that had de-sensationalized the subject matter and had provided a reality-check on standard Hollywood fantasies (Woodson, 1992, p. 151). But for academic critics, it was precisely the sensationalism of the book that located it in a long line of treatises by foreigners stretching all the way back through Seabrook to Spenser St. John in the 1880s (Arthur and Dash, 1999).

For the more sympathetic academic critics, the fact that the film like so many before it mystifies Vodou, transforming it into sensationalistic Voodoo, was not Davis's fault, as he had had no intention to do such a thing, nor had he had any control over the making of the film (Corbett, 1990). Davis (1985, p. 11) had indeed begun *The Serpent and the Rainbow* with the admonition that Hollywood stereotyping of Vodou was endemic, and his study was meant to show the sophistication, even beauty, of Vodou cosmology. Moreover, when the film was finished, Davis very rapidly disowned it publicly. He has subsequently stated that it is "one of the worst Hollywood movies in history" (Davis, 2004), which seems a touch strong given the ample competition in that direction, but at least understandable as the expression of an author hurt by the traduction of his source material. This rather gives the lie to Craven's rather hopeful statement that "Wade Davis was pretty happy with the film. He understood we were making a commercial sort of picture," as if the dictates of commerce had hardly had an impact upon the transition from book to film at all (Robb, 1998, p. 126).

Zombie Disputes

While the Hollywood personnel tended to think of the text of *The Serpent and the Rainbow* as an unproblematic depiction of the zombie-makers of Haiti, academic critics were generally appalled by its cross-pollination of various genres — anthropological treatise and pharmacological/toxicological report on the one hand, first-person narration and adventure story on the other. On this view, the latter elements seriously polluted the former elements, rendering the ethnology fanciful and the pharmacology so much empty hypothesizing. "As much fiction as field work ... the wide eyed narrator wanders through the wilds of Haiti in search of zombies, led by a local Ariadne," goes a typical comment in this vein (Arthur and Dash, 1999, p. 333).

It is indeed the case that Davis's text breaks all the rules of ethnographic writing as then practiced. It may have received a warmer welcome amongst North American anthropologists once the "reflexive turn" had been made in at least parts of that discipline, where the authorial self, far from being excluded from the narrative, is included within it (Rosaldo, 1993). There is a constant oscillation in the text between different authorial modes: fictionalizing of people and places, dramatizing of actions (most notoriously, accompanying a *bokor* and two prostitutes on a midnight expedition to raid what turns out to be a child's grave for materials for the zombie powder); presenting factual information through dialogues the narrator is supposedly having with other "characters"; then moving into the more "straight" presentation of historical, anthropological and medical data, involving veritable firework-displays of inter-disciplinary learning on occasion; then turning back towards novelistic verbal displays, describing, for example, the "extraordinary mystery" that the narrator is engaged in (1986, p. 47) and stopping every so often to comment that "in this surrealistic country, anything might be possible" (p. 61), that he is "stunned by her multitudes, awed by her mysteries, dumbfounded by her contradictions" (p. 72), and that "nothing seemed to happen as it should, but little occurred by chance" in such a country as this (p. 112). Needless to say, Davis's initial admonitions against the stereotyping that have bedeviled previous attempts to write about Haiti in general, and Vodou and zombies in particular, are quite radically contradicted by comments such as these. Equally noticeable is the constant slippage — present already in the original 1983 paper — between presenting what *could* be the case and then assuming that what has been mentioned as a possibility *is* actually the case. A typical Davis passage (e.g., 1988a, p. 9) gives the impression that zombification really does exist, and that such a claim is not a claim at all but unmediated truth. This leads to a central contradiction: despite claiming in various places in both *Serpent* and *Passage of Darkness* that the making of a zombie is a rare event, comments like "undoubtedly *in many instances* the victim does die either from the poison itself or by suffocation in the coffin" (1985, p. 221; emphasis added) rather than being successfully raised from the earth, give the strong impression that zombie-poisonings happen all the time in this peculiar land.

The Serpent and the Rainbow greatly irritated many anthropologists and related others because of its "Indiana Jones bravado" (Corbett, 1990). On this view, Davis had no right to complain about what the film-makers had done to the book, because his text already owed more to Hollywood than to serious scholarship in the first place. Having the temerity to present himself as "a dashing man of action as well as intellect," and to cast himself in the then very current garb of Indiana Jones, combining the role of "average academic turned wily world traveller," Davis had unintentionally cast "an almost comic slant to the 'double persona' problem of anthropologists" (Dutton, 1993, p. 148).

No doubt stung by such criticisms and embroiled in various controversies about the reliability of his claims, Davis published *Passage of Darkness*. This was intended as a text purged of all the fictionalizing apparatus of the earlier book, an orthodox scholarly tract that apparently broke no rules at all, and which would claw back the tarnished respectability of the "zombie project." Some critics accepted that he had indeed successfully achieved this aim (Corbett, 1990). A few even went so far as to proclaim the later book "a masterpiece," wholly shorn of "formula and sensationalism" (Farrer, 1988). A minority also thought that *Passage* "weaves the findings of several disparate academic fields into a provocative argument" (Brodwin, 1992, p. 411). But a more consistently-held view was that the book exhibited, like its predecessor, "a curious mixture of sensationalism and scholarship — and much of the scholarship is questionable" (Lawless, 1989, p. 5). For the majority of critics, either the pharmacology was suspect, or the ethnography was faulty, or both. Far from weaving together the disparate natural and social scientific enterprises, as a good ethnobotanist must, Davis was accused of both falsifying the toxicology results and of producing hopelessly flawed ethnographic data. He was attacked from both wings of the academy that his training had endeavored to allow him to knit together. Moreover, Davis was seen to have gone wrong because of the "collision of two different worlds of research," on the one hand a romantic world of quasi-anthropological adventure where "fame and fortune followed," and on the other "a less glamorous place of mass spectrometers, gas chromatography and mouse bioassays" where his findings were found to be less than satisfactory (Booth, 1988, p. 274).

The most vicious controversy involved the nature and supposed effects of the zombie powders. Eight samples had been collected from a number of *bokors* across Haiti. Various accusations were made against Davis:

1. he had submitted his PhD thesis before the laboratory tests were concluded on the powders to see if they had the properties claimed for them by the *bokors*— and Davis; he had implied that the tests had been carried out already and had shown that they did indeed possess such properties; the reference he gave to the tests in the thesis was to the 1983 paper, but it of course carried no such results as it presented merely interim findings;

2. he had referred in his writings to tests carried out informally by a pathologist at the Columbia Presbyterian Hospital in New York, Leon Roizin, who had carried out the work as a favor to Davis's supervisor; while the tests indicated that the powders examined had traces of tetrodotoxin, which Davis claimed they had, Roizin said that the tests were not formally conducted, and he subsequently declared he wanted nothing more to do with Davis, who had abused an informal agreement;

3. Davis and a colleague had carried out their own tests on the powders, but when they failed to find traces of tetrodotoxin in them, Davis withheld the negative results; Davis retorted that the experiment had been badly conducted (the powders had been put into a solution for testing, inadvertently destroying the TTX), thus invalidating the result, and so there was nothing to report;

4. Davis had implied that TTX was present in all of the samples, but once the lab results were in, it was probably present only in one of them; on this, Davis was alleged to have remained silent;

5. according to the eminent toxicologists, Yasumoto and Kao (1986; also Kao and Yasumoto, 1990), to whom some samples of the powders had been sent for testing, not only were there only insignificant traces of TTX in the samples they examined, the samples were very alkaline in nature, such that the TTX would have become pharmacologically inactive, and if the *bokors* usually made them this way, they could never have worked effectively; Davis responded that the *bokors* could not be expected to make the powders in the same standardized fashion as a pharmaceutical company, and that the fact that *these* powders did not have the capacity to "make" zombies did not rule out the possibility that other powders made by these or other *bokors* could be effective.

This kind of response by Davis particularly enraged the critics: Davis was in effect saying that negative results did not matter, as they could not disprove his claims. For the critics, this went against all the established protocols of science — Davis was requiring the skeptics to disprove his claims, rather than playing by the rules and endeavoring to prove his own claims through well-founded evidence. The debates came to a head when Kao denounced Davis as having perpetuated a major scientific fraud, with Davis subsequently indignantly denying such claims (1988b). He also added that his natural scientific critics had completely failed to engage with the cultural-psychological elements of his argument, remaining bound within the narrow disciplinary boundaries he himself had transcended (Booth, 1988; Davis, 1988b). But the critics were able to respond that the central argument in that regard, namely that TTX had an "ambivalent potential" that could be activated in different ways within different cultures (here, a Vodouisant being led to believe he was becoming a zombie) was absurd, in that all TTX possessed was the capacity to kill if used in sufficient doses, for it was not like some drug that could be taken for psychedelic effects (Anderson, 1988).

The anthropological critics were no less scathing. The most recurrent criticism was that despite his claims to the contrary, Davis had indeed caricatured Vodou, presenting it as a closed cultural system which had not changed since its inception in the late eighteenth-century, and depicting it in a manner that disconnected it from social and political change, and all forms of empirical practice (Brodwin, 1996; Dayan, 1998). As mentioned before, its connections to the Duvalier regime were gestured at but not taken properly into the analysis. He had cavalierly neglected to mention that there existed different schools of thought, both as to the nature of Vodou, its roles in Haitian society and the nature of that society itself, preferring instead to present himself as some *ex nihilo* pioneer treading on virgin territory that was actually already well-trodden. His field work was trounced in various ways. He had no grasp of Creole, the language of the peasantry, so his reliance on an interpreter opened up all sorts of hermeneutic pitfalls. He had spent relatively little time in the field, had carried out little or no preparation beforehand, and was unfamiliar with Haitian society before he landed in Port-au-Prince (Anderson, 1988). He invested far too much credence in the oral testimony of Clairvius Narcisse, and had not taken into account enough that the former was in fact far from a "pristine" informant but had in fact been interviewed by various persons since his reappearance in 1980, not least a BBC TV crew making a documentary about zombification!

Davis's access to the secret societies, which were the hinge of his social structural and functional argument, was very limited, and he was accused both of wildly over-estimating the nature of their activities, of misunderstanding the roles they played in Haitian society, of overemphasizing their supposedly "African" origins, of neglecting the examination of how they had mutated over time, and of not really proving any link between the societies and their alleged justice-giving roles on the one hand, and the creation and utilization of the zombie powders on the other (Lawless, 1989). Indeed he had not witnessed any of the powders he had collected being used, let alone actually witnessing an actual instance of zombification, leaving it open that he might have been bilked by unscrupulous *bokors* taking a rich white man for a ride by selling him powders that could have been made of anything (Brodwin, 1992). Worst of all in the eyes of the critics — worse even than the shameless cultivation of the popular media and releasing his claims through them rather than through the proper scholarly channels (Kao and Yasumoto, 1990) — was his participation in the digging open of the child's grave, the "monstrosity of this moral transgression [being] overwhelming" (ibid., p. 132), making the research "a mockery of science," although some scholars spoke up in Davis's defense, saying that participation in illegal activities was part-and-parcel of ethnographic work in difficult locations (Booth, 1988).

In sum, the general tenor of scholarly criticism was that *Passage* just as much as *Serpent* involved an untenable situation where "fact nestles alongside fiction and warranted generalizations accompany unwarranted ones in a spectacular, though often ungainly, dance" (Anderson, 1988, p. 152). In addition, as "the amount of public information and notoriety" which had been generated was "very much out of proportion to the modest nature of Davis's findings," there was a completely unacceptable "ratio of fact to publicity" (ibid., p. 124). Thus far from advancing knowledge, Davis's contribution had been to "set scientific research on the subject back fifty years" or more (Woodson, 1992, p. 151). Davis meanwhile had gone on an extended fieldtrip to Borneo, no doubt licking his wounds, and wondering if all the notoriety his work had generated had been worth the effort of the field research.

Conclusion: Classifying the Unclassifiable

It is beyond the scope of competence of this paper to adjudicate how accurate or not the claims of Davis's critics were. Even if one were to assume that many of the barbs aimed at his research were valid, it remains the case that when one reads through the controversies of some twenty years ago, one hears the unmistakable crunching sound of disciplinary toes being stepped upon. Perhaps one of Davis's greatest sins was to endeavor to cross established disciplinary boundaries of knowledge. Even if he had done so in a less brash, self-confident, and self-aggrandizing manner, one might surmise that the response from within disciplinary fortresses would have been less than welcoming. Even if he had made claims that were somewhat more nuanced, the fact that he was endeavoring to conjoin areas that normally go unconnected — colonial history and toxicology, for example — meant he was already treading on dangerous ground where few had trod before, but where the risk of offending multiple types of specialist was very great (Woodson, 1992).

But more importantly than that, it was the evocative and provocative zombie subject matter that I think was in part responsible for the vehemence of the responses of his critics. Here was someone who had the temerity to say that zombies were not just folkloric creations, just symbols in a particular tradition or a cheap means of garnering thrills for Western publics, but they were in fact real, and that the life-history cases he was presenting were not only true but also viscerally tragic and empirically factual. Moving away from standard ethnological perceptions that zombies exist symbolically within certain worldviews, towards the radical claim that they *really do exist*, was both troubling and potentially comical at the same time. How could one even begin to think that zombies are "real," when such a thought blows apart so many aspects of the Western university's self-perception, as a place of sober learning rather than a locale for the contemplation of the out-and-out fantastical? This possibility is an outrageous one, and one way of dealing with it is to treat it either with outright contempt, or with nervous and degrading laughter.

It is notable that right from the start of his publishing in this area, the framing by editors and critics of Davis's work, when it was not outright condemnatory, very often seemed to trivialize it with asides akin to a snide snicker. Thus *The Lancet* (1984), as we have seen, felt fit to break with its normal neutral prose to throw in a reference to Ian Fleming and the wilder shores of spy fiction — another despised genre like horror, according to an orthodox "high culture" canonical reading. More remarkably, when the journal *Science* ran a piece summarizing the rancorous debates about the testing of the powders (Booth, 1988), it was accompanied by a still from Romero's *The Night of the Living Dead* depicting the flesh-eating monsters of that film, with underneath the joking caption "Just enough Tetrodotoxin?" So the Haitian *zombi* was, once again, transformed into the zombie of Euro-American fiction, strongly implying that claims as to the existence of zombies belong not in the laboratory but in the movie theater. And the author of the piece was moved to reflect "who does not enjoy a good story about zombies now and then?," implicitly appealing to a commonsense understanding of zombies as only fit for popular fictions and other vulgar recreations. If zombies were to be allowed into academia at all, it would be as symbols and images, dealt with by the more respectable denizens of ethnology departments and by the somewhat less reputable inhabitants of cultural studies outfits. As purely fictive entities in thought experiments, philosophers are allowed today to have debates about zombies.[2] But there is no obvious disciplinary location for *real* zombies, for who under the current social organization of knowledge could, or would want to, study them? They fit nowhere, and like all uncanny things, they are radically "matter out of place" (Douglas, 1966).

Zombies are troubling enough if they are merely symbolic, as both popular fictions and philosophical excurses amply demonstrate (Greene and Mohammad, 2006). As creatures that are neither fully alive nor fully dead, they pose awkward questions about precisely what we, or people in any culture, mean by these terms, a fact that is beginning to be recognized by some more adventurous philosophers in the present day (Thompson, 2006, p. 30). But if zombies were found to be *real*, what consequences would that entail? A *real zombie* (or more accurately, a real *zombi*) would be like the platypus was to eighteenth-century taxonomists: as it did not fit any established categories and disciplinary boundaries, so these would have to be rethought and reconstructed, even if that process was painful and unsettling for those who had stakes in the continuation of the "normal science" of the time (Eco, 2000). What Davis was proposing would have sounded appallingly like the undermining of established notions of what is real and not-real, proper and improper, respectable and not respectable, even if he had had more sound evidential grounds upon which to say it. It suggested bringing into the academy, in an untamed way, an entity that was thought could only exist in folklore, the imagination, and in fiction. A hundred years and more of sensationalizing representations of Haiti, plus the evolution in popular culture of the zombie figure away from its roots in Haitian folk culture towards something that exists *only* in apparently debased commercial, industrial-cultural contexts, ensured that few people, if indeed anyone, could even begin to think that what Davis was claiming could ever be true.

Given its representations either as a folk cultural figment or the kind of thing that keeps teenagers amused in drive-ins and video-consoles, the academic world could not, and I would contend still cannot, possibly conceive of zombies as being "real." That was Wade Davis's provocative challenge to the academy — and it was dealt with as harshly as a heretic might expect. Davis has now moved on to bigger and better things, sponsored by *National Geographic* magazine and representing himself as an eco-warrior for our times (Davis, 2004). He had his fingers badly burnt by his apparently outrageous claims that zombies really walk the turf of Haiti, but in the long-run the publicity generated by the ensuing controversy has led to a successful globe-trotting career. But what the "zombie project" really demonstrated is this: it showed what can happen when the unthinkable is, just for a moment, presented as thinkable, and it demonstrated how established modes of reasoning and fabrications of reality can violently reassert themselves in order to keep out the conceptual darkness that sometimes threatens to pass from their edges to the center of attention.

Notes

1. See http://www.imdb.com/title/tt0096071/

2. Philosophical zombies "raise problematic counterexamples for various positions in metaphysics. These zombies are respiring, fully functional persons in every sense except that they lack subjective states (that is, consciousness). They look and act like everyone else, but have no thoughts, feelings or interior life of any kind. [They] are technically alive, but there is a sense in which they 'shouldn't' be: their existence ... presents a troubling paradox that threatens to upset our most deeply held convictions about what it means to be alive in the first place" (Greene and Mohammad, 2006, xiv–xv).

4

Guess Who's Going to Be Dinner

Sidney Poitier, Black Militancy, and the Ambivalence of Race in Romero's Night of the Living Dead[1]

BARBARA S. BRUCE

The impact Sidney Poitier has had on American cinema and culture is legendary. He was "the first black actor to achieve and maintain true star status within the industry" and "the first black superstar" (Leab, 1975, p. 223); in fact, as Poitier himself has said, throughout the 1950s and until the late 1960s, he was "the only black star out there" (qtd. in Murray, 1973, p. 29). Starting his Hollywood career in 1950 with Joseph L. Mankiewicz's *No Way Out*, Poitier rose to fame in such films as *Blackboard Jungle* (Brooks, 1955), *The Defiant Ones* (Kramer, 1958), and *A Raisin in the Sun* (Petrie, 1961), winning an Academy Award, the first given to an African American actor in a leading role, for *Lilies of the Field* (Nelson, 1963). Poitier's acting career peaked in 1967 with the release of three of his most famous films: *To Sir, with Love* (Clavell), *Guess Who's Coming to Dinner* (Kramer), and *In the Heat of the Night* (Jewison). The box-office success of these films ranked him the seventh-highest money-making star in 1967 and number one in 1968, an achievement that would not be replicated by a black actor for another forty years ("Top Ten").

In the six-month period in 1967 in which Poitier's three films were released — June to December — independent director George Romero was making *Night of the Living Dead*, a low-budget horror film which would alter the trajectory of its genre and which was the first horror film to feature an African American actor, Duane Jones, in the lead role. While critics such as Robert K. Lightning and Richard Dyer have pointed out similarities between Poitier and Jones as the character Ben, they have not sufficiently considered the cultural impact of the Poitier persona in their readings of *Living Dead*. Instead, their studies read Ben in terms of the rising black militancy of the late 1960s and thus as a threat to the film's white characters. In particular, Lightning argues that Ben "occupies a transitional phase (both temporal and in terms of racial signifiers) between the Poitier of 1967 and the blaxploitation hero" of the 1970s (2000, p. 2). I agree to a certain extent with Lightning, but I will in this paper consider Ben not in relation to what followed, but in terms of what he represented at the time of the film's release in 1968, giving greater consideration to the resonances of the Poitier persona in the characterization of Ben. Specifically, I argue that, through its casting and characterizations, *Living Dead* evokes the Poitier persona and black militancy, only to deny both as solutions to the upheavals of the day. Unlike Poitier's 1967 films, relatively conservative studio projects that make race their subject but ignore the reality of increasingly violent black activism, *Living Dead* gives full vent to the anxieties permeating late-'60s American culture, offering a dark, cynical, anti–Hollywood[2] look at "ordinary" Americans and engaging race-based expectations without offering the panacea of a Poitier-like hero or readily identifiable and, therefore, containable black stereotypes. In *Living Dead*, race is thus represented ambivalently, and the binary conceptions of race at play in the film demonstrate the problems associated with depicting "blackness" in American cinema. Furthermore, at a time when (white) audiences had accepted a black hero in mainstream cinema, *Living Dead* ironically suggests that the core values that the hero has traditionally represented in the classic Hollywood cinema no longer have currency.

In the era of the Civil Rights Movement, Poitier "came to personify the Black Man on the Screen" (Leab, p. 223). Talented and handsome, he created a film persona that demonstrated urbanity, reason, and self-control, along with a willingness to temper his individualist impulses for the greater (white) good. Donald Bogle suggests in his seminal work *Toms, Coons, Mulattoes, Mammies, and Bucks* that, for white audiences, Poitier "was the model integrationist hero":

> In all his films he was educated and intelligent. He spoke proper English, dressed conservatively, and had the best of table manners. [...]. His characters were tame; never did they act impulsively, nor were they threats to the system. They were amenable and pliant. And finally they were non-funky, almost sexless and sterile. In short, they were the perfect dream for white liberals anxious to have a colored man in for lunch or dinner [2001, p. 175].

Embodying middle-classness, Poitier also appealed to a "Black America [...] still trying to meet white standards and ape white manners," since "he did not carry any ghetto cultural baggage with him. No dialect. No shuffling. No African cultural past. And he was almost totally devoid of rhythm. In short, he was the complete antithesis of all the black buffoons who had appeared before in American movies" (Bogle, p. 176). Poitier was "the definitive Civil Rights subject," Sharon Willis notes, "embodying the 'sign' of racial difference in a manageable form," and his films of the mid–1960s "work towards fantasmatic reparation of racial conflict, replaying essentially the same drama of reconciliation, offering idealized resolutions that must repress political and material violence around race in the world" (Willis, 2007). By 1967, however, the tenets of integration and passive resistance of the Civil Rights Movement that Poitier embodied were giving way to the more active resistance of Black Power. The success of Poitier's films suggests his persona still had currency with the mainstream American public in 1967, but the criticism leveled at Poitier in the press indicates that his image was quickly becoming passé.

Reviews of Poitier's 1967 films include disparaging and even openly hostile comments[3]: for example, writing in *The Village Voice* in August of 1967, Andrew Sarris labels Poitier "a civil rights commercial" (qtd. in Leab, p. 230), and in a 1969 edition of *Film Comment*, Maxine Hall Elliston describes *Guess Who's Coming to Dinner* as "warmed-over white shit" (qtd. in Guerrero, 1993, p. 76; Leab, p. 230). The most (in)famous attack on Poitier comes from playwright Clifford Mason in his oft-cited 1967 *New York Times* article, "Why Does America Love Sidney Poitier So?" Calling Poitier "a showcase nigger," Mason writes, "it is a schizophrenic flight from identity and historical fact that makes anybody imagine, even for a moment, that the Negro is best served by being a black version of the man in the gray flannel suit, taking on white problems and a white man's sense of what's wrong with the world." Mason's assessment that, at the very least, Poitier was out of touch proved prophetic:

Poitier's mainstream film career faltered after 1967, his idealized characters no longer reconcilable to the reality of late-1960s America, particularly as it involved race relations.[4] For a nation trying to cope with racial tensions and violence, as well as protests for women's and Native rights and against the Vietnam War, daily news of war casualties and American failure, the assassinations of white and black leaders, and the rise of the hippie counterculture, Poitier's characters — their integrationism, ability to solve (racial) problems with a relative gentility and ease, and nearly superhuman sense of restraint — were out of sync with the times. In his article, Mason expresses the desire for a Poitier who is "a real man," suggesting that, in a film like *The Bedford Incident* (Harris, 1965), when faced with an unreasonable and bullying white man whose selfishness and shortsightedness led the entire ship's crew to their deaths, "Poitier should at least have been allowed to bust him one in the jaw." Mason's rather troubling definition of a "real (black) man" as one who solves his problems or at least expresses his negative feelings through violence reflects the growing frustration of black Americans in the latter half of the 1960s. When the passive resistance of Civil Rights failed to resolve the inequities between white and black cultures, African Americans had begun to demonstrate, to riot, and, in some cases, to adopt militant tactics; as Bogle puts it, "black rage, black anger, and black power began their maddening stomp, overturning the old placid way and lifting eyebrows as they introduced to America the deep-seated bitterness so long ignored" (195). With Ben in *Night of the Living Dead*, it seems that Mason gets his wish — a Poitier-like hero who busts white people on the jaw and more — although the horror film form reveals this dream-come-true to be a nightmare, no solution to (black) America's problems.

Romero and other members of the production team have claimed that they cast Duane Jones as Ben, not because of his race, but because he was simply the best actor for the role (Becker, 2006, p. 58); however, while the filmmakers may have achieved a perfect liberal color-blindness, the same cannot be said of the film's viewers. Writing at the time of the film's release about the devastating impact *Living Dead* had on a theatre full of children, Roger Ebert never refers to Ben by his name nor as the "hero" or "protagonist," but always as "the Negro" (1967 [sic]). Similarly, Elliott Stein in his review reveals that the zombies kill all the principle characters "except the leading man, Duane Jones, a black." Later in the piece, he again remarks that the "main character is black — but not only is the point not rubbed in [in the film] — it's not mentioned *once*" (Stein, 1970, original emphasis); the same cannot be said of Elliott's review. In fact, most, if not all, reviewers and critics writing on the film comment on Ben's race. But, how can we — I include myself, of course — not? The filmmakers may not have written Ben as a black character or cast Jones because he was black, but they recognized that Jones/Ben, as the only African American in the film, "gave [the film] some power" (Romero, 2002b), that he would stand out and resonate in particular ways for audiences living in a time of widespread racial conflict in the United States and when only one other black actor was playing lead roles: Poitier, the number-one box-office star. As Nelson George says of Poitier, "No other black actor, and few black figures, was so massive a figure in our (in this case American) psyche. No one else has meant what he did and no one else ever will" (qtd. in Willis). The difference, of course, is that, while most of Poitier's films make his race a primary issue, *Living Dead* "has often been praised for never making an issue of the black hero's color" (Wood, 1979, p. 93). As Wood points out, however, "it is not true that [Ben's] color is arbitrary and without meaning: Romero uses it to signify his difference from the other characters, to set him apart from their norms" (p. 93). I agree with Wood here only in part, because while Ben's "blackness" does signify his difference from the white characters in some ways, the film also undermines those differences to suggest, finally, that all Americans, black and white, are implicated in America's "living dead" culture, an idea I will discuss below.

The similarities between Poitier and Jones/Ben extend beyond their leading roles and their race. As Lightning points out, Ben's casual clothes — "slacks, button-down shirt and sweater"— recall the apparel "habitually worn by the contemporary urbanites Poitier portrayed during the 1960s (e.g., *A Patch of Blue*)" (2000, p. 3). In Ben's case, as it often is in Poitier's, his white undershirt and shirt and light-colored sweater, as well as the grainy black-and-white film stock used to shoot *Living Dead* (Hervey, 2008, p. 50), work to emphasize the very dark complexion he has in common with Poitier. Both men are of similar height and lean build,[5] and both have deep, reassuring voices and speak articulately. Ben's clothing, along with what appear to be a nice watch and a college or wedding ring and way of speaking code him as middle class, which, as I discussed above, is also in keeping with many of the characters Poitier played, most notably his iconic characters of 1967. Lightning further observes that, "Like Poitier, Ben is also placed within a white social world" (p. 3). The similarities between Ben and Poitier, evident from the moment Ben appears onscreen, cannot be ignored, a feature through which the film, consciously or unconsciously, raises the issue of race relations.

The ways in which Poitier's characters and Ben in *Living Dead* make their entrances reveal the films' treatments of racial issues. In her work on Poitier, Willis has observed that his iconic roles depict him as black mentors, who "arrive by accident to enlighten [the white characters]," but who also typically arrive in ways that visually restrict their power. In *To Sir, with Love*, for example, we first see Poitier's Mark Thackeray in the credit sequence in an extreme long shot and silhouetted, boarding a bus on the outskirts of London. Accompanying this image are Poitier's credit, fittingly in large white letters, which clearly identifies this distant figure; the film's title, also in white script; and, the title song. The title and song both assure us that this character will nurture and be respected and beloved. The first clear look at Thackeray comes after several images of the bus traveling into the heart of London: in a long shot followed by cut-ins to a medium shot and then a close-up, we see Thackeray on the bus, surrounded by middle-aged white Cockney women, one of whom makes the crack, "I wouldn't mind having this little lot in my stocking for Christmas." Is it a stretch to read in the negative phrasing of "I wouldn't mind" and her euphemism "little lot" not the idea that the handsome Thackeray would be a nice "gift," but rather a reference to the idea of receiving (a man as black as) coal for being a "bad" girl? However, the potential transgression of a black man/white woman relationship is contained in several ways: the age and unattractiveness of the woman; her abrasive, but joking, manner; her lower-class status, indicated by her Cockney accent; and, Thackeray's mildly amused expression and refusal to engage with her sexual banter. Although the woman is clearly not a potential love interest, this encounter nonetheless foreshadows Thackeray's refusal to "engage" with Pamela (Judy Geeson), the white student who develops a crush on him, or Gillian (Suzy Kendall), his young and attractive white female colleague. In both form and narrative, then, these films reassure their primary audience — the white middle class — that Poitier's black characters pose no threat to the dominant culture.

The Poitier entrance that comes closest to being transgressive occurs in *Guess Who's Coming to Dinner*. In a montage consisting of extreme long to medium close-up shots with the romantic ballad "Glory of Love" on the soundtrack, Poitier's Dr. John Wade Prentice and his pretty, young, white fiancée (Katharine Houghton) walk side by side, talking, laughing, touching, through the San Francisco airport, eventually getting into a cab, where he kisses her. However, the transgressive potential of the interracial couple is also limited by strategies of containment. As in the other two entrances I have mentioned and in many of his other films, Poitier appears in a conservative suit and tie, well-groomed and smiling. As well, while the kiss is transgressive, in the sense that it was the first interracial kiss in a Hollywood film, it is "contained" in the cab's rear-view mirror, in long shot and with their faces in heavy shadow, so that we do not actually *see* the kiss. Prentice is made even safer later in the film when we learn that he is impossibly successful and deferential to the white father's authority; despite his skin color, he embodies white norms and values. In various ways, then, these films and others ensure that Poitier's entrance into, and sojourn within, the white social space are controlled and non-threatening.

Ben's arrival on the scene in *Living Dead*, however, differs significantly, although certainly the Poitier persona has resonance. Barbra (Judith O'Dea), a young white woman, has taken refuge from her living-dead attacker in a remote farmhouse, where she is further terrorized by the sight of a partially eaten corpse she finds upstairs, her state of mind reflected by the dissonant music that begins. Attempting to flee the house, Barbra encounters Ben just outside the door. As she throws herself out the door and onto the porch, we see only the glare of headlights, which cause Barbra to throw her arms over her eyes, a gesture we will later see from the zombies when confronted with fire. As we cut away from Barbra reeling on the porch, Ben bursts from off-screen right into the mostly black frame, in extreme close-up and out of focus, the left half of his face concealed by heavy shadow. Unlike the Poitier films, *Living Dead* refuses us a "safe" distance from which to view and assess the black male character at his first appearance, and it denies us a clear look at his face. In fact, throughout the film, the camera often does not show the details of Ben's face clearly. In part, this is because "Stocks, cameras and lighting were developed taking the white face as the touchstone" (Dyer, 1997, p. 90), so black skin does not register correctly on film. In a sense, then, the film stock itself metaphorizes the problems of representing "blackness" in (white) American cinema. However, Romero often seems to use the limitations of the film stock deliberately, along with shadows and low illuminations, to conceal Ben's expressions from us, making him somewhat inscrutable and denying us complete access to him. In contrast to Poitier's films, *Living Dead* is incapable of containing Ben, but it also refuses to do so.

The remainder of this first scene featuring Ben plays with conflicting racial expectations. From the next shot of Barbra — framed in a canted medium close-up, she stares at Ben and takes a step back, shocked and uncertain, while the disquieting music continues — we cut back to Ben. The camera views Ben from the porch, next to Barbra, and this position aligns the audience with her uncertainty; that we have been with Barbra since the beginning also ensures that we identify with her. Ben, now in close-up and in focus, freezes in place for a few seconds, framed by the headlights and looking off-screen at Barbra. Ben's arrival is thus punctuated by a pause, creating a melodramatic tableau that gives not only Barbra, but also the spectator a moment to wonder if this man is villain or hero — that is, to become aware of our own expectations about the character. The action resumes as Ben looks over his shoulder at the approaching zombie, turns back and steps towards Barbra, hesitates, then, making his decision, manhandles her back into the house. As they enter the house, slam and lock the door, the scene and the dissonant music, having built to a crescendo, come to an end. In 1968, viewers' expectations of Ben would certainly be informed by conflicting cultural models: Ben's aggressive entrance evokes the racist stereotype of the black man as (sexual) threat and the more contemporary image of the black militant, but his clean-cut good looks evoke the non-violent, non-threatening icons of the Civil Rights Movement and integrationism: Martin Luther King and, particularly, Poitier.

Some critics, though, have failed to consider that the impact positive black role models had in the 1960s would make this moment in the film at least ambivalent. Lightning suggests that Barbra reacts fearfully to Ben's arrival because of his race, that she is "product of a culture that has doubtless imbued her with stories of threatening black men": "One notes that she resists him as he takes her into the house," he adds (p. 5). Stephen Harper agrees, reading Barbra as a "progressive" character, because while white women are typically "presented as completely non-racist," Barbra's "clear mistrust of Ben [...] suggests that, for all her docile domesticity, she has been affected by the racism of the world outside" (2005). To support his reading, Harper points to the moment a bit later in the film when Barbra positions the knife she has been carrying for protection since she first entered the house "on the fridge ambiguously, so that the audience is unsure whether she wishes to use it against the zombies or against Ben" (2005). However, nothing in Barbra's initial encounter with Ben or in their subsequent interaction suggests that she is fearful of Ben because of his race. What happens to Barbra before and after Ben's arrival suggests in fact that Barbra is fearful of all men.

From the beginning of the film, (white) male characters subject Barbra to abuse, as Harper himself points out in a second essay on *Living Dead*: in the graveyard, her own brother, Johnny (Russell Steiner), subjects her to "incessant taunting" (Harper, 2003) and then an unknown man — she does not know he is the living dead — kills Johnny and attacks her, prompting her to run for her life. She is quite active and alert when she is on her own, but she becomes less and less active when living men — white or black — are around.[6] Ben's arrival startles Barbra, but he makes no move towards her until he turns and sees the zombie approaching them, indicating that his sole motivation is to remove her, albeit aggressively, from harm's way. Furthermore, Barbra's resistance to being pushed back into the house can be explained by the fact that she knows, where Ben does not, that the house is not safe. She is escaping a house that holds the threat of death when Ben arrives, but he never asks her why she is fleeing, and her instinct proves correct: the house is no safe haven. Once inside, after Ben has assured her that "It's all right" and begins to survey the house, Barbra goes alone to the bottom of the stairs, looks up, and begins to moan and cry, indicating that she is far more disturbed by the half-eaten corpse upstairs than by Ben's presence. In the kitchen, she does hold the knife with the blade towards Ben — he is a stranger who has burst into a horrific situation, after all — but she also sets it down, picking it up again only when the living dead approach the house. The second time Barbra puts the knife down, after Ben has killed several zombies, the blade is turned away from Ben, and she leaves it there, suggesting that she now trusts him, in general and to protect her. The idea that Barbra is fearful of Ben as a black man is further undermined later in the film, when Barbra screams and again attempts to flee as Cooper (Karl Hardman) and Tom (Keith Wayne) — both white men — emerge from the basement. Barbra's fear of men is ultimately realized near the end of the film, when she is pulled outside by Johnny and devoured by a group of white male zombies. The assumption, then, that Barbra is threatened by Ben's blackness or that she is racist relies solely on the *spectator's* association of blackness with threat and danger, and in 1968, given Poitier's currency, the spectator may have been just as likely to associate a black leading man with heroism and altruism. In the absence of any actual signs of racism in the film, Ben's meaning depends on the spectator's own impulses towards race.

Romero's seemingly simple, best-actor-for-the-job casting decision proves to be any-thing but simple, as it shapes the ideology of the film and produces a complex of racial effects. As the readings of Barbra's response to Ben suggest, nowhere are these effects more evident than in what would otherwise be a typical horror-genre scenario, the isolation of the threatened heroic couple[7] — it creates an interracial pairing, which had long been taboo in the classic Hollywood cinema. When Ben takes charge and pushes the reluctant Barbra back into the house to "save" her, it recalls a joke made in 1968 about Poitier "always helping little old ladies across the street ... whether they want to go or not" (qtd. in Leab, p. 231). Inside the house, Ben immediately begins to "secure" the doors and windows and to reassure Barbra, controlling his impatience when she is unable to follow simple instructions or to answer questions. Ben's initial interaction with Barbra seems to indicate that he is a Poitier-esque hero. However, the film refuses to maintain this reassuring association, unsettling the viewer when Ben displays some very un–Poitier-like characteristics as he and Barbra share the stories of their initial encounters with the living dead. Ben tells his story first, becoming a bit emotional when he describes seeing a man die; when Barbra takes her turn, the impa-tience Ben had earlier suppressed resurfaces. Lightning suggests that "Ben and Barbra provide each other a mutual opportunity for emotional release: the shared stories suggest a desperate human need for communication and sympathy brought on by the dire circumstances" (p. 6), but I disagree with this reading, since little communication or sympathy is in evidence. As he tells his story, Ben does not look at Barbra, who is absent-mindedly playing with a button on her coat; as she tells hers, he looks at her warily and then makes agitated move-ments and exasperated expressions. Neither has any interest in the other's story; instead, both characters simply narrativize their chaotic experiences in order to make sense, and thus take control, of them. Their narratives are not about making a connection with another person, but are only self-serving, which is shown most pointedly when Barbra lies to conceal that she had reacted childishly to her brother's taunts. Ben's admonishment to Barbra as she is speaking to "just keep calm," even though she is actually calm at that moment, has the opposite effect: it cues her hysteria. Frantic about Johnny and further agitated by Ben's refusal to let her go to find him, Barbra slaps Ben, which he returns with a punch across her jaw, knocking her out cold. Ben's action effectively subverts any idea that he is a straight-forward Poitier-esque hero, signaling instead to an audience in 1968 that this character brings together, in a never-before-seen mix, Poitier's heroic qualities and a violence evocative of the black militantism that had arisen in recent years.

That is not to say that Poitier's characters do not have their moments of violence, but they are notably different from Ben's violent response to Barbra. *In the Heat of the Night*, for example, is famous for "the slap heard round the world," when Tibbs returns the slap of a rich white man, and certainly it is a Hollywood cliché for the hero to slap a hysterical woman to bring her back to her senses. Ben's punch, however, is not about reestablishing authority or snapping a woman out of her hysteria; instead, it reveals a loss of control and an aggression that we never see in Poitier's characters. Even the famous slap is measured, matching the force of the slap he received, and necessary to declare Tibbs's refusal to be subordinated. After delivering it, Tibbs glares in anger, but he is fully in control of himself, if not the situation. *In the Heat of the Night* gives us another notable example of Poitier's always considered and ideally measured responses, particularly with white women, when Tibbs tells Mrs. Colbert (Lee Grant) about the murder of her husband. Shocked and reeling, Mrs. Colbert remarks, "It's very hot in here. It's very hot in this room," prompting Tibbs to take control and lead her to a chair. He stops her as she tries to rise, and then she clasps his hand. The camera tracks in to emphasize the hands — black and white, united melodramatically in sympathy and understanding — before Tibbs sensitively leaves the room, allowing her to break down in private. In *Living Dead*, Barbra similarly remarks, "Oh, it's hot in here — hot" in the middle of telling her story, but Ben's response is to roll his eyes, which parodies the interaction between Tibbs and Mrs. Colbert and exposes it as idealized and artificial. Ben's exasperation with Barbra and his punch, while disturbing, ring more true than Poitier's characters' controlled responses to tense or emotional situations: even Tibbs might have lost control of himself in the midst of a zombie invasion. *Living Dead* unapologetically casts Ben as a complex and flawed hero, one who defies established stereotypes, positive or negative. It is not only with the living dead, then, that this horror film unsettles its audience: even in scenes in which the main characters are temporarily safe, the racial ambivalence of the hero raises uncertainty as to what to expect from him and from the film. Horror films give vent to the cultural anxieties of their particular time and place — and anxieties were running especially high in the late 1960s — but *Living Dead* breaks new ground by refusing to offer its audience the solace of stock characters and conventional heroic behavior or pat answers to such complex issues as racial and gender relations.

The uncertainty about Ben extends from his status as hero to the implications in the film of the possibility of an interracial coupling. The formulas of the various Hollywood genres differ in some regards, but one commonality is the romantic involvement of the leading male and female characters, even after a slap (although perhaps less so after a punch); *Living Dead* appears to be following the formula, when Ben and Barbra find themselves alone together. Additionally, the "breakthrough" interracial coupling of *Guess Who's Coming to Dinner* the year before *Living Dead's* release and Ben's sheer physical energy would certainly have raised expectations for the audiences of the day that a relationship could develop between Ben and Barbra. Working against this expectation, though, is the specter of Poitier, whose performances, as critics have noted, were often "sexless" (Bogle, p. 175; Walker, 1970, p. 348). Willis reveals numerous strategies that Poitier's films employ to contain him when he interacts with white women. She cites as an example how *To Sir, with Love* deflates any sexual tension between Thackeray and Pamela by showing him dance with an "embarrassing awkwardness that codes the couple as completely mismatched." The film's "flirtation with interracial erotics," Willis continues, "and its clumsy, heavy-handed final disavowal resonate with the strained efforts to manage Poitier's body that mark so many of his films." As well, Poitier's "films seem consistently to manage this erotic pressure through scenarios of 'passing through,' in which he definitively departs the context he has transformed" (Willis, 2007). Like Poitier's characters, Ben is also just passing through, but circumstances beyond his control prevent him from ever departing. Again the film evokes, only to subvert, the typical Poitier characterization, a strategy that creates an unsettled, unknowable scenario for its late-1960s audience.

The ambiguous expectations raised by the interracial pairing of Ben and Barbra is again evidenced in the responses of the film's critics. Lightning reads an erotic tension between Ben and Barbra: he suggests that, when Barbra talks about Johnny, "unaware he is Barbra's brother, Ben's glowering stare at the mention of Johnny's name (and his subsequent withdrawal into his work) suggests sexual jealousy" and that, when Barbra opens her coat, Ben is possibly annoyed at her "unintentionally erotic" gestures because of "his own erotic response" (p. 6). "Ben is the median between two eras," Lightning suggests: "the Poitier era with its (largely implied) sexual restrictions and the blaxploitation era with its hero who dares to desire white women. Ben's emotional state is beautifully summed up at the scene's conclusion when he lays the unconscious Barbra tenderly upon the couch then opens her coat, cautiously, as if afraid to touch her" (p. 6). If Ben is as tender or cautious as Lightning suggests, and I am not convinced that he is, it could also signify in Ben a deeply engrained caution against the long-standing cultural taboo of a black man being coupled with, let alone striking, a white woman. Historically, the punishments meted out upon the violation of those taboos were severe. This moment in the film, when Ben takes great care not to touch the unconscious Barbra as he opens her coat, implicitly raises race as an issue, but ambiguously so, leaving the audience to wonder and to interpret Ben's actions for themselves.

Further complicating Lightning's reading of an erotic tension between Ben and Barbra is the fact that she is unconscious because he has punched her, an act that is shocking today and certainly would have been more so in 1968, not only because of the racial difference, but also because in mainstream cinema, usually only bad guys hit women with enough force to render them unconscious. Ben's punch brings the emotional and defiant Barbra under his control; this fact further implies that he glares at Barbra earlier as she recounts her story not because of sexual jealousy, but because he reads her as a threat to his sense of control. He is patient with her when she is placid and unresponsive, but tenses noticeably as soon as she begins to speak and thus to assert her agency. As I noted above, Ben anticipates that Barbra will become hysterical, and she, like all conventional horror-movie heroines, obliges him. The film, however, parodies the Hollywood cliché when Ben subdues Barbra with a punch, rather than the expected slap. Even before her hysteria, Barbra's "infantilized" behavior (Harper, 2003), which suggests she is in shock, and the fact that Ben's energy is, by necessity, channeled into securing the house and fighting off zombies dissipate any erotic tension that may initially exist between them or, more to the point, that the viewer might expect to exist between them. Later, when Ben puts shoes on Barbra's bare feet, she is unresponsive — no Cinderella — and he shrugs dismissively. Ben's Prince Charming gesture evokes the chivalric behavior of the typical Poitier character — in *The Slender Thread* (Pollack, 1965), Poitier's character fights to keep Anne Bancroft's character on the telephone to talk her out of committing suicide, and in *To Sir, with Love*, Mark Thackeray works determinedly to reach his students through their disdain and indifference — but this image is effectively undermined. Ben does not fight to reach Barbra through her catatonia, but merely leaves her staring off into space and goes about his business. Similarly, when Ben refuses to allow Cooper to take Barbra with him into the basement, it has nothing to do with any erotic feelings he may have for Barbra, nor any chivalric notion about wanting to keep her with him to ensure her safety; in fact, it has nothing to do with her, at all, which is apparent when Ben says to Cooper, "You leave her here. Keep your hands off her, and everything else that's up here, too. Because if I stay up here, I'm fighting for everything up here, and the radio and the food is [sic] part of what I'm fighting for! Now, if you're going down to the cellar, get!" The men make Barbra merely one thing among several that they fight to possess to symbolize their (sense of) power, dominance, and control in an out-of-control situation. Here again, the film may set up formulaic situations, but as Wood argues, the fact that "no love relationship develops between [Barbra] and the hero" is part of "the way in which *Night of the Living Dead* systematically undercuts generic conventions and the expectations they arouse" (1979, p. 91), a strategy that again exposes the artificiality of those conventions. Similarly, the film undercuts the idea, as expressed by Lightning, that the black hero desires the white woman or that an erotic tension exists between them and thus plays on the viewer's own expectations and assumptions about race and interracial relations.

We might assume that the film plays it safe by not depicting a romance between a black man and a white woman, but given that the film does not otherwise shy away from controversial scenarios — the death and cannibalizing of the young lovers, for example, or the Coopers' adolescent daughter murdering her parents and cannibalizing her father — we instead have to consider how the lack of a romance functions in the film. The on-location shooting with mostly non-actors (Jones and Judith O'Dea excepted) and the choice of a low-quality black-and-white film stock give the film a documentary feel and "an uncompromising realism" (Russell, 2005, p. 67). That Ben does not "get the girl" or even desire her in the brief time that they are in a farmhouse surrounded by the walking dead adds to the film's realism, but is also in keeping with "the film's predominant tone of despair" (Lightning, p. 2). Speaking about *To Sir, with Love*, Poitier suggested, "People are not coming to see me [but] to be exposed to a feeling, a reassurance that love is a force in human affairs..." (qtd. in Walker, 1970, p. 338). *Living Dead*, in contrast, does not offer such a reassurance. We realize over the course of the film that the living dead are not only outside the farmhouse, but also within it. The idea of an erotic or romantic connection between Ben and Barbra is not in keeping with the film's bleak view that people have become selfish and that our fundamental humanity has broken down, since it would suggest that people still have the ability to connect and communicate meaningfully with one another. Instead of challenging racial taboos, as *Guess Who's Coming to Dinner* purports to do, *Living Dead* buries race as an issue and makes a broader, pessimistic statement about the state of humanity in an American culture caught up in historic upheavals. A significant part of the impact of this statement comes from the irony that, when a romance between Ben and Barbra does not develop, it actually creates the expectation that Ben will prove to be a Poitier-like character, one who stays focused on the job at hand and who, by not getting side-tracked, will be the victorious hero. This expectation sets the stage for the greatest shock of the film: Ben's death.

I have shown how Ben's place in the white social world and his relationship with the white heroine are fraught with ambivalence, and this remains the case when Ben tries to take the conventional heroic stand by rallying all the living who have taken refuge in the house, leading them to safety and defeating or evading the enemy. The first indication that the film will resist convention and cliché in this regard occurs when Ben works to barricade the doors and windows. In this task, he closely resembles Poitier's character in *Lilies of the Field*, Homer Smith, a traveling contractor who handily fixes a roof for a group of nuns and then designs and builds their longed-for chapel. Taking a job to help support the impoverished nuns, Homer boasts to his boss at the construction company that he can also "handle almost any earthmoving equipment you got," later proving himself to such an extent that the owner offers to make him foreman. In contrast, when Ben nails boards across the windows, he leaves significant gaps, which Cooper correctly predicts will prove no barrier to a zombie invasion. When I screen *Living Dead* for my students, Ben's claim that "this place is boarded up pretty solid" never fails to generate a laugh, particularly since an un-boarded window is visible behind him.[8] Ben is not perfection incarnate; he is fallible, flawed, and vulnerable and thus functions to reveal the artificiality not only of the idealized Poitier hero, but also of the typical hero of the classic Hollywood cinema, as played by such actors as Humphrey Bogart, Gary Cooper, or John Wayne, who faces a crisis, knows exactly what to do, and does it to perfection.

The other tool that Ben employs to attempt to protect the living is fire, and with this, the film creates an association that plays on racially charged media images that would have been very familiar to audiences in 1968. Dyer notes that fire imagery, "particulary [sic] the molotov [sic] cocktail going up around empty cars, seems to recall [...] coverage of the ghetto uprisings of the late '60s," and that "'fire,' as an image of Black Power's threat to white people, had wide currency" (1988, p. 61). This reading is problematic, however, since it assumes the audience identifies with the zombies as the targets of the cocktails, rather than with the living humans who make and throw them. However, in this film, unlike Romero's later *Living Dead* films, the zombies are not portrayed with any sympathy; the living characters in the film repeatedly refer to zombies as "those things": they are "them," not "us," and the viewer identifies with the living. As well, the fires that Ben lights are all safely contained: he starts a fire in the fireplace and sets a chair and a zombie on fire outside the house to deter other zombies from approaching. Ben's fires signify life and safety, as opposed to the fire Tom accidentally lights, which causes the explosion that kills him and his girlfriend, Judy (Judith Ridley), and destroys the truck that could have taken them all to safety. Ben had set the torch down to keep the zombies from coming too close, and he tries to pull it away before it ignites the gas Tom has sprayed all over the truck, but he is too late. Similarly, it is Tom and Judy who assemble, and Cooper who throws, the Molotov cocktails, the image that would best recall the "ghetto uprisings." The film may set up associations *around* Ben that would cue the contemporary audience to think of African American unrest and militancy, but it also specifically undermines those associations.

The film's pattern of the evocation and denial of easy associations between Ben and black militancy and between Ben and the idealized Poitier hero also complicates the conventional scenario of the "the familiar narrative situation wherein a small group is cut off from society and must accomplish a certain dangerous task" (Grant, 1996, p. 204). Barry Keith Grant has noted the influence of Howard Hawks on Romero:

> The world of the living dead films is a brutally Hawksian one, in which the primary task is survival itself. [...] As with, say, the cowboys on the Chisholm Trail in *Red River* or the men in the Arctic in *The Thing*, the characters in the living dead films are cut off from established codes of ethics, forced to survive on an existential precipice even steeper than the mountains surrounding the flyers in *Only Angels Have Wings* [1996, p. 205].

In Hawks's films, the group is able to overcome individual differences and conflicts, rallying under, and because of, the strongest member's "natural" leadership and successfully completing their task. Poitier's characters also routinely demonstrate a "natural" leadership, being able to reason successfully with other characters, to inspire their respect through his credentials and actions, and to mentor them to a more enlightened position. In *Blackboard Jungle*, for example, teacher Mr. Dadier (Glenn Ford) immediately focuses on Poitier's Greg Miller as the one boy in the class who can, and does, inspire the other boys to set aside their delinquent ways. In *Lilies of the Field*, when construction comes to a halt because the workers and the nuns start to bicker among themselves, Homer steps forward to take his deserved place as the boss, and everyone goes back to work in perfect harmony and happiness under his direction. In *Living Dead*, Ben also tries to mentor and "enlighten" the people who have taken refuge in the house, to convince them to work together in order that they may reach safety, but where Ben wants to handle the situation in a conventionally heroic way — to fight and hold their ground until help arrives or escape to a designated shelter — Cooper wants them not to fight and instead barricade themselves in the basement. Here the film recalls, not Hawks's films, but Fred Zinnemann's *High Noon* (1952), a film that screenwriter Carl Foreman intended as a critique of the refusal of Americans, specifically Hollywood, to stand up against Senator Joseph McCarthy's anti-communist "witch hunts" (Costello, 2005,

p. 175), in which Sheriff Will Kane (Gary Cooper), unable to overcome the townspeople's cowardice and self-interest, must face the outlaws alone (his Quaker wife rallies to his cause and shoots one in the back). The image of Harry hesitating in the doorway, afraid to help Ben, brings to mind the image in *High Noon* of Sam Fuller (Harry Morgan) hiding behind a closed door, pretending he is not home when Kane comes to ask for his help. The primary way *Living Dead*, like *High Noon*, undercuts generic conventions, then, is by having the group fail utterly: they are incapable of overcoming their differences and self-preoccupations to get past a group of brain-dead, slow-moving, fire-fearing, easily killed zombies. The film negates the romantic ideals of the Western by denying the expectation that a Hawksian or Poitier-like hero will be able rally the group and save the day. In 1966, President Lyndon Johnson "reassured his countrymen that America was 'strong enough to pursue our goals in the rest of the world while still building a Great Society at home'" (Davies, 1996, p. 105), but two years later, *Living Dead* expresses cynicism over such an idea and despairs that Americans are not capable of pulling together to solve their internal, let alone external, problems.

Readings of *Night of the Living Dead* often consider Ben in conventionally heroic terms and put the brunt of the blame for the group's failure on Cooper (for example, Dillard, 1987, p. 19; Dyer, 1988, pp. 59–60; Grant, 2003, pp. 124–25), but Ben is equally culpable. It is easy to blame Cooper: he is reluctant to cooperate with the others, and he betrays Ben, first by refusing him readmittance into the house after Tom and Judy die and then by holding Ben at gunpoint with the idea of leaving him to the zombies. But Ben, unlike the Poitier hero, does not attempt to reason with Cooper to get him to modify his position; instead, he exhibits exasperation and contempt, yelling at Cooper to shut up and then saying in a more measured tone, "if you're stupid enough to go die in that trap [the basement], that's your business. However, I am not stupid enough to follow you. It is tough for [your] kid that her old man is so stupid. Now get the hell down in the cellar. You can be the boss down there; I'm boss up here." Cooper is cowardly, stubborn, and bullying — the film generates little sympathy for him; Ben is brave, stubborn, and bullying. When Cooper attempts to betray him, Ben turns the gun on Cooper and pauses. As with Ben's entrance, the film gives us a moment to become aware of our expectations: in conventional filmmaking, this would be the moment when the hero masterfully controls his rage and spares the cowardly villain, as Poitier's Dr. Luther Brooks spares the life of the vengeful racist, Ray Biddle (Richard Widmark), at the climax of *No Way Out*. In *Living Dead*, however, when Ben returns to action, he shoots Cooper in a purposeful and punishing, rather than emotional, way. Quite simply, Ben executes him. He is in this moment a far-cry from the typical Poitier hero. Recalling Mason's wish, we can perhaps see in Ben in this moment the Poitier audiences — black audiences, in particular — had wanted to see, a Poitier who faces "the unreasonable and bullying white man" and does more than just "bust him one in the jaw"; however, never having made race an explicit issue, the film casts this climax as a moment, not of (black) victory, but rather of defeat. The use of canted angles in the shots of Ben characterizes him as off-kilter, and after Ben shoots Cooper, he stares at Cooper with the same expressionless look the zombies have throughout the film. In particular, the way Ben raises his chin slightly to stare at Cooper recalls the zombie that grabs Ben through the boarded window: the first two times Ben shoots him, the zombie also raises his head to stare expressionlessly at Ben. With Ben's gesture and dead gaze, the wish has become a nightmare; this moment in the film marks the utter failure of the American hero.

Unlike Poitier's films, *Living Dead* does not affirm a moral high ground. Ben tries but is unable to mentor the group or save anyone; in his frustration and anger, he becomes murderous. He cannot stand apart from the others or raise them up, because he is just as much the living dead as they are, symptomatic of society's decay. Having failed utterly — he is not even able to save Barbra — Ben retreats to the cellar. For Tony Williams, this retreat ironically "shows that father really knows best. Ben finally takes refuge in the basement which aggressive patriarch Harry frequently asserted was the only safe place in the besieged farmhouse" (2003, p. 22). The basement, however, is hardly "safe"; it is, instead, what Ben had aptly called a "death trap," where he again has to shoot Cooper, now a zombie, pumping three bullets into him out of frustration and rage. After reshooting Cooper, Ben buries his head in his arm and heaves a sigh, exhausted and overwhelmed. He must then focus his attention on the now-dead Mrs. Cooper, whose zombie daughter has stabbed her to death with a garden trowel, and he uses just one shot to kill her when she begins to rise. At this moment, Ben begins to cry, throws away the rifle, and pushes over the plywood table on which the Cooper's injured daughter had lain. This breakdown, particularly the gesture of throwing away the rifle, suggests that Ben realizes what he has become, that he is overcome by the horror of the situation and his own part in it. We can read this moment as one of self-awareness, a moment that distinguishes him from Cooper and the white posse that seems to take great pleasure in hunting down zombies who were until recently "the neighbors" (Romero, 1979, p. 62). In *In the Heat of the Night*, Tibbs has a similar moment of self-awareness, when he realizes he has been allowing his own hatred to affect his judgment and to lead him to assume the rich white plantation owner is the murderer; of course, he realizes his error in time and is able to atone for it by catching the real killer. Ben, though, cannot atone for what he has done, and he has solved nothing. That this moment does not represent any kind of moral evolution in the character is emphasized when Ben, quickly remembering the zombie hoard upstairs, retrieves the rifle. When he tries to emerge in the morning, he is mistaken for a zombie and shot by a white posse, although we should perhaps not read it as a mistake at all, given how the film aligns him with the living dead. It may also be that the posse, equally murderous, simply does not bother to distinguish the living from the living dead; and as the film implies, there is little, if any, difference.

During World War II and well into the Cold War, Hollywood had offered easy solutions to difficult problems in the guise of its larger-than-life heroes; in contrast, in the midst of the racially charged chaos of the late 1960s, this low-budget horror film refuses to placate and pander to its audience, portraying instead its own worst nightmare: that such heroes, black or white, are not what they seem and can only fail in their attempts to charge to the rescue. Implied in the irresolvable conflict between Ben and Cooper in *Living Dead* is the idea that the tenets of American individualism, demonstrated by black and white equally, have led to utter selfishness and broken down any sense of group cooperation and social cohesion. As Elizabeth Throop argues it in her psychological study of individualism, "Americans are convinced that, contrary to John Donne, every man (and woman) is an island" (2009, p. 5). Ben and Cooper, each certain he is in the right, are unable, or refuse, to see the other's side; instead, they turn on each other and utterly fail. Ironically, in the expression of their individualism, Ben and Cooper suffer the worst horror imaginable during the Cold War, being "co-opted into the mass" (Russell, 2005, p. 69): Cooper becomes the living dead, and Ben becomes just another anonymous body thrown onto the funeral pyre.

If the film has succeeded in putting race as an issue out of the spectator's mind up to this point, Ben's death brings it back with a shocking impact. As Dillard notes, the film's final images "have all the authenticity of newsreel" (1987, p. 20): the shots of the white posse with police dogs recall images of lynchings and the responses to Civil Rights protests and race riots, and the grainy stills of the posse using meat hooks to throw Ben on the fire, side by side with the graveyard zombie, recall newspaper images of not only racial conflicts, but also "concentration camp footage and Vietnam War photography" (Williams, 2003, p. 30). In short, the images suggest the horrific violence humans inflict on other humans because of differences of race and politics. In Poitier's films, that his characters are "just 'passing through'" reassuringly "casts [the] interracial encounter as a closed episode" (Willis); in *Living Dead*, Ben's death also closes the interracial encounter, but his containment is in no way reassuring. Through Ben, who evokes both the Poitier-esque integrationism of Civil Rights and black militantism, the film cynically suggests that the reactionary white authority will repress any assertion of blackness and anything else that challenges it.

By not explicitly addressing Ben's race at all, the film sets up and then undercuts stereotypes of African Americans as both threat and Poitier-esque hero; that is, the film refuses to contain Ben, to slot him into established categories, depicting him instead as a complex and flawed would-be hero, who tries to maintain his integrity, but fails. The irony of the film is that, at a time in American history when it is finally conceivable for a film to have a black hero, because of Sidney Poitier, the absolutes of the classic Hollywood cinema — hero/villain, white/black, innocent/guilty, selfless/selfish, brave/cowardly, alive/dead — have been revealed as artificial and deconstructed by the upheavals of the 1960s.

NOTES

1. My thanks to Manina Jones and Tim Freeborn for their generous and valuable comments on this essay.

2. Initially, the filmmakers wanted to make a "non-horror, art-house movie," but decided that the best bet for making a return on their low budget was to make an "exploitation movie" (Russell, 2005, p. 66). *Living Dead* was shot in black-and-white on location in rural Pennsylvania for $60,000 (Russell, 2005, p. 68; Romero, 2002a, 162).

3. Ed Guerrero notes that criticism of Poitier "was not unanimous. As evidence of a tension and split in the black community along class lines over the values of Poitier's cinematic contribution, we must contrast these critiques with the consistent position of celebration and support for Poitier and his roles articulated in the principal organ of the black bourgeoisie, *Ebony*" (1993, p. 74).

4. In 1969, Poitier was number six on the list of the top money-making stars, but this ranking would seem to be from the continued success of his 1967 films, since the films he made in 1968 and 1969, *For Love of Ivy* and *The Lost Man*, were not big money-makers. These were the first films to be produced by Poitier's own production company, and their storylines indicate that "Poitier was responding to the altered racial consciousness of Black America" (Walker, 1970, p. 340). Certainly, though, the films did not impact on the public the way his previous films had, suggesting perhaps the reluctance of the audience to accept Poitier in the role of activist, rather than integrationist.

5. Both actors, according to IMDb.com, are 6'2", but Jones is slightly thinner than Poitier.

6. While Gregory A. Waller reads Barbra's passivity as an indicator of the film's sexism (1986, 283), Harper argues, and I agree with him, that the failure of the women to participate in defending the house or trying to get away and the men's failure to include them in their plans implicitly critiques gender role norms of the 1950s and '60s and parodies "traditional representations of women in horror cinema" (Harper, 2003).

7. For example, in *The War of the Worlds* (Haskin, 1953), Forrester (Gene Barry) and Sylvia (Ann Robinson) take shelter in a damaged farmhouse, but are soon forced to flee when the aliens come by for a look. Similarly, Miles (Kevin McCarthy) and Becky (Dana Wynter) hide from the body snatchers in his office, but are soon caught in *Invasion of the Body Snatchers* (Siegel, 1956).

8. His poor workmanship, though, also generates one of the best scares of the film: as Ben walks by one of his boarded windows, one of the living dead suddenly reaches through a gap and grabs him, causing the spectators to jump in their seats.

PART II

The Capital of the Dead

5

Time for Zombies
Sacrifice and the Structural Phenomenology of Capitalist Futures[1]

RONJON PAUL DATTA and LAURA MACDONALD

Introduction: Good Times?

These are fortuitous times for considering zombies. Since Romero's reinvention of the zombie, they have been represented as mindless consumers, habituated into going to the shopping mall even after they are dead. For Romero, shopping is our farcical resurrection. It now appears that much of that mindless shopping was fueled by consumer debt facilitated by what is called the "democratization of credit" in deregulated globalized capital markets, made familiar by ubiquitous credit cards and home equity lines of credit (Harman, 2009, pp. 288–289; Panitch and Gindin, 2009; Blundell-Wignall, *et al.*, 2008). We also have the progeny of Japan's lost economic decade of the 1990s: the "zombie" firms now found globally (Cooley, 2009). What is striking is that the image of the zombie as a dead human that has come back to some semblance of life and then heads to the shopping mall, appears to have been the harbinger of the current recession: people borrowed—"buying on time" (as it used to be called)—to consume. This is why the Great Recession is treated as distinct from other modern recessionary periods with the exception of the Great Depression. Like the latter, it is a balance sheet recession in which households, firms, and governments seek to deleverage and avoid solvency crises, a real possibility given exceptionally high levels of debt (Callinicos, 2010, p. 85). Our *future* promise to pay, as indicated underneath the signature line on a credit card slip, was the fuel for zombie-ish shopping and for global economic growth. Consumption accounts for about 70 percent of GDP in the United States and 60 percent in resource rich Canada. Romero's lesson: consumption has consumed our lives.

Below, we offer our reflections on zombies and the current conjuncture by drawing on Georges Bataille's work as a sociological "stimulus package" not least because consumption, excess, sacrifice, and destruction are his main reference points. We also draw on two of Bataille's main analytical resources: Marx and Durkheim. We contend that zombies, as represented in film and in the current phenomenon of zombie economic agents, mythologize a central temporal contradiction facing the working class, one that cannot be solved within the structure of capitalist futures. Yet, this temporal contradiction remains suggestive of the power of consumption to consume the "brains" of capital that constrain politics. We begin by discussing Bataille's approach to myth as a basis for identifying some key themes in zombie films. His approach to economics is then discussed as a precursor to our Marxian explication of life and death in capitalism, a process we call *zombification*. We contend that zombification is in large measure caused by the imposition of "the future" in capitalism.[2] Bataille's concept of sovereignty, as indicating a possible means of escape from zombification, is then used to analyze the impasses of consumer indebtedness in a neoliberalized world. This then makes it possible to consider the logic of sacrifice, viewed from the point of view of capitalist time. We conclude by discussing how the zombie penchant for eating brains is suggestive of what might be done to return zombies to the human world, thus opening the door for a population to be consumed with democratic politics.

The Timely Profligacy of Zombies

Zombies seem to be appearing everywhere, from pop culture (films, video games) to banking, governments, and households. This circumstance perhaps lends more than a little pertinence to a recent paper by mathematicians that develops an epidemiological model of a zombie attack (Muntz, *et al.*, 2009). Current fiscal policy impasses appear to be hampered by ideological zombification. Reaganite belief in free market unfettered capitalism, "an ideology that says government intervention is always bad, and leaving the private sector to its own devices is always good" is now also described in zombie terms (Krugman, 2009).

In contrast, Le Goff (1990) discusses how lending money at interest was a sin during the Middle Ages precisely because time belonged to God — He alone had sovereign control over the future and fate. To lend money at interest was an incursion on the future, the domain that was the sole prerogative of Providence. To lend money at interest was deemed blasphemous and an extraordinary arrogation by humans of what belonged to God. We see zombies, as popularly found in films and in economic discourse, as intimately connected to the structuring of time, but in a manner that requires us to think beyond a theological framework. The work of the *College de Sociologie*, Georges Bataille especially, is quite suggestive here (Hollier, 1988). They developed the Durkheimian theory of the sacred as a means for understanding the contemporary social world, one wrongly taken to be secular. For them, it is a mistake to conclude that a decline of religiosity means the twilight of the sacred. Moreover, for Durkheim, the primordial form of the sacred concerns temporality. The sacred is constituted and re-energized in exceptional moments of collective effervescence like that found during the French Revolution (Durkheim, 1995, pp. 217–225; Richman, 2002; Datta, 2010). Festivals, as an instance of collective effervescence, are characteristically moments of "debauches of consumption, of the mouth or sex" (Caillois, 1939, p. 298) providing "access to the Great Time" (Pearce, 2003, p. 3). For the Durkheimians, there is a radical difference between regularized profane time, what we call *chronic time*, and the time set aside for exceptional consumption — sacred time.

We see this recent phase of capitalism, better described as one dominated by "finance capitalism" than "consumer capitalism," as *chronic*: zombies (the undead consumers and their cousin firms) are a consequence of the chronic structure of capitalism and how it measures and calculates the time of the return on investments with their spatio-temporal distribution. Significantly, in Marxian terms, "capital is nothing but time (not time in general, not time *as time*, but a specific modality of time) striving continually to go beyond itself. It is the time of production as the time of exploitation, the time of total subsumption" (Gulli, 1999, pp. 16–17; Harman, 2009, pp. 47–50). Time for zombies is a chronic condition, one that won't go away. That's the problem with being "dead"—it tends to go on, just like a chronic condition. Indeed, one of the predominant forms of contemporary zombie films represents "zombification" as a consequence of something like a virus, an infection that creates a chronic condition. We find this kind of figure in both Boyle's *28 Days Later* (2002) and Fresnadillo's *28 Weeks Later* (2007). In both films, once people are bitten by a zombie they become infected with a rage virus that is transmitted through saliva and blood; this instant change to raging in turn manifests as a drive to consume others.

Bataille on Myth

A key component of Bataille's approach to understanding economies of consumption is the sociological analysis of myth. In Bataillean methodology, sociological analysis must deal with the movements of energy, limits and excesses within a societal totality—it is the total movement of a societal organism that must be the object of analysis (Bataille, 1994, pp. 233–234; Bataille and Caillois, [1937] 1988). Myth, in contrast to compartmentalized scientific discourse, is a form of communication about the totality of a community, representing quite radically different types of movements (e. g., movement between sacred and profane places). Consequently, "a myth thus cannot be assimilated to the scattered fragments of a dissociated group [e.g., scientists and politicians]. It is in solidarity with *total* existence, of which it is the tangible expression" (Bataille, 1994, p. 232). Zombie myths are a discomfiting, pervading figure, playing an important role in the *conscience collective* of the Anglosphere especially, since dealing with the consumption of human life as a whole. This proliferation of zombie representations requires us to think in terms of the dynamism of social totalities.

Zombies and Popular Culture: From Romero to Households

Romero's *Night of the Living Dead* (1968) marked a change in the conception of a zombie. It was followed by *Dawn of the Dead* (1979), *Day of the Dead* (1985), *Land of the Dead* (2005), *Diary of the Dead* (2007), and most recently, *Survival of the Dead* (2009). Romero changed the direction of zombie films by emphasizing apocalyptic themes, mirroring the American loss of optimism at the end of the 1960's (Phillips, 2005, p. 100). The linkage between "consumption" and "living" is especially predominant in his work. In Romero's films, the dead come back to life as zombies, devoid of everything but a lust for consuming human flesh. *Dawn of the Dead* in particular considers consumption through the eyes of a zombie. In this film, the human protagonists seek refuge in a local mall. There, they begin to systematically exterminate the zombies who remain in the building until the zombie threat has been abolished within its walls. With the threat diminished, the protagonists are free to wander about the mall and consume with reckless abandon, save for the rationalist, female protagonist, Fran. Fran's rationalist commentary, however, eventually becomes silenced as she too falls into the trap of mindless consumption (Harper, 2002, p. 7). Meanwhile, the mall becomes a target for the zombies outside but not because of the tasty humans inside waiting to be consumed. Rather, zombies appear to flock to the mall out of some sort of distant memory, knowing that the mall was a place they wanted to be, supposedly "out of instinct," suggesting that going to the mall has become as innate in human nature as eating (Loudermilk, 2003, p. 84).

A similar remnant of life-before-zombification is found in *Fido* (Currie, 2006), a film set after a series of "Zombie Wars." Zombies have been domesticated and are used as servants, one of whom, Fido, was apparently a smoker during his human existence. When he reaches for a cigarette, we get some sense of the zombie penchant for consumption as a remnant of human life. This zombie behavior seeks in consumption a way to regain some semblance of living. Edgar Wright's 2004 film, *Shaun of the Dead*, like *Dawn of the Dead*, offers a similar take on the "zombies are us" theme (Harper, 2002, p. 8). Shaun, the half-asleep, hung-over protagonist (rather zombie-ish himself) does not even notice the zombie outbreak until embarrassingly late into the film. This is because most of the zombies are performing exactly the same mundane tasks as they had before they became part of the undead masses, like pushing a shopping cart (Wright, 2004). In our view, the striking feature of the zombie from Romero onward is that it is animated human "meat," an entity that *consumes* just like "real humans" and likes to consume real humans. Crucially, zombies are "once-were-humans"—human existence in the *past tense*. They have, however, cousins in the real world of contemporary capitalism, more specifically, that of the spectral, cybernetic milieu of finance capital—the zombie firms.

Economic Zombies: Firms, Banks, and Homeowners

Zombies too are now a major descriptor of a certain class of economic agents, likely unprofitable ones who continue to function economically on the basis of perpetual borrowing and ever inventive financing and re-financing arrangements. As one commentator defines them:

> zombies are debtors that have little hope of recovery but manage to avoid being wiped out thanks to support from their lenders or the government. Zombies suck the life out of an economy by consuming tax money, capital and labor that would be better deployed in growing companies and sectors. Meanwhile, by slashing prices to generate sales, zombie companies can drag healthier rivals into insolvency [Coy, 2009; cf. Conway, 2009; Cooley, 2009].

The phenomenon first emerged in Japan. After the Japanese financial crisis in 1989, a decade of slow or non-existent growth followed (Harman, 2009, pp. 211–217), generating zombie companies, enterprises "that are competitively dead, but sustained by their banks, continue to walk the Earth and give healthier firms nightmares" (*The Economist*, 2004a). Daiei, one of the largest retailers in Japan, is a case in point since its debt load meant that it could not repay but nevertheless continued its business as usual. It was "bailed out twice, in total receiving 640 billion Yen ($4.9 billion [USD])" and as of 2004, had over 1 trillion Yen in debt. The consequence though is that in the end, the bill will "one day land on taxpayers' doorsteps" (*The Economist*, 2004a).

The U.S. today has its zombie banks:

> Zombie banks—dead but still walking among the living—are, in Ed Kane's immortal words, "gambling on resurrection." Repeating the Savings & Loan debacle of the 1980's, the banks are using bad accounting (they were allowed, for example, to keep impaired assets on their books without writing them down, on the fiction that they might be held to maturity and somehow turn healthy) [Stigliz, 2009].

And, Britain has spawned the zombie household:

> one which by most common sense metrics is at or close to insolvency, but has been kept from official bankruptcy only by dint of extraordinary governmental support. [...] In the case of British

households, it is the extraordinary low level of interest rates which has kept them from either losing their homes, having to trade down or face insolvency. They are dead but undead [Conway, 2009].

Policy makers are now actively trying to conceive of a new regulatory regime "less likely to breed zombies." This might involve "a way to shut down or restructure failing institutions with a minimum of collateral damage to other firms and the general economy" (Coy, 2009). The "future" plays the key role for these zombies, determining a present state of economic "life" or "death"; it is the likely future profitability of an economic agent that plays the decisive role. Time for zombies in this respect means an eternity of non- or under-performance on debt servicing and repayment. These representations of zombies in popular culture are, in our view, myths about an intractable problem of living life in an era dominated by finance capital.

Bataillean Economics: The General and Restricted Economies

Bataillean economics, on the basis of historical, anthropological and sociological analysis, challenge the basic assumptions of modern economics. For instance, while Bataille, like modern economics, sees circulation as important, for him, we are dealing with the circulation of energy in the cosmos, that for humans moves about the surface of the globe. Energy is exchanged and consumed and so transformed to produce life, including social life (Bataille, 1995, p. 27). The movement of energy is determined by limits, pressure, excess and luxury (Bataille, 1995, pp. 27–41). It is this arena that takes ontological priority over conventional conceptions of the economy in which money, goods, and services circulate in markets for human use. Priority is given to *useless, wasteful consumption*, consumption that will not generate an anticipated calculated return and isn't done to do so. *Homo economicus* in Bataille is precisely not the rational utility maximizer. Rather, s/he is displaced in a movement of "general economy," the law of which is the necessary wasteful consumption of surplus energy inherently created by life on the planet. Harman, while no Bataillean, provides further evidence that global capitalist development in the post–World War II era and into the twenty-first century is very much premised on the luxurious consumption patterns of the wealthy and truly massive wasteful military spending (Harman, 2009, pp. 126–132). In the case of the latter, "One estimate is that by 2005 US military spending had risen to a figure equal to about 42 percent of gross non-residential private investment — a big drain on resources that could otherwise have gone into accumulation" (Harman, 2009, p. 234).

The fundamental theorem of general economy is that:

> the living organism, in a situation determined by the play of energy on the surface of the globe, ordinarily receives more energy than is necessary for maintaining life; the excess energy (wealth) can be used for the growth of a system (e.g., an organism); if the system can no longer grow, or if the excess cannot be completely absorbed in its growth, it must necessarily be lost without profit; it must be spent, willingly or not, gloriously or catastrophically [Bataille, 1995, p. 21].

Thus, the basic problem of life concerns of how to dispense with the excess, lest the pressure explode a social system (Bataille, 1995, p. 29). Squander and luxury are potential solutions to the problem of excess. In short, for Bataille, excessive consumption is required in order to solve the problem of the explosive nature of the general economy. (Bataille 1995, p. 30).

The Restricted Economy

The general economy, according to Bataille, has led to a capitalistic development of surplus that reduces the human condition to that of a thing (1995, p. 129), amounting to a surrender to utility instead of a valorization of glorious consumption (Bataille, 1995, pp. 136–7). This includes reducing human subjectivity to one of those things (Bataille, 1989, p. 57). Indeed, technology, far from liberating humans from nature, rather ensconces them in a world of things (Bataille, 1989, p. 41). The subject-object couplet of profane life is one in which a subject is a subject (subjected to; servile) precisely because the world is viewed as an object and tool to be used to achieve instrumental ends. The restricted economy introduces a narrow, chronic form of time governed by a concern for a future result. It is calculated for in terms of the most economical and efficient means for achieving an end. In the capitalist restricted economy, the "end" is that of the further accumulation of the surplus, an excess produced beyond mere subsistence and use-value for people and firms. In accounting terms, that surplus-value is called "profit." The surplus is to again be reinvested in the production process (transforming profit into capital proper) so that a firm may survive in competitive markets and do the same over again.

For Bataille, living within your means-to-an-end as the characteristic ethic of a restricted economy, is precisely *not living*. Instead, it subordinates subjectivity to the object or the tool. In the phenomenology of the restricted economy of capitalist instrumentality, the world is perceived as populated by tools and potential tools for producing things to be sold for a profit. But it is exactly this phenomenology of the world as "tool" and "ends" that constitutes subjectivity itself as among those tools, restricting the development of consciousness to improving instrumental means-ends calculation. The human as thing is thus a consequence of the subjugation of the present general economy to *a* discursively formed calculated future end. It is important to note the often missed *conservative* component of the capitalist phenomenological structuring of time: it presupposes that the world will remain roughly constant and unchanging. Without social stability (i.e., "security"), it is both impossible and futile to make plans about the future. This is the main reason why capitalists abhor political and regulatory instability and uncertainty. We now turn our attention to how capitalist production causes zombification, in which zombies are debtors that have little hope of recovery but continue to economically and socially live as consumers of things, especially their futures.

Capitalism: The Time of Your Life

It is important to distinguish between capital-*ism* and the capitalist mode of production (CMP). With the CMP dominant, capitalism means the positive valorization of capital accumulation and the development of a society that facilitates this. It is accompanied by a normative constraint on alternative means of problematizing, organizing, and coordinating human life. As such, it has a distinct conception of, and fundamental concern with, the future, *a future* that in turn organizes the perception of time. Time, in capitalism, is a means for calibrating rates of return on capital investment, that portion of profits put back into the production process in order to secure a growing rate of return such that production and investment costs are covered and further profits generated. This is what is conventionally meant by the *reproduction of capital*. What we stress though is the *valorization of this telos* of *"development"* as the dominant means for problematizing human existence in capitalist societies. This is the predominant coordinate of the contemporary restricted economy.

The CMP is the totality of social relations and their material institutional supports in and through which *capitalism* is sustained, regardless of the specific content of development goals in various sectors (financial services; resource extraction, manufacturing, agriculture, etc.), hence uneven development. The CMP is a structure dependent on its basic feature of the class constitution of social relations. Substantively this refers to the circumstance that the vast majority of people must work for someone else to provide money incomes needed for them to survive and exist as social persons (i.e., a working class that has nothing but its labor power to sell for money income, thus commodifying its capacity to thoughtfully transform nature into material culture). On the other hand is "capital," i.e., money and means of production (building, technology, computers, etc.) owned and controlled/managed by those who need specific forms of labor power (e.g., "skill sets") to transform capital into further money through the sale of the goods and services, produced by the synthesis between labor power and capital, found in the capitalist division of labor. This produces the transformation of money and capital at one point in time, into more money and potential capital in the future. This allows capitalist enterprise to potentially remain competitive by reinvesting profits back into the production process and so live to fight another day. This is how capital becomes a chronic condition: it organizes time with an eye to future returns on investment. In short, present time is subordinated to a future goal, even if a very abstract goal (future profits). Without this instrumental calculation (e.g., a "business plan") that is the hallmark of capitalism as a restricted economy, no investors would willingly part with their money. Combined, capitalism and the CMP constitute capitalist social life as a totalizing goal-oriented process that subordinates all social activity to a future of development deemed necessary for capital accumulation.

In the *Grundrisse* (Marx, 1973, p. 258; cf. Marx, 1974, p. 233), Marx argues that machines consist of the accumulated dead labor of past and present live workers invested in forces of production in the attempt to reproduce capital accumulation (Marx, 1973, p. 454; Gulli, 1999, p. 16). Previous labor is the condition of possibility for the existence of such capital equipments. This is the Marxian version of the "ghost in the machine," the ontological dualism that arises *from* developments in the capitalist division of labor (e.g., between intellectual and manual labor). Things today have changed somewhat.

Contemporary production involves a high degree of "immaterial labor." Immaterial labor refers to the communicative, creative, social, and emotional components of capitalist production: "Health services, for example, rely centrally on caring and affective labour, and the entertainment industry is likewise focused on the creation and manipulation of affect" (Hardt and Negri, 2000, p. 292). With the spread of immaterial labor, it is no longer enough to simply "do one's job"; one must do so with a smile, be affable and a team-player, a creative and innovative contributor to the enterprise, but only when managers expect one to do so. The social life and social skills that were once the hallmarks of life after work have now been subsumed in capitalist exploitation to "add value" to the sterility of the commodities. Thus, the life that is consumed in the production process has spread to include all facets of human, social being — its corporeal, intellectual, creative, affective, and sociable components. To call work "soul-sucking" is not so far off, especially when Durkheim's concept of the soul and Bataille's concept of the subject are taken into account, as argued below. In this respect, it doesn't matter whether you love your job or not — that you like what you do can be quickly changed since by contractual obligation, as an employee, an employer can command you to do what you don't like. If you don't want to submit to such commands, you are free to resign or be fired. This then begs the question of what "life" means and what kind of life is left for workers whose living labor ("variable capital") ends up as "constant capital"/capital equipments precisely by being consumed by capitalist investment? In effect, their lives, their souls/*Geistes* have been displaced from them, leaving them with their "dead meat" (e.g., "I'm dead tired from work"; "work is killing me").

"Mindlessness" and the Capitalist Division of Labor

While the social relations of production are determined by the ownership of means of production, control over the production process is central to zombification. The calculated control over the production process itself actualizes the soul of capitalist production (Marx, 1974, pp. 362–368). It is control over the division of labor, about what gets produced, how and for what, that produces the experience of workers being alienated from the product of their labor and hence from what else might be produced. Employers have the right to control workers' *labor power* during the time they have purchased from workers, a labor power now subordinated to the demands of capitalist production that partially actualizes that labor power. The mindless nature of capitalist work is thus a consequence of the circumstance that people are excluded from the organization and planning of production.

The Ghost ... in the Ledger?

The marked shift away from industrial manufacturing in advanced societies and rise of service and information sectors of economic activity requires a modified analysis. The accumulated dead labor no longer simply resides in machines *per se* but in the discursive accounting networks that produce the risk-return calculus inherent in an era dominated by finance capital. In finance capital the "M-C-M" (the transformation of money into a commodity that is then sold for more money) refers neither to goods nor services — in the end the "C," yes, refers to a commodity, namely labor-power, but this is not the whole story. What it refers to is the likelihood that a population (a "risk pool") will "perform" i.e., pay its debts. How the money income is generated to make payment is largely irrelevant. What is exchanged, such that M' is generated, is the immanent capacity of a population to pay. Thus, since what is produced by workers under finance capital are their "credit-ratings," all this means concretely is that finance capital *banks* on "the belief" (*credo*/credit) that people will (primarily) work more to gain income to meet terms of repayment to retain access to credit (maintain or better their credit rating, having lenders *believe* in this likelihood of performance), i.e., produce and reproduce themselves as stable risk pools with varying actuarial profiles.

Foucault's concepts of discipline and normalization are useful here (Foucault, 1979). Discipline individualizes and regularizes individual actions whereas normalization tracks the actions of populations and intervenes, using disciplinary techniques, to correct individuals and populations that fall outside of a normal distribution of what gets done and how. Credit-risk in this respect, hinges on the *disciplinary and normalizing* techniques of credit markets and their accompanying risk calculi, that refer in turn to the real social life of groups, perceived from the point of view of the distribution of probabilities on the quality of payment performance in a risk pool (i.e., that loans will continue to perform and that people will pay in a predictable manner).

Capitalism, Governmentality and the Future

There is, moreover, an affinity between capitalism and the liberal form of governmental rationality analyzed by Foucault. This is because they both share a concern with future development, and crucially *securing* the conditions for developing the productive capacities of populations (Foucault, 2006, p. 96, 99; Valverde, 2007, p. 172). We find Foucault's conception of "rationality" quite useful in as much as capitalism depends upon discursive formations that supply a rationality for thinking about how to *govern*, i.e., "structure the possible field of actions of others" (Foucault, 2003, p. 138) so as to make progress toward the goal of improvement in a particular field of social activity. Development has come to mean *perpetuating the accumulation of capital* and securing an investment friendly climate in the society as a whole through governance.

Development is the main goal in capitalist societies because development is always uneven, given the vicissitudes of markets, variations in degrees of competition and perceived varying rates of return in various sectors. Moreover, in an era of highly leveraged firms, development is a "must" because without a sustained and continuing rate of GDP growth, the returns on the monies borrowed (and their costs) to finance capital investment wouldn't exist and the firm would become sunk (Foster, 2008; Murphy, 2009). The emphasis on security is decisive here. The point of government is to *secure* the means of societal development by structuring the fields of people's actions so as to facilitate development. In short, capitalism is about controlling the present in the attempt to secure future capital — there is a clearly defined "end" to the process. In short, the restricted economy of capitalism is one where workers' lives are extracted from them to become the living force of the non-human agents of the CMP (machinery, investment calculus, etc.). With their lives in the machine/ledger, how then do they obtain signs of life?

Get a Life: From Souls to Commodity-Signs

As contemporary zombie films frequently depict, the life that is "left over" after work is the undead life of consumption; it is the one semblance of life that remains. Bataille's reliance on Durkheim's social ontology provides a resource for understanding how life is got: people buy one. For Durkheim, the soul, the personal component of social life (Durkheim, 1995, p. 368), is inherently the product of "collective representations." Souls are a basic stuff of social life. However, because we are born into a social world that will remain after one dies, the social world of collective representations, is, from the point of view of individual perceptions, eternal: it never dies (Durkheim, 1995, p. 271). A simple example of this can be found in one's name and place in a kinship system, e.g., "This is my sister Jenny." The collective representation of "sister" designates relations with other collective representations (brother, mother, father, etc.) and constitutes a social component of an individual. The collective representation of one's first name designates an individualization of a particular empirical person in a generalized, enduring social reality of a kinship system. A central component of Durkheim's sociology is his point that what we are as individuals, as souls, indeed our very human lives, sense of identity, meaning, and values are socially constituted. Durkheim does not thereby reduce the individual to the social. Rather, "In thinking about collective institutions, in assimilating ourselves to them, we individualise them, we more or less impart to them our own personal stamp" (Durkheim, 1982, p. 47). Bataille's reliance on Durkheimian sociology thus helps us understand how the world of signification is the source from which souls are made. Access to collective representations can potentially resurrect workers.

In "consumer capitalism," the collective representations that make it possible to "get a life" are commodified and hence are subjected to the logic of exchange value. This means that the stuff of our souls is commodified and a life can be bought! As both Baudrillard and Negri argue (albeit in different ways), this marks a shift that in turn requires modifying the conventional components of political economy. For Marx, the wages paid to workers are used to buy commodities necessary to the production and reproduction of social life outside of work — "the traditional standard of life" — (Marx, cited in Collier, 2008, p. 93). The commodities that are bought in the domain of exchange value obtain their use-value in how people consume them in the context of living a life within a social formation at a particular point in time. Conventionally, the realm of use-value and consumption refers to systems of values *external* to the logic of capital (Negri, 2003), to things that we would today call a "standard of living." For example, the convention of one's milieu may be to drink lattes or, in another, beer, but Baudrillard and Negri contend that this is no longer the case.

For Baudrillard, for whom Bataille and Durkheim are significant resources (Gane, 1991), the definitive feature of culture in contemporary capitalism is the emergence of the "commodity-sign." The concept indicates that collective representations/signs themselves circulate, are produced and exchanged just like all other commodities. For Baudrillard, we no longer buy things solely for some utilitarian use-value, but for their exchange-value relative to other commodity-signs (Baudrillard, 1981). So, the collective representations that will give people *their* soul and so give them a life, are also commodities in the capitalist nexus. This is similar to Negri's point about the total subsumption of life to capital (Hardt and Negri, 2000, p. 275). It's not just that our "souls" are up for sale (i.e., Marx's point about alienation caused by the social relations of production). Rather, the stuff of the souls *we have* (collective representations) are already "for sale" and hence when we consume commodity-signs the production of our social life is subsumed to capital. Hence, no return to a "life" outside of capital is possible. What we lose in work is got through the consumption of commodified collective representations, allowing us to get "a life."

Consumerism and Sovereignty: A Bataillean Phenomenology of Class Struggle

It is hard to avoid arguing that consumerism lost touch with the "reality principle" of delayed gratification to become squanderous indulgence. It became the driving force of the North American economy in the wake of the Vietnam War (Hedges, 2009, pp. 150–151). A prime example is the remarkable growth in home size. "The average square footage of a North American home has increased by more than 50 per cent in the last thirty years. That means more expensive mortgages and property taxes, and higher costs for everything from utilities to yard care" (Deacon, 2002, p. 35). While this was happening the self-storage business also emerged and grew to house *excess* goods rarely used in daily life. Furthermore, workers in this period came to "define themselves as above all 'consumers' who willingly suffer the 'disutility' of labour to acquire the 'utilities' embodied in consumption" (Wolff, 2005, p. 230). We view excessive consumption as a form of class struggle, not in the conventional sense, but as a struggle for "sovereignty" as Bataille understands the term. For Bataille, sovereignty is a form of subjectivity that is not beholden to instrumental calculability. It is thus a form of subjectivity that lays aside "the future" in favor of the immediate eternal return to the general economic ground of human existence. We thus do not concur with social critics who decry consumerist activities.

Reflexive Sovereignty and Neoliberalism

There is a kind of freedom, an element of sovereignty in the recklessness of consumerist spending because its "essence is to consume *profitlessly* whatever might remain in the progression of useful works" (Bataille, 1995, p. 58; Richardson, 1994, p. 39). The rise to dominance of neoliberalism as the reigning ethical common-sense of our time changes things because it valorizes a kind of "sovereignty" but does so in the context of the increasing valorization of competitive restricted economies. This has changed the struggle for sovereignty.

The pervasive neoliberal attempts to responsibilize people by teaching them, through competitive market mechanisms, that their actions have consequences in the form of money costs, has ironically generated what we call "reflexive sovereignty." By this we mean that people consume without a care, in order to *appear* sovereign, which is to say to appear unconstrained by the mere and dehumanizing effects of restricted economics. In doing so, they *reflexively* increase the appearance to others that, as social beings, *they are worth the risk of socializing with.* The internal (unconscious) dialogue might go something like this: "Look at me, I consume without a thought for the future because I don't need to; my existence is not subjected to calculations. This means that I am successful and sovereign and hence a good risk." Thus, excessive consumption is less about displaying cultural capital and the markings of high social status; rather it is about signifying sovereignty. To signify sovereignty is to demonstrate freedom from profane servility and the restricted economy. Indeed, the *worst* thing that one can signify is that one is exactly a purely instrumentalist miser, or purely instrumentalist out of *necessity* (i.e., not good enough to do more than just get by). Were one to be very frugal (i.e., subject oneself fully to the restricted economy) it would become quite difficult to participate in "normal social life." It would mean only the rare after-work drink with colleagues for instance. Subtract elements like these and cultural reference points no longer resonate, you miss out on the inside-information about changes at the office, or the gossip — all the "good stuff." To live as such is precisely not to live as a social person in our culture; it is to reduce oneself to a mere piece of fleshy accounting software (indeed a cyborg! — the zombie's monstrous double). It is not, in our renovated Bataillean view, that one buys "in order to be cool" (Stoekl, 2007, p. 273); one buys in order to signify sovereignty. It is the *form of the practice*, not the substance, that counts, and that form is one without a regard for *one's own future*, at least the instrumentally calculated future of "ends." The ironic effect of neoliberalism then, is that while it aims to reconstitute individuals as morally responsible subjects, calculating the *costs* of their choices, the effect in the form of a struggle against servile existence is rather the opposite, leading to deresponsibilization in the form of the practice of reflexive sovereignty. Thus, unlike Romero, we situate consumerism as a response to mindlessness, rather than its cause.

The Zombification of the Working Class

The problem with consumerism is its dependence on consumer credit, be it in the form of credit cards or in using one's home as collateral for secured lines of credit in an economic era in which market incomes (the money people make from working) have remained stagnant or have declined, even while people are working more. The appearance of the (sovereign) life that has been got in the market by buying on time only thus means that workers are legally obliged to return to the market to again convert labor power into market income, not just in order to pay, but in order to remain a good credit risk, lest one risk losing the possibility of being able to purchase a reflexively sovereign life. It is precisely this process that we refer to as *the zombification of the working class*.

To this point, perhaps things aren't all that bad: workers used market incomes earned by selling their labor power, have leveraged the evidence of their discipline (facilitated by the risk models of finance capital), and are able to purchase commodity-signs, supplying them with souls. The difficulty is that the struggle for sovereignty, the struggle to wrest oneself from a dehumanizing servility to the restricted economy through excessive consumption without a care, has been fueled by debt. As of January 2009, the total outstanding global credit was estimated to rise to five times of gross domestic product (Harman, 2009, p. 300). Moreover, in the purported "good times" in the U. S., 2003, "consumer debt hit an all-time high of $2 trillion in November, up 41% in five years" (Condon, 2004, p. 48). Between 2000−2003 the sum total of public and private debt in the U. S. grew by 6.5 trillion (*The Economist*, 2004b, p. 83), or about four-and-a-half times the amount of annual GDP in 2007 (Perry, 2008, B2).

This is not a consequence of lack of self-control or the increase in imprudence. Rather, it is a consequence of substantial changes in the political economy, in particular, the portion of wealth being paid to workers relative to basic costs. As the IMF reported in 2007, "labour globalization has negatively affected the share of income accruing to labour in the advanced economies" (Crane, 2007; cf. Krugman, 2009). Incomes in America have declined for more than thirty years, peaking at $33, 000 in 1973, dropping by 2005 to $29, 000, when adjusted (Hedges, 2009, p. 165). So while "productivity grew 46.5 percent between 1973 and 1998 the median wage fell by about eight percent" (Harman, 2009, p. 236). This means that the relative proportion of surplus-value generated by the working-class increasingly goes to capital even while increasing commodities and wealth are produced. For example, while U.S. GDP growth in 2003 was 4.3 percent wage income rose by barely 1 percent (*The Economist*, 2004b, p. 83). This led "buyers to take out large mortgages on expectations of capital gains" but left them vulnerable to potentially higher interest rates and drops in house prices (OECD, 2006, p. 140). Between 2001 and 2006, Americans cashed out an estimated $1.2 trillion in home equity.

By 2001, the signs of a massive pending zombification were present. U.S. consumers then had "$7.3-trillion (US) debt, twice the level they faced in the last recession [of 1991]." For OECD countries, "The percentage of indebted households peaks among young households (less than 35 years) or households in the middle-age groups. Within these age groups, the percentage of indebted households often exceeds 70%" (OECD, 2006, p. 146). A startling report by the Certified General Accountants of Canada calculates that debt loads are the equivalent of 136.5 percent of household disposable income (CGA, 2009, p. 16). Canadian household debt is pegged at $1.3 trillion, equivalent to 100 per cent of annual GDP (CGA, 2009).

As concerns the cybernetics of capitalism, the basic premise of the derivatives models of esoteric investments (e.g., ABCP, "Asset Backed Commercial Paper") assumed a labor market and market income model developed in the early 1970s (see Koza, 2007). This model assumed that the curves on market income would continue to rise (in the aggregate) given then tendencies to GDP growth over medium term. The weakness of economics here is that no one bothered to adjust the maths after the substantial restructuring of labor markets and distributions of market income, especially in the wake of the 1991 recession. Each successive cohort entering the labor market has been subjected to increasingly precarious employment security, and even more so, long-term wealth security, given the proportion of younger cohorts without pension plans. Consequently, while it has been noted by many that the share of income going to all but the top quintile remained stagnant and for the bottom quintile fell even while GDP grew (OECD, 2008), this did not spur a change in the mathematical models. Once the question of the accrual of consumer and public debt that finances this production of capitalist social life is posed, things change. The consumption required to get a life has been financed, first by the working class as consumers and second by the working class again, but as taxpayers who now hold the transfer of liabilities (i.e., "bailouts") in the form of sovereign debt obligations (i.e., government debt). What we are dealing with is the consumptive destruction of the future, i.e., of destruction of the production of the means of *future* consumption.

Sacrifice: Killing Time?

Bataille saw sacrifice as a ritual that showed the most promise for becoming sovereign. Humans search for a lost intimacy with themselves in myths and rituals (1989, p. 57). The sacrificial ritual has the virtue of constituting a form of intimate participation between sacrificer and victim, in which the servile use of both is ended, facilitating a genuine, general economic form of self-consciousness (Bataille, 1989, p. 56). Death is the ultimate squandering of the excesses produced by life, by life itself. However:

> In order for Man to reveal himself ultimately to himself, he would have to die, but he would have to do it while living — watching himself cease to be. In other words, death itself would have to become (self-) consciousness at the very moment that it annihilates the conscious being.... In sacrifice, the sacrificer identifies himself with the animal that is struck down dead. And so he dies in seeing himself die, and even, in a certain way, by his own will, one in spirit with the sacrificial weapon [Bataille, 1990, p. 19].

Zombies as represented in popular culture and economic discourse today are precisely this kind of phenomenological revelation of people to themselves but in a modified/mythic form. Sacrifice amounts to the restoration of the sacred world that makes us fully human, which has been rendered profane by servile use (1989, p. 55). Victims are destined for violent consumption, bringing the sacrificial offering out of the realm of things and radiating intimacy and anguish (Bataille, 1989, p. 59). This is the price to be paid to remove the crushing weight of cold calculation (Bataille, 1989, p. 61).

In the French theory of sacrifice (Pearce, 2003; Richman, 2002), the ritual of sacrifice requires three agents: the sacrifier, the sacrificer, and the victim. The *sacrifier* is the one or the group in whose interest the sacrifice is purportedly conducted. Sacrifiers are also typically the ones that must offer up the victim or the materials to be sacrificed (e.g., the best of the harvest or the herd). The *sacrificer* is the executioner, the one who conducts the ritual that consumes the offering, by killing or burning, for example, and there is the victim/offering so consumed. The victim must be similar enough to the community for the sacrifice to be meaningful, facilitating a moment of sovereign self-consciousness (Bataille, 1989, p. 56). Were we to take this model of the sacrificial triangle and apply it directly to the question of the fiscal sacrifices that must, apparently, be made to atone for the sins of excessive consumption fueled by debt, we run into a structural problem.

When applied to the case of the indebtedness of zombified populations, it would appear to be the case that they must occupy all three positions simultaneously. First, as the sacrifier, people know that things cannot simply return to the way they once were. Households are now going through a process of deleveraging; governments soon will too. Simultaneously, people are now being asked by economists, bankers, bureaucrats, and politicians to prepare themselves for making fiscal sacrifices (i.e., are being interpolated as *sacrificers*), likely in the form of higher taxes and user-fees (or other cost-recovery mechanisms) for public services while at the same time accepting that deep cuts will be needed (Rosenberg, 2010). As sacrificers, people, in the process of deleveraging, will likely themselves have to cut back on discretionary spending, pay higher taxes and user-fees — they will have to give things up. Last, this same zombified population will be the *victims* as well: life will not be as enjoyable; education, childcare, elder care, and health care costs will rise. Strictly speaking, how can the zombified population occupy all three positions? This impossibility only holds in synchronic terms. Once we consider the phenomenological structure of chronic capitalism it becomes possible to see how this sacrifice can be "conducted" while at the same time failing to be effective in generating the intimacy necessary for a sovereign existence. This is because fiscal sacrifice is diachronically structured.

Fiscal sacrifices are no solution to the problem of authentic self-consciousness because of the distributive and extensifying quality of time in chronic capitalism that spreads risks and costs around to wider pools. Debt repayment is less about the deferral of payment and has more to do with *distributing* payments over time and in risk groups. At the level of population, aggregate actuarial statistics provide data about risk factors hence attaching prices (i.e., interest rates) to likelihoods of payment, non- and irregular payment amongst various segments of the population. The contemporary system of debt payment amounts to the phenomenological structuring of time as perceived by debtors in its chronic form.

What the structure of capitalist time does for the zombie-class is defer the "identification" (in Bataille's sense) with the victim: "you will have to make sacrifices" is in the future tense. Indeed, this was Caillois' point about the inadequacy of modern carnivals in contrast to festivals proper: "The moment the human victim is replaced by an effigy, the ritual tends to lose its value for expiation or fertility" (1988, p. 299; Pearce, 2003, p. 3). Without the immediate and intimate communication between sacrificer and victim, no authentic sovereign self-consciousness is possible. The "effigy" in our case is the distribution of payments, its *amortization*. This term itself gives us an etymological clue: it is the point at which the debt obligation is *dead*, and a portion of one's zombie-life ended. The distribution and dilution of debt servicing and repayment costs short-circuits intimacy through repeated, but minimal victimization — a routinized victimization rendering it mundane. The risk calculus that is the key discursive technology of finance capital is exactly a means-ends calculation characteristic of a restricted economy. In short, fiscal sacrifice cannot be an effective sacrifice because in the end it produces its opposite: the re-instrumentalization of social life, imposing a calculated regularity of payment schedules on it.

Brains—Yum! (After All, You Are What You Eat...)

Zombies have a penchant for eating brains and the lesson "you are what you eat" should be taken seriously because it returns us again to the centrality of consumption. Our basic position is this. The discursive coordinates of capitalism (i.e., its risk calculus about the future and liberal governmentality) that dominate the capitalist division of labor (including the work of consuming to get a life) are effectively its "brain." This brain limits possibilities for problematizing any other future than one of development for capital accumulation. To imagine zombies becoming mindful is something of a departure point from the association (unfortunately neglected) of zombies as revolutionaries (Fay, 2008; see also Comaroff and Comaroff, 2002). To eat the brains of capital is to consume the *Geist* that gives "life" to capitalism and become what one eats in the sense of becoming a fleshy discursive machine for differently problematizing societal futures and collective fates. In short, it leads to a political *life* and perhaps a form of political practice that is "life-giving" in Bataille's sense of becoming sovereign. We characterize this as a *sacrificial politics*.

Sacrificial politics would contrast with the persistent valorization of the coordinates of capitalist development and government that imposes a very particular, capitalist future on societies that will continue to generate zombification. The brains of capitalist governance also manifestly excludes public participation, sacrificing democratic processes for conceiving of viable other possible futures and goals (e.g., quality of life *versus* GDP growth). It does so in the name of efficiency and timely responsiveness, i.e., "fast policy" (Jessop, 2007, p. 193).

While fast policy is certainly efficient, democratic policy-making takes a great deal of time and hence is far from "efficient" as far as instrumentally-rational calculation is concerned. Fast policy is efficient precisely because the value of "the goal" is never debated. This, in Bataillean terms, is what can truly give zombies a new form of life because it is *precisely a waste of time* and could consume the excesses our societies have created. Mass participation in political thought, problematizing futures and fates, thinking about any and sundry possibilities for how the massive productive power of contemporary societies can be harnessed (or not, as the case may be), in short, the endless task of thinking about, deliberating, discussing, debating what is possible, would no doubt be a waste of time and people's energy. It cannot but be inefficient *because no goal is assumed*. But in doing so, we suggest, people would truly become sovereign and perhaps the zombies that "are us" would find in the sacrifice of the time that politics takes, an intimacy, the intimacy of the moment of decision about what we should actually do. The moment would come when it would be "time to cut it out" and so sacrifice, for a time, all of the other paths that could be taken. We suggest that this would produce a new kind of intimacy facilitated by the sacrifice of other possibilities we have collectively deliberated in democratic processes. This would be a kind of cybernetic intimacy, taking the domain of the collective representations and the stuff of our souls constituted in political practice and making a sacrificial offering of it. This could constitute a new kind of soul and life for people. This would be a form of truly *popular sovereignty* manifested in an excessive expenditure on the side of an open, aleatory history (cf. Datta, 2010). Such excessive conceptualizations of futures, in contrast to its now *chronic form* would constitute a new phenomenology of time, a new time for the "once-were-zombies," a real resurrection.

Conclusion: Politics as a Luxurious Waste of Time

While the revolution might be a festival (an orgy of consuming the symbols and institutions of subjugation), things need not return to the chronic humdrum of profane existence. Taking time for politics as the concern for, contemplation of, and debate about the collective fate in a general economy means extricating politics from chronic time. Time for politics then becomes a new figure of the sacred, the accursed share of excesses produced that must be consumed. A sacred politics would exactly concern itself with the mindful thought about *possibilities*, rather than the *probabilities* that characterize calculations about risks and futures as found in chronic capitalist form. We are neither enthusiastic about zombies as potentially emancipatory figures, nor moralistic critics of consumerist activity in capitalist societies. Rather, we offer means of analyzing and understanding the general economic conditions of the working class and its struggle for *sovereignty* through an analysis of the mythic significance of popular representations of zombies in films and in economic discourse. Time for some brains!

NOTES

1. We gratefully acknowledge a research grant awarded by the Faculty of Arts and Social Sciences at the University of Windsor, Ontario, Canada, for supporting our research.

2. While our analyses share similar conceptual and explanatory emphases of Chris Harman's recent book *Zombie Capitalism* (2009), it has been developed independently of it. That said, we quite endorse the emphasis on the temporality of capital accumulation in Harman's work, not least since economics orthodox depends so heavily on simultaneity in market activity in its models (see for instance, pp. 42, 74).

6

Zombified Capital in the Postcolonial Capital

Circulation (of Blood) in Sony Labou Tansi's Parentheses of Blood[1]

Elizabeth A. Stinson

"The dead are assholes" [Labou Tansi, 1986 — I, iv, 48].

Throughout Sony Labou Tansi's *Parentheses of Blood* a Fool character talks to the leaves on the ground as if they reside in the world of the undead. The non-sense of his speech makes palpable a world outside of the living. In this sensory and unnamable world, the Fool spots Libertashio, a ghostly revolutionary rebel character that haunts Labou Tansi's one-act play.[2] Libertashio was once alive, but now parts of his body are scattered across his nation. However, he remains un-dead and now appears not only as a leaf but also emerges in the imaginary of the nation's capital as a zombified creature. This creature appears to adhere itself within a concatenation of notions: the un-dead, the nation-state, the postcolony, and the neocolonial drive of global capital. He leaves the earth half-eroded, mutated by nature, and not-quite-dead making his way down the road to feed on and take control of the capital. The idea of him preys on fears and, as the Fool's performance shows, conjures them to the surface and into circulation. The Fool continually exclaims, "not on Libertashio's grave" with some measure of sardonic foreboding, as though the act of bringing him to the surface puts an untenable idea into circulation. Libertashio is consumed by a suspension of death by those in the capital, hovering somewhere around the surface, and yet as a parenthetical figure lingering outside the living, he is also consuming the circulating return of death by *Capital*. This homonym (capital) resides in overlapping instances of space and time; there is the capital seat of government, but then linked in force is Capital, monetary and other assets constituted in the economic and social relations of capitalism.[3] In the imaginary of the capital city in this once colonized nation, Libertashio has the capacity to intimately reproduce himself, build force and family, and become undone.[4] Through the eyes of the capital, these fragmented and zombified identities become bodies to be feared — they are doing something counter. The whole party must be killed again and again as if they are all one, *the one who might infest and infect the future of Capital by unraveling the present economy of blood in the capital.*

Can a zombified nation be a stunted laborer stuck in the circulation of Capital? Congolese writer Labou Tansi, in his play, sketches a zombified space where the neocolonialism of the metropole and the generation of Capital in a postcolonial nation-state come together. The trade center of a former colonist engaging in a somewhat imperial form of exchange with a "peripheral" former colony, the metropole involves itself in the geopolitics and economics of postcolonial nation-states. In most cases, the metropole renders the products of its "workers" entirely as a form of exchange, whereby Capital becomes stunted outside the metropole, a stagnant remainder.[5] The capital of this nation-state becomes a bourgeois proxy, or stand-in, inhabiting the space of the neocolonial and embodying a remainder of Capital that has already been circulating since the colony was founded by force. In what way would Capital then circulate? Within the relationship of a postcolonial nation-state such as this a grotesque manifestation of Capital circulates in opposing and contradictory forces that continually end and begin with blood. A circulation of Capital of this kind becomes the capital's primary concern, the opening and motivating force of its capacity, driving all its endeavors, and globally couched in the closing of parentheses. Within this parenthetical dialectic (capital/Capital) blood still flows red despite the undead appearance of its circulation: we imagine zombies theoretically and we imagine theoretically that zombies can be seen. The parentheses contribute to an understanding of this zombified dialectic by syntactically and figuratively addressing its forged space with a political grammar that demarcates this space as accepted within the polis. The postcolonial capital inhabits the negative space of neocolonial Capital — it could be that the postcolonial capital is parenthetically suspended in neocolonial Capital and that neocolonial Capital produces relations that are somehow antagonistic to those in the metropole. Labou Tansi exhibits this violent and farcical game, the circulation of Capital, in his French-language play, *Parentheses of Blood*. As I follow the zombies circulating in Labou Tansi's play, I will also primarily lean on Marx's *Gründrisse* to read the performance of Capital in a postcolonial capital. Both texts point to the performativity and space of the parentheses on many levels, its opening, and what circulates inside them. With these texts, I want to look at the dynamics and circulation of Capital within the postcolonial capital and point to the mechanisms (such as the military apparatus) that contribute to the space and logic of *zombification*.

Postcolonial theorist Achille Mbembe makes use of this neologism, zombification,[6] to highlight the intimate process tied to a spatial and temporal living space between "gestures in public and covert responses 'underground.'" Mbembe refers to this dynamic as zombification — a logic that has resulted in the mutual loss of vitality and potency in both the dominant power in the capital and those who are ostensibly dominated by the capital (Mbembe, 2001, p. 104). The term conveys the shared space of the postcolony between them, a vulgar and impotent banality that ironically enacts a promiscuous conviviality, a "jarred" and "transgressive disjunction" of participation by both the oppressors and the oppressed. In an interview, Mbembe acknowledges the considerable influence of Labou Tansi's writings in teasing out this dynamic, which composes one of Mbembe's main arguments around how power is exercised in the postcolony (Oboe, 2010). My guiding question is precisely how the logic of zombification plays into (the) capital[7] and circulates in the postcolonial nation-state. I argue that this logic infiltrates (the) capital via the metropole producing a performance of the living-dead. In a sense, the performance generates from a neocolonial imperative, and by that I mean certain development procedures that have been taken up in the postcolonial period, or as an overlapping security measure of Capital (as in the Congo case of the financially-backed secessionist copper-rich southern province of Katanga during

Patrice Lumumba's brief post-independence presidency). These strategies include corporate extraction of resources as well as other suzerain-like government and non-government negotiations. The neocolonial capital seat of the nation is zombified in its global interrelations and those outside the capital are zombified in their intra-national relations. In other words, the metropole becomes the capital's very existence in global relationships. Not only does this status stand outside of power in the context of the neocolonial state, particularly as Labou Tansi portrays it, but the zombie itself haunts power in (the) capital by its own production, circulation and return.[8] As a colonial outgrowth bent on scaring up some Capital, the interaction and familiar exchange of zombification, whether accounted for or not, keeps producing and returning zombies from somewhere. Like Capital, zombification ultimately produces excess, a remainder, leftovers that are omitted in some readings like chemical garbage, oil spills, and violence over resource extraction, especially at the source of Capital gain, which must be guarded at all costs.

In the play, soldiers from the capital city return again one evening to a town where "not a brick or a dick is left standing," searching for the (undead) rebel named Libertashio (I, v, 53). They return to the house where his family lives but, as we learn from the Fool at the beginning of the play, he is already dead. As the soldiers gorge themselves on food and wine, Ramana, one of Libertashio's three daughters, explains that all they were able to bury were his head and clothes. As he vehemently pulls out a huge oversized photo ID, the Sergeant asks, "This head here?" When she confirms its identity match, the Sergeant resigns himself to exhuming Libertashio's head: "I think this time the capital will believe once and for all that Libertashio is dead." However, another soldier immediately shoots the Sergeant dead: "deserters are shot" (I, i, 10). In what subsequently becomes a repetitive shooting-promotion-burial ritual, the newly inducted Sergeant oversees his predecessor's burial — this banal ritual takes place three more times during the play. "The law forbids belief in Libertashio's death," explains the new Sergeant, and any soldier from the capital that denies this imaginary, Libertashio's projected zombie existence, automatically becomes known as a deserter (I, i, 11). Even though his body is in pieces and fragmented, soldiers in the military still must believe he is whole, even death breaks down and cannot kill him as they attempt to control the contingencies and possible outcomes of this remainder. The capital overcomes its individual soldiers to protect Libertashio's zombie state. Where a zombie's head must be destroyed in order to destroy its ability to impact the living, to *see* Libertashio's head would destroy its utility (for the capital) finally, its zombie usefulness that perpetuates the blood-letting that sustains neocolonial Capital.

By the second evening of food and wine with the soldiers Libertashio's nephew by blood relation, Martial[9] is mistakenly identified as Libertashio, and in an act of reproduction, not unlike the characteristic proliferation of zombies, the rest of the family are all tied to stakes facing a firing squad accused of aiding and abetting the condemned. As a stalling ploy, their "last requests" prompt a wedding party for one of the daughters, Aleyo, and the current Sergeant. As Martial begins to realize he will be dying in his uncle's place, a voice suddenly takes over his previously conservative countenance and he begins shouting, "Long live Libertashio" (I, ii, 32). With this insurgence, the last standing Sergeant, Cavacha, commands the other soldiers to cut off Martial's right hand saying, "Don't fool around with useless loss of blood. He must die piece by piece" (I, ii, 33). As Martial moans and screams from the loss of his hand and other body parts — "the time to die is over," he repeats — the wedding plan proceeds into a third evening. The Parson and other guests arrive and eventually they are all calling out, "Long live Libertashio," as Martial did (I, iii, 39). The Sergeant now orders his soldiers to sever all of their ears and with blood running down the sides of their heads, they are thrown in a dark room with Martial. The next scene occurs during the fourth and final evening of the play, and in a state of shock they all attempt to figure out whether they are dead or alive or somewhere in-between. They decide they must be alive, for the morning comes and they are arranged on the grave of Libertashio although they are no longer afraid, "no longer entirely human" (I, v, 53). As the wedding party stands before the firing squad, they consider their humanity, whether they will die inside, and they toy with the lines they can cross verbally with the soldiers. Before the execution begins, however, a soldier from the capital arrives with a message and announces that a new government has been installed in the capital and now considers Libertashio a national hero! Infuriated, the Sergeant rants, "The assholes in the capital have managed to piss in our faces! Not bad!" He shoots them all anyway. As he storms off, he shoots the messenger while awaking the dead by shouting, "Down with Libertashio! ... We'll tear down the capital" (I, v, 56). Now, it is the Sergeant who transforms into the insurgent rebel, and a survivor from the wedding guests ends the play pleading, "You can't close me off in these parentheses.... You can't skip me. No, I want to be reborn" (I, v, 57).

The parentheses become a physicalized space that is skipped, overlooked, zombified, and no longer valorized (always-already). Parentheses materialize in the body and continually appear in the play, not only closing in on intrinsic contradictions, but also opening up potentialities. As the family is preparing for the wedding in handcuffs, the bride asks her cousin Martial why he thinks there is a point to having existed and he replies, "to open the parentheses" (I, ii, 29). Labou Tansi connects power and grammar in this way. Parentheses play with(in) existence, and of course, linguistics — they provide: further explanation, a reference, the meta moment, another level or layer, back story, a revealing secret or joke, a self-conscious aside, a rem(a)inder, a side note or marginalia. They are not supposed to interpret the main flow, but they usually impart something related or supplementary and outside the main throughline, as well as alternative meanings, afterthoughts, contingencies, or incongruities that often take on a larger scope. Figuratively, they have been positioned as veins, eyes with double vision, Fred Moten's "mo(ur)nin(g)," unreleased steam, the traitor within, an entrance or exit, a mass of contradictions, postcoloniality within the neocolonial, dialectical materialism, reproduced coercion, or the liminality between life and death. Nuruddin Farah plays with the space and time encounters of the parentheses in a dialectical style in several of his novels. Jacques Derrida's essay "Signature Event Context" notes several times in parentheses the always-already problem of communication and polysemia, lest we forget in our efforts to deconstruct (1982). Della Pollock mentions "Roland Barthes's rampant parentheticals" as performative form in her essay on "Performing Writing" (1998, p. 83). And Mbembe suggests — echoing Labou Tansi's play — that to open or close the parenthesis is to convey knowledge of "oneself at the crossroads" (2001, p. 203).

Marx's use of parentheses in the *Gründrisse* also tracks similar, multiple meanings and purposes. The *Gründrisse* consists of numerous notebooks or unedited manuscripts that outline much of Marx and Engel's writings on their theories of Capital. There are numerous instances where a parenthetical appears to be in conversation with previously mentioned ideas and opens up the potential for a different direction, such as a rather parenthetical situation in Marx's discussion of exploding out what appears to be fixed bourgeois social relationships of exchange and production:

> ([There are] a multitude of antagonistic forms of the social entity, whose antagonism, however, can never be exploded by a quiet metamorphosis. On the other hand, if we did not find latent

in society as it is, the material conditions of production and the corresponding relationships of exchange for a classless society, all attempts to explode it would be quixotic.) [Marx, 1986, p. 96].

Embedded in Marx's parentheses is an indication of what circulates just below the surface, a prevailing desire within the social mines of circulation underlying Capital cannot coercively change the class society that uses circulation to reproduce Capital. Circulation not only has the capacity to (re)produce Capital, but also classless society. The only reason attempts to explode social antagonisms have any hope of working is that, while latent, circulation also contains the conditions and relations for a classless society. As he hangs on to a revolutionary turn, that conflicts cannot quietly change, he performs the multiple parenthetical mines themselves, silently waiting within the relationships of exchange and production. As a side note in his notebook, this parenthetical stages Marx's philosophy of practice, not necessarily a romantic notion of revolution, nor a kind of movement of the materiality behind these antagonisms, but towards a performance of the multiple conditions that already exist, a latent everyday kind of parenthetical, as if hidden within circulation (the thing itself) lies a way out. In a similar reflective manner Labou Tansi is known for his conscious play and subversion of the rules of French grammar (Yewah, 2002). In relation to *Parentheses of Blood*, what is being performed excavates, resituates, and then reflects what happens inside the parentheses, what and how (the) capital functions within the postcolonial state. The play exemplifies what comes out of Capitalism culturally, as a cultural by-product or surplus of colonialism, or economies of blood.

Parentheses form an enclosure or circle around this remainder (two bloody ears listening for the morning, circulation of Capital, an exchange behind the scenes, a prison, a black hole or any plural place where time does not exist, an obliteration of the delineation between real and actual, and zombification). The physical C of the ear, the stiff cartilage of the pinna, the contour of its helix echoes the C's of (the) Capital in Labou Tansi's play, the severed ears of the parentheses. Disorientation is experienced by the loss of the auricle of the ear. Derrida addresses a related "field of listening" by criticizing the field of philosophy, starting with the verb "to tympanize," which is derived from the archaic French *tympaniser*, ostensibly meaning to criticize. In another serpentine sense Derrida seeks out the affected state of pulling tight the drum within the ear, requiring "the *relevance* of the limit," the external gathering points, the other at the margins. But one continually misses the outer reaches of these parentheses, particularly if they are cut off right at the vestibule — "one misses (the) missing (of) it" (Derrida, 1982, xi). The fourth evening, the last evening before Martial and his family are shot, the wedding party spend the night with no ears locked in a mysterious room "where the condemned are gathered," where the light is blinding "like blood clots," a place where "the world is finished," yet as they decide, they are somehow still alive (I, iv, 43). Embodying Mbembe's notion of "zombification," their personal responses in this public space lack the capacity to open the parentheses:

> RAMANA: Each of us is dying his own death. It's well distributed ... like up there, living our own lives. Loneliness. Our Lady of Solitude. All creation is filled with walls that close us in. You can't go to your neighbor. You can't take part in your neighbor's death [I, iv, 45].

If you go to your neighbor, they too will die. The economy of subjectivity does not exclude complicit or contagious association. The distribution of Capital in a neocolonial space creates an eidolon (a phantasm) of community, a parentheses of individual labor to stay alive, that parallels the distribution of death — a delegation. Death itself, as a reified commodity, is exchanged to ensure the management of and absolve the traces of the capital: open and close.

The capital in this case is Congo-Brazzaville, where Labou Tansi's theatre group, Le Rocado Zulu Théâtre, was formed. "But let's not mention Africa, please! Africa does not enter into this football game that pits two parentheses against each other," as Labou Tansi writes in the prologue of the play (I, i, 1) satirically hinting at the two spaces covered in blood and bowels that engender zombification. Born in 1947 Kinshasa, the capital of the Democratic Republic of the Congo (DRC), which lies on the other side of the Congo river from the city of Brazzaville, he soon moved across that wide river and spent most of his life in and around Brazzaville, the capital of the Republic of the Congo. There, a coup d'état at the end of 1968 inserted Captain Marien Ngouabi, making him the third president after the country's independence from French rule in 1960. The next year, Ngouabi installed the single-party Congolese Labour Party and declared a Marxist/Leninist state named People's Republic of the Congo. The irony of this one-party rule lies in the merging of the gendarmerie with the army yielding a police state, an extreme difference in quality of life in the capital in comparison to the rest of the country, and a subsequently intense deployment of ideology. The privatized ruling class or oligarchy, extended to several metropoles and points of personal capital, cutting off the popular sector and their own foothold in a domestic market. The capital sustained itself on imported French food and wine and most of the capital's budget finances the military and the busy civil service bureaucracy. Despite the rhetoric of development, Capital stays in the capital; there is no integration into the "nation-state" economy, close parentheses. The autocrat Ngouabi was assassinated in 1977; but before his death Ngouabi killed several of Labou Tansi's close friends for allegedly attempting to instigate a coup. Although the capital changed hands, the politics in the Congo remained relatively the same. This action of setting up conspiracy plots matured into a regular device to dispose of potential threats, threats like Libertashio. One of Libertashio's daughters recalls a French teacher who told her "the situation in Africa is entertaining" (I, ii, 32). Referring to this entertaining aesthetic in the prologue as well, Labou Tansi seems to comment on proposing real time as a theatrical temporality, which serves to place all of Africa in parentheses dismissing actual bloodshed and imagining "the situation" without a colonial history or neocolonial relations and destabilizing the ability to distinguish the stage on which "the situation" takes place. When he wrote the play, the capital was a prime example of neocolonial and "socialist" absurdity (with its Capitalist overtones) where the nation-state's self-imposed military violence becomes a travesty — as he writes in his novel *The Antipeople*, "What good is an ounce of justice in an ocean of shit?" (Labou Tansi, 1983). The management and acquisition of military labor and power follows in the footsteps of postcolonial Capital.

When the soldiers from the capital first arrive in *Parentheses of Blood*, the Sergeant calls to another soldier to remind him of what they're looking for ("Libertashio"), who sent them ("the capital"), why ("the capital said to"), and what it wants ("to break our balls"). The commodity of blood bought by the capital in the form of the soldier's labor of bloodshed is then sold as Capital. Whatever foreign investments, installations, or contracts there are based on local resource extraction or other forms of extraterritorialization exit the postcolonial state in the form of Capital, leaving the capital in the Congo region to fight over what remnant bodies in the process of zombification that are all that return. Speaking specifically of Brazzaville, Mbembe contends, "violence is cyclical, and its epicenter is the capital" (Mbembe, 2000, p. 48). The parentheses of blood act as a circulation component of Capital (of continued postcolonialism), preserving the myth of the nation-state capital and in the process reproducing that Capital and class-society that Marx contends is not all that circulation can furnish and restoring the capital's claim to Capital. As a spatial logic, it contains the population in a viscous state of zombification. The first evening prologue: "It's begun — in this sad century. Whether opened or closed — these parentheses of blood, these parentheses of bowels, it's begun, but won't end" (I, i, 1). In this century of neocolonialism, in the capital, as Marx indicated during a time of colonialism, "the interaction of conscious individuals ... their own collisions give rise to an *alien* social power standing above them" (original emphasis). There exists a process, an exchange, which obfuscates and mediates the distinction between individuals, between commodity and labor. Money "whether it is conceived of as a force of nature, an accident, or in any other form, is a necessary result of the fact that the starting point is not the free social individual" (Marx, 1986, p. 132). Through the military arm of the capital, the production of Capital under this 'alien' control performs and provides a misexecution that extorts blood, as well as a subterfuge of circulation, while claiming to lie outside the parentheses of blood. But within these parentheses is a marketplace of the undead. Labou Tansi throws a "parenthetic pass, which either opens or closes; you must choose" (I, iii, 34). And Marx surmises, "so long as money [Capital] remains an essential relation of production, [none of the various forms of money] can resolve the contradictions inherent in the money [capital] relationship, they can all only express these contradictions in one form or another" (Marx, 1986, p. 61). These contradictions, vagarious in their appearance in and around the capital, infuse dangerous social imbalances, hoarding absolute Capital, and "concealing human suffering, burying it in an infinite circle centered, so to speak, everywhere" (Mbembe, 2001, p. 13), for Capital in circulation disfigures, whether opening or closing the parentheses.

Labou Tansi's play exposes an abundance of unconscionable absurdities, just as the structures of Capitalism reveals a mass of contradictions. Contradictions are inherent in the absurd, revealing a cross-eyed vision — a short-sighted, convergent, and folding excess of violence producing a social organization where the value and meaning of life under that vision's assurance is constantly called into question by its lack of focus. This esophoric perversity of perception, where one is making zombies is the excess of Capital. An incommensurable value of blood becomes a deceptive commodification, rendering a world unhinged by the hilarity of officialdom at the mercy of Capital. And, as Marx relates, "...the real value ... negates itself again and brings the real value of the commodities continually into contradiction with its own determination" (Marx, 1986, p. 75). The compensation of one commodity (or body in the process of commodifying zombification) sacrifices another, as in the distinction between use-value and a fetishized value of a commodity where the determination robs what is distinguished of life. All that is left is the fetishized and tendentiously convergent vision of an increasingly "global" space of zombification. The inward violence of the capital and the soldiers' labor turns on the population as a form of use-value (useful for killing), but the new value derived from this labor is questionable in that it is dependent on commodity relations from elsewhere, somewhere outside this particular parentheses. In a sense, the use-value of killing is also an exchange value — Capital opens the parentheses through killing. Similar to Agamben's "state of exception,"[10] where transgression of the law is deemed necessary and the authority of the state claims the right to kill however determined for the sake of nation-state preservation. The bodies of those located outside the capital, whose transgression is also becomes necessary, but may well be met with by death, become a liability to the inhabitants of the capital, a threat to the nation-state consumed with zombified stagnation and neocolonialized stagflation. Hence, an absurd take on bodies, in many contradictory forms, surfaces. As Mbembe contends, "the body more than anything else destabilizes all forms of domination" (Oboe, 2010). The segmentation of the body becomes a metonym for the object (or abject) form of a commodity and the circulation and discourses of blood commandeered by its exchange value. When the Sergeant gives the order to sever Martial bit by bit, starting with his right hand, he call on a tactic leftover from colonial occupation. This gesture and logic is specifically reminiscent of King Leopold II of Belgium's colonial *modus operandi* in the Congo of the nineteenth century. His representatives in the colony and a military formed out of the colonized would cut off the hand of laborers who did not return with the correct amount of rubber extract. Leopold's strategies of colonization and methods of extracting resources were extremely violent as documented and circulated in photographs of accumulated piles of hands. When Mbembe outlines his theory of "necropolitics," he notes the necessity to keep up "the morbid spectacle of severing." Like a zombie body with parts missing, this action performs the walking dead in a ritual that reasserts power, or as Mbembe defines necropolitics itself, reaffirms a "subjugation of life to the power of death" (2003, pp. 35, 39). Death becomes something to be regulated and distributed via various formations: terror, occupation, war, and violence. Not only is politics in the business of death, but it is also through the circulation of death that it actually lives a life.

Mbembe's description of necropolitics positions Capital hovering over the life of the individual, the laborer, the capital, and the nation-state with a net of Capital (like the force of life itself), the parenthetical stranglehold. "Capital does not *exchange* as an individual, but as representing the consumption and the needs of many" (Marx, 1986, p. 506 — original emphasis). The "many" in this case lie outside the postcolonial state. Capital looks beyond the parentheses of blood at a larger exchange, one that benefits the metropole, the capital, and the postcolony with claims toward the freedom of multitudes in poverty and ruin.[11] However, Capital, in this case, portends *consumption* of the Congolese capital as a neocolonial state, a legacy left behind. Neocolonial activity cannot help but engage with Capital in a baleful way, leaving the capital to do its dirty work, which in turn attempts to conceal its own zombie status. The military are an extension of the capital, although they too lie in an uncertain position, where the rules and laws change at a moment's notice producing an affect of irrationality (a revenant of the referent). In Labou Tansi's words, whether Libertashio is dead or whether Martial is not Libertashio does not matter, the capital perceives an antagonism that the soldiers/labor must, but never can, resolve. The circulation of blood becomes the turnover of who is in the capital and "the true nature of Capital only emerges *at the end of its circulation*" (Marx, 1986, p. 439 — original emphasis). When one life is torn to bits, the parentheses close and Capital re-expresses its purpose and valorization.

Marx points out warfare and the military several times as being the first use of wage labor. The military, as a reminiscent form of governance, is a French conquest imperative and highly entangled in the story of colonialism and capital. In the play, the military appear as a never-ending arm of the capital, if not one of the few ways to generate the Capital of a life. If we look at the dual existence of the commodity both as natural and economic/sign (Marx, 1986), we see the feeding of both silence and capacity. In the same way, violence as a form of labor creates the commodity of blood in addition to the mediatizing parasitism of the capital, as exclaimed by the Parson during the third evening, "Men have disappeared, these human forms remain, these human graves, but inside they're no longer human at all. Come back." (I, iii, 40). Marx phrases this duality another way (with an eye on European capital): "One capitalist's raw material is the other's product. One capitalist's product is the other's raw material" (1986, p. 440). This exchange points out the neocolonial capital behind the postcolonial capital (controlling the principal resources, the raw materials) using both Capital and blood as commodities. However, at the same time (in the postcolonial sense), the capital in this case becomes the laborer caught in between the exchange, producing an alienated military laborer in the process of circulation. Marx determines, "In the end, even the illusion that they are *selling* him products disappears. He [the metropole merchant] purchases their labour and takes away first their property in the product, before long in the instrument as well, unless he lets them have it as their *sham property* in order to diminish his own production costs" (1986, p. 434 — original emphasis). As the play reflects, even the soldiers are circulating with mock capacity in the force of circumstance, performing the revolution-restoration cycle, they are eventually caught in the parentheses as well, in between, as Antonio Gramsci points out, "rivalries between cliques at the top: the rank and file splits up behind the various competing leaders" (Gramsci, 1971, p. 215). The Fool sees Libertashio's body move from its grave, like all the fallen leaves the Fool has conversations with, and even his ghostly (dis)appearance becomes subsumed in the unstable Capital of the capital and the subsequent absurdity in the circulation of blood.

With a nation-state capital always on the verge of breakdown of itself, its Capital circulating to another coast, outside the capital the illusion always reappears (like Libertashio). What if there is no labor (other than what the capital provides: military/civic), no market, and a literal (linear) distribution with no production to speak of? Can there be circulation in the country (other than blood)? What is left? Marx's argument that follows would only apply to that one sector of society, the postcolonial capital: "Complete dependence on Capital, complete separation of the workers from the conditions of production, consequently imply their grouping around the individual Capital as the sole source of their subsistence" (1986, p. 509). It is a neocolonial move, a kind of geocapital dependence that is not easy to get out from under and whose residues do not sustain those outside the capital, instead placing them in a state of zombification.

What affects transformation in the capital — by what methods and at what pace? Capital — in the form of lucrative trade (controlled by foreign investors) in mostly crude oil, but also timber, manganese, diamonds, and now coltan and uranium; in return for these Capital investments, the Congolese capital has been established with a heavy dependence on foreign aid and import prices, not to mention the violence associated with neocolonialism. The postcolonial Capitalist sets up parentheses of circulation, accumulating wealth "by a lack of circulation (as in ancient Rome)" (Marx, 1986, p. 61). In parentheses, the location/circulation of the money from oil revenues occupies a space factored out of the equation: the indeterminate dialectic of opposing forces within the parentheses of blood. Capital's "value consists precisely in the process of valorization" (Marx, 1986, p. 469). As long as Capital continues to re-evaluate and re-negotiate the value and terms of the postcolony, the process of sanguinary process will be included in its valorization. Adorno and Horkheimer indicate a similar vein, "multiplying violence through the mediation of the market" (2002, p. 33), the intervention of and into the market (or even a particular market) and its circulation can compound and violently contribute to an unstable scenario. Ultimately, it doesn't matter what the capital wants, it's what *Capital* wants, and valorizes with blood if need be, that really matters.[12] What Capital wants is dependent on zombified relationality between itself and the (in this case, Congolese) capital.

In Labou Tansi's play (perhaps even reflected in his own grave in the Republic of the Congo),[13] we might just find the capitalist system breaking down, in the parentheses of the theatrical production, a circulating, spiraling devolution of postcolonial blood and capital. The capitalist's "universal objectification becomes his total alienation, and the demolition of all determined one-sided aims becomes the sacrifice of the [human] end-in-itself to a wholly external purpose." They posit an end-in-itself, the absolute movement of becoming something other, and return to parenthetical space, where a "complete unfolding of man's inner potentiality turns into his total emptying-out" (Marx, 1986, p. 412). Capital, in the insular existence of its own parenthetical generation, is the valorization of an illusion reflected in the postcolonial state. It holds fast to its return. "The circulation of Capital is simultaneously its becoming, its growth, its life-process. If anything can be compared to the circulation of blood, it was not the formal circulation of money, but the circulation of Capital, which really has a content of its own" (Marx, 1986, p. 441). This content has more to do with the circulation of blood than the capitalist cares to admit, and so, the theatrical and spectral insurrection of zombies[14] continues to haunt Capital's spatial imaginary.

Notes

1. A fervent thank you to José Esteban Muñoz, Fiona I.B. Ngô, Ann Pellegrini, Michael Ralph, Sandra Ruiz, Christopher Moreman, Cory Rushton, Tina Majkowski, and Maya Winfrey for their generous support and feedback.

2. I will be referring to the 1996 Ubu Repertory Theater Publications printing of Lorraine Alexander's 1985 English translation of Sony Labou Tansi's *La Parenthèse de sang*. At the Ubu Repertory Theater in New York, a staged reading (directed by George C. Wolfe) was produced in 1986 as part of a festival of new plays from francophone Africa and the Caribbean. Labou Tansi wrote the play in 1978, the first French publication was in 1981, and the first English publication was in 1986.

3. I will maintain this formatted distinction throughout with the capitalized "c" of Capital signifying the economic value and reproduced process of capitalism. For the most part, there are three "c's": the theoretical system of *Capital*, the *capital* seat of the nation, and *Capital* that flows as money. However, for flow and clarity I am folding Capital that flows into the system of Capital, since I simply find fault with both for the traffic of bloodletting.

4. Considering the Butlerian sense of "undone," now would be an apt opportunity to mark the identity politics that become enmeshed in the (neo)colonial relation of the capital and Capital, those of race and gender in particular. In *Undoing Gender*, Judith Butler argues that gender is an act of doing and analyzes the possibility of becoming undone, of undoing the performativity of sedimented gender roles. Although Labou Tansi does scrutinize gender roles and their politics of interaction in a postcolonial vein, space does not permit a thorough examination of these contributing aspects here. While folding them in as they are I want to also attribute the capacity of becoming "undone" to the contradictory performance that lies in the fragmentation of identities produced by the circulation of the zombie figure in the system of Capital.

5. Ironically, the term "zombie" has developed into a specific definition within economic theory circles recently. Thus, I want to distinguish my usage of the term in the context of Capital, which adheres more to a spatial process or logic reflective in certain postcolonial policies, practices, and politics, i.e., neocolonialism. I will extrapolate this direction and meaning further in the chapter. As an acknowledgment and point of interest, "zombie" firms and banks, as coined by economic researcher Anil K. Kashyap, exemplify a relational effect, a particular economic phenomenon generated with clarity first in Japan. "To study the effect of zombie firms on the Japanese economy, Kashyap, Hoshi, and Caballero began by classifying firms that were *being kept alive with direct interest rate subsidies*. Specifically, zombie firms were defined as *those firms whose borrowing costs were so low that the only possible explanation for the low rates was that the banks were subsidizing them*" (Kashyap 2006 — my emphasis). They found that the prevalence of zombies and their "sham loan restructurings" (from zombie banks) to unprofitable borrowers (zombie firms) lowered the market share as well as job and business production enhancement overall. Granted, I do intend to hint at a similar destructive "feeding" that permeates a neocolonial arrangement, and of course lean on the talk that the Japanese case in the early 1990s has surfaced elsewhere as of late. My meaning takes on more social and political ramifications towards the means of Capital to arise in numerous zombie forms.

6. Haitian writer René Depestre linked colonialism to zombification in a 1971 article, according to Jean and John Comaroff (see footnote 8), and their use of this term was deployed around the same time as Mbembe's *On the Postcolony*, where the term appears in double quotation marks without a reference or any mention Depestre.

7. In this chapter I am evoking both the capital and Capital as well as this parenthetical dialectic within the postcolonial nation-state.

8. For further discussion of zombies in the context of colonialism, immigration, labor, and neoliberal capitalism in South Africa, see Jean and John Comaroff's 2002 essay, "Alien-Nation: Zombies, Immigrants, and Millennial Capitalism." They allude to zombies arising out of colonial encounters and continue to make appearances during "periods characterized by sharp shifts in control over the fabrication and circulation of value" as well as new forms of wealth and changing labor practices in capitalism (2002, p. 783).

9. As Emmanuel Yewah notes, the name of Martial is the theatrical pseudonym used by fellow Congolese writer, journalist, and musician Sylvain Bemba (2002). A strong influence, Labou Tansi dedicates many of his works to him.

10. Agamben positions the "state of exception" as a philosophical problem, one that governments call upon continuously as a de facto or pragmatic right of power to suspend the norm of the law and remove the rights of others. Like Mbembe's notion of "necropolitics," Agamben expands on Carl Schmitt's work on the "state of exception" and the "state of siege." By tracing its extrajuridical and historical inclinations, Agamben demonstrates how "the problem of defining it concerns precisely a threshold, or a zone of indifference, where inside and outside do not exclude each other but rather blur with each other" (2005, 23). Blurred boundaries support a state of exception becoming the rule instead of the exception, like a parenthetical indeterminacy.

11. Tansi writes in *The Antipeople*, "This invasion of money into everyday life is something the Belgians left us as a mark of love. A mark of soul" (1983).

12. In a fairly recent U.S. example, whether a $20 billion program, 25 years in the making, is flawed (as is the case with the introduction of the V-22 Osprey military plane) does not matter. Even though Dick Cheney and the Bush administration attempted to block its development and subsequent release several times, the in-deep (to the tune of $35 billion more), unsafe-landing (30 lives lost so far in training), can't-shoot-straight military wonder will be debuting in an theatre soon, somewhere ... over there.

13. Sony Labou Tansi died in 1995 of complications from AIDS outside the capital of the Republic of the Congo-Brazzaville.

14. Before I end, it seems necessary to reference Jacques Derrida's *Specters of Marx*, particularly his discussion of *incorporation*, a spectral incarnation into an artifactual and fictional body: "For there to be a ghost, there must be a return to the body, but to a body that is more abstract than ever" (Derrida, 1994, 157). This presence, or spectrogenic layering, Marx argues, is all part of a "conjuring trick." This trick is reminiscent of Lisa Lowe's airing of colonialism and Hegel's notion of the dialectic as "a series of phases," frozen in time and space, "in which each subsequent phase emerges as a more explicit or more inclusive whole of which the former phase can be seen in retrospect as one moment" (Lowe, 2006, 200). This process of negation supposedly resolves the individual within a totalizing unity, like the nation-state. Perhaps zombies are all the phases, bodies, and ghosts left behind, which can easily be incorporated into a commodity of glory or conscience.

PART III

Culturally Transplanted Zombies

7

Zombie Orientals Ate My Brain!
Orientalism in Contemporary Zombie Stories

Eric Hamako

Building on Edward Said's concept of Orientalism ([1979] 1994), I suggest that rising fears about Islam are one factor driving the current surge in zombies' popularity. Demonized Muslims and zombies are both Orientalist projections of the negative, repressed qualities that Western Whiteness anxiously denies about itself (Bishop, 2006; Dariotis, 2007; Semmerling, 2006). As a fantastical metaphor, zombies allow audiences to experience and explore their Orientalist fears about terrorism, Islam, and social collapse, while maintaining a comfortable distance from discomforting realities. I also suggest that Orientalist ideas about Islam have influenced a notable evolution in the zombie genre: the rise of the fast, angry zombie.

Some zombie representations paint only the thinnest metaphoric veneer over these Orientalist stories. In *Flight of the Living Dead* (2007), zombies sneak aboard a passenger airplane, take over, and threaten to crash the plane into a city. The political cartoon "Ghoul Academy," depicted three so-called "Axis of Evil" leaders as lumbering zombies with claw-like hands outstretched (Gordon, no date). The cartoon "Night of the Living Guantanamo Detainees," depicting a bearded zombie wearing a turban and robe lurching toward the viewer, mocking U.S. fears of Muslim detainees being transferred to U.S. prisons (Wolverton, 2009). Not all zombie stories are so overt in their conflation of zombies and the Oriental, but the themes do pervade zombie movies. With or without the "Arab kit" (Shaheen, 2003), zombies embody many of the same imaginary qualities as other Orientalized people.

Zombies as the Oriental

To understand the current U.S. fascination with zombies, I'm drawing on Edward Said's ideas about Orientalism (Said, [1979] 1994). Said proposed that European and U.S. imperial powers sought to represent those they were colonizing as Other, as The Oriental, as an ideological means to control them. Imperial powers represent the Oriental Other in ways that suit their own interests. Orientalist representations are often projections of the negative or repressed qualities that imperial powers wish to deny about themselves. So, Western representations of the so-called Orient tell us little about colonized people, but tell us *a lot* about the interests of colonizers.

Western cinema, including the United States and Europe, has created zombies that contain negative, repressed qualities about the West that are displaced onto the Oriental (Aizenberg, 1999). Many of these qualities are also projected onto the United States' Orientalized enemies. Since their first appearances on film, zombies have, in an Orientalist fashion, represented racial Others in ways that serve Western imperial interests. Bishop has called zombies, "the ultimate foreign Other" (Bishop, 2006, p. 201).

In current zombie lore, zombies generally differ from other monsters in several ways. Zombies feed on human flesh. Zombies infect their victims, creating more zombies. Zombies have no superhuman powers, but they gather in hordes and rapidly increase in number. Modern zombie stories generally revolve around social collapse and basic survival (Dendle, 2007). But, there is another, less acknowledged characteristic: zombies are creatures that have lost their sense of self, their unique humanity (Boon, 2007).[1] Zombies' characteristic loss of identity is what links together undead zombies, such as those imagined by George Romero, and living zombies, as in *28 Days Later*. It also links zombies that eat flesh to those that do not, such as "Voodoo" zombies and the "Infected" in *28 Days Later*. Zombies have lost their individual identities and are driven by some enemy Other, whether a Voodoo master, an alien race, a virus, or some unknown cause.[2] The loss of identity also distinguishes zombies from other undead creatures, such as vampires, mummies, and Jesus Christ.

Orientalist Origins: Anti-Colonial Threats by Black Haitians and Black Islam

Since their entry into the U.S. imaginary more than eighty years ago, zombies have expressed U.S. fears about Orientalized peoples and have justified U.S. imperialism. U.S. interest in zombies began when the U.S. invaded and occupied Haiti from 1915 until 1933. While many moviegoers today might not think of the Caribbean as Oriental, the idea resonated for many audience members in the 1920s and 1930s. At the time, Haiti was part of "the West's East," a region more local and accessible to the U.S. empire than the seemingly remote locations in Africa, India, and Asia, dominated by European empires (Bishop, 2008, p. 144). In the 1930s, as Haitian resistance to U.S. occupation increased, U.S. movie producers and consumers began to take interest in zombies (Boon, 2007). Conjured by Orientalist fears, the "Voodoo zombie" genre arose (Aizenberg, 1999).

Voodoo zombie stories articulated White U.S. fears that an independent Haiti might threaten the U.S.'s economic, political, and sexual dominance over Blacks. Films such as *White Zombie* (1932) helped justify U.S. imperialism and its so-called "civilizing mission" in Haiti (Aizenberg, 1999, p. 462). Such stories warned that postcolonial nationalist movements might instate their own exploitative regimes and compete with their former colonizers, perhaps even using their illegitimate Oriental powers to pollute or control the White Christian West (Bishop, 2008). But, in the late 1930s, interest waned as the United States turned its attentions to World War II and the Motion Picture Association of America began restricting representations of non–Christian religions (Whitty, 2004).

In the 1960s, U.S. interest in zombies returned, expressing fears about cultural and political shifts. A host of social movements challenged the United States' wars in Asia, and domestic U.S. racism, sexism, and other forms of oppression. During this period, Islam rapidly gained visibility in the United States, particularly among African Americans disaffected with the White Supremacy of many Christian churches and the integrationist goals of the civil rights movement (McAlister, 2001). The Nation of Islam "defined Islam as the religion of black American militancy," and bolstered what had been a waning anticolonial analysis of both the United States' foreign policy and its colonialist policies toward its own People of Color (McAlister, 2001, p. 91). Mainstream White media reported heavily on the rise of Black Islam; prominent Black Muslims like Malcolm X, Mohammed Ali, and Amiri Baraka aroused White fears of a racial revolution linked to the anticolonial revolutions in Africa, Asia, and the Middle East (McAlister, 2001). In this cultural environment of White fear of another anticolonial, Black, non–Christian revolution, zombies returned.

In 1968, George Romero touched a nerve with his low-budget, black-and-white film, *Night of the Living Dead* (*NOTLD*). Romero's film re-imagined and resurrected the zombie genre. Romero noted that he "ripped off" the idea from Richard Matheson's 1956 novel, *I Am Legend* (Wolfe, 2008). Matheson played on White fears of global revolution and of domestic racial desegregation, using the metaphor of a global pandemic that turned people into vampires.[3] Romero explained that he imagined *NOTLD* as "a parable about revolutionary society coming in and swallowing up the old — in this case literally" (Breznican, 2003). Since *NOTLD*, Romero's re-imagining of zombies has steered the zombie genre and fed a renewed hunger for zombie stories (Paffenroth, 2006, p. 1). Between 1940 and 1968, zombie movies in the U.S. numbered fewer than forty. In the years between *Night of the Living Dead* and September 11, 2001, there were more than two hundred.

"Muslim Rage," 9/11, and the Angry Zombie

In 2001, zombies underwent another change: they got angry. The popular British film *28 Days Later* (2001) was one of the first to re-imagine zombies as fast and angry, a change that has since taken hold in the zombie genre. These zombies are fast, rather than slow; living rather than undead. Infected with a virus, they are motivated by uncontrollable, animalistic rage. *28 Days Later* opens with a monkey strapped to a laboratory table, forced to watch televisions showing angry, rioting Arab mobs that are fighting police, burning cars, waving guns, and beating each other. When accidentally released, the monkey infects humans with an epidemic of rage. If rage is strictly a virus, a biological agent, there's little reason for the opening scene. However, the scene might suggest that the experimenters are presenting Arabs as models from whom the monkey *learns* rage.[4] Zombie scholar Peter Dendle says,

> The zombie has become enraged, feral, frantic, and insatiable: it is a gutted, animalistic core of hunger and fury.... [It's] the lack of control, dignity, direction that scares us. [It] embodies a wanton, unfettered pursuit of immediate physical cravings, a fear of raw power [Dendle, 2007, p. 54].

I believe that this shift toward imagining zombies as motivated by rage is, in part, influenced by contemporary Orientalism. Said observed that popular culture had also revised its representation of Orientalized Islam, with Hollywood films stripping away old ideas of "romance and charm," leaving only "a monolithic, enraged, threatening, and conspiratorially spreading Islam [which would be] more useful and capable of generating more excitement, whether for purposes of entertainment or mobilizing passions against a new foreign devil" (Said, [1981] 1997, pp. xxvii–xxviii).

Recent conservative political theorists have also re-imagined Orientalized Islam as implacably angry. In September 1990, just after the U.S. invaded Iraq, *The Atlantic Monthly* published Bernard Lewis's article, "The Roots of Muslim Rage" (Lewis, [1990] 2001). Lewis proposed that Islamic Fundamentalists hate the U.S., not because of Western sexism, racism, or imperialism — instead, they hate the U.S. because of "a feeling of humiliation — a growing awareness, among the heirs of an old, proud, and long dominant civilization, of having been overtaken, overborne, and overwhelmed by those whom they regarded as their inferiors" (Lewis, [1990] 2001, p. 25). Lewis suggested that Muslims mistakenly believe themselves to be superior to the West — and are enraged and humiliated that the West has forced them to recognize their own inferiority, through military, economic, and cultural domination. According to Lewis, Islamic fundamentalism (which he leaves undefined) has given shape and direction to Muslim's "otherwise aimless and formless resentment and anger" at the West, mobilizing Muslims for a war against secularism and modernism: a "clash of civilizations" (Lewis, [1990] 2001, pp. 24, 26).

Lewis's "clash of civilizations" thesis influenced other conservative theorists and public discourse about the Middle East and Latin America. In 1993, Samuel Huntington took up the thesis in "The Clash of Civilizations?," arguing that Islamic and Confucian (i.e., Chinese) civilizations would become the West's new enemies, taking the place of its Cold War antagonists (Huntington, 1993; Jhally, 1997). In 1996, Huntington expanded on his ideas in *The Clash of Civilizations and the Remaking of World Order*. Huntington repurposed Lewis's discussion of the Christian "Reconquista" of Muslim parts of Europe, warning that Mexicans threatened a "reconquista" of U.S. territory via immigration. Thus, fears about Muslims and fears about Mexicans may be partly linked by Orientalist fear of an inverted "reconquista" of lands that the White West has claimed for itself. In Romero's *Land of the Dead* (2005), humans' looting incursions into a zombie town provoke zombie retaliation. The zombies wade across a large river separating the zombie town from the human city, evoking Mexican "wetbacks" crossing the Rio Grande into Texas. The zombies break down the border's fences and attack the humans, toppling the corrupt oligarchy that rules the human city. The zombies' attack is reminiscent of a sign seen at rallies supporting immigrants' rights: "We are here because you were there." This fear of a "reconquista" has also been repeated and amplified by conservative propaganda films, such as *Obsession: Radical Islam's War Against the West* (2005).

Concluding *The Roots of Muslim Rage*, Lewis argues that through a "legacy of sectarian violence," the West has come to value the separation of church and state (Lewis, 1990/2001, p. 24). Muslims, Lewis proposed, have not learned to value the separation of church and state because they have not experienced comparable "sectarian violence." Without the separation of church and state, Lewis suggests, Muslim theocracies deaden Muslims' minds, turning them into mindless, earthly beings, enraged at secularism and modernity. Lewis' Orientalist characterization of Muslims is not so different, then, from the characterization of modern zombies. The modern zombie embodies Orientalist fears of violent Islamic (and perhaps soon, Chinese) threats to modern, secular (read: Western) society. In a recreational form, the modern zombie genre rehearses *many* of the Orientalist tropes that are also painted onto Muslims.

The generic conventions of zombie stories are suffused with Orientalist notions of the Other. By using conventions that tap popular fears of the Oriental, zombie stories draw popular interest. Through fantasy and metaphor, zombie stories offer audiences an opportunity to indulge in these Orientalist narratives without having to recognize the connection to real-life fears of a current Orientalized villain: Muslims. To explore this idea, I will examine the Orientalist nature of several conventions of the zombie genre.

As with any genre, contemporary zombie stories have particular generic conventions, which may be obeyed, bent, or broken for effect. During the early stages of a zombie outbreak, most people do not realize or refuse to accept the grave nature of the threat, as many zombies bear an uncanny resemblance to humans. With the element of surprise on their side, zombies frequently ambush humans, even once their threat is known. The zombies quickly multiply in number and tear through humanity in ever-increasing hordes. Zombies reveal the corruption and ineffectiveness of modern society, with pillars such as government, corporations, media, and religion failing to protect citizens — or even being revealed as complicit in creating zombies. Without institutional protection, protagonists find one another and form small, motley bands that must learn to work together or die horribly. Soon, the protagonists realize that the zombie apocalypse has destroyed civilization as they know it; they are on their own. All the while, the zombies consume the flesh of humanity, turning lovers and family members into inhuman menaces. Any misguided humans who try to reason with or cure the zombies die horribly and join the zombie horde. Most protagonists come to accept that, regardless of who a zombie once was, all zombies must be destroyed without mercy. In the face of such overwhelming hostility, the protagonists realize that they must make difficult choices, sometimes sacrificing now-outdated morality in the name of survival. Soon, weak links begin to endanger the group; human frailties become lethal. Protagonists learn that, should they falter, a fate worse than death awaits them: zombification. Ultimately, the group realizes that they must leave wherever they are and strike out for the tenuous safety of new frontiers. I suggest that each of these generic conventions tap Orientalist ideas and fears.

Uncanny Monsters and "Hidden Muslims"

During their initial attack, zombies are enabled by their resemblance to humans. Often, early victims are bitten because they do not recognize the nature of the zombie threat (Paffenroth, 2006). Zombie films horrify, in part, because audiences realize and anticipate the danger prior to the protagonists. Zombie films suggest that if humanity had more quickly recognized the zombies for what they were, much of the subsequent catastrophe could have been prevented. Brian Keene, author of numerous zombie novels and stories, linked zombies to Islamophobia, saying, "What I wanted to capture [was] that your wife, your child, your best friend, your pastor, whomever, could suddenly become one of those things.... It's the xenophobia. Americans don't trust Muslims, and Muslims don't trust the West. Everybody is paranoid" (St. John, 2006). *Shaun of the Dead* (2004) paid comic homage to this convention with two slacker-heroes who are so oblivious that they repeatedly mistake zombies for humans. Only when zombies literally invade their backyard do they recognize the danger. A *New York Times* journalist suggested, "The fear that anyone could be a suicide bomber or a hijacker parallels a common trope of zombie films, in which healthy people are zombified by contact with other zombies and become killers" (St. John, 2006). *Flight of the Living Dead* (2007) conjured a zombified version of the 9/11 terrorist attacks. In the film, zombies hijack a commercial airplane in-flight. The pilot makes the fatal mistake of allowing his infected copilot back into the cockpit; the zombified copilot kills him, giving the zombies control of the plane.

Zombies' uncanny resemblance to humans resonates with contemporary Orientalist fears of Muslim terrorism infiltrating the West. In November 2001, the story of John Walker

Lindh fascinated the U.S. media. Lindh, a middle-class White youth from California, was captured by U.S. forces in Afghanistan while fighting on the side of the Taliban. Pundits and the public wondered how a White kid from Marin could wind up a militant Muslim fighting against U.S. forces. Since then, criminal drama television programs have popularized this story, investigating "American Taliban" villains — low-level terrorist agents who are White and American-born, who play on their White privilege to deceive other Whites and perpetrate terrorism.[5] Right-wing propagandists have cautioned against Islam's "infiltration" into Western society (Kopping, 2004). In 2008, CIA Director Michael Hayden reported that Al Qaeda is training fighters who "look western" and could infiltrate the U.S. without attracting attention (Bull, 2008). This was also the plot of the television show *Sleeper Cell* (2005–2006) and the film *Traitor* (2008).

Huntington proposed that Muslim masses were conflicted about the West, both resenting its supposed superiority and comically attempting to ape Western ways (Huntington, 1993, p. 27). I suggest that zombie movies express anxieties about the lower-class racial Other trying (and failing) to take on American values. The Other attempts to mimic the West, which is both comical and threatening (Semmerling, 2006). Comical because the Other is constructed as essentially non–Western and therefore its efforts to be Western will fail. And threatening because the Westernization of the non–Western not only means the possibility of infiltration by non–Westerners who are superficially Western, it also casts suspicion on all Westerners *and* it calls into question the validity of the Western/non–Western distinction.

The fear that any person, even a White person, could be a Muslim terrorist (or zombie) disrupts assumptions about racial loyalty — whether loyalty to White Christianity or to its frequent proxy in fiction, "humanity." People who are supposed, because of their Whiteness, to be trustworthy, may in fact be "infected" and concealing their infection. Conservative suspicions that then-presidential candidate Barack Obama might be a "secret Muslim [or Arab]" bent on overthrowing the United States (Rutenberg, 2008), also show the Orientalist fear of Muslim infiltration into the nation. Like "American Taliban"/"American Al Qaeda" villains, the uncanny resemblance of zombies to humans not only allows them to close in on their victims, it also compels (White) people to interrogate the validity of *every* person's loyalties and "humanity."[6]

Sneak Attacks and Hordes

Zombies often surprise the protagonists and all of Western society by their swift rise and senseless assault on America, a "sneak attack" by a previously unknown enemy. Max Brooks, author of the popular *Zombie Survival Guide*, said, "I think there's also something very American about [a fear of] being attacked when you're minding your own business" (Earl, 2006). Following the 9/11 attacks, the U.S. wondered aloud in many media, not only how the attacks could have happened, but also, "Why do they hate us?" with little understanding of the businesses that the U.S. had been minding in the Middle East. The United States has repeatedly garnered public support for its wars by stirring outrage about supposed sneak attacks. The alleged sneak attack against the USS *Maine* was used as justification for beginning the Spanish-American war. The Japanese sneak attack on Pearl Harbor mobilized American support for entering World War II, drawing on anti–Asian racism and a longstanding narrative about Indians sneak-attacking frontiersmen (MacDougall, 1999). The alleged sneak attack by North Vietnamese torpedo boats against the USS *Maddox*, which the U.S. falsely claimed to have been in international waters in the Gulf of Tonkin, was used as justification for war against Vietnam. And Al Qaeda's sneak attacks on September 11, 2001, were used to justify invading both Afghanistan and Iraq. Each case draws on a deep-seated cultural narrative about war and sneak attacks.

The generic U.S.-American "war story" can be summarized as follows: The White U.S.-American male works to civilize the frontier for settlement. Suddenly, a horde of savage non–Whites, opposed to White civilization, ambush them with a deadly sneak attack. The non–Whites commit atrocities, forcing the settlers to match their barbarism.

> The war story, therefore, portrays the savages as aggressors emerging from the land, and the American man as having the right to react and set out deep into the wilderness on a vengeful, yet defensive and civilizing, campaign against them. The frontiersman is known to set out alone or in a small band of brothers. The difference in numbers between the Americans and the savages is important to the narrative because it casts the American role as defensive [Semmerling, 2006, p. 126].

Like other Orientalized enemies, zombies, too, are a horde of Others, who literally emerge from the land to sneak attack peaceful suburbs, committing savage atrocities, forcing humans to resort to savage acts while under siege, outnumbering the heroes, and warranting a "defensive" genocide. Against a zombie enemy, the West can feel justified in ruthless extermination, in self-defense.

A lone zombie isn't particularly threatening. They tend to be "completely imbecilic, incapable of making plans, coordinating their attacks, or learning from their mistakes" (Paffenroth, 2006, p. 6). Yet, zombies pose a threat, in part, because of their overwhelming numbers. It's common to see even the strongest humans being dragged down by a horde of zombies. These scenes evoke older narratives of Oriental hordes surging over and devouring the West. Hoppenstand argues, "the first characteristic of the yellow peril stereotype [is] the belief that Orientals are part of a great, undifferentiated horde that robs non–Orientals of economic resources" (Hoppenstand, 1992, p. 281). Racist ideas of a Yellow Horde were later transferred onto Orientalized Communists, particularly after China broke with the other Allies of World War II and moved toward Communism: "Racial and ethnic prejudices that had informed American attitudes for centuries would still be used to demonize the nation's foes, particularly after China joined the Communist world in 1949 and reassumed the mantle of America's Yellow Peril" (MacDougall, 1999, p. 72). Sounding a similar alarm, Huntington (1993) warned that the Arab Muslim population was growing and spreading into Western Europe, bringing with it its hostility and alien values. Likewise, U.S. films have often portrayed Arabs as inept and incompetent, yet dangerous due to their numbers and resources (Jhally, 2006). *Rules of Engagement* (2000) featured several "horde" scenes, including one of a mob of Arab Muslims surrounding the White protagonist, attempting to drag him down. Another scene featured a horde of heavily armed Muslim protestors — men, women and young children — surrounding and shooting at a U.S. embassy. The threat of the horde helps explain why a supposedly stupid, weak enemy is a lethal threat: the Oriental/zombie is not superior — that wouldn't make sense within the logic of Orientalism — but, the Oriental/zombie has superior numbers.

Revealing the Oriental Rot Within

Zombies reveal ways that American society has already strayed from its ideals and let Oriental rot take hold within (Paffenroth, 2006). In films ranging from *Dawn of the Dead* (1978) to *28 Days Later* (2001), the government, corporations, media, science and religion are all shown to be corrupt and ineffective in the face of the zombie enemy (Paffenroth, 2006). As the zombies spread, governmental agencies and corporations often disintegrate or abscond to well-stocked hiding places (Paffenroth, 2006). Beyond gross negligence or incompetence, governments and corporations are often *complicit* in creating the zombie menace (Paffenroth, 2006; Williams, 2003). Yet, from a practical standpoint, such complicity is often a moot point to those struggling to survive. Those responsible are generally beyond accountability or the reach of the protagonists — the question "Why?" is overwhelmed by the question of *how to survive* (Bishop, 2006; Paffenroth, 2006). Storytellers use zombies to critique the ways that real social ills (e.g., racism, sexism, capitalism, militarism) weaken society from within, making itself "easy prey for barbarian hordes" (Paffenroth, pp. 17–18). Zombies are apocalyptic in the original meaning of the word: "they 'reveal' terrible truths about human nature, existence, and sin" (Paffenroth, p. 13).

Zombie stories represent popular anxiety that government and corporations are elitist and not looking out for the public's welfare. Following 9/11, many people in the U.S. wondered how the government could have failed them so catastrophically. U.S. media compared the 9/11 attacks to the 1941 Japanese attack on Pearl Harbor. But, few noted that high-level United States officials may have had advance warning about Pearl Harbor and used the attack to galvanize popular support for entering World War II (Stinnett, 1999; Tansill, 1975; Victor, 2007). Similar questions have arisen regarding the United States government officials' foreknowledge of the 9/11 attacks (Bamford, 2004). Regardless of whether such claims are true, their existence and currency speaks to public mistrust of government and large institutions. The Bush Administration *did* use 9/11 to justify implementing pre-existing plans to increase U.S. military presence in the Middle East, including the second U.S. war on Iraq (Earp and Jhally, 2006). Further, the United States *had* helped create and support the Taliban and other Muslim insurgent (now "terrorist") groups during the Cold War, to counter Soviet influence in the Middle East (Chomsky, 2001). As the United States continues its years-long wars in Afghanistan and Iraq, the public may sense that the U.S.'s military may be ill-suited for the types of combat it faces. Max Brooks alludes to this "asymmetric" warfare in his fictional oral history, *World War Z: An Oral History of the Zombie War* — the zombies deal an early and crushing blow to the overconfident U.S. military, which quickly discovers that jet fighters and tanks are near-useless in halting their enemy's advance (Brooks, 2006, p. 92). Similarly, Joss Whedon's Star-Wars-meets-rage-zombies film, *Serenity* (2005), imagined a galactic empire inadvertently creating ultraviolent space-zombies through its attempts to impose a *Pax Americana* on space-frontier settlers. Zombies, then, tap public mistrust of a rotted system that callously endangers the masses.

I suggest that zombie stories express racialized class anxieties about being caught between ruthless elites and underclass hordes. Because of elites' complicity in the zombie menace, the protagonists of zombie stories are usually "everyday people": working-class and middle-class White people, with a few token People of Color (Bishop, 2006). *Shaun of the Dead* spoofed this "everyman" theme in a scene where the protagonists encounter another group of survivors who are their mirror images, down to the shlubby group-member who mumbles a hello while texting a friend.

Apocalyptic Threats

Once the zombie menace begins to spread, chaos quickly follows. Zombies are an apocalyptic threat, ending civilization as we know it (Bishop, 2006; Paffenroth, 2006). Zombies evoke a nightmarish version of Christian myths: the dead rise, but signal humanity's damnation, rather than its salvation (Paffenroth). Although zombies are a global menace, the civilizations that stories depict them ending are almost always modern and Western (Paffenroth). Post-9/11, some zombie movies have adopted imagery from the chaotic aftermath of the attacks. Early in *28 Days Later* (2001), the protagonist, Jim, spends several minutes of screen time wandering the empty, debris-strewn streets of London. At one point, he discovers a fountain-turned-bulletin board, reminiscent of those seen in post–9/11 New York City, complete with family members posting photos and messages asking about missing loved ones or announcing the locations to which they have fled. A similar scene ends *Resident Evil* (2002), with the protagonist, Alice, waking in an abandoned hospital to find a devastated, seemingly empty city that is strewn with the destroyed vehicles of police, emergency, fire, and media. *Resident Evil: Extinction* (2007) depicts Las Vegas as a shattered, empty city overtaken by desert sands. The film also shows a digital image of the zombie infection spreading over the globe like a bloodstain. This visual closely resembles one used in the anti–Muslim propaganda film, *Obsession: Radical Islam's War Against the West*, which showed a global map with red blotches seeping like blood across the world, implying the spread of Muslim terrorist attacks. The image evokes Huntington's often quoted assertion, "Islam has bloody borders" (Huntington, 1993; Krauthammer, 2002; Steinberger and Huntington, 2001)

The Oriental has often been imagined as an apocalyptic threat to Western civilization. In Yellow Peril stories about Asians, the Oriental frequently threatens to conquer the West (Hoppenstand, 1992). As Oriental figures, Arabs and Muslims have been objects of apocalyptic fears in the past. In 1973–1974, the Organization of Arab Petroleum Exporting Countries (OAPEC) limited oil exports to the United States for six months, in response to U.S. support for Israel in the 1973 Yom Kippur War. In response, *Time* magazine published a speculative article imagining a near future in which the rise of Arab/OPEC power collapses the U.S. (*Time*, 1973).

> It is an account that was constructed to inspire fear and ire in Americans and to cultivate the roots of an "evil" Arab character. [It imagined] a man having to resort to making gasoline from wood, leaves, brush, and garbage; Christmas lights being fewer and dimmer; carillon bells at churches cut off; gasoline ration cards imagined to be in the works; town meetings being conducted by candlelight; a professor teaching class in a raccoon coat; women buying long johns; people resorting to attending shelters for heated living ... motorists waiting and fighting amongst themselves in endless lines for gasoline.... The Arabs, in contrast, were show as laughing, gloating, unified, plotting, and powerful enough to push America backward in the modern industrial period that it worked so hard to achieve. A kind of siege mentality was taking hold of America [Semmerling, 2006, p. 16].

In 1976, the Oscar-winning film *Network* starred a news anchor who exposes a secret Saudi Arabian plan to buy out a massive American television network and mobilizes mass audience protests with the now famous cry, "I'm as mad as hell and I'm not going to take it anymore!" Huntington (1993) later warned that the West's power had peaked, while other civilizations, including Muslim civilization, were rising. The West, he said, would need to unify itself and use its military and economic power to hold back the shifting tide.

Fears of the Oriental pushing U.S. civilization backwards resonate with the common images of social collapse seen in zombie films. We also see familiar themes of the degradation of transportation, religion, gender, class, and even civility and solidarity, as desperation and a siege mentality sets in. Peter Dendle connected the current popularity of zombies to fears of Islamic terrorism,

It is not without some justice, then, that the resurgence of zombie movie popularity in the early 2000s has been linked with the events of September 11, 2001. ... The possibility of wide-scale destruction and devastation, which 9–11 brought once again into the communal consciousness, found a ready narrative expression in the zombie apocalypses, which over thirty years had honed images of desperation, subsistence and amoral survivalism to a fine edge [Dendle, 2007, p. 54].

The zombie metaphor also taps economic fears about Orientalized peoples.

All-Consuming Oriental Appetites

The voracious zombie appetite alludes to fears of Oriental consumers of economic resources. Zombies are monsters who consume and consume and are never satisfied — yet nor can they make good use of what they consume. Zombies eat because it's their nature, not because they need sustenance. In this way, they resemble Orientalist stereotypes about oil-rich Arabs. Jack Shaheen observed that, during the 1970s, movies frequently portrayed super-rich Arabs "too rich and stupid to know the value of money," descending to consume massive chunks of the United States' property (Jhally, 2006). The historical representation of the Oriental as a gluttonous consumer is tied to past economic necessities (McAlister, 2001). In the 1890s, the United States reached an economic turning point: its productive capacities began to exceed its domestic consumer market. The United States set out to increase domestic and foreign consumption of its products. Internationally, the U.S. searched for foreign consumers, constructing the Oriental as the lazy consumer contrasting the West's role as producer with its Protestant work ethic (McAlister, 2001). On the home front, the U.S. fought an uphill cultural battle against its own citizens, trying to convince them that increased consumption could be reconciled with their Western self-concept as hard-working producers (McAlister, 2001). To advance this project, "shopping in particular became linked to the exotic pleasures of the Orient, which allowed the new discourse of commodity culture to simultaneously praise the practice of indulgence and disavow it, by linking it to foreignness" (McAlister, 2001, p. 22). So, while Romero's *Dawn of the Dead* (1974) is often read as a critique of U.S. consumerism, McAlister suggests that the U.S. has constructed consumerism *as* Oriental and it is deeply disturbed by consumerism's Orientalizing effects on Western culture. Zombies' voracious consumption resonates with the fear that American society has been infected by an Orientalist disease and has decayed from a robust producer into a monstrous consumer. In creating a domestic market for surplus goods, U.S. corporations encouraged Americans to consume in ways attributed to Orientalized consumers. In doing so, they created a monster: a U.S. culture of consumption that inverted the previous trade imbalance. The United States is no longer the Western producer to China's Oriental consumer; instead, the United States voraciously consumes Chinese goods, becoming further and further indebted to China. Thus, the supposedly Oriental disease of consumerism, attributed to Asians, has infected U.S. society, turning a healthy host into a mindless, hollowed-out monster with an insatiable appetite. This Orientalist narrative underlies Romero's critique of U.S. consumerism in *Dawn of the Dead* (1974). Zombies and their appetites stand in for the Oriental and those Westerners infected by Oriental ways. Zombies' appetites caution viewers against becoming infected by Oriental appetites. Orientalist stories warn of the Oriental's sexual appetites, as well as its material appetites.

Flesh and Blood: Anxieties About Race, Sex, and Family

Zombies' appetite for human flesh symbolizes more than just gluttonous consumption. Flesh may also symbolize sexuality, particularly White women's sexuality. As perversions of humanity, zombies' lust for flesh is also perverse. Zombies are asexual, unable to reproduce sexually; instead, they rely on converting others through infection (Paffenroth, 2006, p. 13). This asexual-yet-sexual threat resembles paradoxical Orientalist Yellow Peril stereotypes of Asian men: asexual, yet also seeking to reproduce "unnaturally" (i.e., interracially), thus threatening White womanhood and White racial purity through miscegenation. Orientalism imagines the Other as perversely lusting for White, Western women. Dong noted, "One of the most potent aspects of the Yellow Peril discourse in American popular culture is the predatory sexual desire from the yellow race that endangers white womanhood and consequently threatens the racial purity of white American society" (Dong, 2008, p. 129). As Hoppenstand pointed out,

> [T]he yellow peril stereotype easily became incorporated into Christian mythology, and the Oriental assumed the role of the devil or demon. The Oriental rape of the white woman signified a spiritual damnation for the woman, and at the larger level, white society. A favorite convention of the yellow peril featured the lone white woman surrounded by a horde of Chinese bent on debauchment. She holds them at bay with a revolver, and that revolver has only a single bullet left. Seeing that her situation is hopeless, she points the barrel of the gun to her temple ... [Hoppenstand, 1992, p. 280].

Resident Evil: Apocalypse (2004) replayed this Orientalist scenario, with zombies standing in for the lecherous Oriental. A terrified White woman flees up a stairwell, to the roof of a high-rise building. A heroic soldier leaps out of a helicopter, shooting the zombies down as he falls. But, he's too late — she's been bitten. As he tries to coax her off the ledge, she trembles, "I've seen what happens once you've been bitten. There's no going back!" and then leaps off the roof to her death. The scene reiterates the idea that White women should choose suicide over racial pollution — and that White men are justified in acts of homicide or genocide in protection of White racial purity.[7] Likewise, the "lecherous Arab" who preys on White women is a common stereotype (Jhally, 2006; Shaheen, 2003, p. 19). *Taken* (2008) abhorrently exemplifies the trope: Albanian Muslims (some of whom pass as White) kidnap young White women tourists in Europe, then sell them to Arab Muslim slavers.[8] Liam Neeson plays the White hero who kills his way through scores of Muslims, finally rescuing his White daughter from the clutches of an obscenely wealthy and fat Arab sheik, narrowly preventing the sheik from raping her. When the sheik attempts desperately to negotiate at knifepoint, Neeson kills him with a shot to the head. The movie evokes current and historical myths about "White slavery," which are shot through with nationalist and racist fears (Doezema, 2000). *Shaun of the Dead* (2004) played more lightly with the interracial subtext constructing a daytime talk show clip, in which a White British woman with a lower-class accent defends her relationship with her zombie husband. The host, disgusted and incredulous, asks, "You go to *bed* with it?" Extending from fears about romantic/sexual relationships, zombie stories also speak to fears about pollution of familial relationships and racial purity.

Zombie stories often tap anxieties about the pollution of romantic and familial relationships. In virtually every zombie story, at least one member of the group will be bitten and infected. Often, the infected person is someone's romantic partner or family member, posing a moral dilemma (Bishop, 2006). Killing a human who's not yet a zombie seems immoral, yet failing to do so will lead to trouble later when that person becomes a zombie, attacks the group and must then be dispatched with violence.

In many films, a person's inability to accept that their infected intimate is no longer "one of us" leads to grisly deaths, sometimes their own, at that intimate's zombified hands. *Dawn of the Dead* (2004) proposed a particularly elaborate case: the interracial relationship between Luda and Andre. Luda is a White immigrant from Russia, pregnant with Andre's child. Andre is a young Black man with a criminal past, desperate to become the father he never had to the family he never had. Together, they conceal the fact that Luda has been bitten. Both literally and figuratively, Luda is racially contaminated: her Whiteness contaminated by her sexual relationship with Andre, evidenced by her miscegenated pregnancy; her humanity contaminated by a zombie's metaphorically sexual bite, from which Andre could not protect her. Andre, driven by guilt and his own hunger for a normal (i.e., White, middle-class) family life, is determined to protect is family, no matter how contaminated or dangerous it may be. As Luda begins turning into a zombie, Andre sequesters her in an abandoned maternity store, to nurse/imprison her until she gives birth. Eventually, the zombified Luda gives birth to a grotesque zombie-baby. When Andre is found out, he makes the "wrong" choice: he chooses family instead of his own race/humanity. To protect his zombie wife and child, Andre shoots one of his fellow survivors and is himself killed. The remaining survivors are left to carry out the task that Andre failed: shooting his zombie wife and their horrific zombie infant.[9]

Zombie stories relate to real-life concerns about the pollution of Whiteness, of family, and of national identity. In zombie movies, the survivors become fictive kin, a family defined by a common enemy and a common race (this time, the human race). This fictive, racial-familial relationship takes priority over actual familial or romantic ties. U.S. racial discourse frames family in racial terms and race in familial terms: a "normal" family should be racially homogeneous and a racial group should treat in-group members as family (DaCosta, 2007). Zombies frequently disrupt the supposed racial homogeneity of the family. In a zombie apocalypse, people must recognize that the only race that matters (here, the human race) must become one's new family, superceding other familial ties. Further, in post–World War II U.S. discourse, "the family" is a key part of national identity; family is understood as a fundamental building-block of the nation, with the imperiled family serving as a metonym of the imperiled nation (McAlister, 2001). Zombies draw on past stories of Orientalist threats to the racial homogeneity and safety of the family, with casts that include Native Americans, opium-pushing Chinese Americans, Arab slavers, and, in cases like *I Married a Communist* (1949), Soviet Communists. But, these zombie threats to family also resonate with recent post–9/11 stories. Google-searching "I married a terrorist," turns up news stories of White Christian women who have married men who secretly are Muslim terrorists (Cruikshank, 2008; Ross and Scott, 2004; Schou, 2007). In the case of John Walker Lindh, the White "American Taliban," Lindh's family was vilified and called on to disavow their son who had — "infected" by Islam — betrayed his race, religion, and nation. Like zombies, the Oriental threatens to infect or disrupt family, forcing family members to choose between familial and racial/religious/national loyalties.

Justifying Genocide

In most zombie films, there's no talking to a zombie, no possibility of dialogue. With few notable exceptions, zombies don't speak — though they may moan, grunt, or roar. Imagining the Oriental as unintelligible is a key part of maintaining emotional distance and dehumanizing the Other. Huntington suggested that cultural differences make it less than "virtually impossible" for a Westerner to "carry on an intellectual debate" with Muslims (Huntington, 1993, p. 45). Ideas about cultural incompatibility also extend to ideas about language. The unintelligibility and humorousness of Arabic is a common theme in United States cinema — exemplified by *Team America: World Police* (2004), made by *South Park's* creators, in which all Arabs speak in gibberish consisting mostly of "durka durka," interspersed with "Allah," "Mohammed," and "jihad" (Shaheen, 2008). On a more literal level, after 9/11, the U.S. military was at a loss to communicate with its "Axis of Evil" enemies, having purged twenty Arabic language specialists, eighteen Korean language specialists, and four Farsi language specialists between 1998 and 2003, for coming out as gay, violating the "Don't Ask, Don't Tell" policy (Murdock, 2005). Try as you might, there's no talking to a zombie.

Even in the few cases when zombies can communicate, its little consolation; the general message is simple: "Let us eat you." Such is the case in the *Return of the Living Dead* franchise, wherein a zombie impersonates a paramedic, using an ambulance radio to tell a dispatcher to "send more paramedics." Reporting on an interview with author Max Brooks, one journalist noted, "You can't bargain with them, because they will eat you. You can't form a pact with them, because they will eat you" (Earls, 2006). Zombies' actions speak louder than any words could (Bishop, 2006). In fact, communicating with zombies might allow them to deceive us. Grace Lee's mockumentary, *American Zombie* (2007), poses the possibility of high-functioning zombies who are struggling to gain civil rights in Los Angeles. Zombie activists have formed the Zombie Activism Group (ZAG) and use the rhetoric of civil rights and oppression to advocate for themselves. However, the film reveals that, for all their civil rights rhetoric, the zombies really *are* plotting to overthrow and consume human (read: American) society. Disappointingly, *American Zombie* portrays conservative rhetoric that the Other does not deserve civil rights and will only use those ill-gotten rights to further their attempts to destroy society. Even when zombies can speak, they're not to be trusted.

Simultaneously, anti–Muslim popular culture has proposed that Muslims are not to be trusted or taken at their word. Films of the 1970s primed viewers to believe "the Arabs were rising up ... infiltrating the security of American lives ... real, powerful, evil, legion" (Semmerling, 2006, p. 58). Then, in 2001, the 9/11 attacks crystallized those sentiments:

> The fears of the 1970s of Middle East violence coming to America had finally been realized: the "evil" Arabs have arrived; they live among us and are funded with the wealth of the oil economy ... these Arabs use our principles of democracy and liberties to plot against us [Semmerling, 2006, p. 23].

In the anti–Muslim propaganda film, *Obsession: Radical Islam's War Against the West* (2004), Christian pundit Brigette Gabriel echoed this idea, saying, "They are using our laws against us. They are using our democracy against us. And they know it. They know exactly what they're doing." Mainstream commercial media have also picked up this story. For example, in an episode of the popular television show *Crime Scene Investigation: Miami*, "Backstabbers" (2006), a White Muslim terrorist suspect denounces the American judicial system, but then pleads the Fifth Amendment and threatens a constitutional lawsuit. The detective retorts, "So, you gentlemen despise our justice system ... until you need it." So, it seems, Western institutions such as due process or rights are not for everyone; the Oriental infiltrates and perverts Western institutions, turning them against the West.

Some zombie stories incorporate do-gooder characters that want to "understand" or "cure" the zombies, unable to accept that the enemy cannot be civilized, only destroyed. Such bleeding heart liberals are destroyed by their own folly, often taking others with them.[10] Christian missionaries cannot "civilize" the zombie (Bishop, 2008). Science cannot cure or control the zombie.[11] You cannot negotiate with a zombie. Save for a few exceptions, which I will explore later, it is their nature to kill the living and destroy civilization.

The Oriental is also often portrayed as verminous, bloodthirsty, suicidal killers bent on destroying civilization (Hoppenstand, 1992; Kopping, 2004; MacDougall, 1999). In imagined Oriental lands, nature and society are inverted; Western strength, individuality, and morality are weakened and overwhelmed by the weak, legion, immoral Oriental (Semmerling, 2006). Thus, attempts to Westernize Oriental lands would fail, strengthening "anti–Western political forces," rather than weakening them (Huntington, 1993, p. 32). Like zombies, Orientalized Asians, Arabs, and Muslims are portrayed as, "childlike, unfeeling automata, puny, incapable of any competencies worthy of notice, bent on world conquest, comical, inscrutable, uniquely treacherous, deranged, physiologically inferior, primitive, barbaric, and devoted to fanatical suicide charges" (Shay, 1994, p. 105). Drawing on this idea, Huntington echoed — perhaps unwittingly — a popular zombie trope,

> In class and ideological conflicts, the key question was "Which side are you on?" and people could and did choose sides and change sides. In conflicts between civilizations, the question is "What are you?" That is a given that cannot be changed. And as we know ... the wrong answer to that question can mean a bullet in the head [Huntington, 1993, p. 27].

Author Max Brooks said, "I think the idea of going up against an enemy with no common ground, no chance of negotiation, that shakes us to our core.... There's no reasoning with them. It's like trying to negotiate with a disease" (Earl, 2006). Coexistence is not an option.

Faced by such implacable, overwhelming enemies, any amount of violence seems justifiable — even genocide. Zombie movies justify all manner of violence. Zombies are frequently destroyed *en masse* with machineguns, armored vehicles, helicopter rotors, missiles, firebombs, and even nuclear weapons.[12] Likewise, the Oriental is often depicted as understanding only violence (Jhally, 1998; Said, [1981] 1997). Said observed, "many films end up with huge numbers of bodies, Muslim bodies strewn all over the place.... So the idea of Islam is something to be stamped out" (Jhally, 1998). In an infamous example, *Rules of Engagement* (2000) climaxes with the justification of a U.S. military officer who orders the indiscriminate slaughter of a crowd of angry Arabs. Zombies seem particularly suited as an Orientalist metaphor for non–White enemies — a fanatical, depersonalized horde requiring extermination.

"Fresh Starts" and "New Frontiers"

As Orientalist nightmares, zombie movies tend to be pessimistic about our current civilization's future and at best cautiously optimistic about the protagonists' futures. Few stories imagine humans regaining control from the zombies. Eventually, survivors must abandon the ruins of their failed civilization, now ruled by zombies, and strike out toward remote areas as pioneers who will build a new society (Williams, 2003). Zombie stories replicate key aspects of the U.S. American frontier narrative, with harried heroes abandoning corrupt and decadent societies to start new civilizations in supposedly empty lands, from which they'll clear away the savage Orientals who ineptly occupy — but do not deserve or shepherd — the land (Semmerling, 2006). In this way, zombie stories express a historical U.S.-American hope for the future.

The current period is not the first time the United States has worried about the collapse of Western civilization. In the 1890s, prominent U.S. historians worried about the eventual end of American democracy: "With 'the close of the frontier' and the rapidly expanding populations of U.S. cities, white Americans were increasingly anxious about what would happen without new territories to settle" (McAlister, 2001, p. 20). In that period, the United States also took interest in the "Orient," as a new frontier into which the U.S. could continue expanding (McAlister, 2001). Today, Western society is again searching for new frontiers to conquer and imagines the Middle East as a new version of the Wild West, complete with savage hordes waiting in ambush (McAlister, 2001). At the same time, the United States is rife with anxieties about its own internal rot — and zombies serve to clear away the rot of the old society, re-creating a mythic wilderness in which the Western hero can again carve out a civilization, but within the nation's boundaries. In true Orientalist fashion, zombie stories project onto an imaginary monster the West's own rapaciousness for land and capital. If the West *is* the zombie of its own imagination, we might say, "When there is no more room in *the West*, White Westerners will walk the Earth."

As the U.S. struggles in its "Great Recession" (Rampell, 2009), and economic and racist anxieties increase, I worry that popular interest in Orientalist zombie stories will continue. This may contribute to public acceptance of even more violent strategies for dealing with Orientalized enemies. The zombie is a flexible villain. Currently, zombies stand in for Orientalized Islam, racialized and religion-ized terrorism — but they may also serve well as metaphor for U.S. fears about the resurging Chinese economy.

Although it's possible to interpret zombies as a call to reflect and then address consumerism, Capitalist exploitation, or other social ills (Comaroff and Comaroff, 2002), audiences' interest in zombies seems less self-reflective and more anxious. Across the United States, zombie fans are massing, not to discuss how to change their spending patterns or working conditions, but to prepare for siege, social collapse, and adventures into new frontiers (Westhoff, 2007). Stories that challenge audiences' Orientalist assumptions about zombies may be met coolly. For example, test audiences demanded an alternate ending to the zombie-flavored remake of *I Am Legend* (2007). In the original ending, when the scientist-hero realizes that the zombie-mutants *do* have their own civilization and *do* have compassion for their own kind, he repents for his violence and his medical experiments on them. He releases the Alpha Female and, in return, the Alpha Male allows the hero to leave unharmed. However, test audiences gave this ending negative reviews, so the filmmakers shot an alternate ending, in which the hero does NOT recognize the zombies' right to exist, but instead martyrs himself as a suicide bomber, killing the invading zombies as well.[13] However, DVD versions did include the original ending, referring to it as "a controversial ending."

Live and Let (Living Dead) Live: Counternarratives

There are a few other zombie counternarratives that challenge Orientalist representations. Here, I will set aside stories that allow for one (or a few) sympathetic zombie that is the exception to the rule,[14] in favor of stories that re-imagine zombies as a group. Several movies do cast zombies as a metaphor for the economically exploited underclass and working class (Comaroff and Comaroff, 2002), even if they still vilify the zombies. In *Shaun of the*

Dead (2004), militarism and capitalism eventually subdue the zombie uprising, enslaving zombies in service industry jobs, which are depicted as so dehumanized that even a zombie could do them. Likewise, *Fido* (2006) and *Resident Evil: Extinction* (2007) both portray evil corporations attempting to tame zombies for use as slave laborers. *Land of the Dead* (2005) expanded this idea to one of class solidarity. In *Land of the Dead*, a hyper-capitalist human society's greed and corruption incurs the wrath of a neighboring town of zombies. The zombies, led by "Big Daddy," a Black working-class zombie, kill their way through the city until they consume the ruling-class villain, Kaufman. In the end, the working-class human hero, Riley, has the opportunity to shoot the zombies that are departing the city. However, instead, Riley orders his crew to stand down, saying, "They're just looking for a place to go, same as us." Big Daddy, leading the zombies away, looks toward Riley's crew, acknowledging them without attacking. Unlike other films, *Land of the Dead*, "was not about whether zombies would 'take over' the world, but rather about how, without the Kaufmans of the world trying to 'take over,' the world could be a place where both living and undead exist together in peace" (Paffenroth, 2006, p. 124). *Land of the Dead* proposed that the human working-class has more in common with the zombie underclass — which just wants to be left unmolested — than it does with the human ruling-class. This call for class solidarity, proposing that White working-class people have more in common with working-class Peoples of Color than they do with ruling-class Whites, is a common anti-racist tenet (Lipsitz, 1998). In a few zombie stories, coexistence *is* possible. And while there are exceptions within any genre, the anti–Orientalist nature of these exceptions make them noteworthy.

Zombie stories are popular because they resonate with pre-existing fears and narratives. I suggest that we can love zombie stories, but also need to understand, critique, and re-imagine the underlying Orientalist narrative. But, I predict that counternarratives like *Land of the Dead* or the original-ending *I Am Legend* will continue to be rare until we deal with the underlying political and economic concerns that mobilize Orientalist fears and stories (Said, [1979] 1994). Huntington himself predicted that governments and societies, "decreasingly able to mobilize support and form coalitions on the basis of ideology ... will increasingly attempt to mobilize support by appealing to common religion and civilization identity" (Huntington, 1993). The United States' corporate capitalism, economic dependence on militarism (Turse, 2008), and its addiction to oil (Klare, 2004) will continue to put it at odds with people around the world, encouraging the Orientalizing and demonizing of those people. And these Orientalist stories already contribute to violence against Orientalized People of Color in the U.S., as well as abroad (Raju and Kuar, 2008). Zombies and other Orientalist monsters will rise again and again, until we aim for the political and economic systems that motivate these prejudicial depictions of the Other.

NOTES

1. There are a few notable exceptions to this theme, which evoke a counter or variant theme: the zombie who retains his/her humanity and consciousness (if not his/her original identity) and who gives their loyalty to humans, not zombies. Examples include the comic book series *Toe Tags* (2005); *Xombie*, a web-cartoon that has spawned a comic book series and may soon yield a movie by a major studio; and *Star Trek: Voyager*, with Seven of Nine distinguishing herself from the zombie-esque Borg. But, even in their own narratives, these zombies are exceptional and tragic because of their inability to fit completely into either human or zombie worlds.

2. Respectively, examples include *White Zombie (1932), Undead (2003)* and *Slither* (2006), *28 Days Later* (2001), and George Romero's films.

3. Notably, when *I Am Legend* was remade as a film in 2007, the vampires were reimagined as zombies.

4. Ironically, the monkey might also stand in for the viewer. The movie suggests that the monkey learns violence and rage by watching Orientalized Arabs. At the same time, the audience learns rage and accepts violent behavior by watching the movie's monstrous metaphor for the same Orientalized people.

5. For examples, see *Law & Order: Criminal Intent* "The Pilgrim" (2002), *CSI: Miami* "Backstabbers," (2006), and *NCIS* "Tribes," (2008).

6. See Palumbo-Liu (1999) for more on White anxieties about non–Whites passing as Whites (and non-humans passing as humans).

7. Zombie movies normally suggest that men and women alike should choose suicide over infection/zombification. In real life, similar sentiments have been expressed about becoming Oriental. For example, in 1877, famous labor activist Denis Kearney said, "To an American, death is preferable to life on a par with the Chinese" (Chacón & Davis, 2006). However, U.S. racial policies and discourses have historically placed additional value (and restrictions) on White women's sexuality and reproductive labor, given its constructed role in the reproduction of Whiteness (Crenshaw, 2000; D'Emilio & Freedman, 1998; Doezema, 2000).

8. McAlister (2001) explains that the Oriental slaver is a common trope in U.S. film, particularly in U.S. Biblical epic films of the 1940s–1960s, where Romans or Egyptians stood in for contemporary Middle Eastern Arab enemies.

9. It seems that zombies, as a racial/religious metaphor, may conform to hypodescent (aka, the One-Drop Rule). The infant's parentage is complex and ambiguous. Racially, its father, Andre, is Black, and its mother, Luda, is White. However, in zombie terms, its "father" (which bit Luda) was a zombie and its mother was (at the time) human. But the movie is clear: the infant is not "half-human" and "half-zombie," it is all-zombie. Likewise, Huntington (1993) questioned the possibility of a person or civilization being half–Christian and half–Muslim. *Dawn of the Dead* leaves open the matter of whether the infant's literal racial identity would have been Multiracial Black and White — or "just Black"— zombie or not.

10. See *Resident Evil: Apocalypse* (2004) and *Diary of the Dead* (2007).

11. See *Day of the Dead* (1985), *Resident Evil: Extinction* (2007), and, again humorously, *Fido* (2006).

12. Respectively, see *28 Days Later* (2001), *Dawn of the Dead* (2004), *28 Weeks Later* (2007), *Land of the Dead* (2005), *Day of the Dead* 2 (2008), and *Resident Evil: Apocalypse* (2004).

13. Christopher Moreman (2008) notes how the strong Christian elements of the film actually work in opposition to Matheson's source text.

14. See *Fido* (2006), *Day of the Dead 2* (2008), *Xombie* (a flash cartoon and comic book series), *George A. Romero's Toe Tags* (a six-issue comic book miniseries), and the *Marvel Zombies* comic book franchise.

8

Post-9/11 Anxieties

Unpredictability and Complacency in the Age of "New Terrorism" in Dawn of the Dead (2004)

BECKI A. GRAHAM

The intimate connections between horror films and the fears, anxieties, and concerns of the audiences for which they are created are firmly established (e.g. Clarens, 1967; Halberstam 1988; and others). While the horror genre and the creatures that haunt it often bring to mind low-budget slashers with little substantial content, deeper examination reveals patterns in films neatly aligned with social apprehensions of the times in which they are released — as Judith Halberstam asserted, "Monsters are meaning machines." (1995, p. 21). A seemingly simple monster, such as a zombie, can demonstrate fears about race, nationality, gender, class, and sexuality; past, present, and future (Halberstam, pp. 19–22). Previous explorations of two eras in zombie films (the 1930s–1940s and the 1950s–1960s) reveal thematic elements timely to concerns of respective social climates. Scholars and critics have asserted that zombie movies of the former era focused on concerns surrounding racial tensions and American colonialism; those of the latter period expressed fears about atomic-age science and the spread of Communism (cf. Bishop, 2006; Dendle, 2001; Halliwell, 1988; Jancovich, 1996; MacDougall, 1999; McIntosh, 2008; Russell, 2005).

Zombie media projects (i.e., feature films and film appearances) have increased substantially in the 21st century. While zombie cinematic representation has risen steadily since the first well-known "zombie movie" (*White Zombie*, 1932), the amount of screen time zombies have claimed in the last eight years is significant. What might be the impetus behind contemporary American audiences' fascination with zombies? Zombies are an ideal "millennial monster"; uniquely suited to expressing the collective fears (e.g. pandemic illness and biological/chemical warfare) of modern society. As creatures "defined by indeterminacy, undecidability, liminality," zombies are figureheads for a cultural and social moment characterized by uncertainty (Leverette, 2008, p. 188). So prevalent are zombies in American culture that a mock-serious *Zombie Survival Guide* (Brooks, 2003) recently sold its millionth copy (Townsend, 2010). While other monsters (e.g., vampires, werewolves, or serial killers) have the capacity to menace their victims, the zombie has the exceptional ability to depict apocalypse, the notion that the world and all its reason is collapsing around itself. Zombie films can fill powerful roles in post–9/11 narratives and discourses, where official communications (such as various Department of Homeland Security media and *The 9/11 Commission Report*) continually assert that citizens are in greater danger than ever before, and that the nature of that danger has changed. U.S. audiences are primed to consume the sort of fears zombie films serve up.

While zombie films have been abundant over the some seventy-five years they have claimed a place in Western cinema, comprehensive studies of the movies' cultural implications have been lacking. In his *Book of the Dead: The Complete History of Zombie Cinema*, film critic and journalist Jamie Russell (2005) asserts that zombies have been largely ignored in academic studies of horror cinema (p. 7). Public and scholarly perceptions of zombies are largely based on experiences with the sort of cut-rate, generally dreadful films in which they tend to appear. In spite of the rather depressing tradition of badly-made zombie movies, the fact that the genre has survived speaks to zombies' capacity to express "the specific fears and anxieties of [the] historical moment[s]" in which those films are created (Russell, 2005, p. 8). The zombie stands as a symbol of large-scale catastrophe, be it grounded in concerns about the effects of American colonialism and related racial tensions (i.e., Haitian zombies that dominated early American zombie films) or Communism and science-gone-awry hysteria (fodder for many of the zombie films of the 1950s and early 1960s) (cf. McIntosh, 2008; Russell, 2005). In the films of the former era, zombies were helpless minions of their masters, and, in American cinema, a metaphor for "the racial Other" (Pagano, 2008, p. 76; Russell, 2005, p. 34). The zombies of Haiti were portrayed almost exclusively as undead slaves; Haitian slaves were understood to be exclusively black. Zombies and the "voodoo" practitioners who created them (regardless of the race of those practitioners) were portrayed as a threat to whites (e.g., in films such as *White Zombie* [1932] and *I Walked with a Zombie* [1943]). The notion of a "white zombie" was thus doubly monstrous: an undead being posing a threat to others in the environment and existing outside of the racial conventions established for such creatures. Zombies were depicted as pawns in hierarchies topped by greed-incensed masters seeking wealth and financial gain — a thinly-veiled reference to slavery in antebellum America (Clarens, 1967, p. 88). Simultaneously, the films contemplated the possibility of unexpected consequences of American economic and military expansion into regions and cultures about which little was known.

By the 1950s, America had other fears in the forefront of her collective mind. Clarens writes that while the horror films of the atomic age primarily featured "creatures of the Bomb" (e.g., giant ants spawned by nuclear testing mishaps in 1954's *Them!*), another, larger fear saturated 1950s horror — dehumanization (pp. 131, 134). Anxieties about possible indoctrination or brainwashing by Communist dogma (or their own government, for that matter), caused Americans excessive worry about issues concerning the appropriation of individual identity and loss of free will. When individuality was sacrificed or stolen for the sake of governmental and political purposes, who those individuals (and those around them) were was called into question. "The zombies are now among us," Clarens notes, "and we cannot tell them and the girl next door apart any longer" (p. 134).

How, then, are post–9/11 film zombies positioned and shaped to represent the anxieties of their audiences? Bishop (2009) provides a superb overview of the ways in which millennial events (e.g., terrorist attacks, pandemic scares such as SARS, and natural disasters such as Hurricane Katrina) have placed audiences in prime position to respond to the brand of horror zombie films offer. The genre holds a unique capacity to function as a stage for apocalyptic/post-apocalyptic narratives. The scenarios commonly posed in zombie cinema (e.g., confused survivors, the failure of critical governmental and social infrastructure, and desperate survival schemes), Bishop (2009) notes, can address modern American audiences in fresh, frightening ways since events like the 9/11 terrorist attacks (p. 22). With terrorism

[handwritten margin note: Cold War Anxieties]

functioning as the "primary metaphor" in post–9/11 society, zombie hordes and the destruction they deliver seem particularly relevant (Bishop, 2009, p. 24). Completely devoid of emotion, rationality, or remorse, zombies' sole ambition is to stalk and kill innocent victims, an apt allegory in a time in which mass media characterize terrorists in very similar terms. It seems an appropriate way to begin to address this question is through a thorough analysis of an influential film in modern zombie cinema: *Dawn of the Dead* (2004), a text which neatly addresses the shock/helplessness/confusion that characterized post–9/11 America. The unpredictable, physical nature of *Dawn*'s zombies themselves (a trend that is making itself known in other recent zombie films, such as *28 Days Later* [2002] and *Resident Evil: Apocalypse* [2004], and *28 Weeks Later* [2007]) and its cinematic disposition underpin the volatility of post–9/11 life. Further, the complacency of the film's main characters is shown to endanger their lives, reinforcing the notion that everyday situations require constant vigilance in societies living under the cloud of New Terrorism. Overall, *Dawn* is a film that can speak to post–9/11 viewers and the concerns they share.

New Terrorism and Unpredictability

September 11, 2001, is marked as the day terrorism as a concrete, physical threat to the continental United States as "homeland" entered mainstream America's consciousness. Terrorism is not a term that can be succinctly defined; whether or not specific acts or the systems of belief that inspire them may be termed "terrorism" or "terroristic" is subject to debate. The sole common denominator of terrorism is "violence or the threat of violence"— the sorts of behaviors that have earned the moniker have been perpetrated for ages and have manifested in an array of strategies (Laquer, 2000, p. 6). Similarly, a degree of controversy has emerged regarding the concept of "New Terrorism," as some authors (e.g., Tucker, 2001; Crenshaw, 2003; Duyvesteyn, 2004) claim that terrorism in the late 20th and early 21st centuries are simply a continuation of attitudes and acts perpetrated throughout human history or is not fundamentally different from "older" terrorism. However, sufficient evidence exists to support an assertion that New Terrorism represents a departure from traditional avenues of dogma and violence.

That the 9/11 attacks were an act of terrorism on a spectacular scale is undeniable. For many, the events of September 11 stand as the most recognizable example of an act of New Terrorism due to their scope, scale, and the motivations behind them. Although the concept of a new form of terrorism had been advanced prior to the 9/11 attacks (e.g., Lesser, 1999; Laquer, 2000), the events sparked an increase in publishing on the topic as analysts attempted to make sense of the incident. Military analyst Matthew Morgan (2004) includes cultural, political/organizational, and technological factors while constructing his argument that New Terrorism is distinct in character from acts of violence in the past. Culturally, Morgan claims that New Terrorism is motivated by primarily religious, rather than primarily political, objectives (p. 32). Modern terrorists "increasingly look at acts of death and destruction as sacramental or transcendental on spiritual levels"; the indiscriminate violence such beliefs spark, coupled with the fact that religiously-motivated groups are not constrained by concerns with public opinion that limited politically-driven factions makes those functioning in a New Terrorism paradigm deadlier than those who came before them (Morgan, p. 32). Such "categorical fanaticism" is seen as one of the hallmarks of New Terrorism by those who embrace the concept (Morgan, p. 41). Technologically, developments in biological, chemical, and nuclear weapons, coupled with the possession of such agents by "non-state" actors has led to a novel, more dangerous context in contemporary terrorism. The relatively ready availability of components to make large-scale weapons for groups unconnected to nations (and thus, again, unconstrained by political considerations typically tied to nations) further destabilizes security in the era of New Terrorism (Morgan, pp. 39–40). Another voice weighing in on New Terrorism, from a distinctly American perspective, is *The 9/11 Commission Report* (The National Commission, 2004).

Prior to 9/11, terrorism, from the perspective of the American public, was typically regarded as an overseas phenomenon, save a handful of appalling domestic examples (e.g., the bombing of the Alfred P. Murrah Federal Building in Oklahoma City, OK in April 1995). Unprepared for such a large-scale tragedy on U.S. soil, a shocked and beleaguered public turned to their government for an explanation. *The 9/11 Commission Report* was created by the National Commission on Terrorist Attacks Upon the United States, an organization charged with conducting an investigation of the "facts and circumstances relating to the terrorist attacks of September 11, 2001," by examining information from a variety of sources relating to the attacks, including hardcopy data collection and analysis and public hearings that featured testimony from 160 witnesses (The National Commission, p. xv). The declassified, public version of the *9/11 Report* was released in July 2004, giving American civilians unprecedented insight into the events leading up to and constituting the attacks. The *9/11 Report* introduces its version of New Terrorism, differentiated in the *Report* from "old" terrorism by its indiscriminate violence and broadening of potential targets. The authors of the *9/11 Report* chose to mark the transition from old terrorism to new by citing a single event: the February 26, 1993 bomb attack on the World Trade Center complex. The explosion, the result of a truck bomb with a timing device planted in a basement garage of the complex, killed six people and injured more than 1,000 (The National Commission, p. 71). While the bombing was not the product of the sort of suicide attacks that have come to be associated with acts of New Terrorism, the *9/11 Report* asserts that the event heralded the a shift in terrorist attitudes. Ramzi Yousef, the al-Qaeda operative who put the bomb in place, indicated that he had planned to kill 250,000 people in the explosion. While the method of the attack was not particularly noteworthy, the *9/11 Report* states, that Yousef's "rage and malice had no limits" (The National Commission, p. 72). His act may be seen as a precursor of an emerging trend in terrorism. Usama bin Ladin, in a 1998 ABC-TV interview in Afghanistan, asserted, regarding governments, military forces, and individuals, "We believe that the worst thieves in the world today and the worst terrorists are the Americans.... We do not have to differentiate between military and civilian. As far as we are concerned, they are all targets" (The National Commission, p. 47). The unpredictability of terrorist forces disinclined to discriminate between enemy governments and civilians under the umbrellas of those governments affected fundamental changes in American views on security. Whether New Terrorism is actually "new," or merely the next chapter of an "old" story, the 9/11 attacks certainly changed the way most Americans viewed terrorism and its potential to affect their daily lives. Experts studying the psychological and emotional aftermath of the attacks (e.g., Boscarino, Figley, and Adams, 2003) noted that the events of 9/11 were typically not perceived as an isolated incident; nearly half of surveyed New Yorkers were "very concerned" about a major attack in the future. Nor are such fears considered to be localized to the regions in which the 9/11 attacks were perpetrated. Silver et al. (2002) found that a significant portion of surveyed respondents (who lived outside the New York City area) experienced 9/11-related posttraumatic stress; the researchers concluded that the negative emotional effects of 9/11 were widespread and not confined to individuals who experienced the attacks personally (p. 1235).

Terrorism in the modern age has become an everyman concern, often perpetrated without warning in seemingly unlikely venues. The 9/11 attacks, along with other unexpected large-scale acts of aggression such as the strikes on the London commuter system on 7 July 2005, illustrate the unstable nature of New Terrorism. Destruction is delivered via many avenues, anyone is a target, and sources of attacks are less foreseeable than in the past. The Department of Homeland Security (DHS), itself an entity distinctive to a post–9/11 landscape, was created through a Presidential proposal in June 2002. The introduction of the proposal justifying the need for the DHS reads, in part, "The changing nature of the threats facing America requires a new government structure to protect against invisible enemies that can strike with a variety weapons. America needs a ... security structure ... to meet the unknown threats of the future": this encapsulates the unpredictability of New Terrorism and its myriad, ambiguous methods of attack (Bush, 2002, p. 2). The proposal reads as a laundry list for post–9/11 fears, referring to chemical, biological, radiological, and nuclear weapons. It alludes to the necessity of stockpiling vaccines as a defense against potential acts of bioterrorism, measures to guard against further strikes to the public aviation industry, and devising timely ways to protect "our critical infrastructure" (Bush, p. 2). It also provides specific examples of the ways in which combining formerly-independent agencies (e.g., the Central Intelligence Agency, Department of Transportation, and U.S. Immigration and Naturalization Services) under a single umbrella will improve the federal government's efficiency in helping citizens protect themselves.

These examples and the situations they outline are disturbing reminders of the ways in which life in America has changed since 9/11. For instance, the proposal points out that without a blanket agency to direct emergency communication to the public, it would be impossible to disseminate timely, reliable warnings and health care information in a chemical or biological attack. The proposal also demonstrates, in disturbing detail, then-current inefficiency in procedures for distributing pharmaceuticals (such as Potassium Iodide, which may check the development of certain cancers) to citizens who live near nuclear power facilities (which are cited as tempting targets for terrorists). Terrorism, the DHS proposal reminds us, is no longer a menace aimed at a military or government target (rather than the larger civilian population); nor is terrorism only a problem "somewhere else." In the age of New Terrorism, *anyone* is a target. The proposal asserts: "Terrorists today can strike at any place, at any time.... The United States is under attack from a new kind of enemy — one that hopes to employ terror against innocent civilians and to undermine their confidence in our institutions and our way of life" (Bush, p. 2). As such, citizens share a responsibility for vigilance. This idea serves as a foundation for a great deal of material distributed through both government and popular sources. The ties between these sentiments and elements of *Dawn* are also plain, as will be explicated shortly.

New Terrorism and Complacency

While the majority of the *9/11 Report* was devoted to examinations and analyses of the origins and modern conditions of radical Islamic terrorism and the events of 9/11, the report concludes with sections exploring ways in which the U.S. government's complacency contributed to the attacks. Perhaps the most recognizable phrase to come from the report in this regard was "a failure of imagination" (The National Commission, p. 339). Despite a series of events and revelations that indicated radical Islamic terrorists were increasingly committed to attacking the U.S. on a spectacular scale, and that a group was considering unconventional means of attack (e.g., commercial airliners), government attention to the matter was lackadaisical. The American public was not afforded sufficient information about the possibility of dramatic action from extremist groups. Intelligence gathered between 1998 and 2001 was ignored or downplayed — complacency that doomed the U.S. to 9/11 or an attack like it (The National Commission, pp. 339–344). Readers of the report were faced with the knowledge that the government, lulled into a false sense of security, ignored warning signs of 9/11 with disastrous consequences. In the aftermath of 9/11, while the government publicly continues to take steps to remedy its mistakes and attempt to prevent future strikes, the American public is regularly warned about the dangers of *personal* complacency. Americans cannot, they are told, expect the government to fight terrorism effectively without their help. Vigilance is the watchword for citizens of a nation targeted by New Terrorism. As such, media outlets continuously advise Americans to be aware of the dangers that face them. A New Year's–themed press release from the DHS dated 11 December 2006 encouraged Americans to make emergency preparedness for themselves, their families, and their businesses their "resolution" for 2007 (Department of Homeland Security, 2006). The statement included a link to www.ready.gov, a DHS-affiliated website that contains checklists to assess preparedness for various emergencies, such as natural disasters, explosions, and biological/chemical attacks. In the event of an emergency, readers are urged to stay informed by watching television, listening to the radio, and checking the Internet for "**official news and information**" (bolding original). Awareness of one's surroundings and keeping up with news are portrayed as essential.

Charges of complacency are also frequently incorporated into the U.S. legislative process. For example, Douglas MacKinnon invoked complacency in a 2005 piece encouraging renewal of the USA PATRIOT (Uniting and Strengthening America by Providing Tools Required to Intercept and Obstruct Terrorism) Act of 2001. MacKinnon wrote, "Because of widespread complacency, we are back to September 10, 2001.... Our very survival as a people, a nation and a democracy depend on never forgetting what happened to us on September 11, 2001" (2005, A21). Citing the increasingly common criticism that lapse of time from the actual events of 9/11 are lulling people into a false sense of security, MacKinnon added ominously, "Complacency, ignorance and passage of time: Those who live to kill us are counting on them" (A21).

Citizens living with the realities of New Terrorism are, then, subject to a barrage of warnings from various media sources. They coexist with ominous-sounding threat notification systems that have drastic effects on security-based aspects of everyday life (e.g., air travel restrictions). As Stuart Croft, Professor of International Security at the University of Warwick notes, news stories, television programming, literary fiction, and other venues reflect and relate pervasive fear. It is natural, then, that horror movies, including zombie films, have evolved to represent the modern concerns of contemporary audiences. Combining the unpredictability of New Terrorism and the dangers of complacency, zombie cinema is perfectly suited to the task.

Dawn of the Dead *(2004)*

Dawn of the Dead (2004) is director Zack Snyder's "re-envisioning" of George Romero's 1978 film of the same name. While fundamental elements of the story remain (a zombie outbreak forces a group of survivors to take refuge in a shopping mall), characters, plot lines, and themes are updated in ways that ensure relevance to post–9/11 audiences. The movie's central character is Ana, a nurse, who, after losing her husband to the zombie epidemic, joins police officer Kenneth, Best Buy employee Michael, reformed gangster Andre, his pregnant wife, Luda, and other survivors in the relative sanctuary of a large mall where the group plans to wait for rescue. Learning, through television news reports and terrifying narratives of other living survivors who join the initial group, that the critical infrastructure of the region has been destroyed, they formulate a plan to flee the city and relocate to a nearby Great Lakes island. Emphasizing the increasingly claustrophobic nature of the characters' circumstances, Snyder neatly weaves in an allusion to the Alamo (e.g., a themed chess set) as the survivors are quickly outnumbered by thousands of zombies who flock to their haven — it seems portentous that Snyder would later go on to direct a re-telling of the Battle of Thermopylae in *300* (2006). The characters settle into a comparatively-normal-given-the-circumstances daily routine of monitoring the news, sharing meals, and taking advantage of the material comforts the mall has to offer until the zombie crisis reaches proportions that necessitate their fleeing the area. After a daring escape from the mall, the audience follows the survivors to a small yacht that is to be their transport into an uncertain future. No final closure is offered: when the survivors reach the island they hope is to be their haven, a hoard of zombies fill the screen, followed by a jump to the film's credits. While viewers do not know how the story will end, it is clear that the survivors will be unable to simply put their terror behind them. Even a remote, isolated island harbors predators; illusions that isolation can provide security are shattered as completely in the film as they were in the continental United States on 9/11. While the 2004 version of *Dawn* does not raise an acerbic eyebrow at consumerism as Romero's earlier vehicle, it is an elegant commentary on post–9/11 and New Terrorism fears and concerns.

Dawn's cinematic elements effectively create a world of fear and anxiety readily recognizable to post–9/11 audiences. Its mise-en-scène (save the obviously theatrical turn of the dead retuning to life) is naturalistic to contemporary audiences. Ana, the character with whom the audience forges the most intimate relationship, resides in a typical suburban home with a green yard and a television in the bedroom, predictably located near hospitals and shopping districts. The survivors have average jobs: nurse, police officer, electronics store employee, truck driver. The mall in which they take refuge is replete with elements an audience would expect to see: an overpriced specialty coffee shop, a sporting goods emporium, and an upscale infant/children's boutique. Life is comfortably ordinary until something unthinkable occurs that compromises the security of that life so completely that the actors are left reeling. As patently absurd as an outbreak of living dead may be, the environment in which they rise and the havoc they wreak is painfully familiar to audiences. *Dawn*'s verisimilitude is based on its ability to remind post–9/11 audiences of the ways in which the world *can* be disrupted in previously unimaginable ways. Post–9/11 audiences are well-equipped to deal with the brand of horror *Dawn* offers. The specific face of the terror is impossible; the nature of the terror is not.

Dawn's opening credits, which are actually situated after the film's initial scenes of zombie attacks and escapes, are germane to audiences literate in media discourses of New Terrorism. A montage of rapidly cut (no shot lasts more than three seconds; most last less than one) stock footage of real-life chaos and portions of the film itself, the credits set a dizzying pace and present material hauntingly familiar to post–9/11 audiences. Police in riot gear, panicked people, and fire are everywhere. Army vehicles career through crowds, scattering chaotic civilians. Some of the footage alludes to overseas settings, including a report from Istanbul; some shows harried local reporters stating that "...shelters have been compromised." The implication of the opening credits is that this crisis is everywhere, all the time. As in the age of New Terrorism, the global and the local have been merged in horrifying ways.

Many of the staged portions of the opening credits are fragments of "news broadcasts" attempting to cover the zombie outbreak. The audience sees news anchors stammer as they struggle to grasp the information they are reporting, scenes which may call to mind television reports of 9/11. When, for instance, United Flight 175 impacted the South Tower of the World Trade Center on 9/11, ABC's *Good Morning America* anchors Charlie Gibson and Diane Sawyer reacted with unmistakable shock. ABC reporter Don Dahler, on a phone call from the scene with Gibson and Sawyer, exclaimed "Oh, my God!" as he witnessed the crash. Others audible in the newsroom gasp and shout; Sawyer murmurs, "My God ... my God." Moments later, Sawyer stammers, "We will ... see that scene again, just to make sure we saw what we thought we..." as ABC aired a replay of footage of the attack. Later in the day, Peter Jennings, who had assumed control of the anchor desk after Gibson and Sawyer departed, was talking with reporters John Miller, who conducted the famous May 1998 interview with Usama Bin Laden, and Pierre Thomas, who covered the Justice Department and the FBI, when the South Tower collapsed. ABC viewers, watching a split screen of the World Trade Center towers and the Pentagon, saw the tower disintegrate, disappearing momentarily below the frame of the helicopter camera filming the scene. Jennings said:

> Let's go to the trade towers again because, John, we now have a — what do we have? We don't... Well, it may be that something fell off the building. It may be that something has fall — yet we don't know, to be perfectly honest. But that is what you're looking at, the current — that's the scene at this moment at the World Trade Center.... Don Dahler from ABC's *Good Morning America* is down in — in the general vicinity. Don, can you tell us what has just happened?

Dahler hurriedly reported:

> I'm four blocks north of the World Trade Center. The second building that was hit by the plane has just completely collapsed. The entire building has just collapsed, as if a demolition team set off — when you see the old demolitions of these old buildings. It folded down on itself, and it's not there any more.... There is panic on the streets....

Jennings, unable to immediately comprehend the enormity of the tragedy asked in astonishment, "The whole *side* has collapsed?" Dahler amends, "The whole *building* has collapsed." Jennings replies, "We are talking about massive casualties here ... and we have ... *whew* ... that is extraordinary" (*9/11 Television Archives*). In addition to newscasters' difficulty in grasping what they were seeing firsthand on screen, there was also an issue with misinformation from secondary sources on 9/11. For example, most of the major U.S. network news agencies (e.g., CNN and ABC, among others) reported that a car or truck bomb had been detonated outside the U.S. State Department in Washington D.C., an account that later had to be recanted. Similarly, initial testimony on the crash of United Airlines 11 (the first flight that crashed into the World Trade Center Complex) on certain networks (e.g., FOX) advanced the notion that a missile, rather than an aircraft, may have struck the tower (*9/11 Television Archives*).

This brand of doubt and hesitation is echoed in *Dawn*'s opening sequence. The audience hears questions being fielded in a news conference setting — although the visual component of the scene is initially missing, post–9/11 audiences have sufficient experience with "breaking disasters" to recognize the format.

MAN'S VOICE: "We'll take your questions..."
REPORTER: "Is it a virus?"
MAN'S VOICE: "We don't know."
REPORTER: "How does it spread — is it airborne?"
MAN'S VOICE: "Airborne is a possibility — we don't know."
REPORTER: "Is this an international health hazard or a military concern?"
MAN'S VOICE: "Both."
REPORTER: "Are these people alive or dead?"

At this moment, the visual element of the news conference is revealed. A bewildered spokesman stands at a podium in front of a Center for Disease Control (CDC) backdrop. Shakily, he replies to the final question, "We ... don't know."

This opening credit montage illustrates the ways in which *Dawn*'s brand of fear is recognizable and relevant to contemporary audiences. These viewers are familiar with situations so frenetic that the most basic questions cannot be definitively answered. The instability of what is trustworthy and what is dangerous can lead to garbled reports by confused media figures. Audiences are likewise familiar with a CDC that has evolved from filling roles focused solely on conventional domestic health care and into the position of a partner in defense against biological/chemical aspects of terrorism. Most of all, viewers have lived through times in which the media has only one story to report — and it's *not* good news. Post-9/11 audiences are accustomed to circumstances so dangerous that the attention of the entire news media is focused upon them. These audiences are ready to consume the fear that *Dawn* offers.

The opening segment of the film can be seen as portraying post–9/11/New Terrorism narratives along two fundamental lines. First, the things about which post–9/11 populations need to be worried and fearful are more unpredictable than in the past. "Old" fears have been rendered obsolete; new concerns are far less obvious and foreseeable. Second, complacency is a luxury they can no longer afford. The need for vigilance and self-awareness is paramount to safety and survival.

Dawn *and Unpredictability*

Unpredictability is a hallmark of *Dawn*'s visual fare and plot development. *Dawn* begins as the audience joins Ana in her car as she leaves her job at a hospital and drives home. An aerial establishing shot orients us in the subdivision in which Ana's home is situated. Before pulling into her driveway, Ana stops her car for a friendly chat with Vivian, a typical suburban kid on roller skates. The brief encounter leads the audience to understand that the two have established a casual, neighborly relationship — Ana suggests rollerblading the next evening and bids Vivian to send her mother Ana's regards. Once inside the house, Ana and her husband Luis engage in small talk about television and a three-day weekend Ana has scheduled at her job. In the space of four-and-a-half minutes, *Dawn* has situated its audience in a familiar, predictable setting of middle-class security and contentment. This is the "pre–9/11 world": things are not perfect, but troubles are conventional — hassles at work or being late for one's favorite TV show.

These peaceful routines are soon shattered. The audience returns to the couple's bedroom through an overhead shot that shows Ana and Luis sleeping. Soft light spills over the bed as a nightstand clock flips from 6:36 to 6:37 — the "dawn" pledged in the film's title. Suddenly, the perspective of the camera changes as the audience finds itself in the hallway, approaching the partially-open bedroom door. Following another abrupt shift to the interior of the bedroom, viewers see the door swing open and the silhouette of a figure standing in the jamb. Luis startles awake, and viewers realize, at the moment he does, that the person in the doorway is Vivian. Puzzled at her early morning appearance in their home, Luis sleepily inquires, "Vivian, honey ... are you OK?" As Vivian enters the light of the room, however, it is apparent that something unspeakable has happened to her. Her pink night-gown is torn and splattered with blood. Her mouth is covered in gore, teeth bared; her expression is predatory as she moves into the room. The audience sees Luis's face register the shock and horror it is feeling as he rises from bed, stumbles toward Vivian, and kneels beside her. As he turns from her, shouting to Ana ("Call an ambulance!"), his neck is exposed and Vivian pounces. The attack is so ferocious that Ana has to intervene to disengage Vivian's jaws, pulling tissue and vascular material away with her from Luis's neck. Ana throws Vivian into the hall; Vivian springs smoothly and athletically to her feet and charges back toward the room. Ana slams the door, which immediately begins to shake violently as Vivian attempts to break through. This brief scene offers the audience a crash course on unpredictability and the "Fast Zombie." Josh Levin, a senior editor at *Slate*, noted, "It's not for nothing that zombies are called the *walking* dead ... but the zombie has a newfound vigor" (Levin, 2004). *Dawn*'s introduction of the fast zombie to its audience is potentially astonishing.

The first onscreen zombie is a central figure in any zombie film: s/he acclimatizes the audience to the "rules" of the crisis and offers a marker for expectations for the undead who will appear later in the film. "First" zombies cue viewers to how zombies may be expected to move, their aggression and efficiency as predators, and how the living might protect themselves. *Night of the Living Dead* (1968), for instance, depicts the first zombie at a comfortable distance from the camera. Set in the cemetery in which Johnny and Barbara, the characters with whom the audience have become acquainted, are visiting their father's grave, an unfamiliar middle-aged man dressed in a suit stalks clumsily into the frame, giving the characters time to see, and even mock him. The figure looks so "alive" that Barbara is halfway through wishing him "Good evening" before she notices he is attempting to assault her. The zombie, though decidedly disturbing, does not pose an imminent physical threat that cannot be anticipated well in advance, once the living have a grasp of the situation. He is, the audience soon learns, an apposite representative of his kind. *Night*'s zombies, while dogged and relentless, are, individually, somewhat laughable predators. They shuffle inelegantly through the film, reacting to stimuli with an almost-comical sluggishness. When Ben, the film's protagonist, has his initial onscreen encounter with a "ghoul" (Romero's moniker for *Night*'s zombies), he is able to dispatch two assailants with relative ease as they lurch toward him in seeming slow motion. If the living are able to patch together a simple plan with elemental organization, it seems they will have a chance of surviving the crisis. These maladroit stiffs bear little resemblance to their 21st century counterparts.

In regard to their physical capacities (e.g., ability to move with speed and agility), *Dawn*'s zombies employ a formulation introduced in another outstanding entry in millennial zombie cinema: Danny Boyle's *28 Days Later* (2002). While quibblers may chafe at *28*'s inclusion in the zombie genre (the "Infected" are victims of a stunningly virulent illness, and not the dead come back to life), popular and scholarly (e.g., Bishop, 2009; Rogers, 2008) perceptions of the film place it securely in zombie cinema. People infected with the

"Rage" virus have a thunderous incubation period of 10–20 seconds, during which they are completely transformed from their former selves into maddened, murderous brutes with a disturbing tendency to indiscriminately vomit blood. The ferocity of the Infected marks them as standouts and precedent-setters in millennial zombie cinema. There is no finesse in the predatory actions of the Infected. They move erratically but with incredible speed, strength, and nimbleness and demonstrate the capacity to jump, tackle, and climb. There is no consistency in their movements and no plans apparent in their actions, save for the manifestation of intense homicidal aggression. *28* raised the threshold of zombie terrorism in contemporary films, paving the way for a new incarnation of the classic hunter — strong, swift, and impossible to read. While *28* provides a startling glace of a post-apocalyptic, manic-zombie infested Great Britain, *Dawn* shows what happens when dynamic, "souped-up" zombies invade the American Heartland.

As *Dawn*'s first (fast) zombie, Vivian represents this unpredictability in two ways. First, she is a child, and a child familiar to the protagonist — quite literally "the girl next door" to whom Clarens alludes (p. 134). She is not an arbitrary stranger lumbering through a cemetery; she is a familiar neighborhood figure with whom Ana and Luis may have attended a barbecue or block party, an established character in their home environment. The nature of Vivian's costume (a pink nightgown) hints that she was attacked in the safety of her home, possibly tucked into bed. A child, who would ordinarily pose the least possible threat to the protagonists, suddenly and inexplicably endangers the life of one while claiming the life of the other. These details are particularly pertinent and poignant to audiences familiar with unexpected, unfathomable attacks on their homeland and with the notion that they can never be completely certain who, precisely, the enemy is. Mundane, commonplace activities such as air travel or going to work have been imbued with high-stakes uncertainty that leave audiences sympathetic to characters dealing with a world rendered deadly and unfathomable with no notice.

The second way in which Vivian exemplifies the unpredictability of *Dawn*'s zombies is through her physical capabilities and demeanor. Although *Night*, with its classic "slow" zombie, depicts increasingly claustrophobic anxiety as survivors attempt to defend an abandoned farmhouse from an undead horde, individual zombies are infinitely out-runable (and usually out-walkable). Detached and impersonal, the strength of classic zombies was in their numbers. Like the conventional armies that characterized pre–New Terrorism forces that were threatening, yet estimable, slow zombies advanced a menace that could be forecast. Characters in zombie films had time to gather information, make plans, and fortify their strongholds. *Night* includes a television news broadcast depicting ghouls being easily defeated by ragtag "clean and sweep" teams consisting of farmers, rural hunters, and low-level law enforcement. *Dawn*'s zombies, tailored to scare a post–9/11, New Terrorism viewership, are monsters that are life-threatening on an individual level. They run, jump, and change course with startling agility. The frenzied strength they exhibit in attacking their victims requires survivors to possess the ability to fight or flee for their lives in the moment, rather than simply requiring a well-conceived defense plan. When *Dawn*'s beleaguered living burst into the shopping mall with zombies sprinting behind them, they scarcely have time to catch their breath before brutal assaults from the small number of undead stalking the center commence. The survivors, who have paused to wash blood from their hands and arms in a decorative fountain, are abruptly battered by a snarling security guard zombie who is able to bite one of the group before Kenneth has time to squeeze the trigger on his shotgun. Distracted from his initial quarry by Kenneth's approach, the zombie tackles him into the fountain. Audiences familiar with Ving Rhames, who portrays Kenneth in the film, know he is hardly a milquetoast subject to overpowering by a tepid opponent. Watching Kenneth's brawny body fly backwards into the water tells viewers that these zombies are a force to be reckoned with; erratic, yet exceptionally robust. While classic zombies typically required substantial numbers to inflict large-scale damage, contemporary counterparts can wreak havoc one-on-one, or even one-on-many.

In the same way, audiences are often reminded, large scale acts of terrorism can be perpetrated by determined individuals with access to a variety of conventional and unconventional weapons. Armies are no longer necessary to inflict large-scale damage; an equally serious threat is posed by individuals or groups who exist below the radar of traditional international politics and relations. As terrorists gain access to novel methods of violence and intimidations (e.g., improvised explosive devices [IEDs]) used frequently against allied forces in Iraq and Afghanistan) and terrorism becomes an end in itself, rather than a means to achieve political goals, the threat is changing faster than targets and victims can adapt (Morgan, p. 30). Potential New Terrorism threats are far less "knowable" than in the past.

The *9/11 Report* notes that between the years of 1988 and 1998, al-Qaeda ("the base" or "the foundation"), under the direction of Bin Ladin, was expanding with disturbing rapidity. The *9/11 Report*'s authors posit that a single event marks the turn "from the old terrorism to the new": the "first" World Trade Center bombing on 26 February 1993 (The National Commission, p. 71). While this operation was not the sort of suicide mission that characterized the 9/11 attacks, the act was planned and perpetrated by radicals whose "rage and malice [toward the U.S.] had no limit" (The National Commission, p. 72). That determined individuals were able to carry out a strike on some of the most high-profile buildings in New York City changed the landscape of safety in the entire nation. Sunni activist Ramzi Yousef, who placed the bomb in an underground garage of the World Trade Center Complex before leaving the scene, later claimed he had aspired to kill 250,000 people and bring both towers to the ground (The National Commission, pp. 71–72). Recalling that remark, FBI officials accompanying Yousef on his 1995 flight to New York to stand trial for the attack lifted Yousef's blindfold as the plane traveled by the World Trade Center towers, pointing out that the building still stood despite Yousef's act. "They wouldn't be if I had more money," Yousef replied (Celona, et al., par. 12). Yousef's embittered lack of remorse, coupled with his expressed desire to kill a quarter-million civilians, marks him in the *9/11 Report* as an archetype of New Terrorist.

Citizen-targets of terrorists operating in the contemporary paradigm described above have less warning of events that are far deadlier and more insidious than in the past. Civilians can never be certain that the mundane spaces they occupy daily are safe. Although an attack on the scale of 9/11 has not been repeated in the U.S. in the years since the tragedy, media reports of foiled terrorist plots of disturbing magnitude are enough to compromise whatever tenuous psychological security that might have developed. The new zombie, with its ability to foil conventional safety measures and its capacity to pose fatal threats on an individual level, is an apt symbol for the apprehension connected with this trend.

Dawn *and Complacency*

As previously noted, complacency is not imagined as tenable in post–9/11 citizens' everyday lives. *Dawn* offers a subtle commentary on personal complacency, primarily through

Ana's actions in the beginning of the movie. As a result of her preoccupation with trivial matters and media, Ana remains unaware of the deadly situation at hand far longer than necessary, thus endangering her life. While she drives home from work early in the film, Ana quickly bypasses two news reports on her car radio ("Unconfirmed reports..." and "...confirmed it is *not* an isolated..."), settling on a station playing a soft rock song. Had she bothered to keep abreast of the news, Ana presumably could have been alerted to the emergency much earlier, increasing her chances of survival. This pattern continues as Ana arrives home to find her husband Luis lying in bed watching television. Alluding to *American Idol* or a show with a similar format, he informs Ana "Richie" has been cut. Upset and disbelieving, Ana replies, "Oh my God! He had such a sweet voice — I can't believe that." In the following scene, programming is interrupted on the television — left on while the couple has sex in the shower adjoining the bedroom — for a "Special News Bulletin," ostensibly about the burgeoning zombie crisis. Settling for an existence in which vital information is ignored in favor of other activities and media fare, *Dawn's* characters leave themselves open to disaster.

The penalty for this complacency is revealed when the audience revisits Ana's neighborhood. Fleeing a freshly-"zombified" Luis, Ana runs to her car to find her environment gone, overnight, to Hell. The camera is positioned behind Ana's head as she pauses, stunned, on her front doorstep; viewers turn with her as she slowly, disbelievingly scans her surroundings. Sirens and screams are heard in the background; several homes are on fire. People rush frantically in all directions, making it impossible to discern who is retreating and who is pursuing. Ana's neighbor, who threatens Ana with a handgun when she approaches him to try to grasp what is happening, is run down in the street by an ambulance careening through the frame. It is, perhaps, this act — drivers of an emergency services vehicle unwilling to slow down to avoid taking a citizen's life — that spurs Ana from her stupor. She escapes the neighborhood in her car, encountering throughout the area the same brand of chaos that was apparent in her front yard. Viewers return to an earlier perspective from the passenger seat of Ana's car, with an entirely different spirit. Ana fights back tears as she madly punches buttons on the radio. This time, however, she doesn't have the option of skipping the news in favor of lighter fare — all stations are airing the same Emergency Broadcast System alert. The audience is resituated in an aerial establishing shot, this time depicting an approach to an urban center. Vast fires and explosions dominate the landscape as viewers realize along with Ana that the turmoil is not isolated to her immediate area.

These scenes have a recognizable message for post–9/11 audiences: complacency and a lack of awareness of issues larger than the self are both a significant social problem and inherently dangerous. Ana's devotion to inconsequential media and entertainment was an obstacle to critical knowledge about more pressing issues. Her sentiments are not unique. One of the most popular recurring segments on *The Tonight Show with Jay Leno* was "Jaywalking," a piece in which Leno would ask people on the street to answer questions about current events, usually with dismally humorous results. One young woman, after responding that she voted for John McCain in the 2008 U.S. Presidential election, was unable to identify a photo of the former candidate, indicating instead that the man in the picture was Dick Cheney. In a similar vein, National Public Radio journalist, David Folkenflik, found that Afghanistan-related reporting accounted for just 2 percent of all coverage; the death of pop music star Michael Jackson in late June 2009 had trumped Afghanistan in U.S. media attention for the year, despite the fact that Jackson's death came six months into the year (Folkenflik, 2009). Americans' propensity to devote greater attention to trifling news than world events is no longer tenable, according to the dictates of the hazardous space we now occupy. The world as we know it can change overnight — worse — in a matter of moments.

Citizens living under the cloud of New Terrorism need not look far for reminders of how dangerous the world in which they live is and how much responsibility they must take for their own safety and security. While the DHS maintains a comprehensive website outlining potential threats and offering suggestions for averting these dangers, the agency also places warnings in such prosaic venues as telephone directories. For instance, a 2008–2009 edition of *Yellow Book* includes in its yellow pages a two-page post from the DHS (listed under "Emergency Preparedness"). The location of this information (i.e., in an ordinary publication such as a telephone book) and the nature of the material makes it an artifact worthy of scrutiny when considering official post–9/11 discourse about the folly of complacency. A large portion (approximately one-third) of the first page is devoted to a quote attributed to former DHS Secretary Michael Chertoff: "Terrorism forces us to make a choice. We can be afraid. Or we can be READY." Directly beneath this banner is a brief section likening individual and family preparation against terrorist attacks to maintaining working smoke alarms in one's home. "We must have the tools and plans in place to *make it on our own*, at least for a period of time, no matter where we are when disaster strikes"; comparing terrorist strikes (which may still seem unlikely to citizens despite the 9/11 attacks) to a fire in their home (which, while fairly rare, is a more common occurrence than such an attack) serves to emphasize the possibility of subsequent strikes on U.S. soil and to make citizens accountable for their own wellbeing.

The announcement goes on to list four steps to "Get ready now" for potential terrorist threats, including making an emergency supply kit (containing items such as drinking water, a flashlight, a battery-powered radio, and filter masks to be worn over the nose and mouth), making a family communications plan (including tips for creating a "shelter in place" if conditions are too unsafe to take flight from the area of an attack), remaining calm, and being informed (emphasizing the notion that attacks can come from a variety of tacks, such as biological, chemical, nuclear, and radiological). That instructions like these are necessary, and that they are so pertinent to common citizens that they warrant publication in something as ubiquitous as a telephone directory speaks volumes to the nature of danger post–9/11. New terrorism and the risks it poses cannot be ignored; its scope of concern and potential effect goes far beyond governments and their direct interests. The danger is now so widespread (and at the same time, so personal) that cautionary material merits space in phonebooks. Ordinary people are charged with being aware of larger national and international issues and with accountability for their own security. It is easy to see how audiences existing in these conditions would be drawn to and compelled by zombie cinema, where characters face unfathomable dangers and survive or die based on their faculties of awareness, vigilance, and adaptability to rapidly changing, deadly circumstances.

Closing Thoughts

This brief exploration into the reasons behind the extraordinary popularity of zombie media and some of the characteristics of this media that diverge from vehicles from previous eras seems to demonstrate a connection between the films and "real" post–9/11/New Terrorism narratives disseminated through such sources as network news and government reports. Terrorism has become an every-person concern in contemporary American society, where citizens must acknowledge a sense of national and personal vulnerability they might have never before experienced. The nature of what audiences must fear has become less predictable, and, thus, more disturbing. Acts of terrorism are no longer things that only happen "somewhere else," to be viewed from a safe distance on the news — they are in the workplace, in the backyard, inside private homes. Media saturation with terrorism-related material serves as a frequent reminder of the dangers surrounding audiences, often without offering concrete information about dealing with threats or, worse, broadcasting information that later must be recanted (e.g., report of an additional plane intended to crash into the Pentagon on 9/11 ["America Under Attack"]). A mock news report included in the special features of the *Dawn* DVD bears striking resemblance to actual reporting from 9/11, both in "factual" content (e.g., the closure of Manhattan area bridges and tunnels), tone (e.g., reporters stammering and gasping, "Oh, my God" when surprised by goings-on) and propensity for mistaken reports (e.g., the news anchor featured in the "report" apologizes for initial reports that the zombie outbreak was a "race riot"). Zombies' facility in serving as the main characters on a stage of apocalypse is well-recognized. They have continued to evolve in ways that ensure their relevance (and scariness) to contemporary audiences. Corrigan and White (2004) note, "Film, like chance, favors the prepared mind" (p. 107); as dangers get harder to track, zombies get faster, as complacency regarding security becomes less tenable, film characters whose lives depend on their awareness resonate with audiences.

As long as audiences continue to live with uncertainty, it is likely that zombies will remain relevant (and thus, frightening). Onscreen zombies continue to show the capacity evolve to reflect collective anxieties of successive generations of viewers. The latest iteration of zombies is ideal for a post–9/11 world and viewership; we are likely to see these monsters continue to stalk screens in the future.

9

The Rise and Fall — and Rise — of the Nazi Zombie in Film

Cynthia J. Miller

"A Nazi Zombie has intent, and that's really frightening" [Director Steve Barker, *Outpost*].

Introduction[1]

In the 1940s, our greatest fear was that the Nazis would win the Second World War. Now, it's that they'll come back from the dead. Nazi zombies — the undead Third Reich — have shambled, lumbered, and run headlong through popular culture since the mid-twentieth century, creating a small but significant sub-genre of films, and raising questions about the nature and function of these recurring social villains. Beginning as a mere allusion, arising from "evil scientist" narratives of the World War II era, and finally making their way to the Sundance Film Festival in 2009, Nazi zombies have wrested a place of note in the horror film genre, drawing on symbols, spectacles, and social fears over half-a-century old, to evoke — and mock — audiences' deepest fears. Why Nazi zombies? As we'll see, the undead of the Third Reich offer the same grotesque parody of death as any other zombie, and then, so much more.

It is no accident that one of Western culture's iconic monster figures, characterized as a relentless flesh-eating ghoul, void of emotion, personality, or free will, has been merged with the image of the Nazi, one of Western culture's most beloved villains, also often framed as relentless, stoic, and succumbing to mass mentality (in sharp contrast with the expressive individualism of American and Western European heroes). As Judith Halberstam (1995) notes, "monsters are meaning machines" that speak to the anxieties of the culture that produced them (p. 21), and Nazi zombies are no exception. Much as zombies have remained on the cultural margins, rejected by the academy in favor of vampires, werewolves, and other more "attractive" undead killers, Nazi zombie films have inhabited the peripheries of the landscape of the living dead, and yet, they ... keep ... coming (Russell, 2005, p. 7; McIntosh, 2008, p. 6). And it is that relentless progression of the Nazi zombie film into the future, along with the evolution of both its creatures and its meaning, which is the focus of this chapter.

Censorship, Science, and the Nation-State

In 1941, the United States was on the verge of entry into World War II, and the motion picture industry was just beginning to flex its muscle against the tight ideological control of the Production Code Administration, which clearly intoned that "the history, institutions, prominent people and citizenry of all nations shall be represented fairly" (Koppes and Black, 1987, p. 29). In spite of this directive, however, the advance of fascism and the outbreak of war in Europe offered enticing subject matter that was difficult to resist: "Wars have obvious dramatic potential, and the studios knew a story 'ripped from the headlines' could draw audiences" (Rostron, 2002, p. 85). At the same time, studios also had tangible reasons for caution. Overseas box-office receipts were a substantial part of their profits, while at home, most of America's heartland was fervently isolationist. Films stepping too far into controversial territory risked hostile reactions, including censorship.

The presumed power of the movies made their content a hot issue. The Production Code, which imposed stringent restrictions on motion picture portrayals of a wide range of subjects, had caused a sharp cutback in the treatment of social and political issues by the major studios in the mid-to-late 1930s (Bernstein, 1999), but as the nation geared for battle, the movies became a prime instrument for public persuasion — so much so that Joseph Breen, the head of the Production Code Administration, accused Hollywood (and in particular the Hollywood Anti-Nazi League) of an attempt to "capture the screen of the United States for Communistic propaganda purposes" (Koppes and Black, p. 22).

In 1939, Warner Bros. broke through the barrier on political topics and premiered the controversial *Confessions of a Nazi Spy*, which revealed, in melodramatic fashion, that Germany sought to conquer the world. The picture's release netted a host of problems for the studio: an injunction from the German-American Bund; official protest from the German Ambassador, Hans Heinrich Dieckhoff; and threats on the lives of Jack Warner and the film's star, Edward G. Robinson (Shane, 1976, p. 40; Birdwell, 1999, p. 76). The stage was then set for the appearance of a rapid succession of major studio releases with pro-intervention themes.[2]

From within this context of wartime commentary, emerged the first associations between National Socialism and zombies; comically at first, with the most subtle of allusions, in the 1941 Monogram release, *King of the Zombies*. Directed by Jean Yarbrough, the production was the first Poverty Row zombie film, and has received more critical and scholarly attention around issues of racism than for its ties to National Socialism (Bogle, 2001, p. 74; Flint, 2009, p. 19). Its narrative turns on the misadventures of Bill (John Archer) and his black valet, Jeff (Mantan Moreland). After the plane carrying the two crash lands on a mysterious Caribbean island during the Second World War, they seek shelter in a nearby mansion, owned by Austrian scientist, Dr. Sangre (Henry Victor), and through a series of comic mishaps, learn that the evil doctor has taken an American admiral captive, and is interrogating him, using voodoo magic — the press kit obliquely states that the evil doctor is a "secret agent for a European government" (Monogram, 1941).

Dr. Sangre has created a cadre of zombies, brought back from the dead to work as slaves. Here, the association with Nazi Germany resides in the evil scientist — controlling the wills of hapless others to do his bidding — zombies in the service of Nazism, rather than Nazi zombies. This is a trope which resurfaces in the film's "sequel," *Revenge of the Zombies* (1943), and again in the post-war period, in *Creature with the Atomic Brain* (1955). The former, released during the war, employs explicit Nazi themes and iconography — including goose-stepping zombies and a heel-clicking Nazi villain (John Carradine)—to create clear ties between malevolent science and the nation-state. Dr. Max Heinrich von Altermann is attempting to create a race of zombie super-soldiers to support the Fatherland in the war: "I am prepared to supply my country with a new army, numbering as many thousands as are required…. Against an army of zombies, no armies could stand … zombies would fight on so long as the brain cells which receive and execute commands still remain intact."

Creature with the Atomic Brain, however, produced and released a decade after the end of the war, returns to a more subtle indictment of Nazi science. When a German scientist, Dr. Wilhelm Steigg (Gregory Gaye), born in Stuttgart, trained in Berlin, and subtly identified as a former Nazi, develops highly advanced atomic technology—vastly exceeding the American government's experiments—which allows him to reanimate the dead and order them to do his bidding via radio control. Steigg, of course, is in league with a criminal (Michael Granger), and sends the zombies on a spree of revenge killings that terrorize the city. Here, in the post-war era, as international relationships with Germany are normalizing, the link between science and the politics of the nation-state is severed, and the zombies' puppet-master is portrayed as duped and laden with misgivings—which ultimately bring about his death at the hands of the true villain, Granger's character, Buchanan.

Taken together, these three films extend familiar themes of mad science (established in the previous decade by notable horror actors such as Lionel Atwill, Lionel Barrymore, Boris Karloff, and Albert Dekker) and the undead (*White Zombie* [1932], *The Walking Dead* [1936], *The Man They Could Not Hang* [1939]), hand-in-glove into the realms of war and politics, setting the stage for the emergence of the Nazi zombie in film. The association of evil (or at least, horribly misguided) science, Nazi Germany, and zombies that these films began continues, initially in not-quite zombie films like *They Saved Hitler's Brain* (1963) and *The Frozen Dead* (1966), to the Nazi zombie's full-fledged screen debut in the late 1970s, and into the present day. Scientific experiments to create unstoppable foot soldiers which would tip the scales of war in the Third Reich's favor—and their hideous results—would become the most common explanatory devices for the appearance of Nazi zombies throughout the genre, thanks in no small part to Hitler's fascination with science, and the real-life experimentation that was carried out during the Nazi era. Marko Makilaakso, director of the 2008 film *Stone's War* (aka *War of the Dead*) relates:

> I was interested about the true stories of Hitler's science experiences during WWII and it was just too damn good an idea to use the Nazis doing secret tests to create the perfect human being but ending up with Zombies and killing everybody. The irony is in there…

So, it began. And it is exactly the persistence of those associations and themes into the future that asks to be explored and understood.

To Die and Live Again

> Gentlemen, in a hundred years still another color film will portray
> the terrible days we are undergoing now. Do you want to play a role in
> that film which will let you live again in a hundred years?
> —Barta, 1998, p. 130

When the Reich Minister of Propaganda, Joseph Goebbels, posed this question to his Nazi comrades in 1945, joining the legions of the reanimated dead was probably the farthest thing from his mind. And yet, the insight that authored Goebbels' question *did* prefigure the persistence of National Socialism in Western popular culture. Indeed, it has not taken a hundred years for those players to live again in film; Nazis have never faded from the Silver Screen. In fact, as Florentine Strzelczyk (2000) observes, they have become embedded as icons and signifiers within popular culture: "Far from being relegated to the garbage dump of history as horrific, yet antiquated monstrosities, the spectacles, visual fantasies, and paraphernalia of National Socialism have assumed a privileged place, not only in entertainment films, but in American mass culture in general." (p. 94) Similarly, in his 1978 review of Hans-Jurgen Syberberg's *Hitler: A Film from Germany* (1977), Nigel Andrews (1978) noted Hitler's (and by extension, the Nazi party's) iconic presence and persistence as part of the film industry, from "chamber melodrama ... to Nazi chic..." is "a startling phenomenon of our times" (p. 53).

Andrew's observation was written in the year following *another* startling phenomenon of our times — the first on-screen appearance of the Nazi zombie, in Ken Wiederhorn's *Shock Waves* (1977).[3] Promoted, in good exploitation style, as "The Deep End of Horror," the film spins a chilling tale of maritime Nazi military science gone awry. The zombies here wear Nazi uniforms and goggles, and lie submerged beneath the water, as if asleep, until they rise up and lumber through the water toward their prey. As Peter Cushing's character, their former commander, relates, the zombies are a division of *Schutzstaffel* (SS) soldiers,[4] "Der Toten Korps,"[5] who are "neither dead nor alive, but somewhere in between," biologically engineered to man U-boats without oxygen or the need to periodically surface. One by one, the passengers and crew of a stranded tour boat are dispatched by the zombies — always drowned — until Cushing, devastated by his role in this abomination, sacrifices himself, so that the tour boat survivors might escape.

These earliest of Nazi zombies deviate from what we now recognize as the template for zombies, the bottom-feeders of cinematic horror. Their grotesqueness derives directly from their crisp, homogenous Aryan appearance, combined with their relentless zombie nature. The goggles serve as eerie signifiers of their impenetrable undead status (so eerie, in fact, that filmmaker Steve Barker recalls his visceral reaction to them when he saw *Shock Waves* video cover art as a 10-year-old), and their removal is the sole means of the creatures' death, when removed. Also unlike more familiar zombies, Weiderhorn's undead are not flesh-eaters — or brain-eaters — or any sort of 'eaters' at all, further removing them from the vulnerabilities of human survival. All of this, combined with their status (both as zombies and as SS) as single-minded killing machines, allowed these Nazi zombies to strike terror into the hearts of their audiences.

In her essay, "Fascinating Fascism," Susan Sontag (1972) explores this association between the SS, terror, and visual fascination, describing them as "supremely violent, but also supremely beautiful":

> Why the SS? Because the SS was the ideal incarnation of Fascism's overt assertion of the righteousness of violence, the right to have total power over others and to treat them as absolutely inferior. It was in the SS that this assertion seemed most complete, because they acted it out in a singularly brutal and efficient manner; and because they dramatized it by linking themselves to certain aesthetic standards [p. 99].

These links to aesthetic standards were a deliberate strategy by the Nazi party in the 1930s to create and perpetuate Nazi ideology "ensuring Nazi ideology prevailed as Nazi aesthetics"— thus consciously creating ideologically-loaded signifiers which would become enduring elements of mass culture (Strinati, 2004, p. 5) And endure, they have, but with what meanings?

In an interesting turn, the Nazi zombies that follow those in *Shock Waves* are creatures of social learning, rather than the results of science-gone-awry — a rare thing in this subgenre, indeed. In two successive Eurocine releases — Jean Rollin's erotically-charged *Le Lac des morts vivants* (*Zombie Lake*) in 1981 and Jesus Franco's 1982 *L'Abime des morts vivants* (*Oasis of the Zombies*)[6]—Nazis caught between the worlds of the living and the dead serve as the avengers and guardians of history, reminding audiences of the inhumanities perpetrated by the living, cautionary figures against heartlessness and greed. The undead of the Third Reich would not take on this role again until 2009, with the production of Tommy Wirkola's *Dead Snow*.

In *Zombie Lake*, Nazi zombies take to the water again. Set in a small village in France, Nazi soldiers who were ambushed by resistance fighters during World War II, their bodies thrown into the nearby lake, rise up to exact retribution against villagers for the inhumanity of their deaths. The lake in question — the Lake of the Damned — has a history that goes back to the Inquisition. It was a site for Black Masses in the Middle Ages, and later, for child sacrifice to appease the spirits who rose out of their watery grave in search of blood, and continues to serve as an archive for the village's history of shameful deeds. A subplot of tragic love, clothed in lush camera work and accompanied by the film's love theme, allows one of the Nazi undead to deviate sharply from characteristic zombie mindlessness, as he encounters and bonds with his illicit child (conceived before his un-death), making him, quite possibly, the only sympathetic Nazi zombie of the sub-genre, and quite definitely, more human than the villagers.

For its part, *Oasis of the Zombies* offers a different sort of morality tale, delivered at the hands of decaying members of the Third Reich. Once again, flashing back to the inhumanities of World War II, a small Nazi squadron carrying gold across the African desert is ambushed and annihilated by Allied troops, and now, its members lie in wait beneath the sand, protecting the valuable shipment from any who dare to search for it. Nazi iconography abounds, with a painted swastika serving as a sign of warning to trespassers, and the worm-infested uniformed zombies are silently relentless. Greed brings about the deaths of nearly all treasure-seekers, except for the son of one of the original American soldiers, for whom the encounter with the Nazi zombies — referred to by the locals as "the sentries who guard the Great Secret"— serves as a *rite du passage*, wresting him away from his avarice, and remedying the selfishness, triviality, and disrespect of youth.

These two Eurocine productions are brimming over with the shoddy production values, wooden acting, and highly sexualized narratives that typically characterize exploitation films of the mid-twentieth century.[7] No small wonder, then, that they would be followed by a film written and directed by the man behind the now-cult classic, *Blood Sucking Freaks* (1976), Joel Reed. Reed's film, *Night of the Zombies* (1981),[8] returns to World War II–era cautionary themes about science gone horribly awry, as both Nazi *and* American zombie soldiers, exposed to Gamma 693, a toxic gas developed for wartime use, carry out nocturnal war games, and plot to take over the world. Reed brought both the budgetary limitations and the unconventionality of the exploitation film industry with him to Bavaria, where the filming took place. Concerns over chemical warfare, the scientific enhancement of troops, and ambitions of world domination that had animated both World War II and Reed's own Vietnam-era service lurked just below the zombies' forays into the world of the living. But even more so, for Reed, zombies "reach out and touch our fear of death ... our panic over our own mortality."

Nazi Zombie Kitsch

Is the horror and attraction of the Nazi zombie the result of confrontation, as Reed suggests, with the nature of our own mortality? A fascination with spectacle? The expression of profound social fears? A yearning for a caricature of evil in the face of contemporary complexities? Or have the symbols, imagery, and psychological evocations of the Third Reich become, as Saul Friedlander (1993) suggests in *Reflections of Nazism: An Essay on Kitsch and Death*, reconfigured into the high drama of overwhelming aesthetic?[9] Tommy Wirkola, director of the sub-genre's most recent addition, *Dead Snow* (2009), recognizes just the type of heightened aesthetic contrast to which Friedlander refers, in his own film: "Seeing the zombies in those uniforms, surrounded by snow and vast nature.... There is just something beautiful and scary about it."

The kitsch appeal of the Nazi as "Hollywood's most beloved villain" (Strzelczyk, p. 94) has captured the imagination of several of the filmmakers behind the most recent waves of Nazi zombies, among them, Wirkola, Steven Barker, director of *Outpost* (2008), and Peter John Ross, director of *Horrors of War* (2006):

> BARKER: The Nazis were simply a cast iron evil, with powerful (and affordable) iconography that hadn't been seen on the big screen for a long time and had a fear factor that came from our childhoods.
>
> ROSS: Lately, it's been harder and harder to think of tried and true "bad guys." There is so much gray area concerning right and wrong that it seems like the Nazis were the last true undisputed "bad guys." No matter how you look at it, Nazis were evil.
>
> WIRKOLA: Well, a Nazi is the perfect movie-villain, no doubt about it. If you combine that with one of the other type of cool "villains"—zombies—then you have the ultimate bad guy. I mean, what is more evil than a zombie? A NAZI ZOMBIE!

Kieran Parker, story-writer and producer of *Outpost* echoed these sentiments, emphasizing that in his conception and writing of the original story, and later, in the film's production, it was not the *reality* of the Nazi character that he and director Barker sought to engage, but its distilled, fantastic form: "...to us the Nazis were very much the Pantomime Villain from our Childhoods—we're not talking about reality Nazis from *Schindler's List* here, we're talking about the bad guys from *Raiders of the Lost Ark* or *Where Eagles Dare*...." For these filmmakers, Nazis are kitsch — Saturday matinee villains — archetypes — caricatures deliberately adopted for their evocative familiarity, as well as the sorts of easily recognized symbols, paraphernalia, and iconography noted by Sontag, Strinati, and others. And while Wirkola credits some of his Nazi zombie inspiration to actual history:

> Since the north of Norway, where I am from, has a strong war history, it felt natural, in a weird way, to make the zombies NAZI ZOMBIES. It just felt right. We could combine one of our favorite types of films, the zombie-movie, with war history that actually occurred in our region.

Others, like Steven Barker, kept a carefully planned distance from political and social realities:

> ... we didn't want to cross the boundaries of taste and disrespect the millions of lives lost to genocide. Nazis are scary enough as it stands we were never, in that movie, going to able to explore anything deeper with regards to their actions so we kept them at the level of Saturday matinee villains.

Joel Reed began *Night of the Zombies* at an even greater remove from real-world politics. Reed's original intention for the film was to draw on imagery spurred by his own experiences during the Vietnam era, writing and directing a Japanese zombie war film. "There was this face, stuck in my mind — the perfect zombie soldier." But, when the financial realities of flying his cast and crew to Japan loomed large, filming in Germany became his fallback. "My travel agent said 'Could they be Nazi zombies instead? I've got a deal here for Germany' and so, we went to Germany and did Nazi zombies."

Nazi Zombies: The Next Generation

Following that trio of films in the early 1980s, cinematic Nazi zombies went under cover for roughly a quarter of a century, finally living again in Peter John Ross's and John Whitney's *Horrors of War* (2006). With promotional materials warning that "In War, Death Is Not the Only Thing to Fear," *Horrors of War* draws together malevolent Nazi science, World War II combat, and evocative SS imagery, but this time Nazi zombies aren't the only undead on the battlefield: "We combined Nazi zombies and werewolves to have a rocking good time like a midnight movie (à la *Grindhouse*) that doesn't take itself too seriously. We just wanted a fun homage to the horror movie hosts from the UHF days and the kinds of movies we loved growing up." With that mingling of monsters, brought forth by a stereotypically evil Nazi scientist to create indestructible soldiers for the Third Reich, Ross and Whitney cause us to think about undead archetypes. As Steve Barker and Marko Makilaakso both point out, there is more "elegance" to vampires: they are sexual beings, with personalities, and they suggest a more "elitist" quality, with new members of their world either choosing or being chosen. In contrast, zombies and werewolves share similar brutal, arbitrary origins, and typically exude a similar rough physicality.

In yet another innovation in the sub-genre, Ross and Whitney usher in a new era for the Nazi zombie, and a new demeanor. The zombies portrayed in *Horrors of War* were zombies in a hurry. Fast zombies. Really fast zombies. *Horrors'* zombies joined the ranks of zombies already rushing around screens, in films such as *28 Days Later* (2002), *House of the Dead* (2003), and of course, Zack Snyder's 2004 remake of *Dawn of the Dead*. In George Romero's zombie classic *Night of the Living Dead* (1968), the ambulatory nature of the zombie is clearly defined in an exchange between a reporter and a law enforcement officer: "Are they slow-moving, chief?" "Yeah... They're dead." From our first glimpses of zombies, with their roots in the lore on Haitian Vodou, until the new millennium, their images have been invoked as metaphors for mindlessness and lethargy. They were creeping, mob-like, diseased. In light of all that, what does it mean to make Nazi zombies *fast* zombies? According to Ross, "We wanted them to be uber-soldiers for the Nazis and wanted them to be faster and just not be affected by bullets as much as regular soldiers. We wanted the 'perfect soldier' as in killing machines with no thought."

The Nazi zombies in Steve Barker's film, *Outpost*, also picked up the pace. Barker hoped to connect with the "creeping, fatal inevitability" of the traditional, Romero zombies, but also the "visceral intensity" of the fast zombies of the twenty-first century, aiming to strike a middle ground: "I wanted them to feel coldly efficient, so that they could pace up if they needed to but generally don't feel that need because they see themselves as so superior." In *Dead Snow*, Tommy Wirkola also saw "fast" as the best characterization for his zombies, specifically because they were Nazis:

> Somehow it just seemed wrong to have slow Nazi zombies. They had to be fast, they had to be merciless, like predators, in order to live up to their name.... I wanted them to be sharp, you

know, bursting with energy, not like Romero's zombies, who almost look tired. These are aggressive, like rabid dogs, and will hunt you down.

Barker (*Outpost*), Wirkola (*Dead Snow*), and Marko Makilaakso (*Stone's War*) are the filmmakers behind the three most recent films in the Nazi zombie sub-genre. In the years 2008–2009, their films have made a substantial contribution to both the sub-genre's quality and visibility, with the Nazi zombies in Wirkola's *Dead Snow* (2009) running headlong into popular consciousness, as a result of the film's debut at the Sundance Film Festival.

The narratives of both *Outpost* (2008) and *Stone's War* (2009) once again address collective fears of Nazi science during World War II. In *Outpost*, the scene is Eastern Europe in the present day, while the cinematic present of *Stone's War* is World War II–era Finland, director Makilaakso's home. Both films portray the devastating outcomes of malevolent science through human experiments, as the protagonists of the two films battle the experimentally undead.

Outpost's narrative unfolds through an atmospheric sepia tint — the result of Barker's desire to move the film "toward a more traditional, almost old fashioned feel, which played with light, shadow and suspense"— as a team of mercenaries investigates a World War II Nazi bunker. Unknown to them, the bunker was the site of human experiments in Unified Field Theory — advanced science again perverted in the service of the Third Reich. The gritty mercenaries are cast as volatile and rugged — blunt instruments — in opposition to the stoic order and control of Nazi science. The team's commander, D.C. (Ray Stevenson), is ignorant of the horror to come as he surveys the laboratory and mutters "I never really trusted science." As the team uncovers documentation and newsreels of the experiments, they are butchered, one by one, confirming the film's tag line: "You can't kill what's already dead." Although director Barker went to great lengths to create an interchangeable villain — one that he felt "didn't really need to be Nazi on any narrative or character level"— the powerful Nazi iconography and themes discussed earlier in relation to the work of Sontag and Strzelczyk seem inseparable from the film's narrative structure and function, and make any zombies other than Nazi zombies in *Outpost* not worth consideration. As in Wiederhorn's *Shock Waves*, terror and the regimented order of Aryan perfection go hand-in-hand.

At another bunker, over half-a-century earlier, Captain Martin Stone (Andrew Tiernan) and his unit join an elite platoon of Finnish soldiers to attack their common enemy. When they do, the soldiers they kill rise up to fight again. Stone and those under his command realize they have awakened an enemy that is tied to one of the War's deadliest and most terrifying secrets — Nazi experiments to create the perfect soldier. Here, *Stone's War*, like *Outpost*, has connected with the sub-genre's roots and traditions, speaking to fears that have remained part of audiences' subconscious landscape for generations. Director Makilaakso noted that archival news accounts of Nazi science informed the back-story of Hitler's plans to create the perfect human being in the film. While not aspiring to the status of historical drama, other aspects of *Stone's War* were inspired by fact, as well, such as the Finnish-American task force, led by Stone, which grew out of the real-life story of a boat that left New York on December 1939, heavy-laden with volunteers to fight with the Finns against the Soviet Union.

In creating *Dead Snow*, the final film in this cluster of cinematic Nazis who refuse to die, director Tommy Wirkola also drew on the landscape and war history of his home region as backdrop and inspiration for the film's horrific narrative. That, however, is where most of the similarities between *Dead Snow* and other contemporary Nazi zombie films end.

Wirkola takes us back to the sub-genre's origins — to the explicit comic sentiment of *King of the Zombies* — to craft a film which utters its messages with tongue-in-cheek, and seeks to leave us gasping from laughter, as much as from horror, drawing more on the comedy of Peter Jackson's *Braindead* (aka *Dead Alive*, 1992) than on *Night of the Living Dead*: "We wanted to make a film that was a tribute to the good old days. A film that would make people laugh seconds after they had seen a head being ripped to pieces. A film that could combine action, horror and comedy."

Unlike the majority of the Nazi zombie films produced since those early days of *King of the Zombies*, *Dead Snow* is not a war film, nor is it a message about science-gone-horribly-wrong. Like its 1980s Eurocine predecessors (*Zombie Lake*, *Oasis of the Zombies*), it is a cautionary message about *human nature* gone horribly wrong, combining a "World War II village uprising" back-story, similar to that of *Zombie Lake*, with morality tales about careless youth and the consequences of greed, reminiscent of *Oasis of the Zombies*.

The story centers on a mountain cabin, where a group of students are gathered to for a vacation of skiing, snowmobiling, and sex. On their first night, a stranger arrives to warn them about the history of the area, and its unsettled souls. During the Second World War, oppressed villagers rose up against Nazi occupiers, who fled to the mountains to escape, ultimately dying there. The heedless youths mock his story and send him on his way. Little time passes before the zombies appear and the killing starts, and the youths are dispatched, one by one — plucked from the outhouse, ambushed from beneath the snow, torn limb from limb. The reason? At the root of the zombies' predatory hunt is the small box of gold found by the vacationers, buried under the cabin floor. Gone is the traditional zombies' mindless, purposeless lumbering. Wirkola's Nazi zombies demonstrate motivations, intentionality, and strategy in their efforts to regain their gold from the careless youths who have unearthed it: "Well, since they are Nazis — German — we figured that they had to be organized. That they worked in groups, like small battalions. They are precise and know what they want, [they're] not just wandering around, looking for fresh meat." Only one student escapes the zombies' carnage and makes his way through the woods, to the group's car. Too late, he remembers the large gold coin that he had earlier taken from the box and hidden in his pocket. Were it not for this act of greed, he might have lived to drive down the mountain to safety.

With its strong visual and narrative similarities to films in the teen horror genre, *Dead Snow* effectively resituates the Nazi zombie in contemporary popular culture. It's strong use of the symbols, icons, and lore of the Third Reich are decontextualized, plucked from the fields of war and inserted into the midst of snow tubing, heavy drinking, and post-adolescent courtship rituals — ghastly caricatures, void of ideological power, which parody, rather than represent, their history — truly, the epitome of Nazi kitsch.

Conclusion: Parodies and Alternatives

As Jamie Russell (2005) points out in *The Book of the Dead*, the zombie is a symbol of a range of anxieties, from our most basic fears of death and deformity, to a host of social issues and ills (p. 8). While this is true of Nazi zombies on many counts, it would be a mistake to oversimplify their role in Western culture, and neglect to examine those things that happen when specifically *Nazi* zombies rise up and walk among us. The brute physicality of the zombie — decomposing predators, "the great unwashed" of horror cinema — combined with the highly stylized, controlled, precise archetype of the Nazi, can, in many cases, be seen as the embodiment of parody itself, both robbing the Nazi image of those elements which give it cultural power, and endowing a classically mindless creature with history and intent. Thought about in this way, Nazi zombies embody the power of both and of neither, creating a hybrid social villain, which, by its very existence, mocks its own origins.

The cinematic image of the Nazi inhabiting the metaphorical "space" between life and death has also worked with other cultural forms (comics, material culture, literature, and in recent decades, video games and new media) in the construction of an enduring niche for National Socialism in popular culture, and particularly, in the realm of the fantastic. For decades, "alternate history," a sub-genre of science fiction, has explored scenarios in which the outcome of World War II was altered, adding to the Third Reich's almost unprecedented entertainment value. The high prevalence of these altered and counterfactual histories moved Gordon Chamberlain, in his "Afterword" to *Hitler Victorious*, to ask "who, outside the literary world, has done more to promote [science fiction] than Hitler?" (Chamberlain, 1986, p. 290) While a case can hardly be made for Nazi zombies as allohistory, their presence in the landscape of cinematic horror contributes both to popular imaginings and conversations about "What if?" (...if the Nazis had engineered an uber-soldier; ... if Nazis still lurked "out there, somewhere"; ... if the war was never *really* over, etc.), and to the firmly situated nature of National Socialism in popular culture, as its symbols, icons, and images are recontextualized and subject to new forms of meaning-making. Nazi zombies, relentless figures of persistent evil, both use and complicate those strong visual elements of National Socialism, highlighting our fears, parodying our monsters, and spinning morality tales, as they menace audiences from the Silver Screen. And as their cinematic history illustrates, they just ... keep ... coming.

NOTES

1. I would like to extend my deepest thanks to Joel Reed, Peter Ross, Steve Barker, Tommy Wirkola, Marko Makilaakso, and Kieran Parker for their generosity of time and spirit in participating in interviews for this article, all of which were conducted in 2009.

2. Charlie Chaplin's *The Great Dictator* (United Artists 1940), *I Married a Nazi* (20th Century–Fox 1940), and *A Yank in the R.A.F.* (20th Century–Fox 1941). In 1939, though, only six titles in all dealt directly with Germany and the European situation, and of those, all but *Hitler, Beast of Berlin*, a low-budget Poverty Row film released by Producers Releasing Corporation (PRC), were tales of espionage (*Television Spy, Espionage Agent, The Lone Wolf Spy Hunt, They Made Her a Spy,* and *Confessions of a Nazi Spy*).

3. Alternately titled *Almost Human* and *Death Corps.*

4. The Nazi party's "Shield Squadron," formed in 1925, numbering nearly one million elite police and military personnel.

5. Literally, the dead corps.

6. The release date for *Oasis of the Zombies* varies by source. IMDB cites 1981, scholarly literature cites 1982, and the DVD release cites 1983.

7. This should not be confused with the trajectory of Nazisploitation films, which blended sexual imagery with Nazi themes, from the late 1960s onward, and resulted in such cult classics as *Ilsa: She Wolf of the SS* (1974). These films were much more deliberate in their linkage of Nazi atrocities, gore, and perverse, sadistic sexuality.

8. Alternately titled: *Gamma 693* or *Night of the Wehrmacht Zombies.*

9. Such that the emotions they invoke cease to have meaning other than as "art." See Friedlander's introduction for more on this.

10

Eating Ireland
Zombies, Snakes and Missionaries
in Boy Eats Girl

CORY JAMES RUSHTON

A woman, surrounded by scaffolding, is painting in a medieval Irish church; the stained glass window behind her depicts St. Patrick stepping on a snake, indicating that the church might be dedicated to the saint who famously threw all serpents out of Ireland. In the course of her work, the woman finds the door into the crypt, and descends into it, seeing lit candles and a shrine to "The Order of Foreign Missionaries, 1804–45." The trope of the old stone church seems to alert the viewer: this horror film will deal with an ancient and European evil. But this is misleading, for the threat will not be in the first instance chronological (from the distant past) but geographical (from the distant places visited by Irish missionaries). Or perhaps it will be both, although the nineteenth century is not as ancient as the medieval invoked by the church itself. There are mixed messages here, even in the opening scene: the missionaries are buried here in the church and candles are lit for them, but are also described as having disgraced themselves by becoming involved in pagan practices abroad; the church's priest, Father Cornelius, describes an old book of "Voodoo" ritual kept below as "a book of pagan trickery," but someone keeps the crypt's shrine lit by candle and looking very much like a functioning place of worship. Further, if the book is full of "pagan trickery," it also does what it says it will do: the rituals within it can help raise the dead, and when performed the ritual resurrection is flawed only because a crucial page is missing. There is a threat here, but its location is ultimately unclear: the book, the church, missionaries, snoopy female painters?

The film is *Boy Eats Girl* (2005), an Irish high school zombie comedy — perhaps, more accurately, *the* Irish high school zombie comedy, being in a category of one. How and why these relics of a pagan faith are kept in the church's crypt, or why the altar is kept stocked with lit candles, is never quite explained; someone has also been feeding an orange and yellow banded snake, which is shown slithering around the crypt and will later be instrumental in resolving the plot. What looks like incoherence — a medieval Irish church venerating the remnants of a despised foreign faith — nevertheless points towards an emergent meaning: why make a point of showing Patrick stepping on a snake before showing an actual snake in the crypt below, unless the juxtaposition is deliberate? It is less about the film's importance than it is about textual production in an age of pop culture and pastiche. This chapter will argue that the film can only be interpreted, in fact becomes interesting, when seen as participating in a number of otherwise independent discourses. Some of these discourses are obvious, as with the film's engagement with the zombie genre (both the Caribbean kind, as in *White Zombie*, and the cannibal/viral kind, as in the films of George A. Romero) and the high school alienation horror-comedy (as in *Buffy the Vampire Slayer*). But there are less obvious discourses which nonetheless play a pivotal interpretive role: the film's Irishness; its emphasis on paralysis and death; the attention paid to the Catholic Church, even if awkwardly expressed; the ways in which a film's thematic interests can be either undermined or paradoxically brought out more clearly by issues of commercial pragmatism. *Boy Eats Girl* is more than simply a film about zombies which takes place in Ireland; it is an Irish film which uses the zombie to say something about Ireland, just as Romero's *Dawn of the Dead* used the zombie to say something about consumer culture and Boyle's *28 Days Later* used the zombie to say something about 21st-century aggression. This chapter will pick up various aspects of *Boy Eats Girl* in an attempt to build a picture of the film, what it tries to do and what it achieves; the aim is to be thorough and suggestive, rather than to produce a definitive interpretation.

Within the Zombie Genre

When *Boy Eats Girl* was first released, the obvious antecedent seemed to be the British *Shaun of the Dead* (2004), the contemporary (and possibly still current) high water mark for zombie comedies. In that, *Boy Eats Girl* is hardly alone, as *Shaun* seems to have inaugurated a trend towards zombie comedies—but it is not an entirely accurate statement, either. The tradition of zombie comedy goes back much further than *Shaun*: arguably, back to the opening scene of *Night*, when Barbara's brother tries to frighten her with a Boris Karloff impression (Badley, 2008, p. 49, n. 1). As Linda Badley argues, with a few serious exceptions like *28 Days Later*, "zombies tend to be stooges—they specialize in stumbling incoherence, sick jokes, and the splatter film equivalent of taking pies in the face" (Badley, p. 35)—in *Dawn of the Dead*, a zombie literally does take a pie to the face. Dan O'Bannon's "Living Dead" series always had comedic elements; just before *Shaun*, the Mexican-wrestling/zombie mash-up film *Enter Zombie King* (also known as *Zombie Beach Party*) was released in 2003. Badley believes that the zombie comedy "shifted over time: from social allegory in the late 1970s to 'splatstick' (splatter slapstick) by the late 1980s and early 1990s, and from concern with the body politic to an obsession with the body itself—the body politicized as a site of anxiety, transgression, adolescent revolt, and liberating laughter" (Badley, p. 36). Although Badley allows that *Shaun* is a "notable exception" to the current (post–90s) crop of unfunny zombie films, she has ignored most of the field to do so: certainly, *Boy Eats Girl* aspires to both social allegory and comedy, as does (even more clearly) *Fido* (2006). Badley quotes director Edgar Wright's assertion that *Shaun* has no "zombie pratfalls" or "funny zombies at all," but *Shaun* is actually full of situational humor at the expense of its zombies: when Shaun and Ed try to kill a zombie with old vinyl records, or more caustically when the unpleasant people Shaun encounters earlier in the film appear in zombified form later.

What *Shaun* really popularizes is the idea of "national" zombie film: the rest of the world exploring how zombie apocalypses affect a series of non–American spaces (one early precursor to this trend is the New Zealand setting of Peter Jackson's 1992 film *Dead Alive*, a production involving, predictably, sheep). *Boy Eats Girl*, partly by accident and partly though some obviously post–*Shaun* marketing, is an Irish zombie film rather than a zombie film that happens to be made by Irish film-makers. In that, it is no different than a host of other recent films: the Japanese *Tokyo Zombie* (2005), New Zealand's *Last of the Living* (2008, but not involving sheep), or Britain's popular *28 Days* films. Each of these films makes some thematic use of their non–American settings, often in ways that are stereotypical enough that North American audiences will catch the clichés. *Tokyo Zombie*, based on a manga from 1999, depicts its two hapless male leads as being obsessed with jujitsu, leading the younger protagonist to survive the apocalypse as a contestant in a fighting arena that feels like the infamous Japanese television game shows frequently parodied in the west; the movie also indulges in a sporadic interest in schoolgirls. The action takes place on Black Fuji, a garbage-clogged parody of Japan's stunning natural feature. *Last of the Living* is noticeably set in Christ Church, and the plot is resolved when the surviving protagonists fly to an island research facility off the coast of Australia. *28 Days Later* engages in long, chilling shots of an instantly recognizable London, and ends when the protagonists escape to distant Scotland (also instantly recognizable). By way of contrast, the Milwaukee of Zack Snyder's *Dawn of the Dead* remake could be any American city, while the Pennsylvania of Romero's films only matters occasionally: when an Amish farmer helps some college kids in *Diary of the Dead*, for example. The recent *Zombieland* (2009), with its narrative built around a quest to reach a Californian theme park, is truly in the tradition of *Shaun* not because it is a comedy but because geography really matters in it (and, in any event, *Zombieland* sees itself in the tradition of *Ghostbusters* rather than *Shaun*, as anyone who has seen the film can readily attest).

Still, because *Boy Eats Girl* is from the British Isles, and because North American audiences do not always distinguish Ireland from England in anything but a superficial way, the film finds itself in direct competition with *Shaun*. The film's director Stephen Bradley notes that *Boy*'s timing was unfortunate: "Slightly frustratingly, we were actually already filming when *Shaun of the Dead* came out so it seemed like we were following the crowd but were actually just slightly and unluckily behind with our timing" (Disgusting, 2007). The long delay in bringing the film both to the screen and to DVD was not the fault of the producers:

> The film was released for the first time in Ireland in September 2005 but it had a difficult birth as it was originally banned by the Censor's Office there. The producers had to appeal the ban to get a release certificate. It eventually received a relatively relaxed 15A certificate, meaning that under 15 year-olds needed to be accompanied by an adult to watch the film in Irish cinemas. However, that decision by the Irish Censor's Office took alot [sic] of the momentum out of the film's release in Ireland and around the world. Fortunately Lionsgate bought the North American rights in 2006 which ensures that after a tricky start the film is going to be seen widely. I think the other issue with the delay has been the huge number of horror films lining up for release. I remember when *Boy Eats Girl* was screening at the Cannes Film Festival in 2005 it was one of 286 new horror films at that market alone [Disgusting, 2007].

Still, the packaging of the Region 1 (North American) release of the DVD, late as it was, borrows from *Shaun* in a way clearly intended to help promote the delayed film: the back cover, and the on-screen scene selection menu, depict zombies on an underground train — a motif entirely out of place, and in fact absent, from a film set in a small Irish town. On the front cover, Nathan sits with knife and fork atop a red telephone box, a well-known unofficial symbol for the British Isles. The back cover pronounces the film to be in the "tradition" of *Shaun*, acknowledging that the film's market in North America was likely to be composed of *Shaun* fans, especially given that the film's big pop cultural attraction — the female lead — had little or no traction outside Ireland and the British Isles.[1]

As Vehicle for Samantha Mumba

Samantha Mumba is solidly, unequivocally Irish; born in Dublin in 1983, her mother is Irish and her father is from Zambia. She came to prominence as a singer, influenced by Aretha Franklin, before moving into film with what is still her most successful project, the 2002 version of *The Time Machine*. She has not had a significant international presence since. Mumba once said that Americans "have a weird perception of Ireland. They think everybody has red hair and there are leprechauns running around" (Huxley, 2000). This is hyperbole, of course: a growing percentage of Americans may think their Christian president is a secret Muslim, but belief in Irish leprechauns remains admirably low. What better way, perhaps, to undermine this false image of contemporary Ireland than to play the romantic lead in the country's first zombie film? What better figure than the hybrid Samantha Mumba, black but Irish, Irish but black, certainly not someone "with red hair" — a new Irish citizen for 2005, when the country was still in its economically vigorous Celtic Tiger period, flexing its muscles on a European and international stage.

This is not to say that Mumba's casting could not simply be the attachment of a young, relatively popular star to a project that looks potentially marginal. It could, of course, be a fortuitous combination of motivations: pragmatic casting, an attempt at colorblind casting, or an advertisement for multicultural Ireland. However it came about, a black heroine potentially participates in a time-honored zombie trope. When Romero cast Duane Jones as the ill-fated hero Ben in *Night of the Living Dead*, he inaugurated a trend in which African Americans would play significant roles not only in Romero's film, but in films derived from his vision; when a white actor was cast as Ben in *Night of the Living Dead 3D*, virtually every review noted the fact. There are two serious reservations when considering Mumba's Jessica as a part of this progressive trend: one, she is the love interest, and not the central protagonist, and thus exists to be alternately threatened and rescued; and two, no character in the film makes any reference to her being non-white, even though her father is white (her mother is absent without explanation; the male lead, Nathan, though having an unexplained absent father, does not seem to immediately raise the same questions). The latter implies that the actress was cast in a colorblind manner — i.e., it may have been her pop star status which mattered to the film-makers, not her skin color or the genre's tradition of central black characters.

And yet, if we consider Jessica's foil — the sexually promiscuous Cheryl, a fellow student identified as being fourteen — Jessica's marks of difference might matter. Cheryl is the perfect stereotype of the Catholic school girl: short skirt, always chewing bubblegum, affecting a precocious kind of faux innocence, and to a degree representing the central symbolic paradox of this trope; the "sexy" schoolgirl outfit which marks the girl (the student and child) wearing it as a sexual object, despite the obvious objection that school outfits are not chosen by the individual but imposed by a system which should probably know better. When one of the film's characters directly addresses Cheryl's sex appeal, it is no coincidence that it is Mr. Frears, Jessica's father. Spotting Cheryl and a friend dressed to the nines in a wine bar, Frears comments explicitly on the chimera of their innocence: telling the two girls they look "extremely elegant with all that skin showing," his half-mumbled observation that "you all walk around acting so innocent" reads precisely like a justification for attempting to take advantage. When they suggest he buy them a drink, Cheryl asks for a "triple vodka with a splash of Red Bull." Frears agrees, the expression on his face testifying to what he thinks their binge-drinking will gain him. Cheryl's role at the film's climax reminds us that she is locked in a binary with Jessica, her fate — she is killed by her possessive boyfriend, Samson — suggesting something about her life, and the impossibility of a woman performing independent and serial sexual acts in a culture where the male is imagined as a predator. Through the shared figure of Mr. Frears, Jessica and Cheryl end up in stark opposition: in the film's economy, Jessica is the modest daughter who must be protected, while Cheryl, somebody else's daughter, is available as "legitimate" prey (shortly before Frears becomes prey himself). With Cheryl representing the well-known schoolgirl trope, Jessica is displaced to a degree, her color a marker which is paradoxically unmarked: she is a good daughter, but maybe not a biological daughter; she is Irish because the film accepts her as such, but our eye — through the camera which picks up her difference — is always thinking twice. This is not to say that the film wants us to notice that Jessica is black, despite the temptation to place her in the tradition of *Night*'s Ben, or to compare her with Naomie Harris's character, Selena, in *28 Days Later* (also black, and also the love interest). The film is content for us to simply register difference itself, to perhaps unconsciously consider Jessica as somehow *new* to Ireland: if Frears is not her biological father, and in the absence of a mother, Jessica seems unanchored to biological parents or traditional Irishness without being in any way marginalized, as paradoxical as that may seem (given that she physically registers difference but is seen nonetheless as an Irish ideal in other ways). Near the middle of the film, as the zombie epidemic is picking up steam, Jessica is seen on a leafy path leading her horse back to a stable: she is framed between green trees and sunlight, in some ways a more accurate depiction of the Irish image than the leprechauns and redhead image Mumba herself invoked. Jessica can contain this positive image of rural Ireland in a film which depicts Irish society, embodied in the school, as largely negative, as if she somehow bypasses the social altogether. Perhaps there is a sense here of Jessica's autochthonous nature: because of her blackness, Jessica is moved into the position of being the best of Ireland, self-created.

So what does Jessica actually do in this film, besides act as Nathan's love interest and potential damsel in distress? Her budding relationship with Nathan is derailed by her father's machinations — he falsely tells Nathan she was picked up by another boy in a nice car — and by an unfortunate, and related, optical illusion: Nathan sees her in another student's car, sitting up from picking up an object. The car's owner, Kennedy, is another of the film's male predators, routinely receiving oral sex in his car from Cheryl's older sister Charlotte even while taking another girl to the school dance; this propensity for automobile extra-curriculars in the school parking lot plays a significant role in Nathan's misreading Jessica's presence in his car. Jessica participates in the school's libidinal economy by not participating in it: she only appears to do so, and Kennedy's bragging that she invited him back to her house for strip poker confirms that she is an object to be fantasized about while remaining in essence untouched.

When Kennedy dies, he dies receiving oral sex — of a distinctly unpleasant but probably predictable kind — from the newly zombified Charlotte, who thus enacts her revenge for Kennedy's neglect. When Charlotte had asked who he was taking to the dance, she had noted that she could finally wear a dress she'd bought earlier — she couldn't before because, by her own admission, she was suffering from bulimia. Charlotte completely lacks a sense of her own worth, manifesting itself in a variety of behaviors. She is jealous of her own sister, and with good cause. Kennedy wipes his mouth with Cheryl's panties after Charlotte has performed oral sex on him, despite his earlier protest that he has had nothing to do with her: she's only fourteen, he protests. It is Charlotte's admission of bulimia that appears most thematically productive, even if it feels as though the film misses a step by not emphasizing it more. Charlotte's body issues are linked to a disease of consumption, of a failure to eat properly, and it is entirely fitting that when we do see her eat she is consuming the instrument of her oppression. For this one moment, shrinking Charlotte, eclipsed by her own sister and used by a man who doesn't even pretend to love her, enacts an overthrow of the film's system of predators.

Another important thing Jessica does is to mow down a whole horde of zombie students with a tractor in her family's yard; if we want to see her as a descendent of Ben, her body count would appear to be much higher. Perhaps she could earn extra points because she knows most of them from school, a place that the film depicts as hyper-sexualized as well as educationally inadequate. This image — Samantha Mumba in a tractor flinging zombie body parts in every direction — lingers, even though she will subsequently be trapped in the barn by two or three zombies and a fire. I suggest that it stays in the mind because, to be honest, it's pretty cool, but also (and more professionally) because it ties together a number of the film's deeper themes (even as Nathan's rescue of Jessica, and subsequent real rebirth, ties together its more explicitly stated themes). If Jessica represents the new Ireland, a place where one doesn't have to be a red-headed leprechaun who burns easily in sunlight, then it would seem significant that she single-handedly destroys most of her white Irish schoolmates in a vehicle made for digging up land in order to build anew. The film's final image is of emo–Irish Nathan kissing an Irish girl played by an actress with a Zambian father, in a town where most of their classmates and teachers (and her father) have been killed. If this is to be read as a happy ending, the focal point must be not on what has been lost, but what has been replaced (and that which replaces it).

St. Patrick

The film's opening sequence takes place in a medieval church, with modern stained glass behind Nathan's mother Grace as she works to restore the paintings. The camera stays on the bottom of this glass for a moment, never overtly showing that the glass depicts Patrick except through one detail: he is standing on a snake. Most western audiences will need no real introduction to Patrick, missionary to the Irish and the man who, legend has it, drove all the snakes from Ireland. It is difficult to think of another saint whose feast day remains so prominent in the western imaginary: St. Nicholas' day is December 6, not the 25th, and his transmogrification is so thorough that Santa Claus is really a separate character. Partly, Patrick's prominence is the result of Irish settlement in the Americas. Scotland's party takes place on poet Robbie Burns' birthday, while Patrick's Welsh analogue, David, cannot come close in prominence: cock-a-leekie soup simply can't compete with cheap lager infused with green food dye. More seriously, as Anthony D. Smith has argued, the growth of nation-states in the west was usually accompanied by a transition from the priest-class to a new class of intelligentsia: "The new motor of ethnic revival is generated by the historical, philological and anthropological researches of the scholars, and the literary and artistic achievements of the poets, musicians, dramatists and painters" (Smith, 1986, p. 160). In Ireland's case, the priesthood remained strong even when the nation engaged in exactly this kind of artistic self-creation (as in the work of James Joyce and W. B. Yeats, as discussed below), and for Smith, Ireland remains a nation with a much stronger clerical class than is found among its European neighbors. Therefore, I would note in turn, Scotland's adoption of a poet, St. David's relative lack of importance in Wales, and Patrick's position in both Ireland itself and within the Irish diaspora would make some sense. In any case, the film can depend on at least a superficial knowledge of Patrick's historical and legendary role in Irish history.

The origin of the story of Patrick's expelling all snakes from Ireland is unknown, although there are many theories: that the story is often seen as a metaphor for Patrick's victory over the Druids, to whom serpents are sacred, for example. There is some evidence that Irish stories of Celtic heroes slaying dragons or serpents were slowly transferred to Patrick over time; the well-known legend of Patrick's Purgatory, a pilgrimage site in the Middle Ages, included Patrick's defeat of a giant serpent whose body became the islands and red waters of Lough Derg or Red Lake, the Purgatory's location (Zaleski, p. 468). When Jacobus de Voragine records the story in the *Legenda aurea*, or *Golden Legend*, the emphasis is less on snakes than on poison: "He also obtained from God that no poisonous reptile could live in the whole province; and it is said that in answer to his prayer even the woods and bark from the trees in that region effectively counteract poison" (Voragine, 1993, p. 194). There is an odd Vodou intertext here: Melville Herskovit's early work (1937) on the propensity of syncretic Caribbean religions to combine elements of African pantheons with Catholicism. Herskovits noted that Patrick appeared in Haiti as an analogue for the West African (Dahomey) snake god, Damballa, clearly on the basis of Patrick's association with snakes (Herskovits, p. 638); while Herskovits' work is now controversial (see Apter, 2005), the existence of work positing a Vodou connection between Patrick and Damballa is intriguing when looking at a film which tries to make a paratactic connection between Patrick's snake, under foot in the church's glass window, and the foreign snake, lurking in the church's crypt. Even if the film-makers only know the legend or its possible Vodou connections in a superficial sense, they know enough: Patrick is involved with snakes and poison, and *Boy Eats Girl* is concerned (in a sense) with both, as we'll see below. The film's Ireland is built in the tradition of twentieth-century Irish texts, which is often a tradition of paralysis, stasis, and the impossibility of a future that is not haunted by the past.

As Irish Text

"If she [Ireland] is truly capable of reviving, let her wake," Joyce wrote in 1907, "or let her cover up her head and lie down decently in her grave forever" (quoted in Kiberd, 1996, p. 328). James Joyce is obviously not thinking of *Boy Eats Girl*, or about zombies at all — but *Boy Eats Girl* is thinking about Joyce. In a very early scene, a class is asked for discussion topics and fails to deliver. The teacher attempts to initiate debate by asking one of the class a deceptively simple question: "Samson, who are you?" Samson responds after a moment of hesitation: "Irish." When Samson cannot answer the follow-up question about nationality, or even what he meant by his own answer ("What does it mean to be Irish?"), the teacher asks for other opinions. Brandon gives what might be considered the safe answer, disguised as something profound: "Myths and legends; scholars and writers; Joyce, Beckett, Yeats." Joyce is the pivotal figure here, the national writer who portrayed Dublin through a "repetitive lexicon" designed to signal its colonized, repressed status: "spectral, shrivelled, stale, vague, mean, dull, dark, melancholy, sombre, sour, sullen, gaunt, bleak, bitter, denuded, pallid, grey, servile, consumptive, narrow, tawdry, gloomy, listless" (Whelan, 2002, p. 65). Toby Loeffler has recently argued that Irish nationalism has historically tried nearly, but not quite, everything in its efforts to define and then build an Irish nation: "parochial essentialism and linguistic revivalism, bourgeois antiquarianism as well as religious sectarianism; it has donned the bloody rags of violence and chaotic rebellion, but it has never been recognized in the Joycean guises of aesthetic experimentation and European cosmopolitan modernity" (Loeffler, 2009, p. 33).

Joyce's Dublin — the setting and indeed subject of most of his novels — is a place of paralysis, haunted and marginal: "'Paralysis' is a key word in the analysis of Irish culture and society; one finds it used by people as diverse in their social and political allegiance as Tone, Lecky, and Joyce" (Sheeran, 1983, p. 102). The 1904 Dublin of *Ulysses* is the "centre of paralysis," a city with a "dead heart" which could "render the discontents and estrangements of the modern world" (Kiberd, p. 329). "Joyce's art, it might be added, is the apotheosis of this paralysis, its transvaluation into stasis, an image of perfect beauty" (Sheeran, p. 102), never more than at the end of "The Dead," with snow falling over the entirety of Ireland, reducing everything (class, history, etc.) to a white sameness, the peace of Michael Furey's grave in distant Galway (Joyce, 1993, p. 256). "The Dead" is the final story in *Dubliners*, and is concerned with an educated Irish man, Gabriel, who is enamored of English and European culture: he is held in Ireland by his family, notably two maiden aunts, and his wife, Gretta, who is from rural western Ireland. In the course of the story, Gabriel is both accused of being a "West Briton" (Joyce, p. 214) — Irish but affecting to be English — and alarmed to discover that his "country cute" (p. 213) spouse has a tragic past in which an early lover dies in the snow after being forcibly separated from her.

Boy Eats Girl is most Joycean in its partial rejection of previous definitions of Irishness, and its acknowledgement that "Irishness" has generally been paralyzing rather than liberating. In the classroom, Cheryl sarcastically asks Brandon whether anyone bothers to read the writers on his *pro forma* list anymore; attempting to head off that particular discussion path (although, in this film, that path might be imagined as potentially fruitful), the teacher asks the question of another student: "What does it mean to be Irish?" The student, Nathan's friend Diggs, answers succinctly if with a question: "Suicidal?" Michael Furey is in some ways an obvious precursor to Nathan: both are teenagers willing to die for a girl they believe they have lost for good (Nathan wrongly, Michael Furey less so — his hold on Gretta remains strong years after his death, but he has still lost her in any way that would have benefited him), both are separated from their love interests by parental interference. Furey's importance to "The Dead" (and to the *Dubliners* collection) cannot be overstated: he is the "Irish past" which "can only return to the present as an absence: the Irish language, love, a national community have all been consigned to the spectral" (Whelan, p. 66). It is a song, "The Lass of Aughrim," which brings Furey back to Gretta's mind. Furey's return is what prompts Gabriel's "Generous tears" at the end of the story, when he imagines all of Ireland under the same snowfall.

Boy Eats Girl reimagines this scene in two key ways. First is Jessica's destruction of her zombified classmates: there are no generous tears shed here, and it is not snow but blood and fire which cover the Frears yard. Second is the reversal of Furey's fate. In the immediate narrative context of *Boy*, the brief conversation that subsequently follows Diggs' tentative suggestion that to be Irish is to be suicidal — and consisting of possible ways Diggs might kill himself — serves to signal Nathan's own eventual suicide attempt, the filmic event which prompted the release of *Boy Eats Girl* to be delayed by the Irish Film Classification Office. Nathan is saved by hanging at the end of the film, an ironic reversal of that which initially killed him — revived by the snake's bite, Nathan's shirt catches on a peg before he can fall into the flames which are consuming the Frears' stable. Neither Furey nor Nathan commits suicide entirely on purpose. Furey's death from exposure is not his primary intent, although Gretta says, "I think he died for me." Already ill when Gretta is to be sent to a convent, Furey appears below her window in the rain, "shivering" and saying he does not want to live (Joyce, pp. 251–53). Nathan prepares a noose and even places his neck within in it when he thinks Jessica has rejected him, but he smiles and starts to remove himself when his mother bursts into his room, the door knocking him from his stool. Both deaths are accidental but with suicidal elements; Furey's afterlife consists of haunting Gretta (and eventually Gabriel), while Nathan's life as a zombie both allows him more agency (he controls his hunger better than anyone else in the film, and remains intelligent and aware) and is eventually cured. Furey, for all the sense of peace that comes with the snow falling on his grave, is consistently associated with the cold of the rain, of shivering, of the ghostly, and through his name with vengeance; Nathan's return, in the end, will not be spectral at all, but a new beginning.

There is another return in the film, although it occurred in the film's diegetic past: the missionaries who went to foreign places and returned with the "Voodoo" paraphernalia in the church's crypt. The dates given on the commemorative plaque seen by Grace (1804–45) may not be random: 1845 is the date on which the Great Irish Famine began, with lingering traumatic effects on Irish society and culture, including the loss of three million people (one million dead, two million emigrating), a loss any country would have difficulty absorbing. As Whelan has put it in a 2002 article, the effect on the population sent Ireland "into a spiral of demographic decline which it has only recently arrested" (Whelan, p. 59), only a few years before *Boy Eats Girl* (a film, as we've seen, very interested in the loss of youth to a kind of hunger). In Whelan's view, the period after the famine (which includes the birth of Joyce in 1882) sees "the creation of an Irish radical memory that sought to escape the baneful binary of modernisation and tradition — the Hegelian view that all that is lost to history is well lost" and can only come back as nostalgia:

> This attitude generated a wistful, rear-mirror view of history where the past stayed firmly in the past, drained of politics and available merely as sentiment. Modernity's nostalgia for its past became a political placebo, sweetening the bitter pill of history and establishing the comfort of distance between past and present. By contrast, radical memory deployed the past to challenge the present, to restore into possibility historical moments that had been blocked or unfulfilled earlier [Whelan, p. 60].

The resulting "Irish Literary Revival was an extravagant discourse in the English language about dumbness in the Irish language," which "restlessly sought access to a world elsewhere — the world of Gaelic civilisation, dismissed, expunged, unknowable, vanished, whose very absence must be articulated or 'summoned' to use a Yeatsian word" (Whelan, p. 62).

It is not difficult to imagine that Irish missionary endeavors might have ended during an intense disaster which lasted seven years, but we do not need to imagine a complicated back story to make use of the 1845 marker. The film itself, as noted above, is confused on the matter of the missionary legacy, and this crypt, which is obviously tended but is also abject in the Kristevan (1982) sense, is denounced by the priest as full of "pagan trickery." The snake seen in the foreground — seen by the viewer, in the opening scene, and not by Grace — is implied as one side of an apparent binary, with Patrick's defeated serpent as the other side of the equation. Yet what looks like a threat — a poisonous snake, a scary Voodoo website Grace visits, skulls and candle in a crypt — is also that which brings Nathan back, at first imperfectly and then fully. Nathan's resurrection is briefly sketched with sudden staccato images and loud noises, the kitchen bearing signs of stress in the aftermath (a huge mess, burnt curtains). It is only after the priest visits, claiming that the Voodoo book is imperfect, that Grace realizes that a crucial page is missing. Who destroyed that page is unknown and unknowable, but it turns out that the snake in the crypt is the agent by which Nathan's zombification can be reversed and his life fully restored; Grace learns this only when the snake bites the zombified priest himself, curing him. That leaves open the strong possibility that the missing page tells the reader that the snake is necessary, is renewed life itself. Snakes have long and near-universally been considered, outside Judeo-Christian culture, to be symbolic of life: they shed their skin and renew themselves (cf. Green, 1992, p. 142).

When juxtaposed with the Patrick legend, however, reconciliation becomes impossible: if Patrick drove the snakes from Ireland, he did so in the service of another theory of life-renewal, the sacrifice of Christ. The film's view of Catholicism does not support a Christian reading, even in severely attenuated form such as that of the snake-handler cults in America. The yellow and orange snake is the return of something to Ireland, something vaguely related to the old Druidic culture supplanted by Christianity; more directly, the missionaries who went out into the world to spread the gospel of resurrection have paradoxically brought resurrection back instead. When Grace visits a "Voodoo" website, she sees a picture of a horned and goat-headed being, highly reminiscent of the Judeo-Christian devil; the viewer who knows Celtic legend might also see the similarities to Cernunnos, the horn-headed god who carries a serpent in his left hand, and is associated with fertility, death and the otherworld (Green, 1992). Filtered through our own western perceptions, the "Voodoo" deity appears Satanic even as that signification is troubled by the ambiguity surrounding the missionaries who brought this knowledge back, and perhaps the feeling that the faith which created the pagan book is not to blame if a page has been lost in Christian hands (who ripped out that page, we ask again). While we do not see the priest's zombification, we see him has a hoarder of knowledge, a keeper of secrets which he only imperfectly understands. He is a barrier rather than a guardian, and (given that he's the most likely candidate for lighting those candles in the den of pagan trickery) at least partially a kind of magician himself.

The priest is revealed to have become a zombie in a scene containing a key Catholic rite: confession. When Brandon, who had introduced some of the film's key Irishnesses in the classroom scene, makes a confession about spying in the women's washroom, the zombie epidemic is moving into full swing; his fate is one of many given in quick succession. The priest has now been infected himself, using his head to burst through the confession screen and attack Brandon; we see blood spill out from under the confessional, accompanied by an eyeball. A keen observer may note the influence of Lucio Fulci and Dario Argento here; Fulci as an early imitator of Romero and Argento as a director famously obsessed with gouging out eyes, especially the eyes of the peeper (perhaps his most famous scene comes in *Suspiria*, in which a woman staring through a door's peephole is shot through the eye, the bullet traveling precisely through the peephole itself). And Brandon is a peeper: he whispers about the "disgusting things" the girls were saying as he listened in. It is perhaps important that Brandon is also seen in the boy's bathroom between the classroom scene and his death: he is behind the cubicle door smashed by Nathan, when the latter overhears Kenneth and Samson discussing Jessica in "disgusting" terms of their own. Unseen, Nathan has listened to the boys' conversation just as Brandon did; but this looks more like a pattern when it comes to Brandon. Brandon's death reminds us that this film is about predators in a dualistic way: Brandon is predator when he spies on the girls in the washroom, and is prey when he goes to an older father-figure for confession. Despite the appearance of the eyeball, it is through the ear that a hierarchy of predators is established.

For Joyce, Roman Catholicism was "yet another insidious snare," something which his most famous protagonist, Stephen Dedalus (from both *Portrait of the Artist as Young Man* and *Ulysses*) must reject in order to grow and move beyond an Irish identity conceived as derivative in its English language and Roman faith (Whelan, p. 66). Irish history and culture become a part of this derivativeness, in something like the terms Mumba derides: red hair, leprechauns, St. Patrick's exiled snakes, and "Joyce, Beckett, Yeats." *Boy Eats Girl* ends with the destruction of all of this: Irish schoolmates, Irish teachers, and the Frears estate. But the priest survives, the only other zombie brought back, and the means by which the flaw in the book's resurrection spell is revealed. A cultural figure who exists to act as a conduit between yet another set of binaries — heaven/hell, past/present, salvation/sin, revelation/ignorance — does indeed function that way, but not between binary terms he entirely understands. Despite his dire warnings when he discovers Grace in the crypt, or when he discovers the book missing, he seems as prone to attack and bafflement as anyone. It is Grace — her name must surely be taken as significant now — who figures out what she's done wrong and how to fix it. In a world of predatory and inadequate fathers, the only mother in the film finds the healing snake and brings her son back to life.[2] Still, Grace disappears at the end of the film, driving away from the barn just as she arrived, not present in the final scene when Nathan and Jessica finally acknowledge their love with a kiss. In this new Ireland beyond binaries, all signs of the earlier generation must be, at least temporarily, suppressed.[3]

For Whelan, Joyce is the author who was initially able to step outside of the system of binaries encoded in Irish society: "The complexity of the Joycean cultural critique was its refusal to inhabit the binaries of Celtic or Saxon, Catholic or Protestant, modern or traditional, national or cosmopolitan, English or Irish — the binaries that so transfixed his contemporaries (and later commentators). Yeats, for example, reversed the value systems of Celtic/Saxon, traditional/modern, but still left the binaries intact" (Whelan, pp. 66–67). *Boy Eats Girl* is fundamentally with Joyce, although it may look otherwise at first.

The Need for Snakes

In this film, the zombie trope begins where it often does: as a signifier for both uncontrolled appetite and uncontrolled rage. At the same time, the film's zombie epidemic looks controlled, even to some degree directed. The first victim — the only person Nathan directly attacks until the end — is Samson, a school bully and nominally Cheryl's boyfriend, who has been threatening Nathan because Cheryl is showing an obvious interest in the latter. From there, the epidemic spreads almost exclusively through the school population, students and faculty: the two most obvious exceptions are the authoritarian male figures, Mr. Frears and the priest, neither associated with the school but sharing with the teachers their control over student lives (again, perhaps, merely a nominal control — just as Samson's "authority" over Cheryl is illusory, so the life of the school seems in no way affected by a set of teachers portrayed as ineffectual at best). The life of the larger community itself is relatively unaffected, the film's climax taking place in the rural space of Jessica's home and garden, in large part because it looks as though the zombified school has pursued her there: the few survivors — Cheryl, Diggs, and Nathan's other friend Henry — have been followed, the epidemic proceeding precisely along the school's social lines. To be a part of this society is to be trapped in it, condemned as it is reduced to living death.

The bite of the snake is the return of something lost when Patrick's Christianity drove all serpents from Ireland. The snake is dangerous, its bite salvific only in the context of the ritual which provides its proper context. Far from being pagan trickery, the missionaries have potentially brought life back to their homeland. The film's happy ending cannot be read in any other way, given that Nathan's resurrection and subsequent kiss with Jessica is entirely contingent on "Voodoo": not only would Nathan still be dead without that book and that snake, his relationship with Jessica is more secure because his male rivals are (and will remain) dead. Irish society — in the form of Mr. Frears and the overly-libidinous Kennedy, and perhaps in the equally libidinous Cheryl when she tries to seduce Nathan herself— is shown as a barrier to the life represented by Jessica and Nathan's kiss. In fact, the new Nathan is the result of two kisses, the snake's touch as well as Jessica's. If the film's imaginary is as I've suggested here, this should not surprise us. The return of the serpent, of pagan trickery, is just what Ireland needs to return to itself, in the idealized form of Jessica, whose difference is revealed to be precisely what, when lost, reduced Ireland to a paralyzed zombie state long before Nathan tried to kill himself.

The sameness of the zombie state does have the potential to move past the various paralyzing binaries of Irish society, but not in a particularly productive way, and it produces a final binary: Jessica's status as the primary distressed character at the end of the film. The last part of the movie is all about Jessica: Nathan wants to save her and simultaneously threatens her as he loses control of his affliction; Nathan's friends want to warn her that the zombies are heading her way. The film appears to indulge in a traditional/modern binary pivoting more than anywhere else on Mumba's Jessica: Voodoo snake/Patrick's snake, Afro-Caribbean religion/Catholicism, black/white, and (finally) living Ireland/paralyzed Ireland. I do not wish my argument, or this film, to be reduced something trite and possibly offensive: "Ireland! Now with Black People!" *Boy Eats Girl* does not directly make anything of Jessica's race, except as a silent marker of change rather than difference: she is Irish, part of the community, but her very presence simultaneously marks how far Ireland has come. Jessica's blackness does not mark *her*: it marks *Ireland*, and it does so positively, as something new in the Irish cultural mix. If the snow at the end of "The Dead" finds a way to short-circuit traditional Irish binaries and impose, temporarily, an equanimity, so Jessica unites in herself elements which short-circuit lingering Irish social binaries — tearing apart all those hungry Irish zombies and returning them to the earth.

NOTES

1. Another possible antecedent film is the American movie *My Boyfriend's Back* (1993), a lackluster Hollywood offering in which a dead teen is resurrected in time to take his dream girl to a high school dance. Outside of the high school setting, however, *Boy Eats Girl* does not resemble *My Boyfriend's Back* in any significant way.

2. It may be worth noting that in *28 Days Later*, it is Selena (a pharmacist with some medical training) who saves the protagonist Jim's life (replacing the film's original ending, in which Jim dies). While this has some interesting resonance with *Boy Eats Girl*, the narrative of *28 Days Later* does not seem to support a closer comparison of Jessica/Selena or Grace/Selena. In *28 Days Later*, the casting appears to be entirely colorblind, reflecting a multi-cultural Britain, which the film assumes to be the norm, unlike the stereotypical view of Irish society in *Boy Eats Girl*.

3. The final fate of Grace is in fact uncertain, I suspect because something was changed near the final editing. Grace jumps back into her car and Samson leaps onto the hood, thrusting a metal pole through the windshield and twisting it as if it has struck Grace; someone dressed the same way as Grace is then seen fleeing the car, but we never see her face. It is clearly meant to be Grace, but her complete absence from the film's final scenes (we do not see her leave the stable, or afterwards when the survivors are seen sitting to catch their breath and then walking slowly down the driveway) seems to require explanation if it is not be simply a weak part of the narrative. The film's final form supports the reading that Grace escapes, but much about the film's ending implies that Grace was meant to die in the original script (and perhaps even up to the very end of filming).

11

It's So Hard to Get
Good Help These Days
Zombies as a Culturally
Stabilizing Force in Fido *(2006)*

MICHELE BRAUN

One of the maxims of the zombie film has been that zombies are a destabilizing force that shatters the everyday lives of those humans who must fight off the menacing bite of the dead. Anagram Picture's *Fido* (2006) moves beyond this narrative of the emergent threat of the zombie to imagine what a post-zombie world might look like. *Fido* is not the first film to narrate the post-zombie threat: the final scene in the parody zombie film *Shaun of the Dead*, released two years before *Fido*, shows the now-zombie Ed "living" on, playing video games in the shed behind the house after the infection has been contained. However, *Fido* goes beyond this limited case to ask what a stable post-zombie culture might look like.

Fido imagines an alternate history for twentieth-century America. Instead of the civil rights movement and second-wave feminism of the 1950s and '60s, America spent the 1950s fighting the Zombie Wars and now survives as a post-zombie white middle-class utopia in which questions of racial and gender equality appear not to have been asked. The zombie's presence in this world allows it to occupy a disenfranchised role like that of the post-emancipation, pre-civil-rights-movement Black subject while the patriarchal control of the zombie threat extends to a heightened control of the women in the film. Despite these controls, it is the women and the children in the film who embrace the equally powerless zombie in recognition of a shared humanity. The recuperation of the zombie back into the human family at the end of the film, despite the quasi-governmental corporation Zomcon's fiscal and physical control of the zombie, actualizes the otherwise invisible social strictures on behavior that control human subjects in capitalist societies.

The visual and cultural cues of the movie, which so clearly set it in an idyllic 1950s setting in the town of Willard, suggest that the zombie can act as a culturally-stabilizing force. Much of the film is focalized through Timmy Robinson's view of the world. Timmy is trying to figure out how the world, and the zombies within in, work, a project his mother Helen eventually fully endorses (and which his father Bill does not). The film opens with a black and white newsreel explaining how the radiation in "space particles" reanimated the dead leading to the Zombie Wars and the fencing in of towns to keep zombies out. According to Zomcon's promotional newsreel, "A Bright New World," Zomcon developed the zombie collar and the town fences as a means of bringing an end to the Zombie Wars. As the newsreel ends, we discover it has been shown to a class of school children by Zomcon's new head of security, Mr. Bottoms. In response to Bottoms's request for questions, Timmy asks Mr. Bottoms: "Are zombies dead or alive?" Timmy's question becomes a persistent theme within the film, but Bottoms avoids directly answering it, responding that although zombies may seem human "these creatures only have one goal, and that is to eat your flesh." When his mother purchases a zombie later that day in response to the social pressure to keep up with the Joneses (or in this case, the Bottomses), Timmy gets the chance to decide for himself first-hand whether his zombie is dead or alive. Timmy names the family's new zombie, Fido, and finds in it a companion who rescues him from the constant torment of two local bullies. Fido's collar, which controls his desire to feed on human flesh, malfunctions so that Fido bites the neighbor, Mrs. Henderson, and unleashes a zombie infestation upon the town. When Mr. Bottoms discovers it is Fido that caused the outbreak, the zombie is taken away, much to Timmy's dismay. Despite Zomcon's confiscation of Fido, Timmy rescues his zombie, who is shown in the final scene participating in a backyard family cookout.

Timmy's befriending of the family zombie, and his recognition of Fido's former humanity by his open-heart-surgery scar, is the beginning of a recuperation of the zombie back into human society. As a former human being, the zombie undergoes a kind of social death like that described in Orlando Patterson's study of slaves and their social position, *Slavery and Social Death: A Comparative Study* (1982); this social death allows the zombie to be exploited as a source of inexpensive labor, performing menial domestic and industrial tasks. The lack of honor and powerlessness that Patterson identifies as the social forces that mark the slave with social death are actualized in *Fido* in the quasi-governmental Zomcon organization, which produces and controls the zombies through technology and intimidation.

To live in a world full of zombies, humans have had to develop several methods for controlling the destructive nature of zombies. Zomcon, whose tagline is "better living through containment," began controlling zombies with security fences around every town in order to separate humans from the zombies in the "wild zone." If the threat that the dead will arise again to become zombies was the only way in which this fictional society had changed, then the town of Willard would be just like any other 1950s era small town in America. However Zomcon's response to the zombie threat helps it establish a utopian vision of community that reveals the dark, dystopic underside of all utopias.

The fences erected by Zomcon divide the idyllic town of Willard from the "wild zone" separate the zombies and the humans into "us" and "them"; this segregation then allows a select few inside who can be controlled and exploited as labor. At one point in the film, we learn that it is illegal for a zombie to be in a public area without a leash, a conjunction of bureaucratic rule-making and an object of control (the leash itself) that constrains the movement of the zombie. When Bill Robinson chains Fido in the backyard, this act of fear creates a kind of ghetto for the zombie while simultaneously reinforcing Timmy's understanding of Fido as a pet. One of the ways we can tell that Fido will be a unique zombie is because he is only minimally constrained in the film; we only see him chained in the backyard and the only leash he ever has attached to him is Cindy's skipping rope, which she throws around Fido's neck when her father approaches to create the illusion that Timmy has Fido on a leash.

With the collars, leashes, and zappers to control zombie behavior, zombies are no longer a threat; in fact, they have become a useful commodity for Zomcon, which controls the distribution and use of zombies in Willard. However, the influence of Zomcon on Willard's citizens extends beyond merely providing a commodity for public consumption. Zomcon's hegemonic control of zombie control technologies that make the zombie "as gentle as a household pet" so that "we can all become productive members of society, even after we're dead" extends beyond simply supplying fences, collars, and leashes. Zomcon retains control of zombies with the power to recall errant zombies as we see when Mr. Bottoms takes Fido away from the Robinsons after discovering that Fido bit Mrs. Henderson.

Zomcon not only controls the use of zombies, but it also controls their production. Because the lingering "space dust" continues to reanimate corpses, there remains a constant threat that those who die within the containment zone will reanimate as zombies. Zomcon thus developed the Zomcon funeral, complete with separate head coffin so that the body cannot be resurrected. The tight control of Zomcon over the production of zombies can be seen in the high cost of funeral payments; Bill's first response to Helen's news that she is pregnant is to object that he doesn't know how he can make another funeral payment. This twist on the usual concern about another mouth to feed nicely captures the way in which the zombie presence and Zomcon's control of zombie use has warped the usual middle-class financial concerns so that they are about the costs of supporting one's death, rather than a new life. It also echoes Freud's early theorizing about the death drive as arising from the fact that "*the aim of all life is death*" and that the instinct of self-preservation ensures that "the organism shall follow its own path to death" (1961, pp. 32–3). With the instincts that preserve life connected to the instincts that lead to death, we see in Willard, or at least in Bill Robinson's attitude, a direct connection between the production of a new life, and its potential death because there is the possibility of a new "life" as a zombie beyond that initial death.

Despite the focus on death in the idyllic town of Willard, the zombie nonetheless makes life easier for its occupants. In the film, we see zombies performing all kinds of manual labor: they are newspaper boys and deliverymen, crossing guards, gardeners, garbage collectors, movers, and butlers. They also have replaced humans in menial factory work. Although the film itself does not show us, in the Zomcon factory to which Fido is sent, they construct the tools of their own oppression: the collars that keep them tame enough to perform all the menial tasks that zombies perform in this utopian post-zombie world ("Audio Commentary," 2007). The exploitation of zombie labor in this alternate-history film is presented in such a way that the zombie acts as a culturally-stabilizing force in the film. The all-white fictional town of Willard appears to have been able to avoid the race relations problems with which the historical 1950s America had to contend. Instead, the zombies of Willard allow racial difference to be subsumed into the narrative of the zombie in a process similar to that which Annalee Newitz suggests allows racial difference in narratives of the undead to be "covertly described as ... the difference between dead bodies and animated ones" (Newitz, 2006, p. 89). The clear difference between a live body and a dead one means that the use of zombies as slave labor in the home, marketplace, or the factory, poses fewer civil rights problems than the use of slaves pre-emancipation, or the sustained limited employment options for Blacks and other minorities in America after that point.

The zombie is more akin to a slave, who is property, than a servant working for minimal wages in dead-end domestic labor; however, the emancipation of the zombie from its condition at the end of the film suggests that if the dead can be recuperated back into the human family, then any other marginal being can as well. Even though the zombie is a second-class citizen, a piece of property that can be bought and sold, in Fido's rudimentary sense of motivation and individuality we see how the zombie can retain some of its humanity. What this humanizing of the zombie does is draw our attention to the ways in which Zomcon's control of both the living and the dead of Willard is oppressive to both groups. In this light, Zomcon's use of collar, leashes, zappers, and fences to contain and control the zombies is an actualization of the kinds of social controls that keep servants and slaves in a socially dead position.

The alternate-history world of *Fido* not only bypassed the civil rights movement, but also first-wave feminism of the 1950s. The patriarchal town of Willard is controlled by men, with Zomcon's head of security, Mr. Bottoms, at the top of it all. Bottoms is a war hero who governs both Zomcon and his own family with an assurance that clearly signals his confidence of his position as head of the factory and the household. But Bottoms's supremacy is gradually challenged by his neighbor, the free-spirited Helen Robinson. At the beginning of the film, the Robinsons appear to be an ideal nuclear family. Bill Robinson works hard to support his family, including funeral insurance so that they don't come back as zombies once they die. Helen Robinson tends the house, baking cookies and welcoming the new neighbors, the Bottoms, with a pie (and a great deal of speculation on how they acquired all their zombies). Helen's pregnancy, which her husband has not yet noticed, will give Timmy Robinson a younger sibling, which would be good for him since he is an isolated little boy who is chastised by his mother at one point for playing ball alone because "it makes you look lonely." Appearances are everything to Helen and, it seems, to much of the rest of Willard; when Timmy comes home and says the bullies dirtied his shirt, Helen's first question is "Did people see you like this? ... Just go and clean up, put on a new shirt, and we won't even have to talk about those bullies." This idealized vision of the nuclear family gradually fragments as first Timmy and then Helen begin to look upon their zombie as more a member of the family than a servant (or even a pet).

The visual look of the film is designed to reinforce the propriety and moral certitude of the period. In the director's audio commentary accompanying the DVD, Andrew Currie suggests that the limited color palate of the film and the meticulous care that went into procuring the period props found in the house interiors and the vintage cars were a deliberate effort to contrast the marginality of the zombie with the rule-bound nature of that historical period. The film's fully-realized 1950s look allows the filmmaker to present a world in which social roles are clearly defined: women are homemakers whose purpose is to make their husband's lives easier, children are to be seen but not heard, and zombies are to be used as manual labor, not befriended. Helen, Timmy, and Fido all resist this standard. Although Helen's response to her son Timmy seems to reinforce her acceptance of these social limitations, her contrast with Dee Dee Bottoms reveals how different her relationship with her husband is from that between their neighbors. During afternoon tea with the Bottomses and Robinsons, John Bottoms suggests that everyone has to be ready to do whatever it takes to keep zombies from infesting the town, declaring that "I'd take Dee Dee's head off in a second if I had to." Despite the nervous laughter this elicits, the seriousness of Bottoms's statement suggests that he has few sentimental thoughts regarding his wife. Dee Dee Bottoms' rejoinder that "He always says that" simply reinforces Mr. Bottoms's lack of emotional attachment to his wife. The contrast between Bottoms's attitude towards his wife and Helen's resistance to such attitudes can be seen when Bottoms tells Dee Dee to get another beer for Bill at their backyard barbecue: Helen stops her, declaring "Get your own beer, Bill," suggesting Helen's resistance to Bottoms's gendered expectations might extend to more than just fetching beverages. By the end of the film, Helen's resistance to patriarchal Willard has extended to empowering zombies as well as other women.

When we first meet Fido, it is in the context of zombie-as-butler. The scene begins in a stereotypical 1950s domestic setting where Helen the housewife, dressed for dinner complete with heels and pearls, greets her husband at the door with a three olive martini. Of course her husband Bill knows something must be up to be greeted at the door this way, but to his query "Helen, what are you up to?" she replies, "If you must know, I have a surprise for you." She leads him into the dining room, pauses dramatically, then rings a small brass bell. On the second ring, Fido emerges from the kitchen, white-gloved, in a Zomcon uniform, carrying dinner on a silver platter.

The white gloves of the butler zombie clearly identify Fido as a servant, but unlike human servants, this zombie is property. As a commodity, the zombie is also a status symbol reminding us that the relationship between zombies and capitalist structures is already a well-established motif. George Romero's *Dawn of the Dead* (1978) set much of that film's action in a suburban mall, and the 2004 remake emphasized the consumerist nature of contemporary culture to an even greater extent. In both versions of the film the shopping mall provides shelter, sustenance, and even the opportunity for entertainment through its cornucopia of consumer goods. Contemporary zombie films have gone so far as to suggest that zombies themselves might contribute, post-death, to the economy, as we see in *Shaun of the Dead* (2004) when, at the end of the movie, Ed remains locked in the shed providing companionship to Shaun while other undead wheel shopping carts or participate in game shows, or, again, in *Land of the Dead* (2005) where zombies act as fodder for bloodsports and sideshow exhibits in the new barter economy of the post-zombie apocalypse. In *Fido*, the film's tagline, "Good Dead are Hard to Find," signals that in this zombie film, the dead may continue to be financial contributors to the economy even when they are no longer living members of its community.

When we first meet Fido, Helen's delight in the zombie can be seen in her exclamation, "Isn't it wonderful? Now we're not the only ones on the street without one!" This line emphasizes ownership, as does her earlier question about whether the new neighbors own all the zombies they are using to unload a moving van. As property, possession of a zombie represents a kind of conspicuous consumption; the fact that the Bottomses have *six* zombies is motivation for Helen to go against her husband's wishes in getting one. Despite her husband's fear of zombies, Helen is willing to risk his disapproval in order to acquire this highly desirable commodity.

The zombie as a commodity highlights the exploitative nature of the zombie's position in this alternate version of mid-century America. In his study of modernism, technology, and the body, Tim Armstrong suggests that "from the point of view of Capital, a zombie is an ideal worker ... [so that] the fragmentation and the promise of restored integrity [of the zombie] renders the commoditization of the body possible" (1998, p. 98). In this case, the flesh of the body is divorced from the humanity of the human body so that the zombie body is just flesh that performs a function in the same way a mechanical device like a robot might. This distinction between flesh and body also informs Abdul JanMohamed's discussion of the "death-bound subject" where he builds on Hortense Spiller's observation that "before the 'body' there is 'flesh'" (qtd. in JanMohamed, 2005, p. 10) to suggest that flesh that is killed becomes meat and that "meat rather than flesh is the absolute zero degree of subjectivity" so that the death-bound subject occupies the zone "between flesh and meat" (p. 10). While JanMohamed defines the death-bound subject as one who is formed "by the imminent and ubiquitous threat of death," we might consider how the zombie, who is formed by the immediate and ubiquitous *fact* of death, might also occupy this zero degree of subjectivity in which the flesh of the body is always susceptible to the possibility of dissolution into mere meat. Once the flesh of the body becomes mere meat, it is available to the labor market just like the body of the animal like the work-horse, oxen, racing dogs and other animals put to commercial use. The fine line between animal flesh and machine (such as one might find when horse and harrow are listed next to each other at an agricultural auction house), emphasizes the descent of flesh into meat that can then be used by humans to perform work. Cindy's revelation to Timmy that her father "says he never wastes a good zombie. He's got him [Fido] working in the factory" reinforces Fido's use-value. The zombie as a form of machine labor in the Zomcon factory in *Fido* aligns the body of the zombie with the industrial machine, threatening to reduce the zombie merely to the materiality of its body, much the same as a robot is of value only in so far as its body performs work.

While this argument that the zombie body represents the meat of a commoditized body began from Armstrong's observations about the worker in a modern rather than a postmodern economy, the zombie also represents an embodiment of production and the (sometimes) impossibility of new forms of wealth in the international and globalized world of the late twentieth century. Zombies interrupt the status quo; they introduce new social and political structures that destabilize old ones. As Ann Kordas suggests in this volume, the zombie of the post–Civil War American South represented fears about African Americans and modern women, both groups that disrupted the means of production in nineteenth-century U.S. history. Similarly, the zombie has recently re-emerged with a vengeance in South African culture in connection with issues of consumption, production, and economic stability because "Although they are creatures of the moment, zombies have ghostly forebears who have arisen in periods of social disruption, periods characterized by sharp shifts in control over the fabrication and circulation of value, periods that also serve to illuminate the here and now" (Comaroff and Comaroff, 2002, pp. 782–3). This focus on the disruption suggests there is an intimate relationship between social and economic disturbances that the zombie might be capable of both representing and responding to. In post-apartheid South Africa the loss of huge numbers of jobs has given rise to the notion of the zombie worker, an immigrant who comes and steals jobs from South Africans. Comaroff and Comaroff suggest that zombies,

> *do* tend to be associated with ... rapidly changing conditions of work under capitalism in its various guises; conditions that rupture not just established relations of production and reproduction, but also received connections of persons to place, the material to the moral, private to public, the individual to the communal, past to future [2002, p. 796].

In South Africa, the end of apartheid has brought immigrants to the region seeking work and in this infiltration, the tradition of witchcraft in the region means that zombie-making is a reduction of individuals "to instruments of production; to insensible beings stored, like tools," controlled by those who create them (Comaroff and Comaroff, 2002). In *Fido*, Zomcon also controls what becomes an essential means of producing value, and this change in the conditions of work reflects a similar anxiety about the means of production. The zombie represents a kind of transitional state which does not necessarily fit neatly into any category, troubling the constructions of those categories as it blurs the boundaries between them.

The alternate-history effect in *Fido* that "freezes" middle-class small-town culture in the 1950s presents a world divided between humans and zombies. This division translates to a social condition where it is us versus the zombie; the human pitted against that which is no longer human. Timmy's persistent question throughout the film — "Are zombies alive or dead?"— suggests that the division between dead and alive may be less important than the shared humanity of the formerly and currently alive. A dead human body becomes a kind of property, but a live human body, even a slave's body, possesses a level of autonomy or integrity, even if that autonomy only remains a potential rather than an actual expression of personhood. As Patterson suggests, the slave is characterized by powerlessness, social death, and a lack of honor. Using Patterson's schema to compare the position of the zombie in *Fido* to that of the slave allows us to mark the places where the zombie resembles the slave as well as the ways in which the zombie is able to transcend the limitations that Patterson identifies. The powerlessness of the slave is relative; it arises as an extension of the master's power. More importantly for Patterson, the slave's powerlessness "originated (or was conceived as having originated) as a substitute for death." This deferred death meant that the slave's life only had meaning in the context of the master's power over that life, such that the slave becomes "a social nonperson" (Patterson, 1982, p. 5). This social death means also that the slave experiences "natal alienation" from all relations, defined as "the loss of ties of birth in both ascending and descending generations" so that the slave has no claim on any relations. Since no relations have a claim on him, everything he produces, including his children, belong to the master (pp. 7, 9). The powerlessness and social death of the slave means that he is dishonored since power and honor are linked so that the master's honor depends on the slave's lack thereof (pp. 10–11).

When considering the zombie in *Fido*'s post-apocalyptic, insular world, the powerlessness of the zombie arises out of an intricate blend of biology and social control. One of the most pervasive and persistent ideas of the zombie is that it is mindlessly controlled by the desire to eat human flesh. The zombie is thus powerless, by nature, over its impulses, and this powerlessness is emphasized in the film from its opening scene. Helen suggests that "zombies kill because it's their nature" leading Timmy to declare: "So then, it's not their fault." As commodities in Willard culture, the zombie is powerless like the slave, however the zombie's powerlessness in the face of their instinct to eat human flesh seems to justify their control (and subsequent loss of power) by those humans who are still living. If this is the case, then we might initially consider whether Fido's ability to override his instinct to eat Timmy and Helen when his collar is turned off by the bullies suggests that Fido is a unique specimen whose status as an object is mis-assigned. We also harbor the suspicion that Fido might not be so unique and that the rationale for subjugating zombies because they are powerless to control their urges might be an illegitimate reason for controlling their every move. The tranquility of the final backyard barbecue scene (including the docile chess-playing and ball-tossing zombies) supports this second explanation; the nature and form of the slave-like oppression of the zombie produces its desire for flesh as a kind of retribution for its wrongful enslavement.

In his discussion of slavery, Patterson does make a distinction between two types of social death: in the intrinsic mode of slavery, the slave was "symbolic of a defeated enemy" (p. 39), while in the extrinsic mode, the slave was "an insider who had fallen, one who ceased to belong and had been expelled from normal participation in the community because of a failure to meet certain minimal legal or socioeconomic norms of behavior" (p. 41). Because the mark of the zombie slave is its physical death, the zombie represents both modes of alienated social death. The zombie's death means that it is expelled from participation in the community, the sign of an extrinsic mode of slavery. The Zombie Wars also clearly signal the zombie as an enemy, an intrinsic mode of slavery, whose defeat is celebrated with all the glory/pomp/admiration that has been a characteristic of war heroes through the ages. The zombie is thus doubly liminal in its ability to be understood as a subject of *both* intrinsic and extrinsic modes of slavery, and it is John Bottoms who intends to keep things that way.

During the Robinsons's visit to the Bottoms's home for a barbecue, Bottoms takes Bill Robinson into his "war room" replete with photographs, weapons, portraits of the war hero in uniform, and trophy zombie heads. The cues in the room suggest that Bottoms is a conqueror who relishes defeat of the enemy. In the case of zombies, it does not seem to matter if the enemy is internal or external to Willard since Bottoms proudly displays the preserved head of "Uncle Bob." In identifying the trophy head as a relative, Bottoms would seem to recognize a natal relation with the zombie. However, a preserved head in a jar also reminds us of the preservation practices of early anthropologists, whose collections often reinforced through the display of difference the subhuman nature of native populations. Displaying Uncle Bob in such a manner disowns any familial relationship, doubly alienating Uncle Bob through both imperial and zombie discourses of the inhuman. In Bottoms's role as head of security for Zomcon and in his "war room," he embodies what Patterson identifies as the "godlike manner [in which the master] mediated between the socially dead and the socially alive" (p. 46).

The zombie is also an insider who has ceased to belong. In ordinary society, an individual may cease to participate in social relations in a number of ways; hermits, homeless individuals, agoraphobics, mentally ill patients, or others who withdraw from what we think of as the normal human relationships in the social realm may all have tentative connections to others within their communities. This situation of social alienation is reversible in these cases; however, death is the one condition that permanently separates the individual from his or her society. That is, it was until the zombies were created by the space dust in this fictional world. Death no longer permanently separates the individual from the social realm, thus the dead, with their failure to meet "certain minimal legal or socioeconomic norms of behavior" (Patterson, p. 41) are estranged from the community to which they once belonged. In this estrangement, the participation of the zombie in the economic life of the community suggests its social condition might be reversible even if its physical condition is not. Regardless, the zombie's ability to be defined by both modes of natal alienation does not negate the effect of that alienation since the result remains the same whether for live human slaves or dead ones.

The slave's powerlessness is directly related to the master's control over the slave so that the master's honor is a direct result of the slave's lack of freedom. We have already seen how the film is focalized through Timmy's interaction with zombies, the experience of a child, who has little power in this culture. According to Patterson, slaves exist in high honor societies; in *Fido*, we see a high honor society in the importance of propriety to those living in Willard. Helen's dismay that someone might have seen Timmy's dirty shirt, or her later admonition to her son not to play ball alone in the yard, reinforce this sense that honor and proper behavior are valued in Willard. However, honor only accrues to the men in the film. While Helen might expect Timmy to follow the rules, the men around her also expect that she will follow their rules. The patriarchal culture of Willard means that despite Timmy's questioning of the status of zombies, he is not encouraged to continue to pursue the question by anyone other than his mother, herself a woman who does not necessarily adhere to the social conventions of the culture. In the film, Fido's recuperation begins through the cooperation between children (Timmy and Cindy), women (Helen), and outcasts (Mr. Theopolis), none of whom have honor in this society.

While the children and Helen stand outside of the power structures of Willard society because of their age and gender, Mr. Theopolis is also located outside of those structures; however, his alienation is a result of his own choices. Theopolis's own relationship with his zombie, Tammy, is the reason why Theopolis no longer works for Zomcon. His affection for Tammy disturbs us as viewers because it goes beyond the familial affection Timmy has for Fido as a substitute father (or even simply as the family pet). Theopolis's desire for Tammy is firmly grounded in the flesh of her body (and his for that matter) so that the sexual overtones of butt slaps, kisses, or even the suggestion that Tammy might be jealous of a younger (fresher) replacement zombie all signal the preoccupation with the flesh of the body inherent in a sexual relationship. Theopolis's relationship with Tammy is deviant in ways that go beyond the simple bending of Zomcom rules that Timmy displays towards Fido, whether we classify Theopolis's behavior as a kind of pseudo-necrophilia or masochism. Our glimpse of Tammy's bite on his shoulder and the shadow in the window that lets us see how Theopolis literally dances with danger by deliberately turning off Tammy's collar suggesting that his deviant behavior was too embarrassing to the company for him to continue to be employed by Zomcon. Theopolis's subsequent displacement outside of the power structure of Zomcon and its principles of control also means that he is not afraid to let Timmy see into those power structures, so that much of what we learn about the company comes from Theopolis's explanation as he fixes Fido's collar.

Theopolis tells Timmy how the creator of Zomcon, Reinhold Geiger, invented the collar because he couldn't stand the loss of his wife who became a zombie, and that Geiger believed that zombies craved human flesh as a way of trying to come back to life. Geiger's very human motivation to create the zombie collar and his ascription of human motivation to the threatening nature of the zombie both suggest that Zomcon's original function was not capitalist, but rather humanist, in nature. The humanist nature of Geiger's original intent for the zombie collar is precisely what Timmy achieves when he and Helen integrate Fido into their family at the end of the film.

What makes the social commentary of *Fido* so intriguing is the way in which the children in the movie are willing to transform the zombies they interact with, from mere flesh or meat, to treasured pets. Timmy's naming of his zombie initiates a "boy and his dog" motif that explains the relationship between the two. Their subsequent disastrous game of catch, or Fido's rescue of Timmy from the zombie cadets, suggest that Fido's status within the Robinson household is that of a pet. The requirement that zombies that are not operating in a work capacity must be on a leash while in public reinforces the notion that Fido is a pet as much as he is a domestic servant. But unlike Donna Haraway's companion species, which is a "permanently undecidable category" that does not "predetermine the status of species as artefact, machine, landscape, organism, or human being" (2008, p. 165), which might free Fido from the capitalist possession of bodies and labor, Fido's position as pet in the film is the indulgent possession of the animal as a replacement for other human relationships.

While the director Andrew Currie suggests that the sweeping crane shots of Timmy and Fido running through open meadows together are reminiscent of the panoramas found in *The Sound of Music*, it seems to me that given the "boy and his dog" motif in the film (which the director also identifies as present within the film), those grandiose crane shots of Timmy and Fido are more evocative of *Lassie*, the ultimate pet of Hollywood cinema.

In particular, Lassie's rescue of Timmy and/or other children in episode after episode of the show is echoed in Fido's fetching of Helen when the bullies turn zombie and try to eat Timmy as he and Fido play in the woods. Timmy's adoption of Fido as a pet reinforces the non-humanity of the zombie, while simultaneously elevating his status within the family above "slave" or "machine" that the film otherwise suggests might be the way to understand the position of the zombie in this post-zombie-threat world.

The persistent question of the film is whether zombies are alive or dead, because as Timmy suspects, the answer to that question will dictate how one should treat a zombie. To decide that zombies are alive, or that at the very least they retain their human characteristics, requires acknowledgement of a shared humanity. Fido's surgical scar indicating he'd had heart surgery, or his predilection for smoking, suggest that Fido retains some of his human characteristics (the vice of smoking for example) even if he has lost others (like the ability to use language). In her study of capitalism and monsters, Annalee Newitz suggests that zombies and other monsters "are allegorical figures of the modern age, acting out with their broken bodies and minds the conflicts that rip our social fabric apart. Audiences taking in a monster story aren't horrified by the creature's otherness, but by its uncanny resemblance to ourselves" (2006, p. 2). In *Fido* the zombies are anything but horrifying because we recognize their shared humanity. It is Zomcon's continued treatment of them as non-human commodities that strikes the viewer as the real inhumanity in this film.

Timmy asks his mother, during one of their weekly visits to watch a funeral, his repeated question concerning whether zombies are alive or dead. Helen suggests that they are more alive than dead and perhaps their zombie status is akin to being in purgatory. This leads to a discussion of sin and human nature and, between them, Timmy and Helen decide that zombies aren't to be held accountable for their killing because it is in their nature. Helen's proposal that Fido might inhabit a kind of purgatory suggests that the zombie might be a human with a sinful compulsion for the flesh, just as Theopolis's desire for Tammy represents an obsession with the flesh. Timmy's declaration to his father that he'd rather be a zombie than dead suggests that Timmy's desire is for more liberal notions of right and wrong rather than a desire for the deviancy of flesh-eating itself. While it is possible that the definition of venial and mortal sins might be up for evaluation in a world where the dead walk the earth (perhaps, as the original *Dawn of the Dead* tells us, because hell is full) so that purgatory might also become a different place, Timmy's growing affection for Fido is validated if there is hope for Fido's eventual preparation for (or recuperation into) a better place. When Bill reassures them that they're all getting funerals so they won't come back as zombies, Helen declares, "Bill, get your own funeral. Timmy and I are going zombie."

Helen's use of the phrase "going zombie" sounds a lot like the colonial accusation of "going native," which, in the context of the film, offers another means for interpreting the zombie's cultural status. As a commodity with a recognized sub-humanity, the zombie resembles the colonial subject, or the slave of the former American South. In declaring they are "going zombie," Helen and Timmy suggest that they would prefer to live on as slaves or pets, rather than ending their existence in the finality of a funeral, complete with head coffin. In a high-honor culture like Willard, it is significant that it is Helen and Timmy who suggest they are "going zombie" since they represent the two classes of people who are recognized as fully human and simultaneously have the least honor and power in that society. They have little to lose in choosing to side with the (former) humanity of the zombie rather than the inhumanity that Zomcon's commodification of the zombie has created.

The zombie's relationship to colonial powers returns us to South Africa where Comaroff and Comaroff note that "zombies themselves seem to be born, at least in the first instance, of colonial encounters; of the precipitous engagement of local worlds with imperial economies that seek to exert control over the essential means of producing value, means like land and labor, space and time" (2002, p. 795). In a postcolonial reading of the zombie, this connection to the means of production results from the clash between different cultures. Just as Comaroff and Comaroff suggest that the zombie in South Africa is best understood in the context of the postcolonial, Annalee Newitz also suggests that "stories about the undead are best understood in the context of anxieties about many kinds of race relationships that develop in the wake of colonialism" (Newitz, p. 90). Newitz's focus on early twentieth-century stories means that her analysis limits itself primarily to Lovecraftian monsters, ghosts and vampires and depictions of Jews and African Americans rather than questions that the zombie raises about the difference between living and dead humans (of any color). With *Fido*, however, we might suggest that zombie's past as a former member of the human race is what generates the fear that the citizens of Willard feel; it's not so much that zombies might cross a color-line, but the line between life and death, blurring the distinction between those two states of being.

The strangeness of the encounters between zombies and humans in this film emerges from the observation that although zombies look and act different from humans, they also resemble humans and respond to commands. They are close enough that we suspect they are (or could be) human, but they are still denied full participation in society. The acknowledgement of shared humanity that the civil rights movement would have in our history is usurped by the presence of the zombie. However, Timmy's questioning of the status of the zombie sets the stage for a potential liberation of the zombie from its status as slave or even pet.

By the end of the film, we see the beginnings of a civilization of the zombie. If the zombie cannot be held accountable for his penchant for flesh any more so than any other person with a disability or condition over which they have no control, then the zombie deserves to be treated in a more equitable manner than it has so far in Willard. Timmy's treatment of Fido suggests that he thinks just like Mr. Theopolis that zombies are human; although Theopolis's relationship with Tammy is considered deviant by those who are aware of it (and is slightly disturbing to us as viewers), that relationship is based on the assumption that Tammy is human in some fundamental way.

Similarly, the ending of the film shows us how the zombie might be civilized and recuperated into the post-zombie-war culture of the movie. The final scene is an idyllic backyard barbecue, with Timmy playing ball with Fido, while another nearby zombie is learning how to play chess. Mrs. Bottoms enters the yard, followed by Cindy, who is leading her now–zombie father on a leash. When Timmy asks Cindy what she's decided to name her zombie she replies, "I don't know. Right now I'm just calling him Daddy." Meanwhile, Fido wanders over to a carriage holding Helen's new baby in order to take a look and touch the child. His guttural cooing and hint of a smile as he reaches into the carriage suggest an affection for, and paternal desire to watch over, the child.

This final scene offers us a vision of the means for recuperating the zombie from the margins of humanity to the center of the nuclear family, with Fido filling in for the now dead and buried biological father. Cindy's arrival with a zombie Bottoms in tow on a leash further seals the idea that the zombie can potentially participate in the family. Cindy's response, "I call him Daddy," to Timmy's question clearly indicates she recognizes at least his former place within the family, even if this recognition relies upon a fluid definition of the nuclear family. Instead of renaming her zombie as Patterson suggests is often the case with slaves (Patterson, pp. 54–55), Cindy allows her father to continue to participate in the family, even if he is now the one controlled by the child and mother rather than the other way around.

Recuperating the zombie back into the realm of the human would then require overturning or reversing the characteristics that Patterson suggests distinguish the slave from those who merely sell their labor or who exist under repressive regimes of various sorts. The powerlessness of the slave in the face of the master's power has been overcome by Fido through his own presumably innate goodness as a human being (regardless of whether he is granted that status by an external agent or not). Fido's ability to control his urges even when the collar is turned off demonstrates his power, which allows him to regain his honor by saving Timmy multiple times and then by replacing Timmy's now completely dead father. Helen and Timmy's invitation of Fido into their family replaces his natal alienation from his former family with a new, adopted one, while Cindy's recuperation of her zombie father back into their family suggests that the natal alienation that Patterson suggests is characteristic of the slave, and which I suggest might be characteristic of the zombie, is reversible.

In *Fido*, the threat of the zombies is still that they will bite and eat you, turning you into one of them, but that threat has been contained in ways that question the place of the zombie in the post-zombie-threat culture of the movie. Even more effectively than the zombie-controlling collar, the incorporation of the zombie into the nuclear family eliminates the threat that this terrifying Other will infect the rest of humanity with its monstrosity. Despite their marginal status, the zombies in *Fido* are a socially-stabilizing force in this alternate history narrative of life after death.

PART IV

The Future of
Zombie Understandings

12

Zombie Categories, Religion and the New False Rationalism

Edward Dutton

Introduction

The sociobiologist E. O. Wilson (1975, p. 574) has summarized much of social science as simply "cross-referencing different sets of metaphors." However, even he would not deny that *some* metaphors can be extremely useful across the sciences in aiding the process of "understanding." We make sense of that which we do not understand by means of comparison. If the comparison is particularly trenchant then it can be built-upon and can develop into a scientific model which becomes central to how we apprehend reality. Rutherford's comparison between the universe and an atom is one such successful academic metaphor (see Gentner, 1982). The comparison between the mind and a computer appears to be another (see Dennett, 1995).

However, some academic metaphors are just not very good. The comparison is superficial, meaning that the more the deeper levels of the metaphor are explored the more difficult it will be to sustain. Other academic metaphors are really just examples of emotional rhetoric. They poison the well of academic debate by implicitly making use of informal fallacies — such as appeal to emotion, insult or connotation — with which to besmirch their academic opponents. Or their metaphor — in its implicit dismissal of a different academic point of view — goes beyond what the empirical evidence would actually permit it to do. Elsewhere, I have discussed the way in which many "death metaphors" in the secularization debate do precisely this, to varying extents (see Dutton, 2008). In arguing that "Christianity in Britain is dying" (Bruce, 2001) or that secularization theory (the theory, in very basic summary, that modernization is leading to the decline of religion) is "dead" and should be "buried" (Stark, 1999), scholars not only attempt to win their argument through methods other than reason but their metaphor is a poor metaphor because it takes us beyond the empirical evidence.

In some respects, Ulrich Beck's "zombie category" is an improvement on these "death metaphors" for secularization, a point which has been argued by Possomai (2007, p. 237). Secularization is the "living dead," it is implied, because it is illogical (academically dead) yet still advocated by scholars — "living." Superficially, the zombie metaphor appears to work in this narrow context. But I will argue in this article that Beck's "zombie category" of academic concepts epitomizes an unsuccessful academic metaphor. The metaphor goes beyond what the evidence allows, simplifies the Zombie concept without accounting for its further connotations, promotes a fallacious form of argumentation and is underpinned by a philosophically unsustainable, "false rationalist" system of categories. We will first look in detail at the nature and scope of academic metaphor and I will present a means by which a good academic metaphor can be identified. We will then examine what we generally mean by the word "zombie" before looking at Beck's "zombie category" idea and assessing the extent to which it is a useful contribution. We will conclude that it is a poor metaphor and that while examining the history or anthropology of zombies may be a contribution to academic debate, using the concept as a metaphor for academic category-employment is quite the opposite.

What Is Academic Metaphor?

Metaphor is useful in the social sciences if it aids "understanding"—making sense of something. Lakoff and Johnson (1980) produced a seminal study of this issue, arguing that a conceptual metaphor involves understanding one conceptual domain in terms of another conceptual domain. Through this, they argued, it is possible to discern the central connecting idea in everyday metaphor. "Life is a Journey" connects two domains through the idea of progression to an end point. Many evolutionary psychologists have argued that human "understanding" is ultimately based around metaphor. The human mind is divided into three "cognitive domains"—social, environmental knowledge and technical. The human mind is distinguished by an ability to apply one cognitive domain over to another — noted, for example, in the tendency to anthropomorphize nature and thus apply social knowledge to the environment. Thought and understanding are ultimately metaphorical (see, for example, Mithen, 1996), a point that has also been argued by Post-Modern scholars such as Derrida (1998).

In examining academic metaphor, Gentner (p. 106) cites a number of different examples of academic analogies such as "Rutherford's comparison between the atom and the solar system" which we have already noted. She observes that some academic analogies have been less than successful. The concept of "urban blight," for example, seems to treat a city as though it were "afflicted" rather than "organically sound": "Some of these analogies have suggested deep research, while others have merely provided a kind of spurious feeling of comfort" (p. 107). A number of other scholars have examined the importance of a base metaphor in theory building in the sciences. Brown (2003, Ch. 1) examines the way in which the metaphor of a "channel" has been employed to understand the operations of a cell membrane. Both Brown (2003) and earlier Bradie (1984) discuss the way in which metaphors in scientific discourse can develop. They both argue that if the metaphor is convincing on a sufficient number of levels then it can develop into a "scientific model" which is further built upon.

But how can we assess whether or a not a metaphor is successful scientifically? Gentner assists us by providing us with a functioning model by which we might be able to assess the usefulness of a particular analogy in scientific terms. Gentner argues that "analogy" is an example of structure mapping between systems, for example between the abstract on the one hand and the visible on the other. Hence, the apparently "known domain"— the visual perhaps — is mapped onto the "domain of enquiry"— the abstract (p. 108). This is as distinct from "similarity," in which the comparable domains are of the same kind. Gentner suggests that it is the "over-lap" between these two different domains which fosters the analogy.

There are a series of qualities that we would expect to find in a successful scientific analogy. Firstly, there is *base specificity*. That is to say that "The better analysed the base (*that is the thing to which the abstract is compared in relation to it*) the clearer the candidate set of importable relations will be" (p. 113). *Clarity* is vital and in assessing an analogy we must ask how clear and how clearly explained it is. Equally important is *richness*, that is to say the extent to which the two domains in question are comparable. Is the comparison a multi-layered one or merely a superficial analogy? The next important factor is *systematicity*. This is the *interrelatedness* of the diverse dimensions of the analogy, as these components would presumably be inter-related in the tangible as well as in the abstract. Thus, to what extent do the aspects of the analogy belong to a mutually constraining system? (p. 114). The *scope and validity* of the analogy must also be considered. Hence, Gentner suggests that we might ask whether a comparison between the solar system and an atom actually only works with a hydrogen atom rather than all atoms. Finally, Gentner (p. 118) argues that we must fully understand whether the purpose of a given analogy is to explain and predict or merely to "express," which would involve "evoking" or "describing."

Criteria for a Successful Academic Metaphor

What is the point of using metaphors in social science? Implicit in Brown, Gentner and others is that the metaphor makes the scientific idea easier to understand, and, so, develop. As social scientists our aim is to better understand social phenomena through detailed empirical research and through the development of scientific models, as occurs in all sciences. Moreover, it is to convey our ideas clearly and accurately to other academics and, ultimately, to the general public. These ideals have been advocated by various scholars as far back as Socrates himself (see Chermiss, 1980; Jaspers, 1960). I appreciate that some scholars — such as those involved in the Frankfurt School or some Post-Modernists — would regard critiquing and changing society as equally important. I would, however, submit that, even from their perspective, we have to "understand" society in order to improve it in some way and our ideas — even if they openly advocate social change or engage in a strong critique of current paradigms — need to nevertheless convey complex information, rendering metaphor a useful tool. Moreover, as Popper (1966) observes, these society-changing philosophies of the Continental School — grounded in Hegelianism — do not, and cannot, prove their premises that, for example, "All history ... is the history of class struggles" (Marx and Engels, 1848, Ch. 1) or "The most natural state ... is a single people with a single national character" (Herder, 1785, in Popper, 1966, p. 52). They are asserted as founding principles just as the Hegelian dialectic is. Popper (p. 21) observes that in Romanticism there is "a new kind of dogmatism ... it confronts us with a dictum. And *we can take it or leave it*." It is an "age of dishonesty" which does little more than "bewitch" the reader. Consequently, there is a good case for arguing that the aim of academia is to critique each generation of knowledge in search of truth. To insert any other aim is philosophically question-begging. With that in mind, I would like to propose and discuss two criteria for a successful academic metaphor.

Richness

This brings together the analyses of Gentner and Brown. In effect, Gentner argues that the successful academic metaphor works on many levels and provides us with a method to produce such a metaphor (clarity, base analysis and so forth). Brown argues that a successful metaphor must be a foundation for future development and must be sufficiently trenchant for this to be possible. I think that both of these ideas can be summed-up as "richness" but I will deal with the question of layers first. A scientific metaphor must work on many layers. If it does not work on many layers then I would suggest that it is potentially confusing and misleading because the reader might have the right to assume, unless otherwise stated, that it would. We would expect academic writing to be of the highest possible quality and we would expect it to be adept at elucidating information. This would be the whole point of a scientific metaphor and a poor metaphor would obviously not help us to understand our object of study in greater depth. Purely from a literary perspective, it is a poor metaphor if does not work on many levels because it does not assist in picturing or understanding whatever it is that it is attempting to describe. These levels would include Genter's conceptions of "richness" and inter-relatedness." However, I will not use "clarity" because I am interested in the success of the metaphor in itself whereas this factor deals with how well it is explained by the author.

But returning to Brown, it must also be possible to develop the metaphor. In a sense, this is a sign of it being multi-layered. It is also indicative of the degree to which it is a contribution to academic discussion. Just as academic research is not especially useful if it cannot be drawn upon and developed, the same may be said to be true of an academic metaphor. If it is genuinely a helpful means through which to understand a concept, then one will be able to develop the metaphor and, through so doing, further understand the concept and, in the case of secularization, *how* institutional religion might decline further. If it is unsuccessful, then developing it will involve moving increasingly away from reality.

Dispassion

While Gentner and Brown provide us with criteria for producing a rich metaphor, I would argue that this should not be the only criterion for an academic metaphor's success. Its success should also be assessed in terms of the degree to which it fulfills the aims of academia. As such, the metaphor must strictly avoid fallacy even by implication. Formal fallacies would obviously not be directly relevant to academic metaphor and dispassion but "informal fallacies" may well be. As noted, these would include "appeal to ridicule," "appeal to emotion" and "retrospective determinism," whereby it is assumed that something was inevitable because it occurred. Lack of clarity in explanation would be a fallacy — whether deliberate or not — as it would, perhaps, be an "appeal to verbosity." A successful metaphor must not be overly emotive and it must not over-reach itself. As the aim of employing the metaphor is that the idea be better understood, an emotive metaphor can be counter-productive. Firstly, an emotive metaphor may lead to an inaccurate picture on the part of the reader — whether an academic or simply an interested party — of the idea that is being discussed. Related to this is the possibility that because the metaphor is emotional — with many associations — it will "stick" in the public's mind — the fallacy of "poisoning the well."

This raises a noteworthy point. Seventeenth century philosopher John Locke was highly skeptical of metaphor, seeing it as a literary device, inappropriate for scientific discussion (Brown, Ch. 1). I think that this point is valid in as much as an emotive image could help to unjustifiably persuade. The sociologist must "get the balance correct" between helping to make a concept easier to understand and unduly influencing the reader. Equally, academic discussion should be about the quality of arguments not about the individuals or groups propounding them. Thus, if one were to produce a metaphor which implied that those with whom one has academic differences are "idiots" then that metaphor, no matter how rich or subjectively accurate, is not appropriate for academic discourse. It is an appeal to ridicule.

Difficulties with the Academic Metaphor Model

It might be countered that emotive metaphors are useful in terms of fostering "understanding" because they are able — if sufficiently disseminated — to provoke public discussion and thus widen understanding of a topic. However, I would argue that an emotive metaphor is only indirectly contributing to knowledge. The emotive metaphor provokes debate and it is this discussion — stimulated by the metaphor — which widens knowledge rather than the metaphor itself. Indeed, it might be argued that it is precisely through nuancing and debating an extreme and emotive metaphor that knowledge is furthered, but this, I think, further demonstrates the importance to understanding of an appropriate metaphor. I appreciate the potential for an emotive metaphor to aid understanding insofar as it stimulates debate but this is an indirect connection and what this article aims to do is understand the kind of metaphor that directly aids understanding. Of course, it might be argued that for an academic to publish an illogical book on a topic would aid public knowledge inasmuch as it might be rigorously critiqued thus highlighting the issues.

Also, I am not suggesting that all metaphors be judged by the criteria that I have outlined. There is a strong rhetorical dimension to metaphor and it might be argued that a metaphor is successful precisely because it stirs up emotions and assists in dissociating a group. But, of course, this again raises my direct and indirect distinction. The ability of a university lecturer to dissociate his students through the use of appropriate metaphors aids their understanding in the sense that they will be more likely to absorb and remember the information helping them to discuss and "understand" it. But there is a difference between that and providing them with a really trenchant and profound comparison which directly assists them in making sense of a topic. Though that latter metaphor may be inherently rhetorical to some extent, it will hopefully directly aid their understanding and — if of sufficient depth — it will be possible to build upon it further. It is metaphors in this context — that attempt to directly aid understanding — that can be judged by their in-depth relationship with the source domain and thus their ability to make ideas easier to understand.

Equally, I appreciate that in writing it might be suggested that it is impossible to get away from metaphor. Post-Modernists such as Derrida (1998) argue that all language is ultimately metaphorical — a view echoed by evolutionary psychologists — and that, moreover, the metaphors of a given text can be dissected to discern the world-view and presuppositions of the writer. Following this, it might be suggested that metaphor — and the use of language itself— is inherently emotional because of the layers of subjective meaning associated with words and the impossibility of not conveying some kind of ideology — albeit unconsciously — through ones use of language. Indeed, it might be submitted that reality itself is simply layer upon layer of metaphor as reality is only apprehended through metaphor. It might even be argued that the very notion of "reality" is an example of metaphor usage and it is therefore impossible to talk about metaphors "successfully" representing some kind of "reality" because we are simply drawn down to a further metaphor through language. I counter that in writing this analysis I am aiming my writing at a community which, I assume, apprehends the world in a relatively similar manner to the way in which I do and shares certain assumptions about logic and the empirical method, though there may of course be variations within the community. It is this — and in particular the use of the empirical method and thus perhaps "Western thought" — that I take as my starting point. Post-Modern scholars might argue that this is basing my analysis on philosophically shaky foundations as they would see Western reasoned argument as ripe for deconstruction. But they are using reason to highlight a fallacy — the circular argument — and therefore are inconsistent. As the biologist Richard Dawkins (2003, p. 15) put it, "Show me a cultural relativist at 3000 feet and I'll show you a hypocrite.... If you are flying to an international conference of anthropologists ... the reason you will probably get there, the reason you won't plummet into the ploughed field — is that a lot of Western, scientifically trained engineers have got their sums right." Or as philosopher Roger Scruton (2000, p. 135) pithily states: "There is no reasoned attack that does not implicitly assume what deconstruction 'puts in question' — namely the very possibility of reasoned attack."

In the following analysis, then, I will assess the success of "zombie categories" according to these criteria. I appreciate that there may well be further criteria and there is always going to be an element of the subjective in suggesting criteria of this kind, hence my drawing upon previous discussions. However, I would submit that the two out-lined above are certainly germane criteria, summarizing previous debate and moving it in a clearer direction.[1]

What Is a "Zombie" and What Are "Zombie Categories"?

If we consult a dictionary, we see that the word is defined as follows: "A supernatural power or spell that according to Vodou belief can enter into and reanimate a corpse or a corpse revived in this way" (The Free Dictionary). Popularly, this is expressed as the zombie being "the living dead." It is also defined as "one who looks or behaves like an automaton."

So, armed with a widely accepted definition of "zombie," let us turn, then, to German sociologist Ulrich Beck's concept of "zombie categories," one which he has outlined in various works and perhaps most usefully in a 1999 interview conducted by sociologist Jonathan Rutherford (Beck and Beck-Gernsheim, 2002). Underpinning Beck's idea is a process which he terms "Individualization" — this is the process (which he argues can be observed in advanced societies and is part of globalization) of people becoming "autonomous individuals." They are, he argues, increasingly removed from "traditional supports and con-straints" and now reflect a "desire to live life on one's own." Beck contends that this is grad-ually leading to "changes in consciousness" which can be discerned in "behaviour and social conditions ... I'm talking about zombie categories," he asserts. "Because of individualization we are living with a lot of zombie categories which are dead and still alive." "Can you name some?" enquires his interviewer. "Yes," he replies, "Family, class, neighbourhood." The interviewer responds that, "Zombies are the living dead. Do you mean those institutions are husks that people have abandoned?" Beck concurs with this. "The family is a good example of a zombie category," he argues, because increasingly we are "transforming" what we mean by "family," it is less and less based around bonds of blood and we are even left in a situation where some children have to "choose" the person they regard as their father.

For Beck (2006), this is the reality of individualization and much sociological discourse is yet to catch-up. It continues attempting to apprehend reality be means of categories which no longer make any sense. These categories are "dead" because they are not logically sustainable but they are living because they are still widely employed. Beck argues that this is because many scholars still base their understanding on "methodological nationalism"—taking categories for analysis from the assumption that the world is composed of nations and imposing them on the world. Beck argues that these categories are no longer useful for social sciences because of the fluidity of modern societies. He instead suggests moving to "methodological cosmopolitanism," reflecting what he sees as the new, post-nationalist reality of a cosmopolitan, globalized world. Citing Kant's dictum, "Observations without concepts are blind, concepts without observations are empty," he argues (Beck and Beck-Gernsheim, 2002, p. 24) that "normal science categories are becoming zombie categories, empty terms in the Kantian meaning. Zombie categories are the living dead which blind the social sciences to the rapidly changing realities inside the nation-state containers and outside as well."

Zombie Categories and Philosophical Rigor

Let me begin by returning to my earlier point about death metaphors in the secularization debate. I would re-emphasize that the notion of "zombie categories" or "zombie theories" may well be useful, at least to some extent, in making sense of how theories live and die. The problem with suggesting that a theory is "dead" is that it raises important questions over what that means. Is a theory dead simply because it is illogical, as Stark (1999) implies? If this is so, it was surely always illogical and so was never alive in the first place. And if that is the case, then "death" is clearly not a rich metaphor. If a theory is alive, regardless of its qualities, because it has advocates then it could conceivably always come back to life even if dead. Consequently, to term a theory such as secularization as "zombie" may work, at least to a degree, with regard to increasing our understanding of how theories rise and fall. If we follow philosophers of science such as Popper (1963) all theories are likely to eventually die as we critique each generation of knowledge.[2] So if people continue to advocate them they are attempting to revive "dead" theories and create the living dead. But even this, as we will see below, is highly contentious. However, I would first like to look at difficulties with "zombie categories" which are far more fundamental.

Beck is arguing that certain categories are underpinned by a worldview constructed around nationalism, globalization challenges this methodology, the categories reflecting the old methodology become inadequate to apprehend the new globalized, "cosmopolitan" reality and, as such, they should be abandoned in favor of new categories. The old categories are, therefore, "zombies"—the "living dead." I would argue that dismissing these "methodologically nationalist" categories as "zombie" goes way beyond what the empirical evidence allows, meaning that the metaphor takes us away from reality. The most obvious problem with it is the way in which it contrasts so starkly "methodological nationalism" and "methodological cosmopolitanism" or the old, pre-globalization world and the new one. Methodological Nationalism is, according to Beck, unable to fully explain sociologically the developments of a "globalized" world. This may be so, but was it really able to provide an entirely accurate method for apprehending reality even when nationalism was more obviously fixed? There were always conceptual difficulties with taxonomizing the world in terms of nations and it is pure idealism to believe that there will be no such conceptual difficulties with looking at the world in terms of "methodological cosmopolitanism." Moreover, previous ideologies which regarded themselves as the mission of modernism — such as nationalism — equally saw the modernism is these revolutionary terms, as fundamentally different from anything before it. It is, therefore, illegitimate for Beck to contrast "methodological nationalism"— which apparently "blinds us" to reality — with "methodological cosmopolitanism"— the divine light that somehow opens our eyes. But this is what Beck does. It is as if he is attempting to argue that perceiving the world through the prism of "methodological cosmopolitanism" will allow us to see the truth. Instead of gradually developing from methodological nationalism following Popper's model of science — by discarding what does not assist understanding and preserving that which does — Beck is advocating a kind of revolution in which a "worthless methodological nationalism" is contrasted with what Chernilo (2007, p. 17) calls "brand-new-world-risk-society methodological cosmopolitanism." There is no logical reason to engage in such violent conceptual iconoclasm but this is what Beck implicitly advocates. What is going on?

Beck's globalization is in-line with the Hegelian theories of the Romantic, Continental tradition. Beck has presented us with a kind of dogma — that we will only understand the world if we completely abandon any attempt to apprehend it in terms of nations. We must get rid of this idea of nations as an analytical tool. There is so little to be gained from employing this category because it makes us *blind*. This is not a rational form of argumentation. It is what Popper terms "false rationalism"— a religious (irrational and asserted as true regardless of evidence)[3] conviction disguised as academic argument. We can either *take or leave* what Beck says just as we can with Marx, Herder or the "cultural relativism" of Margaret Mead. We have to react in this way because we are not going to be able to prove or disprove the premise upon which the assertion is based. As with theories of the Hegelian school, there is a strong-case for arguing that Beck's conception of "globalization" is in the tradition of "historicism." These are worldviews in which the future — such as the development of Communism or "our nation" — is regarded as inevitable. Popper (1957) has criticized historicism in detail because it can lead to self-fulfilling prophecy and is implicitly dogmatic, uncritical and engages in religious assertion rather than carefully critiquing previous knowledge. Beck's "zombie categories" (which express his view that we must abandon numerous long-employed categories to apprehend reality) implies a belief that it is *inevitable* that nationalism will fade away and be subsumed into "globalization." If this is not his view, then it is premature to *absolutely* abandon methodological nationalism (which we have noted only suffers from the same inherent problems as any taxonomy) as *blinding us* to the truth. For these reasons, the notion that certain "categories" are "zombie categories" is constructed on religious and not rational assumptions. Employing the term "zombie category" with regard to these categories involves engaging in a false rationalist, historicist discourse. This is not going to aid understanding and nor, therefore, is the metaphor of zombie categories constructed upon it.

Moreover, as with any Romantic Hegelian-based system, what Beck really presents us with is a form of tribalism. This is inevitable if we follow Popper's (1966) view that all religion is inherently tribal to a certain extent. Not only are Beck's "zombie categories" based around religious assumptions but, as in the Hegelian dialectic, they implicitly create an "other." If we look at this naively, we might simply suggest that the "other" are the people who remain "blind"— who remain unable to apprehend the truth about reality because they have not broken free of the bondage of methodological nationalism. If we examine this with a more paranoid eye, we might suggest that dismissing the category system (the way of understanding the world) of these people as being like "zombies" is not that far, if we return to our discussion of Haitian Vodou, from implying that they are, in some sense, wicked. They are like evil sorcerers who keep the dead alive for their own unspeakable purposes. This is precisely how every Hegelian ideology has treated its opponents — with moralistic smears. The opponents of Marxism are "enemies of the people," the opponents of nationalism are "traitors," the opponents of Cultural Relativism are "racists, imperialists ... Neo-Nazis" (see Ellis, 2004; Sandall, 2001).

Indeed, in presenting the "zombie categories" which he does, Beck appears to heavily simplify or misrepresent the process of nationalism. It is implied that the term "family" is a zombie category, underpinned by methodological nationalism. Globalization means that we must find a new concept to replace the methodologically nationalist category of family. But the only way we can justify this reaction is if we insist that the past was always nationalistic. This would be strongly disputed by numerous social scientists. There is considerable debate, for example, with modernists such as Andersen (1983) arguing that nationalism developed as a consequence of the process of modernization. This leads to ethnic groups — and society in general — being brought together through phenomena such as the mass media and the development of a written language as well as mass education. As a consequence, there developed the mass internalization of being part of one nation. However, some scholars such as Smith (1999) are skeptical of this "modernist" position. Known as "primordialists," they argue that nationalism or proto-nationalism can be traced back considerably further than the nineteenth century, especially amongst certain social classes, and is rooted in older ethnic identities. It may be that the nineteenth century saw the "mass" internalization of nationalism which had already occurred earlier amongst the elite, something with which "the masses" were gradually inculcated and I would suggest that this allows us to reconcile the two positions to a certain degree. But, nevertheless, the concept of the family is not underpinned by methodological nationalism. It follows that even if we accept that methodological nationalism is useless, that is no reason to dismiss the concept of the "family."

And there is another fundamental philosophical issue at hand here. We have come-up against a relic of a debate which has been raging since the time of Plato. On the one hand, *essentialists* — following the Platonic view — insist that every concept is an imperfect reflection of the ideal of that concept (which, according to Plato, can be found in the world of forms accessible through the intellect). These forms are unchanging and it is the task of science to describe the true nature of things (and here is the relic) and thus focus on the definitions of terms. Dennett (1995, p. 95) observes that scientists should "of course" define their terms but "only up to a point." He provides a modern version of the so called *nominalist* critique. *Nominalists* are more interested in understanding how something behaves in different circumstances and they make use of a concept if it is helpful. There will always be different ways of defining a set term and different definitions will be useful in different circumstances. But to insist, in an essentialist fashion, that terms must always be perfectly defined before being employed leads us to a situation where we can do very little. It also means that our categories — and everything else — remained "fixed," meaning that we cannot criticize knowledge and hope to get closer to the truth; something essential to academic discourse. As Dennett (p. 39) observes, there are manifold difficulties defining a word such as "island" but, aware of the intellectual difficulties, we can still use the concept as a tool to further our understanding. Some form of essentialism is necessary in order to taxonomize the world and further understand it but focusing so intensely on the precise meaning of words leads us to a situation where we cannot really go any further. It is the fallacy of "Loki's Wager."

The Norse god, who lost his wager, was happy for the dwarves to cut off his head but insisted they not touch his neck. They discussed where his neck ended for eternity.

Beck is defining words such as "family" in an essentialist fashion. Rather than employing the term and concept in different ways and according to different definitions depending on whether or not it is useful in answering discrete questions, he is defining the word in an essentialist way. He is therefore arguing that anything that deviates from the essence of "family" is something else. This essentialism requires new concepts and new words — and I would agree with Lumsden and Wilson (1981, p. 26) that "jargon is the anaesthetic of scholarship." Indeed, the fact that this metaphor — following its essentialist assumptions — implicitly encourages us to dismiss widely understood words and concepts (which have not become overly-emotive and which can be developed) in favor of completely new ones means that it encourages the proliferation of jargon and the cutting-off of sociology so that many people cannot understand it. Andreski (1974, Ch. 6) notes that sociology has a long history of doing precisely this — attempting to make relatively menial insights seem revolutionary and profound by obscuring them with an incomprehensible smoke-screen of jargon. This would not aid "understanding" which, as we have discussed, is a central justification to employing academic metaphor. If new terms are to be introduced, it should be a slow, cautious process which occurs when absolutely necessary to summarizing a complex idea, distinguishing it from other concepts and so aiding understanding (see Lumsden and Wilson, 1981, p. 26). To absolutely dismiss older terms as useless, however, betokens dogmatic essentialism.

And it is also quite unnecessary. The concept of "family" is central to how many of us apprehend reality — so, in that sense, it a useful grappling hook in gaining "understanding" of the world. Moreover, it has the potential to be malleable. This kind of dogmatic essentialism is not scientific. It is scientific to draw upon established knowledge and develop it by answering discrete research questions employing (carefully) essentialist concepts to the extent that they are useful. Utterly dismissing certain concepts as completely useless forever more — something surely implicit in asserting that they are "dead" — seems to be rather at odds with this. To give another example, Beck (1994, p. 40) asserts that "social class" is a "zombie category": "take class parties without classes." This is, he writes, one of many "zombie institutions which have been clinically dead for a long time but have been unable to die." How can we interpret the previous sentence? I assume that Beck means that changes in work-life and social fluidity mean that your social class (formerly defined by your profession and your background) is no longer as clear-cut as it once was. Indeed, Hayward and Yar (2006) have observed that social class in England is increasingly defined not in terms of profession but in terms of consumption-practices as an expression of social-background. But this does not mean that the "class" category is "clinically dead." It has evolved, for sure, and it is more complex than it was but there have long been different ways of defining social status which have been, to a great extent, culturally contingent. The evolution, if this has occurred, in the means by which social class is negotiated and perceived may have changed but this does not mean social class is "dead" as a useful means of apprehending reality. As discussed, to interpret it in this way is unjustifiably essentialist. Moreover, Beck's assertions further indicate the superficiality of his zombie metaphor. For "class" to be a zombie it would have to be dead — he would have to prove it was not a useful sociological category — and it would then have to be brought back from the "dead," employed once again as a sociological category. But as critical rationalists, we must always accept that our assertions may be proven wrong — otherwise we are asserting dogmas. Asserting that these categories are dead, even if they are maintained as "zombies," is final because death is final. If they are dead, they are absolutely useless, or brain-dead automata useful for wicked purposes. So, if we follow Beck's notion of dead categories it leads to an implicit worldview which is uncritical, dogmatic ... ultimately unscientific and opposed to understanding. As we have discussed, under-pinning Beck's zombie metaphor is globalization-historicism. Popper's (1957) summary of this — highlighting the implicit essentialist view that history is divided into dramatic and quite separate eras which are literally revolutions apart — could almost have been written about Beck's zombie categories:

> They believe — and what else could their deification of modernism permit?— that their own brand of historicism is the latest and boldest achievement of the human mind, an achievement so staggeringly novel that only a few people are sufficiently advanced to grasp it.... Contrasting their "dynamic" thinking with the "static" thinking of all previous generations they believe that their advance has been made possible by the fact that they are now "living in a revolution" [p. 160].

There is, moreover, no rational reason for this total dismissal of "family" other than, possibly, that Beck — with his Hegelian ideology — is opposed to nationalism, committed to globalization as a revolutionary ideology and understands that if you remove the concepts which are central to those who oppose you (this is not just nationalists but anyone opposed to globalization) it becomes easier to pull apart their "opposing" ideology. While "family" has existed far longer than "nationalism," it is true that the "family" — and bonds of blood more broadly — are central to certain conceptions of nationalism and certainly to Paganism, the intellectual revival of which might to appear to be a modern revival of Herderian nationalist ideals (see, for example, Benoist, 2004; Bar-On, 2007). By dismissing the concept of "family," you dismiss the importance of blood-bonds and you move towards creating a society — Benoist would argue a kind latter-day Judaeo-Christian society — where you are bonded by something other than blood; very possibly the acceptance of some dogma. Outsiders are not outsiders because they are not related to you but because they do not accept the manifest "truth" which the insiders all realize. Jettisoning such categories is a way of making a clean break with the past and rendering the past "other" — something crucial to ultimately Hegelian-based "cultural revolutions" (see Gabb, 2007 for discussion of this process in relatively recent history).

Zombie Categories and Informal Fallacy

However, there are further problems with the term and to some extent I have already touched on these. The metaphor is not dispassionate. In many ways, it implicitly attempts to destroy the arguments of academic opponents — of those who criticize globalization or maintain that nationalism is a useful taxonomy — other than through reason.

Most of obviously, it commits the fallacy of "poisoning of the well" through its implicit appeal to insult and ridicule. If you disagree with Beck, he has already made clear that your entire system of making sense of reality is composed of "zombie categories." Your concepts are the "living dead," they may appear "alive" but they are really just controlled by a Vodou priest (perhaps your own childhood inculcation with a sense of nationalism). The broader associations with the term zombie are many but we might associate it with clichéd horror-movies (your ideas are clichéd and unoriginal), that which is philosophically inconsistent (your concepts are likewise inconsistent) and even that which is controlled in order to do evil (your "nationalist" concepts will lead to "evil"—the fallacy of "appealing to consequences"). I am not necessarily suggesting that Beck is aware of all of these connotations to terming concepts "zombie categories"—though surely we have the right to assume that he would have thought extremely carefully before disseminating this idea and, as such, he most certainly should be aware of them. Even if we define "zombie" in Beck's narrow terms as the "living dead," then this is still "poisoning the well" when we consider that Beck has not proven the uselessness of "methodological nationalism." And, in fact, even if he had proven it, "zombie" still has the potential to be an insult. It is dismissing a person's category system as "dead"—this is a very strong rhetorical term. And it is not a huge leap from calling a person's categories "zombie" to implying that those who employ them are kind of zombies themselves, without any real capacity for thought.

But I would pursue Beck further. The word "zombie" has numerous other connotations and even if you define "zombie" in a narrow way those connotations are still there, in the background, when the term is employed. This further proves the degree to which the term "zombie category" is poisoning the well, as we have already discussed. Pursued, as it surely can be as to be a useful academic metaphor it must be rich and work on many levels, further than simply "the living dead" we can discern the implication that those who support "zombie categories" have at best failed to understand the truth and are at worst wicked, just like the Haitian Vodou priests. It follows that not only is this metaphor not "rich"—unless we accept all these implications as true—but it is not dispassionate either. Terming certain categories as "zombie" does not assist us in apprehending reality. If anything, it creates an atmosphere of ridicule, insult and intimidation which is in no way conducive to the aims of academia which we have already outlined. Tomlinson (2007, p. 149) writes rather euphemistically that "Ulrich Beck makes the point (*about globalization challenging the assumptions of sociology*) even more forcefully in his critique of the adequacy of 'normal social science concepts' to the analysis of rapid and perplexing changes set in train by globalization." Indeed he does. With his "zombie categories," Beck puts it too forcefully, so forcefully—going so beyond what the evidence and scientific method permit—that his metaphor becomes a means of rhetoric rather than an aid to understanding.

Another False Rationalist Dogma

In last ten years, Post-Modernism has been gradually exposed for what it is: yet another Post-Hegelian, Romantic philosophy of the Continental School; a false-rationalist dogma which—when we make the effort to cut through the appeals to jargon and verbosity—is inconsistent, epistemologically pessimistic and implicitly religious (For detailed critiques of Post-Modernism see Wilson, 1998; Scruton, 2000, Ch. 12). "Globalization" now appears to be replacing Post-Modernism as the new, cutting-edge false rationalist dogma. As with its predecessors it employs not the logical, critical methods of scholarship but the fallacies and unsustainable assertions of religion. Beck's "zombie categories" are underpinned by the globalization historicist dogma—by an implicit belief that globalization is positive, inevitable and in some sense the "mission" of modernism. We have assessed them in terms of our model of a useful academic metaphor and we have found that the metaphor is not rich because if followed it leads to fallacy and the need to justify a philosophically unsustainable world-view which, accordingly, does not assist us in "understanding" the world. And we have agreed that an academic metaphor is only useful if it further aids our "understanding."

To recapitulate in more detail, Beck's "zombie categories" are in line with the false-rationalist dogmas of the Continental School because they implicitly engage in conceptual iconoclasm presenting us with historicist dogmas that we can take or leave rather than gradually developing and critiquing knowledge in search of truth, they create a kind of "other" outside the tribe who they regard as not having understood the manifest "truth" thus appealing to ridicule, insult and so on; they are dogmatically essentialist — a way of thinking which stands in contrast to academic pursuit and accordingly they attempt, without good reason, to dismiss the categories of those who disagree with them (possibly in an attempt to wipe-out the world-view sustained by them). Moreover, the term "zombie category" poisons the well of academic debate. Most obviously it commits the connotation fallacy — implying that those who disagree, or their categories at least, are mindless and even dangerous. Legitimately pursuing this analysis — in line with our discussion of richness — zombie categories may even imply that academic opponents are "evil." It is difficult to escape these implications and for this reason alone the "zombie category" is not a useful metaphor in measured, academic discourse. It seems to be more a way of promoting globalization.

As social scientists we should be very careful with our language and very careful with our metaphors if we want to ensure that we can continue to operate in an atmosphere of rationalism and reason. Some metaphors are extremely helpful to achieving this, others are not and "zombie theories" falls into the latter category. There have always been what Popper (1966) calls "false rationalists" and what Andreski (1974, p. 238) terms "sorcerers clad in the latest paraphernalia of science" in the social sciences. They tend to employ rhetoric rather than reason and their metaphors are likely to reflect that. The idea of "Zombies" has been popularized by Hollywood movies, but it has ultimately emerged from the Vodou religion practiced in Haiti. "Zombie categories" are the descendents of Hegelianism and therefore, ultimately, religious-perspectives such as that of Vodou. This is because "zombie categories" are underpinned by a world-view which is "religious" or "tribal" rather than rational; a world view with certain unfalsifiable founding dogmas which are defended not with reason but rhetoric.

We could follow this metaphor to argue that Beck is a kind of priest of globalization attempting to steal the souls — the category system — of people in the tribe that oppose him. But there's no point doing that, it is an appeal to insult and it would probably collapse as a useful metaphor fairly quickly. We should only attempt to construct an academic metaphor if we have really thought it through and if it genuinely contributes to understanding.

"Zombie categories" do not contribute to understanding. They contribute to a religious way of apprehending reality comparable to that held by those who genuinely believe in zombies. The genuine belief in zombies is a religious belief in the broad sense of being a belief which is held very strongly, relates to a "hidden hand" (in Boyer's terms) and is by its very nature irrefutable. As we have discussed, this is also true of Romantic ideologies such as Marxism and we have argued that Globalization is in this tradition.

In refuting "zombie categories," we are helping, then, to foster a more rational atmosphere for academic debate. This is of considerable significance to scholarship. I think this discussion has demonstrated that "zombie categories" are a danger to scholarship. They replace reasoned argument with fallacy such as smearing academic opponents, they ultimately promote a worldview based on dogmatic, false rationalist foundations of the kind developed from the Romantic School, they attempt to jettison the concepts of their academic opponents in order to remove any opposition to what is seemingly a new historicist cultural revolution. "Zombie categories" are — to use a well-worn metaphor — the tip of an iceberg which would ultimately sink the kind of open, rational analyses that we are aiming for in volumes such as this and throughout the academic world.

NOTES

1. The above section is an abridged version of a section of my article "Death Metaphors and the Secularisation Debate: Towards Criteria for Successful Social Scientific Analogies," originally published in the journal *Sociological Research Online* (Dutton, 2008).

2. I am familiar with the criticisms of Popper's "Critical Rationalism." For a detailed refutation of the criticisms see Dutton (2009) or Popper (1966).

3. I am aware of the debate over how "religion" should be defined. When it is useful to do so in this article I will employ the phenomenological definition (which contrasts religion with the secular). In general, I am employing the functionalist definition. I would agree with Wilson (1975) that "religion" refers to the aspects of culture that people are the most strongly and irrationally attached to. Thus, if something is believed strongly and it is not empirically justifiable this is matter of religion. Even if it is empirically justifiable, believing 'strongly' demonstrates centrality to world-view and possible irrational attachment. However, I am also sympathetic to Boyer's (2001) point that, in addition to strength of feeling, "religion" is defined by perceiving a sense of agency in the world. This would include historicist ideologies whereby history's course is inevitable and there is a kind of "hidden hand" behind the scenes.

13

Nothing but Meat?
Philosophical Zombies and Their Cinematic Counterparts

Dave Beisecker

Preview. "The Death That Will Not Die"

My work in the philosophy of mind frequently exposes me to zombies. Indeed, one might suspect that I've become infected with a very peculiar strain of the zombie virus, one which suffuses philosophical discussion about the nature of consciousness, and which is responsible for an equally peculiar form of zombie: the *philosophical zombie*.

At first blush, philosophical zombies appear the antithesis of their more familiar, cinematic counterparts. Zombies on screen are horribly unlike ordinary folk. They shamble about in a blood-lust devouring any and all souls unfortunate enough to come within their grasp. By contrast, zombies in philosophy are not nearly so easy to spot (at least not from the "outside"). They are not rotting corpses. In all their mundanely material aspects — their physiology, their linguistic and non-linguistic behavior, even in the thoughts that they seem to express — they are completely indistinguishable from ordinary folk such as (presumably) you and me. In that respect, they have more in common with the "pod-people" of *Invasion of the Body Snatchers* (1956) or maybe Stepford Wives — except that they're composed of real live flesh and blood. Still, they lack something with which (again, presumably) we are intimately familiar and treasure: consciousness or "phenomenal experience." They wholly lack subjective feeling. As folk in the philosophy biz put it, there's "nothing it's like" to be a philosophical zombie or "all is dark and silent within." So like their cinematic counterparts, one wouldn't ever want to be a philosophical zombie.

In philosophical circles, it has been argued that the bare conceivability of such creatures spells the end of the world for materialistic theories of consciousness.[1] If such creatures are so much as metaphysically possible, then it can seem that the totality of mundane material facts in our own world could not guarantee that consciousness as we are inclined to understand it is also a feature of our world. So (it is argued) the fact that consciousness is a part of our world must be due to some additional *non-material* aspect of reality. For now, I'll skip the details of this ongoing debate in contemporary philosophy of mind (though I'll have more to say at the end). The zombie argument against materialism is the latest and most vivid reincarnation of a family of arguments that can trace its roots to the seventeenth-century. In his *Sixth Meditation*, Descartes ([1641] 2005) confidently affirmed that he could "clearly and distinctly conceive" both of his mind existing separately from the totality of his material body and the totality of his material body existing independently of his mind. From that intuition Descartes eventually concluded that his mind and his material body must in fact be distinct from one another (since God could distinguish "in reality" what we could clearly distinguish in imagination). Now what Descartes said he could conceive of was not exactly a philosophical zombie, for he thought that a mere material body could not be capable of the thoughtful speech he took to be criterial for genuinely mental activity. Nevertheless, Descartes' argument stems from the same sort of dualistic intuitions that also animate the zombie argument, intuitions which have proven to be remarkably hard to kill. Aptly, then, the zombie argument against materialism is just that: a "zombie" argument.

I often encounter non-philosophers who are amazed that contemporary philosophers of mind are vexed about the conceivability and possibility of philosophical zombies. Confusing philosophical zombies with their cinematic counterparts, they find it hard to believe that philosophers would worry that the dead will start coming back to life and devour the living. Is that where all their hard-earned tax and tuition dollars are going? Here I plan to lay their doubts to rest. In this paper, I will suggest that despite their vast behavioral and physiological differences, philosophical zombies play much the same role in debates about consciousness that cinematic zombies do in film. It's just that philosophy renders tediously explicit what films choose to leave so delightfully implicit. The challenge for philosophers and film buffs alike is to describe in suitably enlightening terms just what makes us the fully conscious, distinctly human creatures that we are by providing a specification of what it is exactly that makes us so distinct from zombies. At least in the more "deliciously cerebral" zombie flicks (those that offer up the social commentary for which the genre is so justly famous) the difference is not nearly as stark as it might at first seem. At the end of *Diary of the Dead* (2007), Professor Maxwell observes that "mornings and mirrors typically reveal much in us that we'd prefer not to see." In that vein, I propose that the zombies are the ones holding the mirrors up to us.

Scene I. "They're Evolving, Changing, Getting Smarter"— *Land of the Dead*

The rage these days is to think of the items coursing through our minds as outcomes of an evolutionary process akin to biological natural selection (Dawkins, 2006; Blackmore, 2000; Brodie, 2009). The various creatures of our imaginations (or "memes") spread like viruses from person to person by means of our intellectual products (such as books and films). In this process of memetic self-replication, our conceptions or "mind-children" occasionally spawn mutations, a few of which prove more adaptable — better equipped to invade and colonize our minds and brains. They are more gripping or infectious.[2] We're unable to put them to rest, and they reappear again and again in our artistic creations and other endeavors. Now it must be granted that the "zombie meme" is a stunning memetic success story as it continues to insinuate itself into our imaginations and capture ever-increasing screen time. Zombies are no longer confined to B-level status. Not only have they broken into the Hollywood high-rent district, their comic potential has been fully recognized, as evidenced by recent spoofs like *Shaun of the Dead* (2004), *Tokyo Zombie* (2005), and *Zombieland* (2009), films which give up any pretense to horrifying their audience.

In short, zombies have burst out of their subgenre and are now on the loose. They've gone viral. Like Elvis, references to zombies are everywhere. The *Wall Street Journal* now refers to "zombie banks" (those that can't be allowed to die), "zombie debt" (that which never seems to go away) and "zombie brands" (those such as Schlitz beer, which get brought back from the dead). The recent, stunning success of *Pride and Prejudice and Zombies* (Austen and Grahame-Smith, 2009) attests that they've infiltrated highbrow literary culture. And of course, this very volume testifies to the inroads zombies have made into academic circles.

Given their humble origins, this might seem surprising. Staying true to their Vodou-inspired roots (and their name), the first zombies on film were mindless puppets — reanimated corpses or near-corpses that have fallen under the spell of some nefarious master or witch-doctor. Such zombies were usually the victims of poison or witchcraft, not infection, and they were far from contagious. Mostly, they were dull and boring — much like their undead mummy cousins. The real monsters in these films are their masters, such as Bela Lugosi in *White Zombie* (1932).

The more recognizably modern conception of a zombie is arguably an offshoot of the vampire family tree, which has taken off on a distinct evolutionary path. In Richard Matheson's *I Am Legend* (1954 — which *must* not be confused with any of its film adaptations, including the 2007 one bearing the same name), one sees an early articulation of the notion that eventually animates Romero's living dead series. While Matheson's creatures are "vampires" (of sorts) — they feast upon the blood of the living, they cannot abide sunlight or garlic, and they can be killed with a stake driven through the chest cavity — they behave in other ways that we now associate as more characteristic of zombies. They are the victims of an apocalyptic infection that brings down civilization and threatens the extinction of the entire human race. Moreover, they aren't particularly powerful as individuals; their strength, rather, is in their numbers, which requires Robert Neville, the lone remaining uninfected human, to barricade himself in his house against their nightly assaults.

Acknowledging that his original inspiration came from the Matheson novelette, Romero (2006) tells us that he sought to free himself from the vampire paradigm by confecting a new sort of monster that carried less conventional baggage in its train. Instead of drinking blood, Romero has his creatures eating flesh. Whereas Matheson's story focuses upon the very end of the human catastrophe, Romero preferred to chronicle the crisis as it begins and unfolds. Initially, in *Night of the Living Dead* (1968), Romero doesn't connect his creatures to any Vodou-inspired precursors, referring to his creatures not as "zombies," but rather "ghouls" or simply "those things." Even *Dawn of the Dead* (1978) contains but a single reference to zombies as such.[3] Of course, by the time *Night* achieved its status as a cult classic and began to spawn sequels, remakes, and imitations, our ideas and expectations about "those things" had insinuated itself into the popular consciousness and coalesced into a distinct monster paradigm unto its own.

Given its relatively recent origin along with the natural flux of our conceptions, I'm perfectly happy to allow for genre-bending variations deviating from Romero's initial blueprint. Mutations, after all, are the engine of most evolutionary processes, and zombies continue to evolve and adapt to prevailing cultural trends and phobias. The recent trend, exemplified by *28 Days Later* (2000), *Pontypool* (2008), and *Quarantine* (2008) is to portray what are in effect zombies as not quite dead yet, but "merely" afflicted by some sort of rage-inducing virus. Zombies of this more recent ilk defy reigning zombic conventions by being able to run, jump, and even have pulses. Still, while the conventional notion of a zombie might not be fixed, there are central, stable features of zombies, which help to explain why they have invaded our minds and movies as much as they have. Indeed, this stability governing our expectations of how zombies *should* be and how zombie outbreaks *should* go has allowed zombies to burst onto genres beyond the horror.

Scene II. "Now It's Us Against Them ... Except They Are Us"—Diary of the Dead

So what are some of the key features of a cinematic zombie? My purpose here isn't legislative, so much as elucidative. Romero might tell us (Curnette, 2004; Biodroski, 2008) that he deplores the trend towards the more agile zombies that have recently popped up on screen, especially the remakes of *Dawn* and *Day of the Dead* (2004, 2008). Insisting that fast-moving zombies make no sense to him, he has Jason Creed (the student director of *The Death of Death*, *Diary of the Dead*'s film-within-the-film) cheekily remark that dead things have to move slow; otherwise, their ankles would break.[4] Despite these admonishments from the master who gave us the reigning conception of the movie zombie, I'm not interested in protecting the purity of the subgenre by laying out necessary conditions for what counts as a bona-fide or genuine cinematic zombie. Such essentialist attitudes don't do justice to the idea above that the creatures of our collective imagination are just as fluid and evolving as biological species.

Nevertheless, one key, enduring facet of the reigning zombie paradigm is their very personal, intimate connection to us. By that I mean that we are all potentially zombies — they are recognizably what we can become. In making this claim, I don't mean to take on any grand metaphysical commitments concerning personal identity. We can obviously *become* a zombie, even though our own personal identities might not *survive* such a change. In many if not most interesting senses — those to which various philosophers have turned to pin the notion of personal identity — it is clear that we *wouldn't* survive zombification. Our bodies are no longer alive, our memories have all but vanished, and our emotions and desires have (I would hope) changed beyond recognition. Indeed, much of the tragedy of such a metamorphosis lies in its utter irreversibility. So while there might not be enough in what remains of us to *identify* those remains *with* us, we can nevertheless saying of our remains that it has become a zombie.

Zombies do not simply replace us — as a robot might assume the place of one's spouse, or an alien doppelganger might snatch our bodies and take on our social roles. Rather, they are whatever *remains* of us. One cannot deny one's personal connection with that body of remains. Moreover, we care about what becomes of those remains — as well as the remains of our loved ones. Without the threat of potentially becoming one of them, we lose much of the true awfulness of a zombie attack. Being devoured alive is a gruesome enough fate to contemplate. But that could happen to you at the claws, pincers, or mandibles of any garden-variety mutated superbug or alien. It's all that much worse when you are forced to consider the fact that what remains of you will eventually rise up and join in on the feast. Equally distressing is the thought that in fighting off such a gruesome fate, you might have to desecrate what remains of your spouse or grandmother. Whatever else might befall us, then, we don't want either us or our loved ones winding up as one of "those things." Better to put a bullet through our brains beforehand.

Scene III. "Man, They Are All Messed Up!"— Night of the Living Dead

The point is that the possibility of becoming a zombie is supposed to be one of the most horrible and terrifying fates to contemplate, one that no rational creature would ever wish on their remains. This idea is reinforced by another central feature of the zombie paradigm: the "ick factor." Everything about zombies is meant to be loathsome, disgusting, and utterly repellant. As such, zombies fit perfectly Noel Carroll's definition of the classic horror monster. Carroll defines the horror genre in terms of the emotional responses that horrific creatures or "monsters" are meant to provoke in their audiences, chiefly fear and disgust (Carroll, 1990, p. 52). While horrific creatures are supposed to be terrifying in the sense that they pose some sort of threat to a film's protagonists, Carroll spends more time emphasizing the disgust or revulsion that we are supposed to feel toward them. For Carroll, our disgust is a characteristic reaction to what we find impure or otherwise unnatural. We tend to revile those things that resist categorization or transgress conventional boundaries in a way that defies ready explanation "according to reigning scientific notions." We flinch or shudder at things that are categorically interstitial, contradictory, incomplete, or formless (e.g., The Blob). Cinematic zombies epitomize each of these characteristics. They are both alive and dead. Their maimed, mangled bodies have no business ambulating. With their exposed innards, what should be inside them is on the outside. Their gooey, oozing, decaying bodies lack form and integrity. They are diseased, polluted, their flesh contaminated. In short, you just wouldn't want to touch one if you didn't have to. Speaking for us all, Kaufman, the bossman of Fiddler's Green in *Land of the Dead* (2005), says of zombies, "Man, they give me the creeps!"

As if by design, then, zombies are utterly repulsive. Not only do they appear as rotting, fetid, disease-ridden carcasses, often horribly mangled and sometimes even with entrails spilling out, their behavior is equally vile and despicable. It's not just that they're single-mindedly bent on cannibalism; it's also the appalling manner in which they carry out the practice, gnawing and munching on their still-living victims while remaining oblivious to their writhing and screaming. In this respect, the very concept of the zombie actually justifies the graphic, gory spectacle for which the zombie subgenre is infamous, and on account of which such films are often dismissed as irredeemably juvenile or second-rate. Aristotle might tell us that spectacle is the lowest form of entertainment, but that dismissive attitude overlooks the fact that in many zombie movies, the gore and spattering are more than just aesthetic set pieces to display the creative talents of a makeup artist or sick, uncanny mind of a director. Though they can be that, they also serve to amplify the fear and disgust Carroll tells us is so crucial to the genre. The blood, guts, and gore advance a narrative by conveying the true horribleness of the catastrophe threatening to engulf the protagonists (and possibly all of humankind). Certain themes simply call for spectacle. The "rout of civilization and massacre of mankind" isn't for the squeamish; it cannot be refined.

In this vein, it's instructive contrasting the zombie with their undead cousin, the vampire. For despite the common origin mentioned above, vampires and zombies have embarked on vastly divergent, perhaps even opposing, evolutionary paths. Like zombies, vampires have also witnessed an onscreen resurgence, but unlike the vile and repulsive zombie, the cunning and seductive vampire has now become the glamorous cool-kid on the undead block.[5] Vampires possess superpowers, which allow them to overcome the limitations of ordinary human embodiment. They can impose mastery over us. They have sex appeal. As

True Blood and the *Twilight* franchise attest, we swoon for vampires; they're dreamy and charming.

While they terrify us and threaten our well-being, vampires might well elude Carroll's definition of the movie monster, for they might well be too charming and fascinating to meet his requirement that genuine monsters be repellant and disgusting. Since the bulk of their characteristics are such as to evoke awe and admiration, authors and filmmakers feel compelled to convince us how truly awful it would be to endure the rest of eternity cut off from the rest of humanity, slinking around in the shadows preying upon the blood of the living. But these arguments are typically flimsy, failing even to convince the humans onscreen. Though perhaps damningly hubristic, it isn't that crazy to think that overcoming our bodily limitations and imposing mastery over others as a vampire would be worth whatever price we'd have to pay. Perhaps none of us actually possess what Anne Rice calls "the stamina for immortality," but surely, a great many of us would give it a shot. However, in order to become a vampire one needs to be chosen, a feat which requires one to charm a sexy, predatory superior being who can have virtually anybody they desired. Consequently, most of us can only dream of becoming vampires. They are out of our league.

The wretched zombie, by contrast, possesses virtually none of the admirable qualities of the vampire. The notion of a "glamour zombie" seems every bit a play on words as the notion of the "living dead." They are utterly devoid of any physical or social grace. Zombies are plodding and not at all plotting. Their desires — their hunger — cannot be satisfied, not even temporarily. While vampires salaciously savor their victims, zombies unceremoniously gobble them down with no hint of aesthetic appreciation. Their tormented, inarticulate moaning conveys how much they *suffer* their bodily limitations. I suspect that this (and not broken ankles) is a chief reason Romero chides those who try to pack their zombies with extra speed or punch. *Nothing* about zombies is supposed to evoke envy, awe, or admiration. There's even something wrong with their dogged tenacity and resilience. By design, they are the losers, the bottom-feeders, of the undead pantheon. We laugh at their antics in a way we wouldn't dare laugh at a vampire — their feeble attempts to cross the ice rink in *Dawn*, for example, or at how they get trapped in the swimming pool in *Diary*. While a zombie horde might eventually overcome or supplant us, one wouldn't be inclined to say that they've achieved *mastery* over us. Individually, they cannot outwit or overpower us. Since their strength lies in overwhelming numbers, the zombie fraternity cannot afford to be as selective as that of the more individualistic vampire. So if the vampire is the undead emblem of the aristocracy, then the lowly zombie is the undead representative for the vast majority of us unwashed commoners.

Thus there's little need to convince us we wouldn't want to wind up becoming a zombie. Compared to vampirification, zombification is much more clearly a fate worse than death. While some might fantasize about becoming a vampire, fantasies about the zombie apocalypse have us assuming the role of zombie *killers*. The continuing success of first-person zombie shooters attests to how absorbing and widespread this fantasy is.[6] Let's face it; how fun would it be to emulate Bruce Campbell or Woody Harrelson — to strap on leather and arm oneself with shotguns and chainsaws for the purpose of mowing down a host of slower-moving, dim-witted foes hell-bent upon our destruction? Some of us might occasionally explore our zombie potentials by posing for a "zombie pin-up" or going out on a "zombie walks," but after such adventures we always get to return from the undead. There's something clearly wrong with the eponymous vixens who choose to become zombies in *Zombie Strippers* (2008). They were obviously messed up to begin with. Even when the occasional zombie film portrays zombies as sexual beings — David Cronenberg's *Shivers* (1975), for instance, in which an orally transmitted wormlike parasite turns its victims into lumbering sex-maniacs — their very sexual indiscrimination and licentiousness is in no ways erotic, but rather repellant and discomfiting.

Scene IV. Evil Dead?

As Romero takes us through the course of his vision of the zombie apocalypse, his zombies recover more and more of their former selves. As early as *Dawn of the Dead*, they are returning to the mall. In *Day of the Dead* (1985), the zombified veteran Bub returns salutes and mourns the loss of Dr. Logan. In *Land of the Dead*, Big Daddy "relives" his former life as a gas station attendant, while others recall how to play instruments and push lawnmowers. My personal favorites are the two hand-holding sweethearts who've carried their mutual affection over to the other side. Riley remarks, "It's as if they're pretending to be alive."

When such vestiges of their former humanity break through, zombies emerge as more sympathetic creatures. Their moaning becomes less menacing, and more pathetic — a disconsolate cry of longing for lost soul. We cheer Bub as he shoots the deserving Captain Rhodes, and see the justice when Big Daddy incinerates Kaufman and Cholo. So maybe we can find something redeeming in zombies after all. While the scheme to domesticate them in *Day of the Dead* fails, *Fido* (2006) treats us to a scenario in which zombies are brought into compliance by shock collars developed by the Zomcom corporation. The zombie Fido is clearly an endearing figure: a kindly, protective old cadaver who just wants to find love and acceptance in his new family. Showing this very sympathy at the end of *Land of the Dead*, Riley declines to shell Big Daddy and his wandering band. "They're just looking for a place to go, same as us."

While we may still find them largely disgusting, zombies thus become more objects of pity than terror. Though they continue to menace us, they aren't truly villainous. Having lost any real intentionality, they aren't nearly cunning or sadistic enough, and they're much too ineffective, at least individually. Being victims themselves, they can't help it when in turn they victimize others. Focusing on the evil embodied by the monsters of various horror classics, Cynthia Freeland claims that "Most of all, horror movies are about the very picturing of evil" (2000, p. 275). Freeland's purpose is partly to argue against Carroll's conception of the horrific by showing that horrific evil can exist in a thoroughly naturalistic setting. We can still feel horror at monsters that aren't exactly impure or interstitial in Carroll's sense. However, zombies aren't really compelling sources of evil. I find it telling that while she devotes whole chapters to vampires, psycho-killers, and the like, she doesn't include a distinct section on zombies. And in the chapter devoted to the director David Cronenberg, she has but one fleeting reference to the aforementioned *Shivers*. Zombies just don't fit particularly well with her chosen focus, namely the concept of evil.[7]

At most, zombies are the instruments of someone else's diabolical scheming. For instance, *Resident Evil* (2002) traces the source of a zombie outbreak to the efforts of a greedy military corporation trying to genetically engineer the ultimate super warrior. This sort of explanation has by now become cliché; it was offered before in *Return of the Living Dead* (1985) and its campy spawn, and it has been revived in countless others. There can be a strong temptation to pin the blame of a zombie outbreak on the morally dubious activities of some individual or organization in what is basically an updated, hackneyed version of the Frankenstein theme, with the usual suspects playing the role of the overreaching "mad scientist." However, there is a threat that such explanations for why the dead have suddenly come back to life only distract from the zombies themselves. Indeed, as the *Resident Evil* series progresses, the story line focuses more and more upon the struggles between Alice and the nefarious Umbrella Corporation as it tries to design evermore powerful Frankensteins to defeat her. The zombies themselves become increasingly incidental and less threatening. By the time we reach *Resident Evil: Apocalypse* (2002) and *Extinction* (2007), they've been reduced to mere distractions as we await the arrival of the next "real" threat to pop out of the Umbrella Corporation's labs.

When we pin the blame of an outbreak on the nefarious activities of an individual or organization, we revert back to the original Vodou-inspired notion of a zombie. Again, such zombies are boring and dull. But we don't need to succumb to the temptation to invoke evil or human hubris as the explanation for a zombie outbreak. Indeed, in *Day of the Dead*, Romero hints that perhaps we're simply not destined to find any explanation at all. In fact I'm inclined to think it's a step backwards for the subgenre. Perhaps the cause is just radioactive spacedust from a rogue comet, maybe the Creator is punishing us, or there's no more room left in hell (even these last two possibilities injects distracting evil connotations). Romero himself eschews offering any specific explanations for the sudden uprising.

> ... the *T.V. Guide* blurbs on *Night of the Living Dead* begin with, "A returning Venus probe brings this plague...," and I never meant to imply that. When we originally shot the *Night of the Living Dead* thing, there were three proposed causes, and we cut two of them out because the scenes were boring and the scenes around them were boring, and that one we left in because it was part of that newscast and it made it seem a little bigger. And that became for a while, people said, "Oh, that's what happened." You know, some Venus probe came back and brought some kind of bug. And so I was determined ... I don't want there to be a cause, it's just something that's happening, it's just a different deal, it's a different way of life. If you want to look at it as a revolution, a new society coming in and devouring the old, however you want to look at it. That's really my take on it, it doesn't matter [Curnette, 2004].

One of the more remarkable things about Romero's Dead films is the extent to which evil is absent at the outbreak's onset. As he mentions in the passage above, the zombie plague is akin to a revolution, in which different ways of "living" struggle to supplant one another. Though revolutions claim victims, there needn't be anything inherently good or evil about them. Such struggles for survival are perfectly natural, and it really doesn't matter in the cosmic scheme of things whether they succeed or fail.[8]

Accordingly, it has become commonplace — even cliché— to construe a zombie outbreak as a metaphor for some particular perceived social threat. Indeed, zombies are so regnant with symbolism that it can be hard to view them literally — or just as they are. Zombie uprisings in various films have been taken as allegories for the seemingly inexorable spread of communism, fascism, McCarthyism, crass commercialism, AIDS, even the sexual revolution. Zombies have also been taken to represent specific despised, "untouchable" segments of the populace: homosexuals, drug addicts, immigrants, the homeless, even returning war vets.

To be sure, these kinds of interpretations can work well for specific films, but we should be wary about taking this line generally. For they threaten to obscure the potential zombie lurking in each and every one of us. If zombies symbolize the insidious fifth-column of some identifiable social threat, then we will be inclined to saddle them with unflattering moral characteristics inherited from that which they represent, thereby excavating a moral gulf between us. How, for instance, can one resist seeing the Nazi zombies in *Dead Snow* (2009) as inherently evil, or question the morals of stripper zombies? But it's not their zombie aspect that is responsible for such negative assessments. They were bad before the change, and their zombification serves only to accentuate their moral shortcomings. Consider instead how we would regard zombies if they represented an elderly population threatening to overwhelm our health-care system. After all, in their ceaseless wandering and bewildered expressions, they bear a striking resemblance to Alzheimer's patients. From that angle, zombies are much more likely to spark our sympathies; aging is common to us all, not just strippers or nazis.

Steering us away from overtly moral or political interpretations, Romero encourages us instead to view zombie outbreaks along the lines of a more natural disaster.

> I mean I don't care what they are. I don't care where they came from. They could be any disaster. They could be an earthquake, a hurricane, whatever. In my mind, they don't represent anything to me except a global change of some kind. And the stories are about how people respond or fail to respond to this and that's really all they've ever represented to me. It's what I thought in Richard's book, in the original book *I Am Legend*, that's what I thought that book was about. There's this global change and there's one guy holding out and saying "Wait a minute. I'm still a human." He's wrong. I mean, go ahead, join them, you'll live forever. In a certain sense he's wrong. On the other hand, you've got to respect them for taking that position. And zombies to me don't represent anything in particular. They are a global disaster that people don't know how to deal with and that's what it's about because we don't know how to deal with any of this shit, man [Romero, 2007].

That is, the focus is on how we deal with disaster generally, and not on any specific potential threat to society. To be sure, zombie movies don't assimilate well to other types of disaster films, for there is the additional supernatural or paranormal element of reanimated dead, coupled with the spattering of blood and guts. But the overall point is that we needn't posit any nefarious source of the catastrophe, even metaphorically. As Romero tells us, it really doesn't matter what the cause is, or whether we can offer some sort of naturalistic or pseudo-naturalistic explanation for the outbreak.[9] All we need to know is that something extraordinary has happened, and our zombie potentials have become realized in at least a few of us. The afflicted have begun to feast upon — thereby converting — the flesh of the living.

Scene V. "Are We Worth Saving? You Tell Me"— *Diary of the Dead*

My interest is in how we might try to distinguish living humans from zombies, for the obvious differences might turn out to be merely skin (plus viscera) deep. Earlier I argued that cinematic zombies are meant to be utterly repellent with few redeeming features. At least as horror monsters go, they are wretched, pathetic, utterly ungraceful and laughably inept. However, I suspect many of us harbor, deep down in our souls, doubts of being pathetic losers as well. When we look at them, we see aspects of ourselves — perhaps as through a magnifying glass, but aspects of us nevertheless. Zombies might suffer their bodily limitations, but don't we all? We too sometimes stumble about, slip on the ice, and have trouble emerging from the pool. And our ankles might break if we try to move too fast. Even the "ickiness" we see in them might just be a "projective disgust" of our own bodily functions.[10]

Our mental faculties are often equally pathetic. We're not particularly thoughtful or articulate, and our psychologies are not as robust as we might wish. In a zombie's hopeless quest to satiate "the hunger that will not cease,"[11] we can see some of our own forlorn attempts to fulfill superfluous desires, the satisfaction of which really isn't necessary for our continued existence. When zombies press their faces against the windows of the JC Penney at the Monroeville Mall, they bear an uncanny resemblance to those of us who press our noses up against the window displays at Macy's or who stampede the doors of the local Walmart on "Black Friday" for the latest "must-have" gew-gaw. As in the wickedly funny opening scenes of *Shaun of the Dead*, many of us sleep-walk through lives of quiet desperation, mindlessly shambling through daily routines to an extent that we would not recognize an outbreak, even were one to occur right under our noses. In short, we've already lost our souls, but are just too slow to catch onto the fact.[12] So while there might be something tragically and horribly missing in zombies, it isn't altogether clear that we aren't missing it as well. Despite our pretensions and protestations of superiority, the seemingly vast differences between us and zombies show up as differences, not in kind, but merely of degree.

Not only do zombies reflect our own limitations, there is another way they can be revealing, which is much more subject to directorial control. In our imagined *reactions* to zombie outbreaks, zombie movies have us disclosing, once again, just how pathetic we can be. After all, if we can be overwhelmed by a horde of lowly zombies, then what does that say about us? Recall that in the second passage quoted a section back, Romero tells us that his films are as much about humanity's inability to cope with crisis as with any particular political theme. The message is that as we react to a zombie attack, our propensities for mass hysteria actually threaten to facilitate the disaster's spread. Infected flee in hope and panic to the same places where the uninfected congregate. In turn, the uninfected are too slow, stupid, unwilling, or otherwise unable to implement measures necessary to contain the outbreak. Ironically, then, the very characteristics we are tempted to attribute to zombies show up in us and hasten our doom. It isn't as if containment is impossible. Zombies are slow, stupid, and not very dangerous as long as we keep their numbers to a manageable level. The problem is that we're just as inept and ineffectual as they are. Simple human shortsightedness leads to debacle and tragedy, and ultimately threatens wholesale social collapse.

Like other apocalyptic films, zombie movies express anxieties about our dependence upon social institutions that could, as with Hurricane Katrina, prove either too fragile or callous to deal humanely with crisis. Thus these films warn us about being too comfortable, confident, and complacent in our ordinary lives. Moreover, zombie films warn us about being too trusting of or engrossed by an all-too-deceptive media. We're told to remain isolated in our homes, and are reassured that "they are coming to get us," but when they finally arrive, we discover, to our horror, that it's the wrong them (or that "they" have been converted). The protagonists of *Diary of the Dead* feel compelled to document the spectacle for others and upload it to the internet, as if their own experience is really all that significant. Jason Creed takes the fact that his chronicle of the disaster has generated 7500 hits in only 8 minutes as testament that others are starving to learn "the truth" about what's going on. But it's more likely that he's just generating more of the chatter, spam, and spectacle that paralyzes and dooms us all. In any event, Jason's single-minded obsession with getting the truth "out there" ultimately turns him and most of his unfortunate compatriots into another form of spam fit for undead consumption.

Those lucky enough to survive will be the proactive ones who take their security into their own hands. Zombie outbreaks offer survivors a chance to recapture some semblance of a humanity that has been stultified by social ills and addictions threatening to make zombies of us all. In their efforts to separate themselves from the living dead, survivors are forced to transform themselves — perhaps to a greater degree than if they had joined the ranks of the undead. Liberated from dehumanizing social influences, the most unheroic of us all have an albeit brief, fleeting opportunity to exercise in a most glorious fashion the very values espoused (if not possessed) by the American Transcendentalists: the self-reliance of Emerson and the economy of Thoreau, that inspires those of us who pretend to prepare for an impending zombie apocalypse by perusing the *Zombie Survival Guide* (Brooks, 2003) or thinking through the scenarios presented on the Zombie Hunter's website.

So as the affliction spreads and hope for rescue or containment is lost, we may finally begin to see differences emerging between the remaining living and the living dead. But zombie films warn us that not all of these differences speak well for humanity. Zombies bring out the worst in us. Even as they are hemmed into increasingly tight spaces, survivors lose precious time squabbling with one another and jockeying for position. Do they remain upstairs and relatively mobile, or do they barricade themselves in the cellar? Do they remain at the mall or do they take a chance on finding more fuel? Do they continue their scientific mission to tame the zombies, or do they flee north in the whirlybird? As we all know, these decisions are tainted by extraneous personality concerns about who gets to be in charge. Ben tells Mr. Cooper, "You can be the boss down there: I'll be the boss up here." Humanity's penchant for internal dissent stands in stark contrast to the terrifying "group-think" of a zombie horde. Sarah sums it up in *Day*: "we're all pulling in different directions," and that only contributes to our eventual demise.

It is here, of course, that evil emerges in many zombie films, and once again it doesn't come primarily from amongst the murderous ranks of the living dead. Zombie films thus voice a fear and loathing of humanity as a whole that rivals any similar attitudes we might have toward a zombie horde. The outbreak has released the id in all of us, living and dead alike, and any pretension we might have of moral superiority ring hollow. Lovers of the subgenre know that the survivors have just as much to fear from each other as they do from the undead horde. As Dr. Logan notes, "we descend into attacking ourselves." In *Dawn of the Dead*, the protagonists take refuge at the mall in part because they don't like their chances with the rednecks shooting up the Western Pennsylvania countryside. Peter then has the survivors at the mall conceal their refuge, not from the zombies, but rather from roving gangs of looters, a precaution that proves all too warranted when Pasquale's gang breaks in and compromises their refuge. In *Day of the Dead*, Dr. Logan rewards his star pupil, the aforementioned zombie Bub, with the flesh of the recently deceased soldiers who died in the service of Logan's protection. This gruesome practice eventually leads to his demise, not at the hands of zombies, but rather by the horrified Captain Rhodes. In *Land of the Dead*, class division between the haves in Kaufman's Fiddler's Green and the have-nots immediately outside ultimately leads Cholo to hijack Kaufman's Dead Reckoning, leaving downtown Pittsburgh and Fiddler's Green defenseless in the face of Big Daddy's oncoming zombie horde. The protagonists of *Diary of the Dead* are waylaid by bushwhackers masquerading as the National Guard, who in turn are caught up in familial infighting in *Survival of the Dead* (2009). And so it goes. In sum, just as zombies appear ever-more redeeming and sympathetic, the dwindling remnants of humanity appear ever-less worthy of redemption. The distinction between humans and murderous zombies blurs once again, and our efforts to separate ourselves from the undead seem only to hasten the inevitable.

Zombie films are justly famous for their ambiguous dystopian endings; this nihilism is a big part of their charm. Protagonists typically do not survive their ordeal. If they do not wind up being chewed apart by zombies, then they might, as in the original *Night of the Living Dead*, end up being shot by rednecks. Even when a director is tender-hearted enough to allow survivors, it's typically unclear where they are going, or whether the afflicted will already be there to greet them when they arrive. Like other revolutions, zombie attacks eventually run their course, but it doesn't really matter who prevails. The mop-up operation at the close of the original *Night of the Living Dead* (which "accidentally" claims Ben) suggests that the zombie threat has dissipated. Romero's other contributions, however, paint a much bleaker future for the living. Even in films where the infection appears contained, campy gratuitous codas hint that this happy state is only temporary. If the outbreak spreads out of control, then we'll all be zombies in the end. But even if humanity manages to put the threat down, a new post-zombie world order emerges in the aftermath, a more brutal one in which we can no longer be innocent of the flesh-hungry zombie latent within.[13]

Scene VI. "These Are the End Times. Get on Your Knees and Pray!"—Diary of the Dead

Let's return at long last (like *Diary of the Dead*) to the beginning, to my intellectual home in the philosophy of mind and the dwelling place of philosophical zombies. For it's not an incredible stretch to view on-screen themes as an allegory for what has recently happened in consciousness studies. My narrative about cinematic zombies takes the following trajectory. Zombies are abjectly disgusting and pathetic creatures, even though we might see aspects of ourselves in them and perhaps despise them all the more for it. Moreover, we are all potentially zombies, but fervently hope that will not be our fate. However, though in the face of an outbreak we might strive to maintain some semblance of a humanity apart from our zombie selves, this cherished hope typically cannot be sustained, usually on account of warring tensions or inconsistencies within the very idea of humanity to which we so desperately cling. Humanity contains within it the seeds of its own destruction at the hands of its zombie successors. Ultimately, we're destined to be nothing but meat — mere animated flesh.

Philosophy recapitulates something resembling this narrative arc, only worked out in logical space. Several philosophers have found the very idea of materialism intellectually repugnant. Opposition to materialism can (but needn't have to) come from those seeking to establish the existence of an immaterial soul or an aspect of our being that could survive the inevitable dissolution of our material bodies. Or it might stem from a deep-seated suspicion of a scientism that appears prevalent in mainstream analytic philosophy. Whatever the motivations, several are repelled by the view that we're nothing more than animated flesh.

The zombie argument against materialism might offer these folk some comfort. As Descartes observed so long ago, the satisfaction of material and phenomenal descriptions appear to come apart from one another. Given any material description, one can seemingly envision a situation in which consciousness fails to attend the satisfaction of that material description. Thus purely materialistic explanations about how mere flesh can give rise to conscious experience all seem to fall flat. It's as if we are no more destined to explain conscious experience than Romero's characters are able to explain why the dead have come back to feed upon the living. Philosophical zombies — complete physical or material duplicates of us, except that they altogether lack what we refer to as consciousness or subjective feeling — are the very embodiment of this so-called "explanatory gap" between the material and the phenomenal. They are merely animated flesh with no consciousness added. From the fact that they seem so readily conceivable, the argument goes on to affirm the metaphysical possibility of philosophical zombies. The idea is that insofar as these creatures are genuinely possible, then the totality of material facts concerning us cannot necessitate or entail the facts about our conscious mental lives. A complete material description of our bodies would thus fail to capture an aspect of ourselves with which we are intimately acquainted, and so such descriptions must be incomplete. In addition to the material composition of our world, there must be something which is responsible for the evident presence of subjective feeling in our world.

Traditionally, materialists have regarded philosophical zombies to be a menace that must be eradicated. Accordingly, they've either tried to stamp it out at the onset by denying that proponents of the zombie argument can clearly and distinctly conceive of philosophical zombies after all, or they've attempted to block the inference from their apparent conceivability to their genuine possibility.[14] However, the squabbling amongst materialists in how exactly to deal with the threat serves only to give the argument greater force. It's as if in their zeal to lob grenades at zombies, they wind up hitting each other.

Another form of materialist response can take an altogether different cue from cinema. By explicitly raising and affirming the possibility of philosophical zombies, a question for the proponent of the zombie argument inevitably arises: why couldn't we turn out to be the very kinds of creatures that they have taken such great pains to conceive (and traditional opponents to stamp out)? Why aren't we zombies in actuality, who turn out to lack subjective feeling —*at least of the sort that anti-materialists think we have?* After all, absolutely nothing would change in what we seem to say or do. So this form of materialism fully acknowledges — indeed, embraces — the potential zombie lurking within each and every one of us. All is supposed to be "dark and silent" within the mind of a zombie; yet maybe the same is true of us as well.

The unsettling possibility, then, is that the zombie argument undermines itself, and that its proponents have unleashed the seeds of their own destruction at the hands of their overly active imaginations. In defense, proponents like to appeal to the authority of a powerful intuition on their side, indeed the one that never seems to die. While there might not be any behavioral differences between us and zombies, there is nevertheless a clear difference in how we *feel*, for in their very conception or definition they must *lack* the subjective feeling or consciousness that we evidently have.[15] That is, our evident "acquaintance" with phenomenal consciousness — with how it feels to have the conscious experiences that we have — clearly elevates our mental lives onto a higher plane than that of philosophical zombies. To think otherwise only goes to show that one hasn't accurately grasped the relevant conception of a philosophical zombie.

Still, there is a lingering suspicion that the apparent authority of this intuition is but a sham, and will ultimately fail to provide those hoping to separate themselves from zombies much salvation. This enduring faith in an evident "acquaintance" with phenomenal consciousness might just be so much hollow pretension, and just as in the movies, our human perspective need not be nearly as lofty as proponents so smugly suppose. The worry is that the definition or conception of zombie that proponents work with smuggles in illicit preconceptions about the nature of consciousness that just won't survive sustained scrutiny.

Thus the way in which the proponent frames the intuitions that are supposed to inoculate themselves from zombification is bound to collapse under the weight of its own internal tensions. Conscious people are the problem, not zombies. The strange thing about the zombie argument is that its proponents are awkwardly hemmed into a position in which they must maintain that an admittedly *metaphysically possible* world is not really a *logical possibility* after all. And here the problem is that any definition of zombie which logically excludes the possibility of the materialist begs the question by illicitly centering the actual world on a *non*-zombie world. It threatens to beg the question from the outset in much the same fashion that the ontological argument uses a suspiciously ampliative definition of God in order to affirm his existence. Once again, we see this by looking at the argument through a zombie's eyes. For any zombie is bound to find the zombie argument against materialism just as compelling as we would. After all, they are disposed to behave and say exactly the same sorts of things that we do. But for them at least, the argument is bound to be unsound simply because the conclusion is, by definition, false. Though they seem to talk about subjective feelings just as we do, their constitution is wholly material. So the question, then, is why shouldn't the zombie argument be unsound for us as well?

There are two distinct perspectives and ways of talking in play here, that of the zombie and that of the non-zombie. The conclusion of the zombie argument is true for the latter, but false for the former. And now, the whole question about the truth of materialism for us turns on whether our own *way of talking* accords with that of a zombie or that of a non-zombie with an acquaintance with an immaterial consciousness. The trouble is that by design, we just can't *say* all that much about what it is with which we are supposedly acquainted, and which is supposed to prevent us from zombification. More and more of us are now exploring the zombie way of talking about their subjective feelings (e.g., Beisecker, 2009; Beisecker, 2010; Stalnaker, 2002; Lynch, 2006). Like *Colin* (2008) or Cholo in *Land of the Dead*, we've "always wanted to see how the other half lives." And when we seriously consider the zombie perspective, we find it much more congenial than we initially might have supposed. Once you get to know them, zombies are not so horrible after all, and being one wouldn't be such an awful fate. Indeed, the admitted possibility of zombies shows that the acquaintance with consciousness demanded by the antimaterialist isn't required by the way in which we talk about our so-called "conscious" experience. We are thus forced to question whether we actually possess the acquaintance with a non-material consciousness that the non-materialist insists we have. When we look deeply into our minds and souls, we find it to be as dark as that of a zombie. It should comes as no surprise then that the nature of our conscious experience would be somewhat opaque to us. In essence, then (again, like Cholo), we've "gone zombie" and now take our task to be that of recruiting others to the ranks of living dead (or walking unconscious) by infecting them with the idea (or "meme") that they too are philosophical zombies.

Coda: "Long Live the New Flesh!"— Videodrome[16]

The zombie wars in philosophy are far from over. It remains an open question which side will eventually overwhelm the other by the force of better argument. Ultimately, proponents of the zombie argument might prevail and force philosophical zombies to do their conceptual bidding (à la *Fido*). But I doubt it. In any event, one must admit that in philosophy, as in film, it can prove deceptively hard to say anything constructive about the difference between zombies and humans. The distinction between the living and the undead is a fine one indeed, so much so that in philosophy some of us have quite literally given up the ghost. In other words, we bet that the trajectory in philosophy and film will be the same. We're all destined to be zombies — nothing but meat.[17]

NOTES

1. I highly recommend Alter and Howell (2009) as a quite readable introduction to conceivability arguments against materialism. For more extended discussions of the contemporary zombie argument, see David Chalmers (1996, 2006).

2. Indeed, the recent Canadian film *Pontypool* (2008) is an interesting addition to the zombie corpus, in which a rage-inducing infection is spread *memetically*, not virally.

3. It is often wrongly believed that *Land of the Dead* features the first use of the term "zombie" in Romero's series. The reference in *Dawn* occurs once: as the bikers burst into the mall, when Peter says: "With those bay doors open, there's going to be a thousand zombies in here." Ed.

4. By using a film-within-a-film (a meta-film?) to foreshadow events within the larger film, Romero follows the lead of the original *King Kong* (1933), as well as many of Shakespeare's plays.

5. They weren't always this way. Just look at *Nosferatu* (1929), or consider that Bram Stoker's Dracula was originally portrayed as a hideous and repulsive monster, a far cry from the beautifully seductive beings that now lay claim to the Dracula character and other vampires. For a nice discussion of how the vampire character has evolved, see Chapter 4 of Freeland (2000).

6. Saying that "zombies are simply fun to shoot at," during a recent horror convention in Las Vegas (Oct. 31, 2009), Romero attributed the current popularity of zombie films to such video games (*Resident Evil I–V, Left 4 Dead, House of the Dead,* and *Dead Space*).

7. By no means is this a knock on Freeland's study, which I like immensely. She freely recognizes that not all horror-movie monsters need to be evil (pp. 10–11). In this respect, her project is no more legislative than mine (and much less so than, say, Carroll's).

8. The phrase, "struggle for survival" or existence is a key component of Darwin's theory of natural selection. It also appears in the movie poster for *Night of the Living Dead.*

9. In this respect, Romero's understanding of the zombie appears to break a bit from Carroll's understanding of the horror monster. It isn't as if Romero thinks that zombies must have an *extra*-scientific explanation; it's just that he's not interested in their origins at all. Here I find it telling that when Romero does offer an explanation for a zombie-like uprising in *The Crazies* (1973), he pointedly does not have his victims turn into his living dead (well, at least not "literally").

10. See, for instance, Martha Nussbaum's (2004) account of how discriminatory attitudes are reinforced and maintained by a disgust of the messier animal aspects of ourselves, which are then projected upon others who subsequently bear the brunt of such disgust.

11. The phrase comes from Stephen King's monologue in *Diary of the Dead.*

12. A related sub-genre of horror film, exemplified by *Invasion of the Body Snatchers* has protagonists realizing that some dehumanizing change has already made most of us zombies of a sort, and that it is now likely too late to do anything about it, except for trying to save oneself by assimilating or secluding oneself away. One of my favorites of this ilk is Michael Haneke's *Seventh Continent* (1989), based on the true story of a young family who commit suicide after barricading themselves in their home against the dehumanizing forces of modern, capitalistic society (especially money!) before committing suicide.

13. *Fido* likens such a post-apocalyptic world to the supposedly halcyon times of post–World War II America, in which close human attachments are virtually impossible. The message is clear: friends, family, neighbors, corporations, and the government (and *especially* the elderly!) simply cannot be trusted.

14. Chalmers dubs these "Type A" and "Type B" materialists respectively. Once again, I'll spare you the intricacies surrounding the conceivability and possibility spawned by the burgeoning discussions of the zombie argument. The curious can review Chalmers (2006) for an overview.

15. As an aside, we might not be totally sure that others have subjective feelings like we do, but that is beside the point. All we need in order to get the anti-materialist conclusion off the ground is that in at least one case — namely our own — there is feeling. Thus we must not confuse the zombie argument in philosophy with another philosophical canard — the problem of other minds.

16. I realize this is not a zombie movie. Still, it seems fitting.

17. Many folk helped me bring this project to fruition. I'd especially like to acknowledge Jen Beaty, Tim Connolly, Jenn Neal, Mark Rauls, Michael Wolf, and Ron Wilburn, as well as the bartenders at the Pioneer Saloon in Goodsprings (Cindy, Deanna, LeeAnn, and Tracy), where the vast bulk of the writing actually transpired.

Bibliography

9/11 Television Archives. Online: <http://www.archive.org/details/sept_11_tv_archive>. Accessed Sept. 8, 2010.

Aching, Gerald. (2002). *Masking and Power: Carnival and Popular Culture in the Caribbean.* Minneapolis: University of Minnesota Press.

Ackermann, Hans W., and Jeanin Gauthier. (1991). "The Ways and Nature of the Zombi." *The Journal of American Folklore*, 104 (414): 466–494.

Adorno, T. W., and M. Horkheimer. (2002). *Dialectic of Enlightenment: Philosophical Fragments.* Stanford: Stanford University Press.

Agamben, G. (2005). *State of Exception.* Kevin Attell (Trans.). Chicago: University of Chicago Press.

Aizenberg, E. (1999). "'I Walked with a Zombie': The Pleasures and Perils of Postcolonial Hybridity." *World Literature Today*, 73 (3): 461–466.

Alter, Torin, and Robert Howell. (2009). *A Dialogue on Consciousness.* Oxford: Oxford University Press.

"America Under Attack." (2001). *CNN.* Sept. 11. Online: <http://transcripts.cnn.com/TRANSCRIPTS/0109/11/bn.04.html>. Accessed Sept. 8, 2010.

Anderson, W. H. (1988). "Tetrodotoxin and the Zombi Phenomenon." *Journal of Ethnopharmacology*, 23: 121–26.

Anderson, Benedict. (1983). *Imagined Communities: Reflections on the Origins and Spread of Nationalism.* London: Verson.

Andreski, Stanislav. (1974). *Social Sciences as Sorcery.* London: Penguin.

Andrews, Nigel. (1978). "Hitler as Entertainment." *American Film*, 3 (6): 50–53.

Apter, Andrew. (2005). "Herskovits's Heritage: Rethinking Syncretism in the African Diaspora." In Anita M. Leopold and Jeppe S. Jensen (Eds.), *Syncretism in Religion: A Reader* (pp. 160–184). London: Equinox.

Armstrong, Timothy. (1998). *Modernism, Technology, and the Body: A Cultural Study.* Cambridge, UK: Cambridge University Press.

Arthur, C., and M. Dash. (1999). *Libète: A Haitian Anthology.* Kingston, Jamaica: Ian Randle.

"Audio Commentary." *Fido.* Dir. Andrew Currie. Lionsgate, 2007. DVD.

Austen, Jane, and Seth Grahame-Smith. (2009). *Pride and Prejudice and Zombies.* Philadelphia: Quirk Books.

Badley, Linda. (2008). "Zombie Splatter Comedy from *Dawn* to *Shaun*: Cannibal Carnivalesque." In Shawn McIntosh and Marc Leverette (Eds.), *Zombie Culture: Autopsies of the Dead.* Lanham, MD: Scarecrow Press. 35–53.

Bamford, J. (2004). *A Pretext for War: 9/11, Iraq, and the Abuse of America's Intelligence Agencies.* New York: Doubleday.

Bar-On, Tamir. (2007). *Where Have All the Fascists Gone?* Aldershot: Ashgate.

Barta, Tony. (1998). *Screening the Past: Film and the Representation of History.* Santa Barbara, CA: Praeger.

Bataille, Georges. (1995). *The Accursed Share.* San Francisco: Zone Books.

_____. (1990). "Hegel, Death and Sacrifice." *Yale French Studies*, 78: 9–28.

_____. (1989). *Theory of Religion.* New York: Zone Books.

_____. (1994). *Visions of Excess.* Minneapolis: University of Minnesota Press.

_____, and Roger Caillois. ([1937] 1988). "Sacred Sociology and the Relationships Between 'Society,' 'Organism,' and 'Being.'" In Denis Hollier (Ed.), *The College of Sociology.* Minneapolis: University of Minnesota Press.

Baudrillard, Jean. (1981). *For a Critique of the Political Economy of the Sign.* Ann Arbor, MI: Telos Press.

Bearden, Romare, and Harry Henderson. (1993). *A History of African-American Artists from 1792 to the Present.* New York: Pantheon Books.

Beck, Ulrich. (1994). "The Reinvention of Politics." In Ulrich Beck, Anthony Giddens and Scott Lash (Eds.), *Reflexive Modernization: Politics, Tradition and Aesthetics in the Modern Social Order.* Stanford, CA: Stanford University Press. 1–55.

Beck, Ulrich, and Elisabeth Beck-Gernsheim. (2002). *Individualization: Institutionalized Individualism and Its Social and Political Consequences.* London: Sage.

Becker, Matt. (2006). "A Point of Little Hope: Hippie Horror Films and the Politics of Ambivalence." *Velvet Light Trap* 57: 42–59.

Beisecker, David. (2009). "Zombies and the Phenomenal Concepts Strategy." *Southwest Philosophy Review*, 25: 1: 207–216.

_____. (2010). "Zombies, Phenomenal Concepts, and the Paradox of Phenomenal Judgment." *Journal of Consciousness Studies*, 17, 3–4: 28–46.

Bell, Ernest A. (1911). *Fighting the Traffic in Young Girls*. Toronto: A. Sims.

Bellegarde-Smith, Patrick. (1984). "Overview of Haitian Foreign Policy and Relations: A Schematic Analysis." In Charles Foster and Albert Valdman (Eds.), *Haiti: Today and Tomorrow: An Interdisciplinary Study*. Lanham, MD: University Press of America. 265–281.

Benoist, Alain de. (2004). *On Being a Pagan*. Atlanta: Ultra.

Bernstein, Matthew. (1999). *Controlling Hollywood: Censorship and Regulation in the Studio Era*. New Jersey: Rutgers University Press.

Biodroski, Steve. (2008). "Interview: George Romero Documents the Dead." *Cinefantastique Online*: Online: <http://cinefantastiqueonline.com/2008/02/15/interview-george-romero-documents-the-dead-part-1/>.

Birdwell, Michael. (1999). *Celluloid Soldiers: Warner Bros.' Campaign Against Nazism*. New York: New York University Press.

Bishop, Kyle W. (2009). "Dead Man *Still* Walking: Explaining the Zombie Renaissance." *Journal of Popular Film and Television* 37: 16–25.

_____. (2006). "Raising the Dead: Unearthing the Nonliterary Origins of Zombie Cinema." *Journal of Popular Film and Television* 33: 196–205.

_____. (2008). "The Sub-subaltern Monster: Imperialist Hegemony and the Cinematic Voodoo Zombie." *The Journal of American Culture*, 31, 2: 141–152.

Blackmore, Susan. (2000). *The Meme Machine*. Oxford: Oxford University Press.

Blee, Kathleen M. (1991). *Women of the Klan: Racism and Gender in the 1920s*. Berkeley: University of California Press.

Blundell-Wignall, Adrian, Paul Atkinson, and Se Hoon Lee. (2008). "The Current Financial Crisis: Causes and Policy Issues." *Financial Market Trends*. Paris: OECD. 1–21.

Bogle, Donald. (2001). *Toms, Coons, Mulattoes, Mammies, and Bucks: An Interpretive History of Blacks in American Films*. 4th ed. NY: Continuum.

Boon, K. A. (2007). "Ontological Anxiety Made Flesh: The Zombie in Literature, Film, and Culture." In N. Scott (Ed.), *Monsters and the Monstrous: Myths and Metaphors of Enduring Evil*. Amsterdam: Rodopi. 33–43.

Booth, W. (1988). "Voodoo Science." *Science*, New Series, 240 (4850). 274–77.

Boscarino Joseph A., Charles Figley, and Richard Adams. (2003). "Fear of Terrorism in New York After the September 11 Terrorist Attacks: Implications for Emergency Mental Health and Preparedness." *International Journal of Emergency Mental Health*, 5: 199–209.

Bough, Geoff. (2006). "Interview with Mark Kidwell, Nat Jones and Jay Fotos, Creators of the Upcoming Comic '68." *Revenant: The Premiere Zombie Magazine*. Online: <http://www.revenantmagazine.com/68interview.htm>.

Boyd, Valerie. (2003). *Wrapped in Rainbows: The Life of Zora Neale Hurston*. New York: Scribner.

Boyer, Pascal. (2001). *Religion Explained: The Human Instincts That Fashion Gods, Spirits and Ancestors*. London: William Heinnemann.

Bradie, Michael. (1984). "The Metaphorical Character of Science." *Philosophica Naturalis*, 21: 229–243.

Breznican, Anthony. (2003). "Zombie Movies: A Feast for (and of) the Mind." *The Topeka Capital-Journal Online*. June 29. Online: <http://cjonline.com/stories/062903/art_zombies.shtml>. Accessed Sept. 10, 2010.

Brodie, Richard. (2009). *Virus of the Mind: The New Science of the Meme*. Carlsbad, CA: Hay House.

Brodwin, P. E. (1996). *Medicine and Morality in Haiti*. Cambridge: Cambridge University Press.

_____. (1992). "Review of Passage of Darkness." *Medical Anthropology Quarterly*, New Series, 6 (4). 411–13.

Brooks, Max. (2006). *World War Z: An Oral History of the Zombie War*. New York: Crown Publishers.

_____. (2003). *The Zombie Survival Guide: Complete Protection from the Living Dead*. New York: Three Rivers Press.

Brown, Karen McCarthy. (1989) "Afro-Caribbean Spirituality: A Haitian Case Study." *Second Opinion*, 11: 36–57.

_____. (2005). "Vodou." In Lindsay Jones (Ed.), *Encyclopedia of Religion*. 2nd edition. Volume 14. New York: Thomson Gale. 9634–9639.

Brown, Theodore. (2003). *Making Truth: Metaphor in the Sciences*. Champaign: University of Illinois Press.

Bruce, Steve. (2001). "Christianity in Britain: RIP." *Sociology of Religion*, 62 (2): 191–203.

Buck-Morss, S. (2009). *Hegel, Haiti and Universal History*. Pittsburgh: University of Pittsburgh Press.

Bull, Alister. (2008). "Al Qaeda Recruiting 'Western' Fighters: CIA Boss." *Reuters*. March 30. Online: <http://www.reuters.com/article/idUSN3032631620080330>. Accessed Sept. 10, 2010.

Bush, George W. (2002). *The Department of Homeland Security (Proposal)*. DHS. June. Online: < http://www.dhs.gov/xlibrary/assets/book.pdf>. Accessed Sept. 12, 2010.

Butler, Judith. (2004). *Undoing Gender*. London: Routledge.

Cabin in the Cotton. (1932). *Daily Capital News and Post-Tribune* [Jefferson City, MO]. Oct. 16, 6. Advertisement.

Caillois, Roger. (1988). "Festival." In Denis Hollier (Ed.), *The College of Sociology*. Minneapolis: University of Minnesota Press. 281–303.

Callinicos, Alex. (2010). *Bonfire of Illusions: The Twin Crises of the Liberal World.* Cambridge: Polity Press.

Carroll, Noel. (1990). *The Philosophy of Horror or Paradoxes of the Heart.* London: Routledge.

Celona, Larry, Murray Weiss, and Kati Cornell. (2009). "City Blocks Are Locked and Loaded." *New York Post.* Nov. 15. Online: <http://www.nypost.com/p/news/local/city_blocks_are_TpEAXSmorGa3k6xDzO4INP>. Accessed Sept. 8, 2010.

Césaire, Aimé. (1972). *Discourse on Colonialism.* Tr. Joan Pinkam. New York: Monthly Review Press.

CGA. (2009). *Where Has the Money Gone: The State of Canadian Household Debt in a Stumbling Economy.* Burnaby, ON: Certified General Accounts Association of Canada.

Chacón, J. A., and M. Davis. (2006). "The Yellow Peril." In J. A. Chacón & M. Davis (Eds.), *No One Is Illegal: Fighting Racism and State Violence on the U.S.-Mexico Border.* Chicago: Haymarket Books. 27–31.

Chalmers, David. (2003). "Consciousness and Its Place in Nature." In Stephen Stich and Fritz Warfield (Eds.), *The Blackwell Guide to the Philosophy of Mind.* London: Blackwell. 102–142.

_____. (1996). *The Conscious Mind: In Search of a Fundamental Theory.* Oxford: Oxford University Press.

Chamberlain, Gordon. (1986). "Afterward: Allohistory in Science Fiction." In Gregory Benford and Martin Greenberg (Ed.), *Hitler Victorious: Eleven Stories of the German Victory in World War II.* New York: Garland. 281–300.

Chermiss, H. (1980). *The Riddle of the Early Academy.* New York: Garland.

Chernilo, Daniel. (2007). *A Social Theory of the Nation-State: Political Forms of Modernity and Beyond.* London: Routledge.

Chesnutt, Charles W. (1898). "The Wife of His Youth." *Atlantic Magazine,* June. Online: <http://www.theatlantic.com/magazine/archive/1969/12/the-wife-of-his-youth/6658/>. Accessed Sept. 11, 2010.

Chomsky, Noam. (2001). *9-11.* New York: Open Media/Seven Stories Press.

Christol, Hélène. (1991). "DuBois and Expansionism: A Black Man's View of Empire." In Serge Ricard and Hélène Christol (Eds.), *Anglo-Saxonism in U.S. Foreign Policy: The Diplomacy of Imperialism 1899–1919.* Aix-en-Provence: Publications de l'Université de Provence. 49–63.

Clarens, Carlos. (1967). *An Illustrated History of the Horror Films.* New York: G.P. Putnam's Sons.

Collier, Andrew. (2008). *Marx.* Oxford: One World.

Comaroff, Jean, and John Comaroff. (2002). "Alien-Nation: Zombies, Immigrants, and Millennial Capitalism." *The South Atlantic Quarterly* 101 (4): 779–805.

_____ and _____. (1999). "Occult Economies and the Violence of Abstraction: Notes from the South African Postcolony." *American Ethnologist,* 26 (2): 279–303.

Condon, Bernard. (2004). "Till Debt Do Us Part." *Forbes Magazine,* 173 (3): 48–49.

Conway, Edmund (2009) "The Rise and Rise of Zombie Households" *Telegraph.co.uk.* Online: <http://blogs.telegraph.co.uk/finance/edmundconway/100000592/the-rise-and-rise-of-zombie-households/>. Accessed Sept. 8, 2010.

Cooley, Thomas. (2009). "Zombie Firms and Zombie Banks." *Forbes.com* (Feb. 11,). Online: <http://www.forbes.com/2009/02/10/recession-tarp-japan-opinions-columnists_0211_thomas_cooley.html>. Accessed Sept. 8, 2010.

Corbett, Bob. (1990). "Review of Wade Davis, *Passage of Darkness.*" *Bob Corbett's Home Page.* Webster University. Online: <http://www.webster.edu/~corbetre/haiti/bookreviews/davis1.htm>. Accessed March 4, 2010.

Corrigan, Timothy, and Patricia White. (2004). *The Film Experience: An Introduction.* 8th ed. Boston: Bedford/St. Martin's.

Costello, Matthew J. (2005). "Rewriting *High Noon*: Transformations in American Popular Political Culture During the Cold War, 1952–1968." In Peter C. Rollins and John E. O'Connor (Eds.), *Hollywood's West: The American Frontier in Film, Television, and History.* Lexington: University Press of Kentucky. 175–97.

Cott, Nancy F. (1987). *The Grounding of Modern Feminism.* New Haven: Yale University Press.

Cowley, John. (1996). *Carnival, Canboulay and Calypso: Traditions in the Making.* Cambridge, UK: Cambridge University Press.

Coy, Peter. (2009). "A New Menace to the Economy." *Business Week,* 4117 (Jan. 29, 2009): 24–26.

Crane, David. (2007). "Workers Get Smaller Slice of Bigger Pie." *The Toronto Star,* star.com. Apr. 16. Online: <http://www.thestar.com/article/203409>. Accessed Sept. 8, 2010.

Cranford, Cynthia J., et al. (2003). "Precarious Employment in the Canadian Labour Market: A Statistical Portrait." *Just Labour,* 3: 6–22.

Crenshaw, K. (2000). "Demarginalizing the Intersection of Race and Sex: A Black Feminist Critique of Antidiscrimination Doctrine, Feminist Theory, and Antiracist Politics." In J. James & T. D. Sharpley-Whiting (Eds.), *The Black Feminist Reader.* Malden, MA: Blackwell. 208–238.

Crenshaw, Martha. (2003). "'New versus 'Old' Terrorism." *Palestine-Israel Journal.* 10 (1): 48–53.

Croft, Stuart. (2006). *Culture, Crisis, and America's War on Terror.* Cambridge: Cambridge University Press.

Cruickshank, P. (2008). "I Married a Terrorist." *Marie Claire.* June 1. Online: <http://www.marieclaire.com/world-reports/news/international/married-to-terrorist_?click=rel>. Accessed Sept. 8, 2010.

Cunard, Nancy, (Ed.). (2002). *Negro: An Anthology.* New York: Continuum.

Curnutte, Rick. (2004). "There's No Magic: A Conversation With George A. Romero." *The Film Jour-*

nal, 10: Online: <http://www.thefilmjournal.com/issue10/romero.html>. Accessed Sept. 8, 2010.

DaCosta, K. M. (2007). *Making Multiracials: State, Family, and Market in the Redrawing of the Color Line*. Stanford: Stanford University Press.

Dariotis, W. M. (2007). "Crossing the Racial Frontier: *Star Trek* and Mixed Heritage Identities." In L. Geraghty (Ed.), *The Influence of Star Trek on Television, Film and Culture*. Jefferson, NC: McFarland. 63–81.

Dash, Michael. (1988). *Haiti and the United States: National Stereotypes and the Literary Imagination*. New York: St. Martin's Press.

Datta, Ronjon Paul. (2010). "From Political Emergencies and States of Exception to Exceptional State and Emergent Politics." *International Social Science Journal*, 185: 169–183.

Davies, Gareth. (1996). *From Opportunity to Entitlement: The Transformation and Decline of Great Society Liberalism*. Lawrence: University Press of Kansas.

Davis, Wade. (1983). "The Ethnobiology of the Haitian Zombi." *Journal of Ethnopharmacology* 9 (1): 85–104.

_____. (2004) "The Ethnosphere and the Academy," Keynote address, Interinstitutional Consortium for Indigenous Knowledge conference, Pennsylvania State University. Online: <http://www.ed.psu.edu/icik/2004Proceedings/section7-davis.pdf>. Accessed Sept. 8, 2010.

_____. (1988a). *Passage of Darkness: The Ethnobiology of the Haitian Zombie*. Chapel Hill: University of North Carolina Press.

_____. (1985). *The Serpent and the Rainbow*. New York: Warner Books/Simon & Schuster, 1985.

_____. (1988b) "Zombification," *Science*, New Series, 240 (4860): 1715–1716.

Dawkins, Richard. (2003). *A Devil's Chaplain: Reflections on Hope, Lies, Science and Love*. New York: Basic Books.

_____. (2006). *The Selfish Gene* (30th Anniversary Edition). Oxford: Oxford University Press.

Dayan, Joan. (1993). "France Reads Haiti: An Interview with Rene Depestre." *Yale French Studies*, 83: 136–53.

_____. (1998). *Haiti, History, and the Gods*. Berkeley: University of California Press.

Deacon, James. (2002). "The Joys of Excess." *Maclean's*, 115 (31): 34.

Deleuze, Gilles, and Félix Guattari. (1983). *Anti-Oedipus: Capitalism and Schizophrenia*. Trans. Robert Hurley, Mark Seem, and Helen R. Lane. Minneapolis: University of Minnesota Press.

Del Guercio, Gino. (1986). "The Secrets of Haiti's Living Dead." *Harvard Magazine*, January/February. 31–37.

D'Emilio, John, and Estelle Friedman. (1988). *Intimate Matters: A History of Sexuality in America*. New York: Harper & Row.

Dendle, Peter. (2007). "The Zombie as Barometer of Cultural Anxiety." In N. Scott (Ed.), *Monsters and the Monstrous: Myths and Metaphors of Enduring Evil*. Amsterdam: Rodopi.

_____. (2001). *The Zombie Movie Encyclopedia*. Jefferson: McFarland.

Dennett, Daniel. (1995). *Darwin's Dangerous Idea: Evolution and the Meaning of Life*. New York: Simon and Schuster.

The Department of Homeland Security. (2008-2009). "Emergency Preparedness." *Yellowbook*. Wilkes-Barre, PA.

_____. (2006). "Resolve to Be Ready in 2007." *DHS*, Dec. 11. Online: <http://www.dhs.gov/xnews/releases/pr_1165851559816.shtm>. Accessed Sept. 12, 2010.

Derrida, Jacques. (1982). *Margins of Philosophy*. Chicago: University of Chicago Press.

_____. (1998). "The Originary Metaphor." In Julian Wolffreys (Ed.), *The Derrida Reader*. Edinburgh: Edinburgh University Press.

_____. (1994). *Specters of Marx*. London: Routledge.

Descartes, René. ([1641] 2005). *Meditations on First Philosophy*. David B. Manley and Charles S. Taylor, (Eds.). *Descartes' Meditations Home Page*. Online: <http://www.wright.edu/cola/descartes/intro.html>. Accessed Sept. 15, 2010.

Dillard, R. H. W. (1987). "*Night of the Living Dead*: It's Not Like Just a Wind That's Passing Through." In Gregory A. Waller (Ed.), *American Horrors: Essays on the Modern American Horror Film*. Urbana: University of Illinois Press. 14–29.

Disgusting, Mr. (2007). "Boy Eats Girl: Director Stephen Bradley." Bloody Disgusting. Online: <http://www.bloody-disgusting.com/interview/437>. Dec. 12. Accessed Sept. 16, 2010.

Doezema, J. (2000). "Loose Women or Lost Women? The Re-emergence of the Myth of 'White Slavery' in Contemporary Discourses of 'Trafficking in Women.'" *Gender Issues*, 18 (1): 23–50.

Dong, L. (2008). "Cinematic Representation of the Yellow Peril." In L. Lewis, G. Griffith & E. Crespo-Kebler (Eds.), *Color, Hair, and Bone: Race in the Twenty-First Century*. Lewisburg, PA: Bucknell University Press. 122–146.

Douglas, M. (1966). *Purity and Danger*. London: Routledge and Kegan Paul.

Duncan, Andy. (2008). "Zora and the Zombie." In John Joseph Adams (Ed.), *The Living Dead*. San Francisco: Night Shade. 377–93.

Durkheim, Emile. (1995). *The Elementary Forms of Religious Life*. New York: The Free Press.

_____. (1982). *The Rule of Sociological Method*. New York: The New Press.

Dutton, Edward. (2008). "Death Metaphors and the Secularisation Debate: Towards Criteria for Successful Social Scientific Analogies." *Sociological Research Online*, 13. Online: <http://www.socresonline.org.uk/13/3/3.html>. Accessed Sept. 16, 2010.

_____. (2009). *The Finnuit: Finnish Culture and the Religion of Uniqueness*. Budapest: Akadémiai Kiadó.

Dutton, W. (1993). "The Problem of Invisibility:

Voodoo and Zora Neale Hurston." *Frontiers: A Journal of Women Studies*, 13 (2): 131–52.

Duyvesteyn, Isabelle. (2004). "How New is the New Terrorism?" *Studies in Conflict and Terrorism*, 27 (5): 439–454.

Dyer, Richard. (1988). "White." *Screen* 4: 44–64.

_____. (1997). *White*. New York: Routledge.

Earls, Stephanie. (2006). "Zombie Fever: Everything I Needed to Know I Learned from the Undead." *The Times Union*. Albany, NY. Oct 29.

Ebert, Roger. (1967 [*sic*]). "Review of *The Night of the Living Dead* [*sic*], dir. George Romero." *Chicago Sun Times*. Jan. 5. Online: <http://rogerebert.suntimes.com/apps/pbcs.dll/article?AID=/19670105/REVIEWS/701050301/1023>. Accessed Sept. 8, 2010.

Eco, U. (2000). *Kant and the Platypus: Essays on Language and Cognition*. New York: Harvest Books.

The Economist (2004a) "Dead Firms Walking." September 23, Vol. 372, Issue 8394, pp. 81–83.

The Economist (2004b) "A Phoney Recovery." February 26, Issue 8364, p. 83.

Ellis, Frank. (2004). *Political Correctness and the Theoretical Struggle: From Lenin and Mao to Marcus and Foucault*. Auckland: Maxim Institute.

"Extracts from the Modern Traveler." (1845). *American Freeman* [Plainville, WI]. May, 15. 1.

Farmer, Paul. (1992). *Aids and Accusation: Haiti and the Geography of Blame*. Berkeley: University of California Press.

_____. (2006). *The Uses of Haiti*. Monroe: Common Courage Press.

Farrer, C. (1988). "New and Noteworthy." *Western Folklore*, 47 (3): 224–226.

Fatton, R., Jr. (2002). *Haiti's Predatory Republic*. Boulder: Lynne Rienner.

Fay, Jennifer. (2008). "Dead Subjectivity: *White Zombie*, Black Baghdad." *The Centennial Review*, 8 (1): 81–101.

Flint, David. (2009). *Zombie Holocaust*. London: Plexus.

Folkenflik, David. (2009). "Hey, Media: Where's the Afghanistan Coverage?" *NPR Online*, Aug. 24. Online: <http://www.npr.org/templates/story/story.php?storyId=112030088>. Accessed Sept. 8, 2010.

Foster, Charles, and Albert Valdman, (Eds.). (1984). *Haiti: Today and Tomorrow: An Interdisciplinary Study*. Lanham, MD: University Press of America.

Foster, Ernest. (1942). "Around Hollywood." *Olean* [New York] *Times Herald*. Nov. 14. 7.

Foster, John Bellamy. (2008). "The Financialization of Capital and the Crisis." *Monthly Review*, 59 (11): 1–19.

Foucault, Michel. (1979). *Discipline and Punish*. New York: Vintage Books.

_____. (2006). *Security, Territory, Population*. New York: Palgrave.

_____. (2003). "The Subject and Power." In Paul Rabinow and Nikolas Rose (Eds.), *The Essential Foucault*. New York: The New Press. 126–144.

Freeland, Cynthia. (2000). *The Naked and the Undead: Evil and the Appeal of Horror*. Boulder, CO: Westview.

French, Scot. (2004). *The Rebellious Slave: Nat Turner in American Memory*. Boston: Houghton Mifflin.

Freud, Sigmund. (1961). *The Pleasure Principle*. Trans. James Stracey. New York: W.W. Norton.

Friedlander, Saul. (1993). *Reflections of Nazism: An Essay on Kitsch & Death*. Bloomington: Indiana University Press.

Gabb, Sean. (2007). *Culture Revolution, Culture War: How Conservatives Lost England and How to Get It Back*. London: The Hampden Press.

Gane, Mike. (1991). *Baudrillard: Critical and Fatal Theory*. New York: Routledge.

Genovese, Eugene D. (1972). *Roll, Jordan, Roll: The World the Slaves Made*. New York: Random House.

Gentner, Dedre. (1982). "Are Scientific Analogies Metaphors?" In David Miall (Ed.), *Metaphor: Problems and Perspectives*. Brighton: Harvester Press.

Gikandi, Simon. (1992). *Writing in Limbo: Modernism and Caribbean Literature*. Ithaca: Cornell University Press.

Gordon, R. (Artist). (no date). *Ghoul Academy*. Political cartoon.

Gramsci, Antonio. (1971). *Selections from the Prison Notebooks*. New York: International Publishers.

Grant, Barry Keith. (2003). "Experience and Meaning in Genre Films." In Barry Keith Grant (Ed.), *Film Genre Reader III*. Austin: University of Texas Press. 115–29.

_____. (1996). "Taking Back the *Night of the Living Dead*: George Romero, Feminism, and the Horror Film." In Barry Keith Grant (Ed.), *The Dread of Difference: Gender and the Horror Film*. Texas Film and Media Studies Ser. Austin: University of Texas Press. 200–12.

Green, Miranda. (1992). *Symbol and Image in Celtic Religious Art*. London: Routledge.

Greene, R., and K. S. Mohammad, (Eds.). (2006). *The Undead and Philosophy*. Chicago: Open Court.

Greenfield, W. (1986). "Night of the Living Dead II: Slow Virus Encephalopathies and AIDS: Do Necromantic Zombiists Transmit HTLV-III/LAV During Voodooistic Rituals?" *Journal of the American Medical Association*, 256: 2199–2200.

Grittner, Frederick R. (1990). *White Slavery: Myth, Ideology, and American Law*. New York: Garland.

Guerrero, Ed. (1993). *Framing Blackness: The African-American Image in Film*. Philadelphia: Temple University Press.

Gulli, Bruno. (1999). "The Labour of Fire: On Time and Labour in the *Grundrisse*." *Cultural Logic*, 2 (2): 1–20.

Halberstam, Judith. (1995). *Skin Shows: Gothic Horror and the Technology of Monsters*. Durham, NC: Duke University Press.

Hale, Grace Elizabeth. (1998). *Making Whiteness: The Culture of Segregation in the South, 1890–1940*. New York: Vintage Books.

Halliwell, Leslie. (1988). *The Dead That Walk: Dracula, Frankenstein, the Mummy, and Other Favorite Movie Monsters*. New York: Continuum.

Hardt, Michael, and Antonio Negri. (2000). *Empire*. Cambridge, MA: Harvard University Press.

Haraway, Donna. (2008). *When Species Meet*. Minneapolis: University of Minnesota Press.

Harman, Chris. (2009). *Zombie Capitalism*. London: Bookmarks Publications.

Harper, Stephen. (2005). "*Night of the Living Dead*: Reappraising an Undead Classic." *Bright Lights Film Journal*, 50. Online: <http://www.brightlights film.com/50/night.php>. Accessed Sept. 8, 2010.

_____. (2003). "'They're Us': Representations of Women in George Romero's 'Living Dead' Series." *Intensities: The Journal of Cult Media*, 3. Online: <http://intensities.org/Essays/Harper.pdf>. Accessed Sept. 8, 2010.

_____. (2002). "Zombies, Malls, and the Consumerism Debate: George Romero's *Dawn of the Dead*." *Americana: The Journal of American Popular Culture*, 1 (2). Online: <http://www.americanpopular culture.com/journal/articles/fall_2002/harper.htm>. Accessed Sept. 8, 2010.

Harris, Wilson. (1999). *Selected Essays of Wilson Harris: The Unfinished Genesis of the Imagination*. Andrew Bundy (Ed.). New York: Routledge.

Hayward, Keith, and Majid Yar. (2006). "The 'chav' Phenomenon: Consumption, Media and the Construction of a New Underclass." *Crime, Media, Culture*, 2 (1): 9–28.

Hedges, Chris. (2009). *Empire of Illusion: The End of Literacy and the Triumph of Spectacle*. Toronto: Knopf Canada.

Heffernan, Kevin. (2002). "Inner-City Exhibition and the Genre Film: Distributing 'Night of the Living Dead' (1968)." *Cinema Journal*, 41 (3): 59–77.

Hemenway, Robert E. ([1977] 1988). *Zora Neale Hurston: A Literary Biography*. Urbana: University of Illinois Press.

Herder, J. G. von. (1795). *Ideas Toward a Philosophy of the History of Man*. Riga.

Herskovits, Melville J. (1937). "African Gods and Catholic Saints." *American Anthropologist*, 39 (4.1): 635–43.

Hervey, Ben. (2008). *Night of the Living Dead*. BFI Film Classics. Houndmills, UK: Palgrave Macmillan.

Herzberger-Fofana, Pierrette. (1999). "Un entretien avec Sony Labou Tansi, Ecrivain." *Mot Pluriels*, 10. Online: <http://motspluriels.arts.uwa.edu.au/MP 1099slt.html>. Accessed Sept. 8, 2010.

Heuvel, Katerina Vanden, (Ed.). (1990). *Selections from The Nation Magazine 1865–1990*. New York: Thunder's Mouth Press. Online: <http://www.third worldtraveler.com/Independent_Media/Selections_ TheNation.html>. Accessed Sept. 11, 2010.

Higham, John. (1963). *Strangers in the Land: Patterns of American Nativism, 1860–1925*. 2nd ed. New York: Atheneum.

Hollier, Denis. (1988). *The College of Sociology*. Minneapolis: University of Minnesota Press.

Hoppenstand, G. (1992). "Yellow Devil Doctors and Opium Dens: The Yellow Peril Stereotype in Mass Media Entertainment." In J. Nachbar & K. Lause (Eds.), *Popular Culture: An Introductory Text*. Madison, KY: Bowling Green State University Press. 277–291.

Huntington, S. P. (1993). "The Clash of Civilizations?" *Foreign Affairs*, 72 (3): 22–49.

Hurston, Zora Neale. (1935; 1990). *Mules and Men*. New York: Harper Perennial.

_____. (1938; 1990). *Tell My Horse: Voodoo and Life in Haiti and Jamaica*. New York: Harper & Row.

_____. (1937). *Their Eyes Were Watching God*. Philadelphia: J.B. Lippincott.

Huxley, F. J. H. (1966). "The Ritual of Voodoo and Symbolism of the Body." *Philosophical Transactions of the Royal Society of London, Series B Biological Sciences*, 251 (772): 423–27.

Huxley, Martin. (2000). "Samantha Mumba." *Broadcast Music, Inc.* Nov. 30. Online: <http://www.bmi.com/news/entry/233559>. Accessed August 23rd, 2010.

"Interesting Facts About Zombies — the Walking Dead." (1943). *Cumberland* [Maryland] *Evening Times*. May 1. 3.

Jackson, Rosemary. (1988). *Fantastic: The Literature of Subversion*. London: Routledge.

Jancovich, Mark. (1996). *Rational Fears: American Horror in the 1950s*. Manchester: Manchester University Press.

JanMohamed, Abdul. (2005). *The Death-Bound-Subject: Richard Wright's Archaeology of Death*. Durham, NC: Duke University Press.

Jaspers, Karl. (1960). *The Idea of the University*. London: Peter Owen.

Johnson, F. Roy. (1966). *The Nat Turner Slave Insurrection*. Murfreesboro, NC: Johnson Publishing.

Jordan, Winthrop D. (1968). *White Over Black: American Attitudes Toward the Negro, 1550–1812*. New York: W.W. Norton.

Joyce, James. (1993). *Dubliners*. New York: Vintage Premier Classics.

Kao, C. Y., and T. Yasumoto. (1990). "Tetrodotoxin in 'Zombie Powder.'" *Toxicon*, 28 (2): 129–32.

Kashyap, Anil K. (2006). "Zombie Lending in Japan: How Bankrupt Firms Stifle Economic Reform." *Capital Ideas: Selected Papers on Macroeconomics*, The University of Chicago Graduate School of Business, September. Online: <http://www.chicago booth.edu/capideas/sep06/3.aspx>. Accessed Sept. 8, 2010.

Kiberd, Declan. (1996). *Inventing Ireland: The Literature of the Modern Nation*. London: Vintage.

Klare, M. (2004). *Blood and Oil: The Dangers and Consequences of America's Growing Dependency on Imported Petroleum*. New York: Metropolitan Books.

Koppes, Clayton, and Gregory Black. (1987). *Hollywood Goes to War*. New York: The Free Press.

Koven, M. J. (2008). "The Folklore of the Zombie Film." In S. McIntosh and M. Leverette (Eds.), *Zombie Culture: Autopsies of the Living Dead*. Lanham, MD: The Scarecrow Press. 19–34.

Koza, Harry. (2007). "Statistics 101." *GlobeInvestor-Gold*. Nov. 15. Toronto.

Krauthammer, Charles. (2002). "Violence and Islam." *The Jewish World Review*, Dec. 6. Online: <http://www.jewishworldreview.com/cols/krauthammer120602.asp>. Accessed Sept. 8, 2010.

Kristeva, Julia. (1982). *Powers of Horror: An Essay on Abjection*. New York: Columbia University Press.

Krugman, Paul. (2009). "All the President's Zombies." *The New York Times*, August 23. Online: http://www.nytimes.com/2009/08/24/opinion/24krugman.html>. Accessed Sept. 8, 2010.

Labou Tansi, Sony. (1983). *The Antipeople*. Trans. J. A. Underwood. London: Marion Boyars.

_____. (1986). *Parentheses of Blood*. Trans. Lorraine Alexander. New York: Ubu Repertory Theater Publications.

Laguerre, M. (1989). *Voodoo and Politics in Haiti*. Basingstoke: Macmillan.

Lakoff, George, and Mark Johnson. (1980). *Metaphors We Live By*. Chicago: Chicago University Press.

Laquer, Walter. (2000). *The New Terrorism: Fanaticism and the Arms of Mass Destruction*. Oxford: Oxford University Press.

The Lancet. (1984). "Puffers, Gourmands and Zombification," *The Lancet*, June 2: 1220–1.

Laroche, Maximilian. (1976). "The Myth of the Zombi." In Rowland Smith (Ed.), *Exile and Tradition: Studies in African and Caribbean Literature*. London: Longman.

"Last of the Caribs: A Romance of Martinique." (1879). *Decatur* [Illinois] *Daily Review*. July, 26. 2.

Latham, Angela J. (2000). *Posing a Threat: Flappers, Chorus Girls, and Other Brazen Performers*. Hanover, NH: University Press of New England.

Lauro, Sarah Juliet, and Karen Embry. (2008). "A Zombie Manifesto: The Nonhuman Condition in the Era of Advanced Capitalism." *boundary 2*, 35 (1): 85–108.

Lawless, R. (1989). "Review of The Serpent and the Rainbow; Passage of Darkness." *Latin American Anthropology Review*, 1 (1): 5–6.

Leab, Daniel J. (1975). *From Sambo to Superspade: The Black Experience in Motion Pictures*. Boston: Houghton Mifflin.

Le Goff, Jacques. (1990). *Your Money or Your Life*. San Francisco: Zone Books.

Lesser, Ian O. (1999). *Countering the New Terrorism*. Santa Monica, CA: RAND.

Leverette, Marc. (2008). "The Funk of Forty Thousand Years; or, How the (Un)Dead Get Their Groove On." In Shawn McIntosh and Marc Leverette, (Eds.), *Zombie Culture: Autopsies of the Living Dead*. Maryland: Scarecrow Press.

Levin, Josh. (2004). "Dead Run: How Did Movie Zombies Get So Fast?" *Slate*, March 24. Online: <http://www.slate.com/id/2097751/>. Accessed Sept. 8, 2010.

Lewis, B. (1990/2001). "The Roots of Muslim Rage." *The Atlantic Monthly*, 17: 17–26.

Lightning, Robert K. (2000). "Interracial Tensions in *Night of the Living Dead*." *CineAction* 53: 22–29.

Lipsitz, G. (1998). *The Possessive Investment in Whiteness: How White People Profit from Identity Politics*. Philadelphia: Temple University Press.

Littlewood, R., and C. Douyon. (1997). "Clinical Findings in Three Cases of Zombification." *The Lancet*, 350: 1094–96.

Litwack, Leon F. (1979). *Been in the Storm So Long: The Aftermath of Slavery*. New York: Random House.

Liverpool, Hollis "Chalkdust." (2001). *Rituals of Power and Rebellion: The Carnival Tradition in Trinidad and Tobago, 1763–1962*. Chicago: Research Associates School Times Publications and Frontline Distribution Int'l Inc.

Locke, Alain, (Ed.). (1968). *The New Negro*. New York: Atheneum.

Loeffler, Toby H. (2009). "'Erin go bragh': 'Banal Nationalism' and the Joycean Performance of Irish Nationhood." *Journal of Narrative Theory* 39 (1): 29–56.

Loudermilk, A. (2003). "Eating 'Dawn' in the Dark." *Journal of Consumer Culture*, 3(1): 83–108.

Lowe, Lisa. (2006). "The Intimacies of Four Continents." In Ann Stoler (Ed.), *Haunted by Empire*. Durham, NC: Duke University Press. 191–212.

Lumsden, Charles, and Edward O. Wilson. (1981). *Genes, Mind and Culture: The Co-Evolutionary Process*. Cambridge, MA: Harvard University Press.

Lynch, Michael. (2006). "Zombies and the Phenomenal Pickpocket." *Synthese*, 149: 37–58.

MacDougall, R. (1999). "Red, Brown, and Yellow Perils: Images of the American Enemy in the 1940s and 1950s." *Journal of Popular Culture*, 32(4): 59–75.

MacKinnon, Douglas. (2005). "The Danger of Complacency." *The Washington Times*. May 6, op ed.: A21.

Marx, Karl. (1974). *Capital, Volume 1: A Critical Analysis of Capitalist Production*. New York: New World Paperbacks.

_____. (1973). *The Grundrisse*. Middlesex: Penguin Books.

_____. (1986). *Karl Marx, Frederick Engels Collected Works (Grundrisse): Volume 28, Marx: 1857–1861*. New York: International Publishers.

_____, and Frederick Engels. (1848). *The Communist Manifesto*. Online: <http://www.anu.edu.au/polsci/marx/classics/manifesto.html>. Accessed Sept. 8, 2010.

Mason, Clifford. (1967). "Why Does White America Love Sidney Poitier So?" *New York Times* Sept. 10. Online: <http://www.nytimes.com/packages/html/movies/bestpictures/heat-ar.html>. Accessed Sep. 8, 2010.

Matheson, Richard. (1954). *I am Legend*. Garden City, NY: Nelson Doubleday.

Mbembe, Achille. (2000). "At the Edge of the World: Boundaries, Territoriality, and Sovereignty in Africa." S. Rendall (Trans.). In Arjun Appadurai (Ed.), *Globalization*. Durham, NC: Duke University Press. 22–53.

_____. (2003). "Necropolitics." L. Meintjes (Trans.). *Public Culture*, 15(1): 11–40.

_____. (2001). *On the Postcolony*. Berkeley: University of California Press.

McAlister, M. (2001). *Epic Encounters: Culture, Media, and U.S. Interests in the Middle East Since 1945*. Berkeley: University of California Press.

McIntosh, Shawn. (2008). "The Evolution of the Zombie." In Shawn McIntosh and Marc Leverette (Eds.), *Zombie Culture: Autopsies of the Living Dead*. Lanham, MD: The Scarecrow Press. 1–18.

McIntosh, Shawn, and Marc Leverette (Eds.). (2008). *Zombie Culture: Autopsies of the Living Dead*. Lanham, MD: Scarecrow Press.

Mehta, Brinda. (2002). "Re-creating Ayida-wédo: Feminizing the Serpent in Lilas Desquiron's *Les Chemins de Loco-Miroir*." *Callaloo*, 25 (2): 654–670.

Metraux, Alfred. (1972). *Voodoo in Haiti*. New York: Schocken Books.

Mintz, S., and M.-R. Trouillot. (1995). "The Social History of Haitian Vodou." In Donald Cosentino (Ed.), *Sacred Arts of Haitian Vodou*. Los Angeles: UCLA Fowler Museum of Cultural History. 123–147.

Mitchell, W.J.T. (2003). "The Work of Art in the Age of Biocybernetic Reproduction." *Modernism/Modernity* 10 (3): 481–500.

Mithen, Steven. (1996). *The Prehistory of the Mind: A Search for the Origins of Art, Religion and Science*. London: Thames and Hudson.

Mohammad, K. S. (2006). "Zombies, Rest and Motion: Spinoza and the Speed of Undeath." In R. Greene and K. S. Mohammad (Eds.), *The Undead and Philosophy*. Chicago: Open Court. 91–102.

Monogram Studios. (1941). *Press Kit: King of the Zombies*. California: Monogram Studios.

Moore, A., and R. LeBaron. (1986). "The Case for a Haitian Origin of the AIDS Epidemic." In D. Feldman and T. Johnson (Eds.), *The Social Dimensions of AIDS*. New York: Praeger. 77–93.

Moreman, Christopher M. (2008). "Review: *I Am Legend*. Dir. Francis Lawrence." *Journal of Religion and Film* 12 (1): Online: <http://www.unomaha.edu/jrf/vol12no1/reviews/ILegen.htm>.

Moretti, Franco. (2005). *Signs Taken for Wonders*. Trans. Susan Fischer, David Forgacs, and David Miller. London: Verso.

Morgan, Matthew J. (2004). "Origins of the New Terrorism." *Parameters* Spring: 29–43.

Muir, J. K. (1998). *Wes Craven: The Art of Horror*. Jefferson, NC: McFarland.

Muntz, Philip, et al. (2009). "When Zombies Attack! Mathematical Modelling of an Outbreak of Zombie Infection." In J. M. Tchuenche and C. Chiyaka (Eds.), *Infectious Disease Modelling Research Progress*. New York: Nova Science Publishers. 133–150.

Murdock, Deroy. (2005). "Don't Ask, Don't Tell, Don't Translate Terrorist Secrets." *Independent Gay Forum*. Jan. 13. Online: <http://www.indegayforum.org/news/show/26846.html>. Accessed Sept. 9, 2010.

Murphy, R. Taggart. (2009). "Beyond Bubblenomics." *New Left Review*, 57, May-June. Online: <http://www.newleftreview.org.proxylib.csueastbay.edu/?page=article&view=2787>. Accessed Sept. 8, 2010.

Murray, James P. (1973). *To Find an Image: Black Films from Uncle Tom to Superfly*. Indianapolis: Bobbs-Merrill.

The National Commission on Terrorist Attacks Upon the United States. (2004). *The 9/11 Commission Report*. New York: W.W. Norton.

Negri, Antonio. (2003). *Time for Revolution*. New York: Continuum.

Newitz, Annalee. (2006). *Pretend We're Dead: Capitalist Monsters in American Pop Culture*. Durham, NC: Duke University Press.

Nicholls, David. (1979). *From Dessaline to Duvalier: Race, Color and National Independence in Haiti*. Cambridge: Cambridge University Press.

Niehaus, Isak. (2005). "Witches and Zombies of the South African Lowveld: Discourse, Accusations and Subjective Reality." *Journal of the Royal Anthropological Institute* 11: 191–210.

Nkrumah, Kwame. (1966). *Neo-Colonialism: The Last Stage of Imperialism*. New York: International Publishers.

Nussbaum, Martha. (2004). *Hiding From Humanity: Disgust, Shame, and the Law*. Princeton, NJ: Princeton University Press.

Oboe, Annalisa. (2010). "Africa and the Night of Language: An Interview with Achille Mbembe." *The Johannesburg Salon* 2. Online: <http://jwtc.org.za/the_salon/volume_2/annalisa_oboe_africa_the_night_of_language.htm>. Accessed Sept. 10, 2010.

OECD. (2008). *Growing Unequal? Income Distribution and Poverty in OECD Countries*. Paris: OECD.

_____. (2006). *OECD Economic Outlook*, 80. Paris: OECD.

Olsen, L. (1986). "Zombies and Academics: The Reader's Role in Fantasy." *Poetics*, 15: 279–85.

Paffenroth, Kim. (2006). *Gospel of the Living Dead*. Waco: Baylor University Press.

Pagano, David. (2008). "The Space of Apocalypse in Zombie Cinema." In Shawn McIntosh and Marc Leverette (Eds.), *Zombie Culture: Autopsies of the Living Dead*. Lanham, MD: Scarecrow Press. 71–86.

Palumbo-Liu, D. (1999). "Double Trouble: The Pathology of Ethnicity Meets White Schizophrenia." In D. Palumbo-Liu (Ed.), *Asian/American: Historical Crossings of a Racial Frontier*. Stanford, CA: Stanford University Press. 295–336.

Panitch, Leo, and Sam Gindin. (2009). "The Current

Crisis: A Socialist Perspective." *Studies in Political Economy*, 83 Spring: 7–31.

Patterson, Orlando. (1982). *Slavery and Social Death: A Comparative Study*. Cambridge, MA: Harvard University Press.

Pearce, Frank. (2003). "Introduction: the College de Sociologie and French Social Thought." *Economy and Society*, 32 (1): 1–6.

Pernick, Martin. (1985). *A Calculus of Suffering: Pain, Professionalism, and Anesthesia in Nineteenth-Century America*. New York: Columbia University Press.

Perry, Ann. (2008). "Is This Canada's 'Last Hurrah'?" *The Toronto Star*, Saturday, Nov. 15: B2.

Philippe, J., and J. B. Romain. (1979). "Indisposition in Haiti." *Social Science and Medicine*, 13B: 129–33.

Phillips, K.R. (2005). *Projected Fears: Horror Films and American Culture*. Westport: Greenwood.

Pollock, Della. (1998). "Performing Writing." In P. Phelan and J. Lane (Eds.), *The Ends of Performance*. New York: New York University Press. 73–103.

Popper, Karl. (1963). *Conjectures and Refutations: The Growth of Scientific Knowledge*. London: Routledge, Kegan and Paul.

_____. (1966). *The Open Society and Its Enemies II: The High Tide of Prophecy: Hegel, Marx and the Aftermath*. London: Routledge, Kegan and Paul.

_____. (1957). *The Poverty of Historicism*. London: Routledge, Kegan and Paul.

Possomai, Adam. (2007). "'Secularisation' and 'Religion' as Zombie Categories?" *Australian Religious Studies Review*, 20 (2). 233–242.

Poulantzas, Nicos. (1980). *State, Power, Socialism*. London: Verso.

Putney, Clifford. (2001). *Muscular Christianity: Manhood and Sports in Protestant America, 1880–1920*. Cambridge, MA: Harvard University Press.

Raboteau, Albert J. (1978). *Slave Religion: The "Invisible Institution" in the Antebellum South*. Popper, Karl: Oxford University Press.

Rampell, Catherine. (2009). "'Great Recession': A Brief Etymology." *The New York Times*. March 11. Online: <http://economix.blogs.nytimes.com/2009/03/11/great-recession-a-brief-etymology/>. Accessed Sept. 8, 2010.

Reed, Ishmael. (1990). "Foreword." In Zora Neale Hurston. (1938; 1990). *Tell My Horse: Voodoo and Life in Haiti and Jamaica*. New York: Harper & Row. xi–xv.

Rey, T. (2004). "Marketing the Goods of Salvation: Bourdieu on Religion." *Religion* 34 (4): 331–343.

Rhodes, Gary D. (2001). *White Zombie: Anatomy of a Horror Film*. Jefferson, NC: McFarland.

Ricard, Serge, and Hélène Christol, (Eds.). (1991). *Anglo-Saxonism in U.S. Foreign Policy: The Diplomacy of Imperialism 1899–1919*. Aix-en Provence: Publications de l'Université de Provence.

Richardson, Michael. (1994). *Georges Bataille*. New York: Routledge.

Richman, Michele. (2002). *Sacred Revolutions: Durkheim and the College de Sociologie*. Minneapolis: University of Minnesota Press.

Robb, B. J. (1998). *Screams and Nightmares: The Films of Wes Craven*. London: Titan Books.

Rogers, Martin. (2008). "Hybridity and Post-Human Anxiety in *28 Days Later*." In Shawn McIntosh and Marc Leverette (Eds.), *Zombie Culture: Autopsies of the Living Dead*. Lanham, MD: Scarecrow Press. 119–133.

Romero, George. (2007). "George Romero Interview, Diary of the Dead." *Horror-Movies.ca*. Feb. 13. Online: <http://www.horror-movies.ca/horror_10828.html>. Accessed Sept. 8, 2010.

_____. (2002a). "George A. Romero's Fears for Horror and Hollywood: The Underbelly of the Monster." Interview with Priscella Engall. *Metro: Media & Education Magazine*, 1 (June): 158–63.

_____. (2002b). Interview. *Masters of Horror*. Dir. Mike Mendez and Dave Parker. Universal.

_____. (1979). "Morning Becomes Romero." Interview with Dan Yakir. *Film Comment*, 15 (3): 60–65.

Rosaldo, R. (1993). *Culture and Truth: The Remaking of Social Science*. Boston: Beacon Press.

Rosenberg, David. (2010). "Shared Sacrifice Will Be the New Economic Order." *The Globe and Mail*, July 6. Online: <http://www.theglobeandmail.com/globe-investor/investment-ideas/features/experts-podium/shared-sacrifice-will-be-the-new-economic-order/article1629347/>. Accessed July 12, 2010.

Rosenfeld, Gavriel. (2005). *The World Hitler Never Made*. Cambridge: Cambridge University Press.

Ross, B., and D. Scott. (2004). "An American Married to Al Qaeda: Woman Says Her Husband Helped Set Up Sleeper Al Qaeda Cell." *ABC News*, (December 23).

Rostron, Allen. (2002). "'No War, No Hate, No Propaganda': Promoting Films About European War and Fascism During the Period of American Isolationism." *Journal of Popular Film and Television*, 30: 85–96.

Russell, Jamie. (2005). *Book of the Dead: A Complete History of Zombie Cinema*. Godalming, UK: FAB.

Rutenberg, Jim. (2008). "The Man Behind the Whispers About Obama." *The New York Times*. Oct. 13. A1, Online: <http://www.nytimes.com/2008/10/13/us/politics/13martin.html>. Accessed Sept. 9, 2010.

Said, E. W. ([1981] 1997). *Covering Islam: How the Media and the Experts Determine How We See the Rest of the World*. New York: Vintage Books.

_____. ([1979] 1994). *Orientalism*. New York: Vintage Books.

St. John, Warren. (2006). "Market for Zombies? It's Undead (Aaahhh!)" *The New York Times*, March 26. Online: <http://www.nytimes.com/2006/03/26/fashion/sundaystyles/26ZOMBIES.html>. Accessed Sept. 9, 2010.

Sandall, Roger. (2001). *The Culture Cult: On Designer Tribalism and Other Essays*. Oxford: Westview Press.

Schele DeVere, Maximilian. ([1872] 2009). *Americanisms: The English of the New World*. New York: C. Scribner & Co.

Schou, Nick. (2007). "So I Married a Terrorist: Saraah Olson's Strange Trip Through the U.S. War on Terror." *OC Weekly News*. April 19. Online: <http://www.ocweekly.com/2007-04-19/news/so-i-married-a-terrorist/>. Accessed Sept. 8, 2010.

Scott, Helen. (2004). "Haiti Under Siege: 200 Years of U.S. Imperialism." *International Socialist Review*. May-June. Online: <http://www.thirdworldtraveler.com/Haiti/Haiti_Under_Siege.html>. Accessed Sept. 8, 2010.

Scruton, Roger. (2000). *Modern Culture*. London: Continuum.

Seabrook, William B. (1929). *The Magic Island*. New York: The Literary Guild of America.

Semmerling, T. J. (2006). *"Evil" Arabs in American Popular Film: Orientalist Fear*. Austin: University of Texas Press.

Shaheen, J. G. (2008). *Guilty: Hollywood's Verdict on Arabs After 9/11*. Northampton, MA: Interlink.

_____. (2003). *Reel Bad Arabs: How Hollywod Villifies a People*. Gloucestershire: Arris Books.

Shane, Russell. (1976). *An Analysis of Motion Pictures About War Released by the American Film Industry, 1930–1970*. New York: Arno Press.

Shaviro, Steve. (2002). "Capitalist Monsters." *Historical Materialism* 10 (4): 281–90.

Shay, J. (1994). *Achilles in Vietnam: Combat Trauma and the Undoing of Character*. New York: Atheneum.

Sheeran, P. F. (1983). "Colonists and Colonized: Some Aspects of Anglo-Irish Literature from Swift to Joyce." *Yearbook of English Studies* 13: 97–115.

Sheller, M. (2003). *Consuming the Caribbean*. London: Routledge.

Silver, Roxane Cohen, et al. (2002). "Nationwide Longitudinal Study of Psychological Responses to September 11." *Journal of the American Medical Association*, 288 (10): 1235–1244.

Smith, Anthony D. (1986). *The Ethnic Origins of Nations*. Oxford: Blackwell.

Sontag, Susan. (1972). "Fascinating Fascism." In *Under the Sign of Saturn*. New York: Farrar, Straus, and Giroux. 73–105.

Stalnaker, Robert. (2002). "What Is It Like to Be a Zombie?" In Tamar Szabo Gendler (Ed.), *Conceivability and Possibility*. Oxford: Clarendon. 385–400.

Stark, Rodney. (1999). "Secularization: RIP." *Sociology of Religion*, 60 (3): 249–275.

Stein, Elliott. (1970). "Review of *Night of the Living Dead*, dir. George Romero." *Sight and Sound* 39 (2): 105.

Steinberger, Michael. (2001). "Interview with Samuel Huntington: So, Are Civilisations at War?" *The Observer*, Oct. 21. Online: <http://www.guardian.co.

server, Oct. 21. Online: <http://www.guardian.co.uk/world/2001/oct/21/afghanistan.religion2>. Accessed Sept. 9, 2010.

Stevenson, Burton E. (1906). "The Marathon Mystery: A Story of Manhattan." *Racine* [Wisconsin] *Daily Journal*. Feb. 20. 14.

Stiglitz, Joseph E. (2009). "Spring Is Here, but Contain Your Excitement." *The Economists' Voice*, 6 (5). Online: <http://www.bepress.com/ev/vol6/iss5/art6/>. Accessed Sept. 8, 2010.

Stinnett, R. (1999). *Day of Deceit: The Truth About FDR and Pearl Harbor*. New York: Free Press.

Stoekl, Alan. (2007). *Bataille's Peak*. Minneapolis: University of Minnesota Press.

"A Story of Murillo's Pupil." (1879). *Sioux County* [Iowa] *Herald*. March 13.: 6. Online: <http://siouxcounty.newspaperarchive.com/PdfViewer.aspx?img=107007731&firstvisit=true&src=search&currentResult=0&currentPage=0>. Accessed Sept. 10, 2010.

Strinati, Dominic. (2004). *An Introduction to Theories of Popular Culture*. London: Routledge.

Strzelczyk, Florentine. (2000). "Fascism — Fantasy — Fascination — Film." *Arachne: An Interdisciplinary Journal of the Humanities*, 7 (1–2): 94–111.

Tait, R. Colin. (2007). "(Zombie) Revolution at the Gates: *The Dead*, the 'Multitude' and George A. Romero." *Cinephile* 3 (1): 61–70.

Tansill, C. C. (1975). *Back Door to War: The Roosevelt Foreign Policy, 1933–1941*. Santa Barbara, CA: Greenwood.

"Theatre and Stage News of Current Import." (1932). *Mansfield* [Ohio] *News*. Aug. 21. 4.

Thompson, H. (2006). "'She's Not Your Mother Anymore, She's a Zombie': Zombies, Value and Personal Identity.'" In R. Greene and K. S. Mohammad (Eds.), *The Undead and Philosophy*. Chicago: Open Court. 27–38.

Throop, Elizabeth A. (2009). *Psychotherapy, American Culture, and Social Policy: Immoral Individualism*. New York: Palgrave MacMillan.

Thurman, Wallace. (1929). *The Blacker the Berry*. New York: The Macaulay Company.

Time Magazine. (1973). "Energy: The Arabs' New Oil Squeeze: Dimouts, Slowdowns, Chills." *Time Magazine*. Nov. 17. Online: <http://www.time.com/time/magazine/article/0,9171,944743-1,00.html>. Accessed Sept. 8, 2010.

Todorov, Tzvetan. (1973). *The Fantastic: A Structural Approach to a Literary Genre*. Ithaca: Cornell University Press.

Tomlinson, John. (2007). "Globalization and Cultural Analysis." In David Held and Anthony McGrew (Eds.), *Globalization Theory: Approaches and Controversies*. Cambridge: Polity Press.

"Top Ten Money Making Stars." (2009). *International Motion Picture Almanac*. Quigley Publishing. Online: <http://www.quigleypublishing.com/MPalmanac/Top10/Top10_lists.html>. Accessed Sept. 8, 2010.

Townsend, Allie. (2010). "Q&A: Zombie-Survival Expert Max Brooks." *Time*. 26 July. Online: <http://

www.time.com/time/arts/article/0,8599,2006405, 00.html?artId=2006405?contType=article?chn= arts>. Accessed Sept. 8, 2010.

Trefzer, Annette. (2000). "Possessing the Self: Caribbean Identities in Zora Neale Hurston's *Tell My Horse*." *African American Review*, 34: 299–312.

Tucker, David. (2001). "What's New About the New Terrorism and How Dangerous Is It?" *Terrorism and Political Violence*, 13. 1–14.

Turse, Nick. (2008). *The Complex: How the Military Invades Our Everyday Lives*. New York: Metropolitan.

Ullman, Sharon R. (1997). *Sex Seen: The Emergence of Modern Sexuality in America*. Berkeley: University of California Press.

"The Unknown Painter." (1838). *Alton* [Ohio] *Telegraph*. Sept. 26. 1.

Valverde, Marianna. (2007). "Genealogies of European State: Foucauldian Reflections." *Economy and Society*, 36 (1): 159–178.

Victor, G. (2007). *The Pearl Harbor Myth: Rethinking the Unthinkable*. Dulles, VA: Potomac Books.

Voragine, Jacobus de. (1993). *The Golden Legend: Readings on the Saints*. Trans. William Granger Ryan. Princeton, NJ: Princeton University Press.

Walker, Alexander. (1970). *Stardom: The Hollywood Phenomenon*. London: Michael Joseph.

Waller, Gregory A. (1986). *The Living and the Undead: From Stoker's* Dracula *to Romero's* Dawn of the Dead. Chicago: University of Illinois Press.

Webb, Jen, and Sam Byrnand. (2008). "Some Kind of Virus: The Zombie as Body and Trope." *Body & Society* 14 (2): 83–98.

West, M. Genevieve. (2005). *Zora Neale Hurston and American Literary Culture*. Gainesville: University Press of Florida.

Westhoff, Ben. (2007). "Doomsday Disciples: Be It Nuclear Holocaust or Hurricane, St. Louis' Zombie Squad Is Ready for Anything — Even an Attack from the Living Dead." *Riverfront Times*. Feb. 7. Online: <http://www.riverfronttimes.com/2007-02-07/news/doomsday-disciples/>. Accessed Sept. 8, 2010.

Whelan, Kevin. (2002). "The Memories of 'The Dead.'" *Yale Journal of Criticism* 15 (1): 59–97.

White Zombie. (1932). Advertisement. *Daily Capital News and Post-Tribune* [Jefferson City, MO]. Oct. 16. 6.

Whitty, Stephen. (2004). "What Zombie Movies Tell Us About Ourselves." *Houston Chronicle*. March 15. Online: <http://www.chron.com/disp/story.mpl/headline/entertainment/2455845.html>. Accessed Sept. 8, 2010.

Williams, Tony. (2003). *Knight of the Living Dead: The Cinema of George A. Romero*. London: Wallflower.

Willis, Sharon. (2007). "Black Mentors and White Redemption: The Extraordinary Career of Sidney Poitier." The University of Western Ontario, London, ON.

Wilson, Edward O. (1998). *Consilience: The Unity of Knowledge*. New York: Alfred A. Knopf.

_____. (1975). *Sociobiology: A New Synthesis*. Cambridge, MA: Harvard University Press.

Wolfe, Ron. (2008). "The Not-So-Quick and the Dead." *Arkansas Democrat-Gazette*. June 6. Style, 53–54.

Wolff, Richard D. (2005). "Ideological State Apparatuses, Consumerism, and U.S., Capitalism: Lessons for the Left." *Rethinking Marxism*, 17 (2): 223–235.

Wolverton, M. (Artist). (2009). *Night of the Living Guantanamo Detainees*. Political cartoon.

Wood, Robin. (1979). "Apocalypse Now: Notes on the Living Dead." In *American Nightmare: Essays on the Horror Film*. Toronto: Festival of Festivals. 91–97.

Woodson, D. G. (1992). "Review of *Passage of Darkness*." *Africa: Journal of the International African Institute* 62 (1): 151–154.

Yasumoto, T., and C. Y. Kao. (1986). "Tetrodotoxin and the Haitian Zombie." *Toxicon*, 24 (8): 747–49.

Yewah, Emmanuel. (2002). "Congolese Playwrights as Cultural Revisionists." In F. Harding (Ed.), *The Performance Arts in Africa*. London: Routledge. 208–221.

Zaleski, Carol. G. (1985). "St. Patrick's Purgatory: Pilgrimage Motifs in a Medieval Otherworld Vision." *Journal of the History of Ideas* 46 (4): 467–85.

Žižek, Slavoj. (1992). *Looking Awry: An Introduction to Lacan Through Popular Culture*. Cambridge, MA: MIT Press.

Zolberg, Aristide R. (2006). *A Nation by Design: Immigration Policy in the Fashioning of America*. New York: Russell Sage Foundation.

Filmography

American Zombie. Dir. Grace Lee. Perf. Austin Basis and Jane Edith Wilson. Lee Lee Films, 2008.

The Bedford Incident. Dir. James B. Harris. Perf. Richard Widmark and Sidney Poitier. Columbia Pictures, 1965.

Blackboard Jungle. Dir. Richard Brooks. Perf. Glenn Ford, Anne Francis, and Sidney Poitier. MGM, 1955.

Blade Runner. Dir. Ridley Scott. Perf. Harrison Ford, Rutger Hauer. Warner Bros. Pictures, 1982.

The Blob. Dir. Irvin S. Yeaworth, Jr. Perf. Steve McQueen and Aneta Corsaut. Paramount Pictures, 1958.

Blood Sucking Freaks (AKA *The Incredible Torture Show*). Dir. Joel M. Reed. Perf. Seamus O'Brien and Viju Krem. AFDC, 1976.

Boy Eats Girl. Dir. Stephen Bradley. Perf. Samantha Mumba, David Leon, Deirdre O'Kane. Maple Pictures, 2005.

Confessions of a Nazi Spy. Dir. Anatole Litvak. Perf. Edward G. Robinson. Warner Bros., 1939.

Colin. Dir. Marc Price. Perf. Alastair Kirton. Nowhere Fast Productions, 2008.

The Crazies. Dir. George A. Romero. Perf. Lane Carroll, Will MacMillan, and Lynn Lowry. Pittsburgh Films, 1973.

Creature with the Atom Brain. Dir. Edward L. Cahn. Perf. Richard Denning. Clover Productions, 1955.

Dawn of the Dead. Dir. George A. Romero. Perf. Ken Foree and Gaylen Ross. Laurel Group, 1978.

Dawn of the Dead. Dir. Zack Snyder. Perf. Sarah Polley and Ving Rhames. Strike Entertainment, 2004.

Day of the Dead. Dir. George Romero. Perf. Lori Cardille. Dead Films Inc., 1985.

Dead Alive (AKA *Brain Dead*). Dir. Peter Jackson. Perf. Timothy Balme and Diana Peñalver. WingNut Films, 1992.

Dead Snow. Dir. Tommy Wirkola. Perf. Vegar Hoel. Euforia film, 2009.

The Defiant Ones. Dir. Stanley Kramer. Perf. Sidney Poitier, Tony Curtis, and Lon Chaney, Jr. United Artists, 1958.

Diary of the Dead. Dir. George A. Romero. Perf. Michelle Morgan, Shawn Roberts and Josh Close. Artfire Films, 2007.

Divided We Fall: Americans in the Aftermath. Dir. Sharat Raju. New Moon Productions, 2008.

Edward Said—The Myth of the "Clash of Civilizations." Dir. S. Jhally. Media Education Foundation, 1998.

Edward Said on Orientalism. Dir. S. Jhally. Media Education Foundation, 1998.

Enter ... Zombie King (AKA *Zombie Beach Party*). Dir. Stacey Case. Perf. Jules Delorme, Jennifer Thom, and Rob "El Fuego" Etcheverria. El Zorrero Productions, 2003.

Fido. Dir. Andrew Currie. Perf. Carrie-Anne Moss, Billy Connolly, and Dylan Baker. Lionsgate, 2007.

For Love of Ivy. Dir. Daniel Mann. Perf. Sidney Poitier and Abbey Lincoln. Cinerama, 1968.

The Frozen Dead. Dir. Herbert J. Leder. Perf. Dana Andrews. Gold Star Productions, 1967.

Flight of the Living Dead. Dir. Scott Thomas. Perf. David Chissum and Kristen Kerr. Imageworks, 2007.

Ghostbusters. Dir. Ivan Reitman. Perf. Bill Murray, Dan Ackroyd, Sigourney Weaver, and Harold Ramis. Black Rhino Productions, 1984.

Guess Who's Coming to Dinner. Dir. Stanley Kramer. Perf. Sidney Poitier, Spencer Tracy, and Katharine Hepburn. Columbia Pictures, 1967.

High Noon. Dir. Fred Zinnemann. Perf. Gary Cooper and Grace Kelly. United Artists, 1952.

Hijacking Catastrophe: 9/11, Fear & The Selling of American Empire. Dir. Jeremy Earp and Sut Jhally. Media Education Foundation, 2006.

The Hills Have Eyes. Dir. Wes Craven. Perf. Susan Lanier and Robert Houston. Blood Relations, 1977.

Hitler: A Film from Germany. Dir. Hans-Jürgen Syberberg. TMS Film GmbH, 1977.

Horrors of War. Dir. Peter John Ross. Perf. Jon Osbeck and Joe Lorenzo. Arbor Ave. Films, Sonnyboo Productions, 2006.

House of the Dead. Dir. Uwe Boll. Perf. Jonathan Cherry. Boll KG Productions, 2003.

I Am Legend. Dir. Francis Lawrence. Perf. Will Smith and Alica Braga. Warner Bros., 2007.

I Married a Communist (AKA *The Woman on Pier 13*). Dir. Robert Stevenson. Perf. Laraine Day and Robert Ryan. RHO Radio Pictures, 1949.

I Walked with a Zombie. Dir. Jacques Tourneur. Perf. James Ellison, Frances Dee, and Tom Conway. RKO Radio Pictures, 1943.

In the Heat of the Night. Dir. Norman Jewison. Perf. Sidney Poitier and Rod Steiger. United Artists, 1967.

Invasion of the Body Snatchers. Dir. Don Siegel. Perf. Kevin McCarthy and Dana Wynter. Allied Artists, 1956.

King Kong. Dir. Merian C. Cooper and Ernest B. Schoedsack. Perf. Fay Wray and Robert Armstrong. RKO Radio Pictures, 1933.

King of the Zombies. Dir. Jean Yarbrough. Perf. Dick Purcell and Joan Woodbury. Monogram Pictures Corporation, 1941.

Land of the Dead. Dir. George Romero. Perf. Simon Baker, John Leguizamo, and Dennis Hopper. Universal, 2005.

Last of the Living. Dir. Logan McMillan. Perf. Morgan Williams, Robert Faith and Ashleigh Southam. Gorilla Pictures, 2008.

Lilies of the Field. Dir. Ralph Nelson. Perf. Sidney Poitier and Lilia Skala. United Artists, 1963.

Live and Let Die. Dir. Guy Hamilton. Perf. Roger Moore, Yaphet Kotto, and Jane Seymour. United Artists, 1973.

The Lost Man. Dir. Robert Alan Aurthur. Perf. Sidney Poitier and Joanna Shimkus. Universal Pictures, 1969.

The Man They Could Not Hang. Dir. Nick Grinde. Perf. Boris Karloff and Lorna Gray. Columbia Pictures, 1939.

Masters of Horror. Dir. Mike Mendez and Dave Parker. Universal, 2002.

My Boyfriend's Back. Dir. Bob Balaban. Perf. Andrew Lowry, Traci Lind, and Mary Beth Hurt. Touchstone Pictures, 1993.

Night of the Living Dead. Dir. George Romero. Perf. Duane Jones, Judith O'Dea, and Karl Hardman. Image Ten, et al., 1968.

Night of the Living Dead 3D. Dir. Jeff Broadstreet. Perf. Sid Haig, Brianna Brown, and Joshua Des-Roches. HorrorWorks, 2006.

Night of the Zombies (AKA *Battalion of the Living Dead*). Dir. Joel M. Reed. Perf. Jamie Gillis, Samantha Grey, and Ryan Hilliard. N.M.D. Distributing Company, 1981.

A Nightmare on Elm Street. Dir. Wes Craven. Perf. Robert Englund and Johnny Depp. New Line Cinema, 1984.

No Way Out. Dir. Joseph L. Mankiewicz. Perf. Richard Widmark, Linda Darnell, and Sidney Poitier. Twentieth Century–Fox, 1950.

Nosferatu. Dir. F. W. Murnau. Perf. Max Schreck. Jofa Atelier Berlin-Johannisthal, 1929.

Oasis of the Zombies. Dir. Jesus Franco. Perf. Manuel Gélin and France Lomay. Eurocine, 1982.

Obsession: Radical Islam's War Against the West. Dir. Wayne Kopping. G-Machine, 2005.

Ouanga. Dir. George Terwilliger. Perf. Fredi Washington and Marie Paxton. George Terwilliger Productions, 1936.

Outpost. Dir. Steven Barker. Perf. Ray Stevenson. Black Camel Pictures, 2008.

A Patch of Blue. Dir. Guy Green. Perf. Sidney Poitier and Shelley Winters. MGM, 1965.

Pontypool. Dir. Bruce McDonald. Perf. Stephen McHattie and Lisa Houle. Ponty Up Pictures, 2009.

Quarantine. Dir. John Erick Dowdle. Perf. Jennifer Carpenter and Steve Harris. Andale Pictures, 2008.

Raiders of the Lost Ark. Dir. Steven Spielberg. Perf. Harrison Ford, Karen Allen, and John Rhys-Davies. Lucasfilm, 1981.

A Raisin in the Sun. Dir. Daniel Petrie. Perf. Sidney Poitier, Ruby Dee, and Louis Gossett, Jr. Columbia Pictures, 1961.

Reel Bad Arabs: How Hollywood Vilifies a People. Dir. S. Jhally. Media Education Foundation, 2006.

Resident Evil. Dir. Paul W. S. Anderson. Perf. Milla Jovovich and Eric Mabius. Constantin Film Produktion, 2002.

Resident Evil: Apocalypse. Dir. Alexander Witt. Perf. Milla Jovovich and Sienna Guillroy. Constantin Film Produktion, 2004.

Resident Evil: Extinction. Dir. Russell Mulcahy. Perf. Milla Jovovich. Constantin Film Produktion, 2007.

The Return of the Living Dead. Dir. Dan O'Bannon. Perf. Clu Gulager and James Karen. Hemdale Film, 1985.

Revenge of the Zombies. Dir. Steven Sekeley. Perf. John Carradine and Gale Storm. Monogram Pictures Corporation, 1943.

Revolt of the Zombies. Dir. Victor Halperin. Perf. Dorothy Stone and Roy D'Arcy. Halperin Productions Academy, 1936.

Schindler's List. Dir. Steven Spielberg. Perf. Liam Neeson, Ben Kingsley, and Ralph Fiennes. Universal Pictures, 1993.

The Serpent and the Rainbow. Dir. Wes Craven. Perf. Bill Pullman. Universal Pictures, 1988.

The Seventh Continent. Dir. Michael Haneke. Dir. Dieter Berner and Birgit Doll. Wega Film, 1989.

Shaun of the Dead. Dir. Edgar Wright. Perf. Simon Pegg, Kate Ashfield, and Nick Frost. Alliance Atlantis, 2004.

Shivers (AKA *They Came from Within*). Dir. David Cronenberg. Perf. Paul Hampton and Lynn Lowry. Cinépix, 1976.

Shock Waves. Dir. Kenneth Wiederhorn. Perf. Peter Cushing and Brooke Adams. Zopix Company, 1977.

The Slender Thread. Dir. Sydney Pollack. Perf. Sidney Poitier, Anne Bancroft, and Telly Savalas. Paramount, 1965.

Stone's War (AKA *War of the Dead*). Dir. Marko Makilaakso. Perf. Andrew Tiernan and Mikko Leppilampi. Leituvos Kinostudija, 2010.

Sugar Hill (AKA *The Zombies of Sugar Hill*). Dir. Paul Maslansky. Perf. Marki Bey. AIP, 1974.

Survival of the Dead. Dir. George A. Romero. Perf.

Alan Van Sprang and Kenneth Welsh. Blank of the Dead Productions, 2009.

Suspiria. Dir. Dario Argento. Perf. Jessica Harper, Stefania Casini, and Flavio Bucci. Seda Spettacoli, 1977.

Taken. Dir. Pierre Morel. Perf. Liam Neeson and Maggie Grace. Europa Corp., 2008.

Team America: World Police. Dir. Trey Parker. Perf. Trey Parker and Matt Stone. Paramount, 2004.

Them! Dir. Gordon Douglas. Perf. James Whitmore, Edmund Gwenn, and James Arness. Warner Bros., 1954.

They Saved Hitler's Brain. Dir. David Bradley. Perf. Walter Stocker and Audrey Claire. Paragon Films, 1968.

300. Dir. Zack Snyder. Perf. Gerard Butler and Lena Headey. Warner Bros. Pictures, 2006.

The Time Machine. Dir. Simon Wells. Perf. Guy Pierce, Samantha Mumba, and Mark Addy. Warner Bros., 2002.

To Sir, with Love. Dir. James Clavell. Perf. Sidney Poitier and Judy Geeson. Columbia Pictures, 1967.

Tokyo Zombie. Dir. Sakichi Satô. Perf. Tadanobu Asano, Shô Aikawa, and Erika Okuda. Tôkyô Zonbi Seisaku, 2005.

Traffic in Souls. Dir. George Loane Tucker. Perf. Ethel Grandin and Matt Moore. Universal, 1913.

28 Days Later. Dir. Danny Boyle. Perf. Cillian Murphy and Naomie Harris. British Film Council, 2002.

28 Weeks Later. Dir. Juan Carlos Fresnadillo. Perf. Robert Carlyle. Fox Atomic, 2007.

Twilight. Dir. Catherine Hardwicke. Perf. Kristen Stewart and Robert Pattinson. Summit, 2008.

The Walking Dead. Dir. Michael Curtiz. Perf. Boris Karloff and Edmund Gwenn. Warner Bros., 1936.

The War of the Worlds. Dir. Byron Haskin. Perf. Gene Barry and Ann Robinson. Paramount, 1953.

Where Eagles Dare. Dir. Brian G. Hutton. Perf. Richard Burton and Clint Eastwood. MGM, 1969.

White Zombie. Dir. Victor Halperin. Perf. Bela Lugosi, Madge Bellamy, and Joseph Cawthorn. RKO-Pathé Studios, 1932.

Zombi 3. Dir. Lucio Fulci. Perf. Deran Sarafian and Bearice Ring. Flora Film, 1988.

Zombi 2 (AKA *Zombie*). Dir. Lucio Fulci. Perf. Tisa Farrow and Ian McCulloch. Variety Film Production, 1979.

Zombie Lake. Dir. Jean Rollin. Perf. Howard Vernon. Eurocine, 1981.

Zombie Strippers. Dir. Jay Lee. Perf. Jenna Jameson and Robert Englund. Stage 6 Films, 2008.

Zombieland. Dir. Ruben Fleischer. Perf. Woody Harrelson, Emma Stone, Jesse Eisenberg, and Bill Murray. Columbia Pictures, 2009.

Zombiez. Dir. John Bacchus. Perf. Jenicia Garcia. Purgatory Blues LLC, 2005.

About the Contributors

Dave Beisecker is an associate professor of philosophy at the University of Nevada, Las Vegas. His work is primarily in the philosophy of mind and language, and he's been commissioned to write an entry on philosophical zombies for the *Internet Encyclopedia of Philosophy*. He received his Ph.D. at the University of Pittsburgh.

Michele Braun teaches in the English Department at Mount Royal University in Calgary, Alberta, Canada. Her research interests include monsters and technologies. Her dissertation, "Cyborgs and Clones: Production and Reproduction of Posthuman Figures in Contemporary British Literature," explored the relationship between technology and notions of representation and inclusion as they emerge in twentieth and early twenty-first century literature. She also researches contemporary narratives about vampires, zombies and werewolves.

Barbara S. Bruce teaches film studies and English literature. In her work on film, she specializes in American cinema, particularly classic Hollywood and the horror and disaster genres. She is co-authoring a book on Hollywood disaster films of the 1930s at Carlton University and the University of Western Ontario.

Ronjon Paul Datta is an assistant professor of social theory and culture in the Department of Sociology at the University of Alberta. His recent publications discuss a range of theorists and topics including Foucault, Agamben, Durkheim, Althusser, critical theory, social justice and realist philosophy of social science. He is a recipient of a Governor General of Canada Academic Gold Medal for his doctoral work in social theory and political sociology.

Edward Dutton has a Ph.D. in religious studies from Aberdeen University and is adjunct professor of the anthropology of religion at Oulu University (Finland). He has published *Meeting Jesus at University: Rites of Passage and Student Evangelicals* (Ashgate, 2008) and *The Finnuit: Finnish Culture and the Religion of Uniqueness* (Akademiai Kiado, 2009) and is writing a study of Sudanese Christian refugees in northern Finland. He has written for *Times Higher Education* (London), *The Times Educational Supplement* (London), *The Daily Telegraph* (London) and *The Chronicle of Higher Education* (DC).

Becki A. Graham is pursuing her doctorate in rhetoric and professional communication in the English Department at New Mexico State University. Her research interests include popular culture, mass media, and horror cinema. In addition to teaching courses in rhetoric and composition and technical writing, she works as a technical writer and editor.

Eric Hamako is a doctoral candidate in the University of Massachusetts Amherst's Social Justice Education Program. He is studying how community education can support mixed-race people's political movements in the U.S. and ways to incorporate stronger antiracist frameworks into those educational efforts. His essay "For the Movement: Community Education Supporting

Multiracial Organizing" appeared in the journal *Equity & Excellence in Education* in 2006. He has also presented on multiraciality and identity development, community education, and pop culture.

David Inglis is a professor of sociology at the University of Aberdeen. He is a graduate of the University of Cambridge and the University of York. He is an Academician of the UK Academy of the Social Sciences. Research interests include the history of social thought, historical sociology, the sociologies of culture, art and aesthetics, and the cultural sociology of globalization. He has been on several editorial and advisory boards, most recently of the *European Journal of Social Theory* and the *Journal of Sociology*.

Rita Keresztesi is an associate professor of English at the University of Oklahoma. She is the author of *Strangers at Home: American Ethnic Modernism between the World Wars* (University of Nebraska Press, 2005). She is writing a work on transnational dialogues: black power in the diaspora. Her research and teaching focus on issues of race and ethnicity and African American and Afro-Caribbean literary and cultural studies.

Ann Kordas received her Ph.D. in history from Temple University in 2002. She is an assistant professor in the Department of Humanities at Johnson & Wales University in Providence, Rhode Island. Most of her research and writing is in the field of American cultural history and gender history. She contributed the chapter entitled "'The Blood Is the Life': Roman Catholic Imagery in American Vampire Films of the 1930s" in the anthology *Roman Catholicism in Fantastic Film* (forthcoming). She is writing a book on occult beliefs of women and people of color in the United States.

Laura MacDonald is a graduate (B.A.) of Mount Allison University, with a major in psychology, and minors in sociology and anthropology. Her research interests include popular culture, religion and psychoanalytic theory.

Cynthia J. Miller is a cultural anthropologist, specializing in popular culture and visual media. She is a scholar-in-residence at Emerson College, in Boston, and is associate editor of *Film & History: An Interdisciplinary Journal of Film and Television Studies*. She has written and spoken extensively on the B-movie and exploitation film genres, and her writing has appeared most recently in *Heroes of Film, Comics, and American Culture* (McFarland, 2009), *Sounds of the Future: Essays on Music in Science Fiction Film* (McFarland, 2010) and *Science Fiction Across Media* (Gylphi, 2010).

Christopher M. Moreman is an assistant professor in the philosophy department at California State University, East Bay, teaching courses in comparative religion. He wrote *Beyond the Threshold: Afterlife Beliefs and Experiences in World Religions* (Rowman & Littlefield, 2008) and edited *Teaching Death and Dying* (Oxford University Press, 2008) and articles on death and the afterlife.

Cory James Rushton is an assistant professor of English at St. Francis Xavier University in Antigonish, Nova Scotia, Canada. He is co-editor of *A Companion to Middle English Romance* (with Raluca Radulescu) and *The Erotic in the Literature of Medieval Britain* (with Amanda Hopkins), both from Boydell Press; and editor of *Disability and Medieval Law: History, Literature, Society* (forthcoming). He has written on Sir Thomas Malory, Terry Pratchett, and the legend of the Holy Grail in Canada.

Elizabeth A. Stinson is a Ph.D. candidate in performance studies at New York University, writing a dissertation on transnational networks, globalization, and postcoloniality. She holds an M.F.A. from the University of California, Irvine, and a B.A. from California State University, Los Angeles, in theatre arts and dance. She participates on the editorial collective for the *Women and Performance: A Journal of Feminist Theory*.

Index

academic metaphor, defined 178–82
Afghanistan 112, 113, 114, 127, 135, 136
African American zombie films 5, 6
African zombies 3
Agamben, Giorgio 99, 103n10
AIDS 45, 47, 103n13, 198
Al Qaeda 112, 113, 135
Alexander, Lorraine 102n2
Ali, Muhammad 109, 126
American Zombie (film) 119
Antoine, LeRoy 27
apocalypse: and fears of racial pollution 118; as generic convention 111, 124, 125, 138; George Romero's emphasis on 79, 197; in *I Am Legend* (Matheson) 193; and nationalism 150, 151; and Orientalist threats 114–16; preparing for 201; in *The Walking Dead* (comics) 9; and zombie killers 196; in *Zombi 3* 4
Arab stereotypes: as enraged 109; as hordes or mobs 113, 120; and oil industry 115, 116; as slavers 117, 118, 123n9; as unintelligible 119; zombies as Arab terrorists 107; *see also* Islamophobia
Archer, John 140
Argento, Dario 158
atomic technology *see* nuclear technology
Atwill, Lionel 141

Bakhtin, Mikhail 32
Bancroft, Anne 68
banks, zombie 77, 78, 80–81, 102n5, 193
Baraka, Amiri 109
Barker, Steve 142, 144, 145, 146
Barry, Gene 73n7

Barrymore, Lionel 141
Bataille, Georges: and Durkheim's concept of the soul 83, 85, 86; on economics 81–82; main analytical resources 77; on myth 79; on sovereignty 78, 87, 89, 91
Baudrillard, Jean 86
Beck, Ulrich *see* zombie categories
Beckett, Samuel 155, 159
The Bedford Incident (film) 62
Bell, Ernest A. 27–28
Bemba, Sylvain 103n9
bin Laden, Osama 127, 131, 135
biocybernetics 33–34, 36
Bizango societies 37, 49
Blackboard Jungle (film) 60
Blade Runner (film) 38
The Blob (film) 195
Blood Sucking Freaks (film) 143
Bogart, Humphrey 69
bokors *see* zombie masters
Borg 4, 122n1
Boy Eats Girl (film) 149–61; Grace's uncertain fate 161n3; and Irish national identity 12, 150–51, 155–59, 160; Samantha Mumba in 152–54, 159, 160; Voodoo in 5, 149, 155, 157, 158, 160; zombie film antecedents 150–52, 160n1
Boyle, Danny 79, 150; *see also 28 Days Later* (film)
Bradley, Stephen 151; *see also Boy Eats Girl* (film)
Braindead (film) 10, 147
brands, zombie 193
Breen, Joseph 140
Brooks, Max: on reasoning with zombies 119, 120; *World War Z* 5, 6, 114; *The Zombie Survival Guide* 5–6, 10, 112, 124, 201
Brown, Theodore 178–80

Buffy the Vampire Slayer (TV series) 150
Bush, George W. 103n12, 114
Butler, Judith 102n4

Campbell, Bruce 196
Cannes Film Festival 151
cannibalism: as capitalist consumption 7; in *Day of the Dead* 201; in *Night of the Living Dead* 69; as Romeran zombie trait 5, 43, 150; in sensational Voodoo tales 46; and zombies' repulsiveness 195
capitalism: capitalist division of labor 83, 84, 91; capitalist mode of production (CMP) 82–83, 85; commodity-signs 85–86, 88; economic zombies and global recession 77, 78, 80–81, 88–89, 90, 102n5; as economy of blood 93–94, 95, 97, 98–99, 100–102, 102n3, 103n12; origination of capitalist zombie trope 1, 7, 11; and sacrifice 89–91; in *The Seventh Continent* 205n12; zombies commodified by 122, 163–64, 166–67, 171; zombification and capitalist futures 77, 78, 82, 89–92, 92n2; *see also* consumerism
Caribbean zombies *see* Haitian zombies
carnival 32, 41, 90
Carradine, John 141
Carroll, Noel 195, 197
cartoons 107, 122n1, 123n15; *see also* comic books
Catholicism: African vs. Haitian 3; in *Boy Eats Girl* 149, 150, 152, 158–59, 160; and Caribbean syncretic religions 155; as Haitian state religion

2, 45, 52; and white fears of immigrants 23, 30n4
censorship 140, 151, 157
Chamberlain, Gordon 148
Chaplin, Charlie 148n2
chemical origins of zombies 4–5, 143
Cheney, Dick 103n12, 136
Chertoff, Michael 137
Chesnutt, Charles W. 41n4
Chinese, fear of: as enemy of the West 110, 113, 115, 116, 121; and immigration laws/quotas 23; and white fears of racial pollution 117, 118, 123n8; and Yellow Peril stereotypes 113, 115, 117; see also Orientalism
The Clash of Civilizations and the Remaking of World Order (Huntington) 110
class struggles: and circulation 97; vs. civilizational struggles 120; and consumerism 86–87; in Haiti 32–33, 37; in *Land of the Dead* 9, 122, 201; and white fears of immigrants 22–23; working-class viewpoint of zombie films 114, 121–22; zombies as eliminating 11
Claybourne, Doug 52
Colin (film) 204
Collège de Sociologie 78
colonialism/neocolonialism: American occupation of Haiti 32–33, 34–36, 37, 39, 41, 46, 108; and Catholicism 2; as economy of blood 93–94, 95, 97, 100–102; neocolonial zombies vs. economic zombies 102n5; neocolonialism, defined 41n6; and Orientalism 107, 108–09; postcolonial view of zombie trope 1, 171–72; and Wade Davis controversy 44; Z. N. Hurston's critique of 32–33, 34–36, 37, 39–41; and zombies' periodical resurgence 108–09, 125; as zombification 93–95, 99–100, 101, 102n6, 103n8; see also slavery
comedy see humor
comic books: by Dynamite Entertainment 9; by Image Comics 8, 9; manga 151; by Marvel Comics 6, 123n15; Nazi villains in 148; *Toe Tags* series 122n1, 123n15; *Xombie* 122n1, 123n15; *The Zombie Hunters* (online) 201
Communism: and film censorship 140; and *High Noon* 70;

and *Invasion of the Body Snatchers* 3; and Orientalist fears 113, 118; zombie outbreaks symbolizing spread of 124, 125, 198
Confessions of a Nazi Spy (film) 140, 148n2
Congo 94–95, 98, 100, 101, 103n9, 103n13; see also *Parentheses of Blood* (Labou Tansi)
consciousness: and death 89; materialistic theories of 12, 191–92, 202–04, 205n15; zombies' lack of 4, 7, 34, 191, 203; zombies who retain 122n1
consumerism: and Bataillean economics 81, 87; and credit availability 77, 84, 88–89; George Romero's critique of 1, 7, 77, 79–80, 108, 116, 130, 150, 166; post-Vietnam War increase in 86–87; and social class 186; zombies as mindless consumers 3, 7–8, 77, 79–80, 116, 168; and zombies as reflections of ourselves 200; see also capitalism
Cooper, Gary 69, 71
Craven, Wes 44, 52–54
The Crazies (film) 5
Creature with the Atomic Brain (film) 140–41
Cronenberg, David 197
Cunard, Nancy 35, 38
Currie, Andrew 165, 170; see also *Fido* (film)
Cushing, Peter 142
cybernetics 33–34, 36, 80, 89
cyborgs 4, 33–34, 36, 87, 122n1
Dahler, Don 131

Darwin, Charles 205n8
Davis, Wade 42–59; controversy surrounding 5, 11, 42, 44, 51–52, 53–57; and disciplinary boundaries of knowledge 42, 44, 57–59; zombie research, summarized 43, 47–51
Dawkins, Richard 182
Dawn of the Dead (1978 film): and consumerism 1, 3, 7, 79, 80, 116, 150, 166; as entertainment vs. sociopolitical commentary 9; and fears of racial pollution 118, 123n10; hell as full in 171; humor in 150, 196; and Lucio Fulci's films 4; and Max Brooks 6; and public mistrust of government 113–14; remake of 11, 129–30; survivors' dissension in 201; and

zombie agency/individuality 197; "zombie" as term in 193, 205n3; zombie genocide in 123n13
Dawn of the Dead (2004 film) 129–38; and complacency about terrorism 135–37, 138; and consumerism 166; and geographical significance 151; vs. original film 11, 129–30; post-9/11 elements in, summarized 129–32; and unpredictability of post-9/11 life 126, 132–35, 138; zombies' speed of movement in 134, 145
Day of the Dead (film): Mark Kidwell's reimagining of 9; and Max Brooks 6; and mindless consumption 79; science's failure in 123n12; survivors' dissension in 201; and zombie agency/individuality 197; zombies' origin in 198
Day of the Dead 2 (film) 123n13, 123n15
Dead Alive (film) 10, 147, 150
Dead Snow (film) 143, 144, 145–47, 199
The Defiant Ones (film) 60
Dekker, Albert 141
Democratic Republic of the Congo 94–95, 98
Depestre, René 44, 102n6
Derrida, Jacques 96, 97, 103n14, 178, 181
Descartes, René 191–92, 202
Diary of the Dead (film): and consumerism 79; and do-gooder characters 123n11; film within the film 194, 205n4; geographical significance in 151; humor in 196; Stephen King in 205n11; and zombies as reflections of ourselves 192, 200, 201
Dieckhoff, Hans Heinrich 140
Dracula 8
Dubliners (Joyce) 156
DuBois, W. E. B. 36
Duncan, Andy 5
Durkheim, Emile 77, 78, 83, 85–86
Duvalier, François (Papa Doc) 52, 56
Duvalier, Jean-Claude (Baby Doc) 47
Dyer, Richard 60
Dynamite Entertainment 9

Ebert, Roger 62
EC Comics 6

economic zombies 77, 78, 80–81, 88–89, 90, 102*n*5; *see also* capitalism; consumerism
Elliston, Maxine Hall 61
Emerson, Ralph Waldo 201
Enter Zombie King (film) 5, 150
essentialism 185–86
etymology of "zombie" 3, 17
evolution of the zombie *see* history of zombies in American culture

false rationalism, defined 184
Farah, Nuruddin 96–97
Felix-Mentor, Felicia 5, 31, 32, 34, 36, 38–39
Fido (film) 162–73; and consumerism 80, 166, 168; gender roles in 162, 165–66, 169–70; human attachments as impossible in 205*n*13; and Max Brooks 6; and philosophical zombies 204; science's failure in 123*n*12; social commentary and humor combined in 10, 150; zombies as enslaved laborers in 122, 163, 164–65, 168–69, 171, 172–73; zombies as stabilizing force in 12, 162, 164, 173; zombies as sympathetic in 123*n*15, 197
Fighting the Traffic in Young Girls (Bell) 27–28
Flight of the Living Dead (film) 107, 111
Folkenflik, David 136
For Love of Ivy (film) 73*n*4
Foran, Michael 23
The Forest of Hands and Teeth (Ryan) 8
Foucault, Michel 84–85
Franco, Jesus 143
Frankenstein 8, 198
Franklin, Aretha 152
Freeland, Cynthia 197, 205*n*7
Fresnadillo, Juan Carlos 79
Freud, Sigmund 164
The Frozen Dead (film) 141
Fulci, Lucio 4, 158

Gaye, Gregory 141
Geeson, Judy 63
gender: Caribbean gender discrimination 32–33, 40–41; *Fido*'s patriarchal society 162, 165–66, 169–70; Judith Butler on 102*n*4; *Night of the Living Dead*'s critique of gender norms 67, 73*n*6
genocide 113, 117, 120, 123*n*13, 144

Gentner, Dedre 178–80
German-American Bund 140
Ghostbusters (film) 151
Gibson, Charlie 131
Godsmack 5
Goebbels, Joseph 141–42
Golden Legend (Jacobus de Voragine) 155
gore 9–10, 133, 148*n*7, 158, 195
government, U.S.: and Chinese immigration laws 23; in *Creature with the Atomic Brain* 141; and economic zombies 78, 80, 81, 89, 90; military spending 81, 103*n*12; and 9/11 attacks 114, 124, 127–29, 131, 135, 137; and occupation of Haiti 35; public mistrust of 111, 113–14; *see also specific government officials*
Granger, Michael 141
Grant, Lee 66–67
The Great Dictator (film) 148*n*2
Guantanamo detention camp 107
Guess Who's Coming to Dinner (film) 60, 61, 63–64, 67, 69

Haiti: American occupation of 32–33, 34–36, 37, 39, 41, 46, 108; Duvalier regimes 47, 52, 53, 56; foreign stereotypes of 44–47, 54; Haitian American Sugar Company (Hasco) 21; religion in, summarized 2, 45, 52; revolution 2, 3, 12, 15, 17, 45, 51; St. Patrick in 155; as *White Zombie* setting 24–25; zombification outlawed in 3, 48
Haitian zombies: vs. African zombies 3; and class struggles 9; different forms of, summarized 16; as enslaved laborers 3–4, 24, 36–38, 42–43, 125; and foreign stereotypes of Haiti 44–45, 46–47, 54; Hollywood zombies' eclipse of 2, 5, 6, 15, 58; and mindless consumption 7; and Romeran zombies 5, 150; William Seabrook's account of 17–18, 19, 20, 21, 27; as Voodoo cyborgs 33–34, 36; Wade Davis's research on 43, 47–51; Z. N. Hurston's case study 5, 31, 32, 34, 36, 38–39; in *The Zombie Survival Guide* 5–6, 10
Halperin, Victor 19, 21; *see also White Zombie* (film)
Haneke, Michael 205*n*12

Hardman, Karl 65
Harman, Chris 92*n*2
Harrelson, Woody 196
Harris, Naomie 153
Hawks, Howard 70, 71
Hayden, Michael 112
Hayti, or the Black Republic (St. John) 46
Hegel, G. W. F.: dialectic as series of phases 103*n*14; on lost history 157; master-slave dialectic 45; and social critique/change 179; and Ulrich Beck's zombie categories 184, 187, 189
Herskovit, Melville 155
The Hills Have Eyes (film) 9
history of zombies in American culture 15–30; and anticolonial threats 108–09; George Romero's influence on 1, 2, 5, 42, 60, 77, 79, 193; as meme 192–94; and mid–20th-century fears 124, 125; and Nazi zombie films' emergence 139–41, 148*n*2; and nineteenth-century "zombi" tales 16–17; and Voodoo in New Orleans 2, 15, 31; and white fears in New South 18–22, 125; and white fears of immigrants 22–26; and women's changing roles 26–29
Hitler, Adolf 141, 142, 146, 148
Hitler: A Film from Germany (film) 142
Hitler, Beast of Berlin (film) 148*n*2
Holmes, Oliver Wendell 23
horror genre, defined 195, 197
Horrors of War (film) 144, 145
Houghton, Katharine 63–64
The House of Bondage (Kauffman) 26
House of the Dead (film) 145
humor: and Arab stereotypes 119; emphasis on, in recent zombie films 192; in *Fido* 10, 123*n*12, 150; in George Romero's films 69, 133, 150, 196; in Nazi zombie films 12, 140, 147; in *Shaun of the Dead* 10, 111, 192, 200; zombie comedy tradition, summarized 150
Huntington, Samuel: on civilizational conflicts 120, 122, 123*n*10; on Mexican immigrants 110; on Muslims 112, 113, 115, 119, 123*n*10
Hurricane Katrina 125, 200
Hurston, Zora Neale 31–41;

controversy surrounding 11, 32, 33; on neocolonialism 32–33, 34–36, 37, 39–41; Vodou research 5, 31, 36–39, 41, 41*n*2; and Wade Davis's research 48
Hutchins, Grace 35–36, 38
hypodescent ("one drop rule") 123*n*10

I Am Legend (film) 121, 122, 123*n*4, 123*n*14
I Am Legend (Matheson) 109, 123*n*4, 193, 199
I Married a Communist (film) 118
I Married a Nazi (film) 148*n*2
I Walked with a Zombie (film) 21, 27, 28–29, 43, 125
ideological zombification 78
Ileus, Francine 48
Ilsa: She Wolf of the SS (film) 148*n*7
Image Comics 8, 9
In the Heat of the Night (film) 60, 66–67, 72
infection *see* zombie infections
Invasion of the Body Snatchers (film) 3, 73*n*7, 191
Iraq 109, 113, 114, 135
Islamophobia: and apocalyptic threats 115; and communicating/reasoning with the enemy 119, 120; and "hidden" or "secret" Muslims 111–12, 117, 118, 123*n*6, 152; and "hordes" of Muslims 113; and "Muslim rage" 109–10, 123*n*5; zombies' popularity due to 107, 121

Jackson, Michael 136
Jackson, Peter 10, 147, 150
Jacobus de Voragine 155
Jamaica 31, 32, 39, 41*n*2
Japanese financial crisis 77, 80, 102*n*5
Jennings, Peter 131
Jesus Christ 108, 158
Johnson, Lyndon 71
Jones, Duane: George Romero's casting of 10, 62, 152; and Judith O'Dea 69; Sidney Poitier compared with 11, 60, 62, 63, 73*n*5; *see also Night of the Living Dead* (film)
Joyce, James 155–56, 159

Kant, Immanuel 183
Karloff, Boris 141, 150
Kashyap, Anil K. 102*n*5
Katrina, Hurricane 125, 200

Kauffman, Reginald 26
Keene, Brian 111
Kendall, Suzy 63
Kidwell, Mark 9
King, Stephen 205*n*11
King Kong (film) 205*n*4
King of the Zombies (film) 140, 147
Kline, Nathan S. 48–49
Kristeva, Julia 37, 39–40, 157
Ku Klux Klan 30*n*4

Labou Tansi, Sony: and Achille Mbembe 94, 96; *The Antipeople* 98, 103*n*11; birth and homeland 98; death 103*n*13; grammatical playfulness of 97; grave site 101; and Sylvain Bemba 103*n*9; *see also Parentheses of Blood* (Labou Tansi)
Ladd, David 52
Laguerre, Michel 49
Land of the Dead (film): class struggles in 9, 122, 201; and consumerism 79, 166; and materialism 204; and Max Brooks 6; and Mexican immigration 110; and zombie agency/individuality 197; "zombie" as term in 205*n*3; zombie genocide in 123*n*13; and zombies' repulsiveness 195
Lassie (TV series) 170–71
Last of the Living (film) 151
Lee, Grace 119
Leno, Jay 136
Leopold II, King of the Belgians 100
Lewis, Bernard 110
Lewis, Edmonia 19, 30*n*4
Lightning, Robert K. 60, 65, 66, 67–68
Lilies of the Field (film) 60, 69
Lindh, John Walker 111–12, 118
Live and Let Die (film) 6
Locke, Alain 35
Locke, John 180
Loederer, Richard 46
London bombings (2005) 128
The Lost Man (film) 73*n*4
Lugosi, Béla 8, 24, 28, 46, 193
Lumumba, Patrice 95

The Magic Island (Seabrook) 17–18, 19, 21, 46; *see also* Seabrook, William
Makilaakso, Marko 141, 145, 146
Malcolm X 109
The Man They Could Not Hang (film) 141

manga 151
Mankiewicz, Joseph L. 60
Maroons 37, 39, 43
Marvel Comics 6
Marx, Karl: Bataille's reliance on 77; on capitalist production 83, 84, 86; Frankfurt School 179; on *homo laborans* 4; and *Parentheses of Blood* 94, 96–97, 99, 100–102; and spectrogenic layering 103*n*14
Mason, Clifford 61–62
master figures *see* zombie masters
materialism 12, 191–92, 202–04, 205*n*15
Matheson, Richard 109, 123*n*14, 193, 199
Maxwell, Richard 52
Mbembe, Achille 94, 96, 97, 100, 102*n*6, 103*n*10
McCain, John 136
McCarthy, Kevin 73*n*7
McCarthyism 70–71, 198
memes 192–94, 204, 205*n*2
mental illness 30*n*2
Mexicans, fear of 110
militarism: in Mark Kidwell's work 9; in mid–20th-century zombie films 125; and public mistrust of government 114; in *Shaun of the Dead* 121–22; U.S. military spending 81, 103*n*12; in *Zombi 3*, 4; zombies as super-soldiers 21, 141, 143, 148, 197; *see also* colonialism/neocolonialism; Nazi zombies
Moreland, Mantan 140
Morgan, Harry 71
Motion Picture Association of America 108, 140
Mules and Men (Hurston) 34–35
Mumba, Samantha 152–54, 159, 160
mummies 108, 193
Murillo, Bartolomé Esteban 16
My Boyfriend's Back (film) 160*n*1

Narcisse, Clairvius 48, 49–50, 56
nationalism: Irishness in *Boy Eats Girl* 12, 150–51, 155–59, 160; and Ulrich Beck's zombie categories 183–85, 187, 188
Nazi zombies 139–48: emergence of, as film sub-genre 139–42, 148*n*2; evolution of, as film sub-genre 142–43, 145–47; kitsch appeal of 12,

144–45, 147; and moral interpretations of zombies 199; and Shield Squadron (SS) 142, 148*n*4; and World War II allohistory 148

Nazisploitation films 143, 148*n*7

Neeson, Liam 117

neocolonialism *see* colonialism/neocolonialism

neoliberalism 78, 87

Network (film) 115

Ngouabi, Marien 98

Night of the Living Dead (film) 60–73; Ben's death, significance of 10, 72–73; Ben's interracial relationship 63–69; Ben's leadership, and black militancy 62, 69–72; Ben's status in white world 61–64; and black protagonists in later zombie films 152, 153; and *Dead Snow* 147; and dystopian zombie film endings 201; filming location and budget 69, 73*n*2; and *I Am Legend* (Matheson) 109, 193; and mindless consumption 7; and natural selection 205*n*8; reason for zombie outbreak in 198; as redirecting popular views of zombies 1, 2, 42, 60, 79; sexism alleged in 73*n*6; and Vietnam War 9, 62, 73; and Wade Davis controversy 58; zombies' first appearance in 133; zombies' slowness in 134, 145

Night of the Living Dead 3D (film) 152

Night of the Zombies (film) 143, 144–45, 148*n*8

A Nightmare on Elm Street (film) 52

9/11 attacks *see* September 11, 2001, attacks

No Way Out (film) 60, 71

nominalism 185

Nosferatu (film) 205*n*5

nuclear technology: in *Creature with the Atomic Brain* 141; in *The Hills Have Eyes* 9; in mid-20th-century zombie films 124, 125; and 9/11 attacks 127, 128, 137; and zombie genocide 120

Oasis of the Zombies (film) 143, 147, 148*n*6

Obama, Barack 112

O'Bannon, Dan 150

Obsession: Radical Islam's War

Against the West (film) 110, 115, 119

O'Dea, Judith 64, 69

Oklahoma City bombing 127

Orientalism 107–23; and American frontier narrative 120–21; and anticolonial threats 108–09; and apocalyptic threats 114–16; and communicating/reasoning with the enemy 118–20; and consumerism 116; and fears of racial pollution 11–12, 108, 117–18, 123*n*8; and "hidden" or "secret" Muslims 111–12, 117, 118, 123*n*6, 152; and "hordes" of Orientals 113, 120, 121; and "Muslim rage" 109–10, 123*n*5; and public mistrust of government 113–14; Said's concept of, summarized 107; stereotypes, summarized 11–12; zombie counternarratives to 121–22

Other: Oriental Other 11–12, 107–08, 110, 112, 113, 117, 119, 122; and Ulrich Beck's zombie categories 184, 187, 189; zombies as both self and 4, 173; zombies as racial Other in the 1930s–1940s 125; *see also* race and racism

Ouanga (film) 21, 22, 29

Outpost (film) 144, 145, 146

Paffenroth, Kim 8

Parentheses of Blood (Labou Tansi) 93–103; and Brazzaville politics and violence 98, 101; Libertashio as zombified creature in 93, 95, 101; and Marxist theory 94, 96–97, 99, 100–102; publication and staging details 102*n*2

Parker, Kieran 144

Passage of Darkness (Davis) 42, 51, 54, 55, 57

Patterson, Orlando 163, 168, 169, 173

pharmaceuticals *see* potions, to induce zombification

philosophical zombies 191–205; defined 59*n*2, 203; and evolution of zombie meme 192–94; and materialistic theories of consciousness 12, 191–92, 202–04, 205*n*15; metaphysical problems raised by 58, 59*n*2, 204; and personal identity 194; and zombies as evil vs. sympathetic 197–99, 201, 204; and zombies as reflections of

ourselves 192, 199–202, 204, 205*n*12; and zombies' repulsiveness 195–97, 199, 205*n*10

Plato 185

Poitier, Sydney 60–73; and Ben's death in *Night of the Living Dead* 72–73; and Ben's status in *Night of the Living Dead* 61–64; criticism of 61–62, 73*n*4; as first black superstar 11, 60, 62; and interracial couple in *Night of the Living Dead* 63–69; and leadership/black militancy in *Night of the Living Dead* 62, 69–72; physical stature 73*n*5

political cartoons 107

Pontypool (film) 193, 205*n*2

A Portrait of the Artist as a Young Man (Joyce) 159

postmodernism: and academic metaphor 178, 179, 181–82; and biocybernetics 33–34; as false-rationalist dogma 188; Z. N. Hurston's writings as postmodernist 31–32, 33; zombies as postmodernist 12; *see also specific postmodern scholars*

potions, to induce zombification: and original film zombies 193; Wade Davis's pharmacological research on 42, 43, 48–49, 50–51, 54, 55–56; in *White Zombie* 25, 28, 30*n*4; Z. N. Hurston's ethnographic research on 37, 38; and zombie agency/individuality 7

Poverty Row film studios 140, 148*n*2

Pride and Prejudice and Zombies (Austen and Grahame-Smith) 193

Product Code Administration 140

al-Qaeda 112, 113, 135

Quarantine (film) 193

race and racism: African American zombie films 5, 6; and Ben's death in *Night of the Living Dead* 10, 72–73; Ben's interracial relationship in *Night of the Living Dead* 63–69; Ben's leadership and black militancy in *Night of the Living Dead* 62, 69–72; Ben's racial status in *Night of the Living Dead* 61–64; in *Boy Eats Girl* 152–54, 160, 160*n*2; in *Fido* 162, 164, 172; George

Romero's casting of black protagonist 1, 10, 62, 66, 152; in
King of the Zombies 140;
Nation of Islam's rise 108–09;
"Voodoo" as racist construction 2–3; white fears in New
South 18–22; white fears of
immigrants 22–26, 30n4, 110;
white fears of racial pollution
11–12, 108, 117–18, 123n8,
123n10; *see also* Orientalism;
slavery
rage viruses 79, 109, 133–34,
193, 205n2
Raiders of the Lost Ark (film) 144
A Raisin in the Sun (film) 60
Reagan, Ronald 78
Reed, Joel 143, 144–45
religion: and American immigration 22–23; defined 190n3;
in Haiti, summarized 2, 45,
52; Nation of Islam's rise 108–
09; as powerless against zombies 111, 113–14; resurrection
40, 115, 149, 158, 159; Satanism 158; secularization debate
177, 180, 183; sin, views of 27,
78, 171; and Ulrich Beck's
zombie categories 184, 189; *see
also* Catholicism; Islamophobia; Vodou/Voodoo
Republic of the Congo 98, 101,
103n9, 103n13; *see also Parentheses of Blood* (Labou Tansi)
Resident Evil (film series) 5, 6,
198
Resident Evil (2002 film) 115,
197
Resident Evil: Apocalypse (film)
117, 123n11, 123n13, 126, 198
Resident Evil: Extinction (film)
122, 123n12, 198
resurrection 40, 115, 149, 158,
159
The Return of the Living Dead
(film) 4–5, 119, 197
Revenge of the Zombies (film) 140
Revolt of the Zombies (film) 21,
22, 23, 29
Rhames, Ving 135
Rice, Anne 196
Ridley, Judith 70
Robertson, Pat 2
Robinson, Ann 73n7
Robinson, Edward G. 140
Roizin, Leon 55
Rollin, Jean 143
Romero, George: casting of
black protagonist 1, 10, 62, 66,
152; critique of consumerism
1, 7, 77, 79–80, 108, 116, 130,

150, 166; and geographical significance 151; and *I Am Legend*
(Matheson) 109, 193, 199; and
Lucio Fulci 158; as redirecting
popular views of zombies 1, 2,
5, 42, 60, 77, 79, 193; satiriza-
tion of 5, 6; and *Toe Tags*
comic books 123n15; and
Westerns 70–71; and zombie
agency/individuality 7–8, 108,
122n2, 197; and zombie as
both Other and self 4; on
zombie origins 198, 199,
205n9; on zombies' current
popularity 205n6; on zombies'
speed of movement 194, 196;
see also Dawn of the Dead
(1978 film); *Day of the Dead*
(film); *Diary of the Dead*
(film); *Land of the Dead*
(film); *Night of the Living
Dead* (film)
Roosevelt, Theodore 23
Ross, Peter John 144, 145
Rules of Engagement (film) 113,
120
Russell, Jamie 1, 125
Russo, John A. 4, 9–10
Rutherford, Ernest 177, 178
Ryan, Carrie 8

sacrifice 6, 37, 39, 89–91, 143,
158
Said, Edward 107, 109, 120; *see
also* Orientalism
St. John, Spenser 46, 53
Sarris, Andrew 61
SARS pandemic 125
Satanism 158
Sawyer, Diane 131
Schindler's List (film) 144
Schlitz beer 193
Schmitt, Carl 103n10
Schultes, Richard Evans 48, 49
science: atomic-age fears in
zombie films 124, 125; chemical compounds unleashed by
4–5, 143; in *Day of the Dead*
9; in *I Am Legend* 121;
mad/evil scientist narratives
139, 140–41, 198; and
metaphor 178–79, 180–81;
myth vs. scientific discourse
79; Nazi scientists 140–41,
142, 143, 145, 146; as powerless
against zombies 113–14, 120,
123n12; Z. N. Hurston's scientific proof of zombies 34; *see
also* Davis, Wade
Scruton, Roger 182
Seabrook, William: introduction

of Haitian zombies to American public 17–18; and sensational Voodoo tales 46, 52,
53; and sexual transgression
27; and white fears in New
South 19, 20, 21; on zombies
as mentally ill 30n2
September 11, 2001, attacks: and
apocalyptic film scenes 115;
and communicating/reasoning
with the enemy 119; and fears
of racial pollution 118; and
Flight of the Living Dead 107,
111; *The 9/11 Commission Report*
124–25, 127, 128–29, 135; and
public mistrust of government
114; and sneak attacks 112–13;
television coverage of 131, 138;
unpredictability of life following 126–28, 132–35, 138;
zombies' popularity due to
115–16, 124–25, 137–38
Serenity (film) 114
The Serpent and the Rainbow
(Davis) 42, 44, 49, 51–52,
53–55, 57
The Serpent and the Rainbow
(film) 5, 44, 52–54
The Seventh Continent (film)
205n12
sexuality: in *Boy Eats Girl* 152,
153–54; in Nazisploitation
films 143, 148n7; in *Shivers*
197; of vampires 145; of
Voodoo priests 47; and white
fears of racial pollution 123n8;
zombie females as sex objects
41, 170, 196, 199; zombie outbreaks symbolizing sexual revolution 198; zombies and
female sexual transgression
26–29; zombies as asexual-
yet-sexual threat 117–18
Shakespeare, William 205n4
Shaun of the Dead (film): and
Boy Eats Girl 150–52; and
fears of racial pollution 117;
and *Fido*'s post-zombie world
162, 166; lack of horror in 192;
and Max Brooks 6; oblivious-
ness of protagonist in 80, 111;
as satirizing George Romero's
films 5; social commentary
and humor combined in 10,
200; working-class characters
in 114, 121–22
Shivers (film) 197
Shock Waves (film) 142, 143, 146,
148n3
sin, views of 27, 78, 171
slavery: and American occupa-

tion of Haiti 35–36; in American South 18–20, 22, 171; film zombies as enslaved laborers 122, 163, 164–65, 168–69, 171, 172–73; and Haitian revolution 2, 3, 12, 15, 17, 45, 51; Haitian zombies as enslaved laborers 3–4, 24, 36–38, 42–43, 125; sexual slavery 26, 27–28, 117; and social death 163, 165, 168; and Vodou origins 2, 15, 32; white guilt over 16, 19; white slavery 26, 27–28, 117; zombie outbreak as slave uprising 10, 17

The Slender Thread (film) 68
Slither (film) 122n2
Snyder, Zack 129, 130, 145, 151; *see also Dawn of the Dead* (2004 film)
Sontag, Susan 142, 144, 146
The Sound of Music (film) 170
South Africa, zombies in 167, 171–72
speed of zombies' movement: and complacency about terrorism 138; George Romero on 194, 196; in Nazi zombie films 145–46; and Orientalist fears 107; in *28 Days Later* (film) 109, 133–34, 193; and zombie agency/individuality 7
Star Trek (TV and film series) 4, 122n1
Stein, Elliott 62
Steiner, Russell 65
Stevenson, Ray 146
Stoker, Bram 205n5
Stone's War (film) 141, 146
Streiner, Russell 10
Sugar Hill (film) 6
Sundance Film Festival 139, 146
Survival of the Dead (film) 79, 201
Suspiria (film) 158
Syberberg, Hans-Jurgen 142

Taliban 112, 114, 118
Tansi, Sony Labou *see* Labou Tansi, Sony
Team America: World Police (film) 119
Tell My Horse: Voodoo and Life in Haiti and Jamaica (Hurston) 31–41; Felicia Felix-Mentor as zombie in 5, 31, 32, 34, 36, 38–39; Z. N. Hurston's critique of neocolonialism 32–33, 34–36, 37, 39–41

terrorism: and apocalyptic film scenes 114–15; and communicating/reasoning with the enemy 119; complacency about 128–29, 135–37, 138; in *Dawn of the Dead* (2004) summarized 129–32; and fears of racial pollution 118; New Terrorism, summarized 126–28; and public mistrust of government 114; sneak attacks by terrorists and zombies 112–13; and unpredictability of post–9/11 life 126–28, 132–35, 138; zombies as Islamic terrorists 107, 111; zombies' popularity due to threat of 12, 115–16, 121, 124–25, 137–38
tetrodotoxin (TTX) 37, 43, 50, 51, 55–56, 58
Their Eyes Were Watching God (Hurston) 33
They Saved Hitler's Brain (film) 141
Thomas, Pierre 131
Thoreau, Henry David 201
Thurman, Wallace 41n4
Tiernan, Andrew 146
The Time Machine (2002 film) 152
To Sir, with Love (film) 60, 63, 67, 69
Tokyo Zombie (film) 151, 192
Traffic in Souls (film) 26
transcendentalism 201
True Blood (TV series) 196
Turner, Nat 19, 22
28 Days Later (film): black lead character in 153, 160n2; geographical significance in 151; and "Muslim rage" 109, 123n5; and 9/11 attacks 115, 126; and public mistrust of government 113–14; as social commentary 123n5, 150; viral infection in 3, 5, 79, 108, 109, 133–34, 193; and zombie agency/individuality 122n2; zombie genocide in 123n13; zombies' speed of movement in 109, 133–34, 145, 193
28 Weeks Later (film) 79, 123n13, 126
Twilight novels and films 196

Ubu Repertory Theater, New York 102n2
Ulysses (Joyce) 156, 159
Undead (film) 122n2
U.S. government *see* government, U.S.

vampires: in Cynthia Freeland's work 197; as glamorous 195–96, 205n5; in *I Am Legend* (Matheson) 109, 123n4, 193; and individual identity 8, 108, 145, 196; vs. other monsters 124, 139, 145, 193, 195–96
Victor, Henry 140
video games 42, 59, 78, 148, 162, 205n6
Vietnam War: and consumerism 86; and Joel Reed 143, 144–45; and *Night of the Living Dead* 9, 62, 73; and sneak attacks 112–13
viral zombies: and class struggles 9, 11; prevalence of, in films 5, 79; as Romeran zombie type 1, 5, 7–8, 150; in *28 Days Later* 3, 5, 79, 108, 109, 133–34, 193; in *The Zombie Survival Guide* 5–6, 10; *see also* zombie infections
Vodou/Voodoo: and academic truisms about zombies 1; in *Boy Eats Girl* 5, 149, 155, 157, 158, 160; differences between Vodou and Voodoo 2–3, 15, 41n1; and foreign stereotypes of Haiti 45–47, 54; in Marvel Comics 6; in New Orleans 2, 15, 31; and original film zombies 193, 198; origins of 2, 15, 32, 43; in *The Serpent and the Rainbow* (film) 5, 52–53, 54; in *28 Days Later* 108; and Ulrich Beck's zombie categories 185, 187, 188, 189; Wade Davis's research on 43, 47–51, 56–57; and Z. N. Hurston controversy 11, 32, 33; Z. N. Hurston's research on 5, 31, 36–39, 41, 41n2; *see also* Haitian zombies
Voodoo Fire in Haiti (Loederer) 46

The Walking Dead (comic book series) 8, 9
The Walking Dead (film) 141
The War of the Worlds (film) 73n7
Warner, Jack 140
Wayne, John 69
Wayne, Keith 65
werewolves 124, 139, 145
Westerns (film genre) 69–71
Whedon Joss 114
Where Eagles Dare (film) 144
White Zombie (film): and American occupation of Haiti 108;

Béla Lugosi in 8, 24, 28, 46, 193; as first well-known zombie film 124; and Haitian vs. Hollywood conceptions of zombies 43, 46, 150; and Nazi zombie films' emergence 141; as redirecting popular views of zombies 2; and white fears in New South 19, 20–21, 125; and white fears of immigrants 22, 24–26, 30*n*4; and white slavery 27–28; and zombie agency/individuality 122*n*2

Whitney, John 145

Widmark, Richard 71

Wiederhorn, Ken 142, 146; *see also Shock Waves* (film)

Wilson, E. O. 177

Wirkola, Tommy 143, 144, 145–47

Wolfe, George C. 102*n*2

World Trade Center bombing (1993) 127, 135; *see also* September 11, 2001, attacks

World War II: Hollywood heroes during 72; Nazi Shield Squadron (SS) 142, 148*n*4; Nazi zombie films' emergence 139, 140–42, 148*n*2; Nazi zombie films' evolution 142–43, 145–47; Nazi zombie kitsch 12, 144–45, 147; and Orientalist fears 112, 113; in science fiction 148; and September 11 attacks 114; and zombies' wane in popularity 108

World War Z (Brooks) 5, 6, 114

Wright, Edgar 80, 150; *see also Shaun of the Dead* (film)

Wynter, Dana 73*n*7

X, Malcolm 109

A Yank in the R.A.F. (film) 148*n*2

Yarbrough, Jean 140

Yeats, W. B. 155, 157

Yousef, Ramzi 127, 135

Zombi, Jean 17

Zombi 2 (film) 4

Zombi 3 (film) 4

zombies: academic truisms about 1–2; in Africa 3; agency/individuality of 3, 4, 7–8, 108, 122*n*2, 157, 194, 196, 197; as asexual-yet-sexual

threat 117–18; as brain eating 78, 91; commodification of 122, 163–64, 166–67, 171; communicating with 118–19; and consciousness 4, 7, 34, 122*n*1, 191, 203; defined 182; etymology 3, 17; fear of, vs. fear of zombification 42–43, 49, 53; first appearances of 133; generic conventions, summarized 108, 111; in Hegelian dialectic 103*n*14; and hypodescent ("one drop rule") 123*n*10; as Islamic terrorists 107, 111; as meme 192–94; as mentally ill 30*n*2; as mindless consumers 3, 7–8, 77, 79–80, 116, 168; as only modern myth 1, 2, 10–11; vs. other monsters 124, 139, 145, 193, 194, 195–96; photographic evidence of 5, 31, 34, 36, 39; popularity of, due to Islamophobia 107, 121; popularity of, due to terrorism 12, 115–16, 121, 124–25, 137–38; popularity of, due to video games 205*n*6; as postmodernist 12; rage associated with 79, 109, 123*n*5, 133–34, 159, 205*n*2; as reflections of ourselves 192, 199–202, 204, 205*n*12; as sex objects 41, 170, 196, 199; in South Africa 167, 171–72; as super-soldiers 21, 141, 143, 148, 197; symbolism of, surveyed 3, 125, 198; as sympathetic 70, 121, 123*n*15, 143, 197, 199, 201; *see also* economic zombies; Haitian zombies; history of zombies in American culture; Nazi zombies; philosophical zombies; speed of zombies' movement; viral zombies; zombification

zombie banks 77, 78, 80–81, 102*n*5, 193

Zombie Beach Party (film) 5, 150

zombie brands 193

zombie categories 177–90; academic metaphor, defined 178–82; connotation fallacy of 187–88, 189; defined 12, 182–83; and essentialism 185–86; as false-rationalist dogma 188–90; and "methodological nationalism" 183–85, 187, 188; and secularization debate 177, 180, 183

zombie comedies *see* humor

The Zombie Hunters (online comics) 201

zombie infections: and consumerism 116; and dystopian zombie film endings 202; and fears of racial pollution 112, 117–18, 123*n*8; as generic convention 8; memetic spread of 192, 204, 205*n*2; and 9/11 attacks 111, 115, 132; in *Parentheses of Blood* 93; and philosophical zombies 191; rage viruses 79, 109, 133–34, 193, 205*n*2; in *Shaun of the Dead* 162; and zombies as reflections of ourselves 200; *see also* viral zombies

Zombie Lake (film) 143, 147

zombie masters: appetites of 7, 47, 125; Béla Lugosi as 8, 24, 46, 193; *bokors*, described 3, 22, 37; *bokors'* use of potions 37, 48–49, 50–51, 54, 55–56; and female sexuality 29; as more terrifying than zombies 21, 42, 193; and racial fears 16, 21, 22, 26; in Tonton Macoute (secret police) 52; viral zombies' elimination of 8

Zombie Strippers (film) 196

The Zombie Survival Guide (Brooks) 5–6, 10, 112, 124, 201

zombie walks 196

Zombieland (film) 151, 192

Zombiez (film) 5

zombification: and capitalist division of labor 84; and capitalist futures 77, 78, 82, 89–92, 92*n*2; through chemical exposure 4–5, 143; colonialism as 93–95, 99–100, 101, 102*n*6, 103*n*8; as eroticization 27–29, 41; as family punishment 40; fear of, vs. fear of zombies 42–43, 49, 53; ideological 78; infection as common cause of 5, 79; laws prohibiting 3, 48; and personal identity 194; vs. vampirification 196; of working class 88–89; *see also* potions, to induce zombification

zombiis 4, 11

zombis astrals 3, 51